MOON

COASTAL CAROLINAS

JIM MOREKIS

NORTH CAROLINA COAST

Roanoke Rapids

Corolla

158

Elizabeth City

Hertford

13

Kitty Hawk

Edenton

17

Nags Head

Windsor

Roanoke Island

64

Creswell

12

Hatteras Island

Greenville

Avon

Bath

264

Cape Hatteras

Swan Quarter

Pamlico Sound

Ocracoke Island

Kinston

Portsmouth Island

70

New Bern

Croatan National Forest

Core Banks

24

Beaufort

Morehead City

Cape Lookout

17

Topsail

ATLANTIC OCEAN

0   25 mi

0   25 km

© AVALON TRAVEL

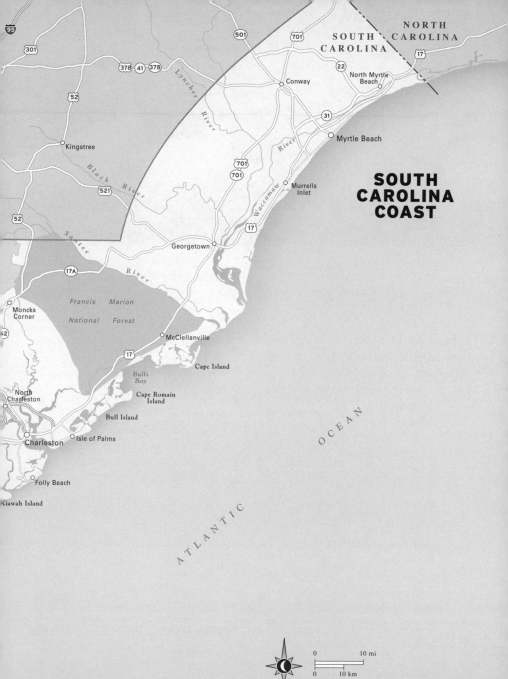

NORTH
SOUTH CAROLINA
CAROLINA

North Myrtle
Beach

Conway

Myrtle Beach

**SOUTH
CAROLINA
COAST**

Kingstree

Murrells
Inlet

Georgetown

Moncks
Corner

Francis   Marion

National   Forest

McClellanville

Cape Island

*Bulls
Bay*

Cape Romain
Island

North
Charleston

Bull Island

Charleston

Isle of Palms

Folly Beach

Kiawah Island

ATLANTIC

OCEAN

Lynches   River

Black   River

Santee   River

Waccamaw   River

0   10 mi

0   10 km

© AVALON TRAVEL

Contents

DISCOVER THE
Coastal Carolinas

From the wide, deep waterways of North Carolina on down to the South Carolina Sea Islands, there's a shared, effortless mystique over the 500-mile stretch of Carolina coast—a sense of time standing still that is both poignant and palpable. No mere poet's license, it's something you feel here, whether in the bracing tang of the sea breeze or the oddly comforting whiff of pluff mud at low tide.

The chronicle of this stretch of the Eastern seaboard includes some of the United States' oldest and most important recorded history. The names from its past echo on today: Sir Walter Raleigh, Blackbeard, Francis Marion, Fort Sumter, the Wright Brothers.

But outdoor recreation is by far the chief passion, almost all of it having to do with the waterways that virtually define the region. Swept by a constant, cooling breeze off the Atlantic and crisscrossed by hundreds of rivers, creeks, and marshes, the Carolina coast is an aquatic wonderland for boaters, kayakers, and naturalists alike.

Clockwise from top left: carriage ride in Charleston; Edisto Beach State Park; Bodie Island Lighthouse; Charleston's Pineapple Fountain; sweetgrass baskets; kayakers on Bald Head Island.

If you want family-themed vacationing, there are the commercial areas of Myrtle Beach, Hilton Head Island, or Wrightsville Beach, with their user-friendly stretches of sand and tourist infrastructures. For a more challenging journey, put the kayak on top of the car and head to the Great Dismal Swamp of North Carolina or the blackwater ACE Basin of South Carolina. For a remote, laid-back beach experience, hang out on the Outer Banks, or take a jaunt down to Edisto Island or Hunting Island and enjoy the beachfront life, South Carolina-style.

Locals and visitors alike also enjoy the fruits of the sea in the fresh catch that exemplifies the coastal Carolina plate. From Elizabeth City to Charleston to Port Royal, from fried to grilled to boiled, you can be assured of a tasty nautical treat at nearly every meal—though the barbecue around here is not too shabby, either!

Another common denominator along the Carolina coast is the people themselves. All have their distinctive identities, and they go by many names: the "wreckers" of the Outer Banks, the Down Easterners of the Core Sound, the Gullah of the South Carolina islands, even the "snowbirds" of Hilton Head. But the thread linking them all together—and infusing the atmosphere of the coastal Carolinas—is a gusto combining a gregariousness of spirit with a love of the simple pleasures of life.

Clockwise from top left: Wright Brothers National Memorial; the Angel Oak on Johns Island; Arthur Ravenel Jr. Bridge; Cape Lookout Lighthouse.

5 TOP EXPERIENCES

1 **Beaches:** Relax, play, or just admire the view at some of the best beaches in America (page 18).

2 **Historic Charleston:** Enjoy this historic city's well-preserved sights with a walking tour of its charming, winding streets (page 143).

3 **Marine Morsels:** From fresh oysters to shrimp & grits, the Carolinas are a haven for seafood lovers (page 19).

^
^
^
4 **Lighthouses:** Each one has a story to tell and a view to admire (page 21).

5 **Golf Galore:** Tee up a links-centric vacation at top-ranked, public courses, especially around Charleston, Myrtle Beach, and Hilton Head Island (page 241).

<<<

The Best of the Coastal Carolinas

From Nags Head to Hilton Head, this journey down the coast hits all the hot spots and highlights the region's culture, history, natural beauty, and rich maritime legacy.

North Carolina Coast

DAY 1

Begin at **Nags Head** on North Carolina's Outer Banks, your home base for the next couple of days, and enjoying the beach and the key local sights, **Jockey's Ridge State Park** and the **Wright Brothers National Memorial.**

DAY 2

This morning head down to windswept **Cape Hatteras National Seashore** and climb the historic lighthouse. Then, in the afternoon, head to Roanoke Island's **Fort Raleigh National Historic Site.** At night, perhaps take in a performance of "The Lost Colony" historical drama.

DAY 3

This morning enjoy the exquisite historic district in **New Bern,** with a visit to the gorgeous gardens at **Tryon Palace.** After a tasty lunch downtown, head to the ocean again and walk the waterfront at **Beaufort.** Don't miss a visit to the **North Carolina Maritime Museum** and the **Old Burying Ground.** Tonight drive down to **Wilmington** for the first of two nights at a fine B&B, such as the **Rosehill Inn.**

DAY 4

This morning tour Wilmington's historic homes: **Bellamy Mansion, the Burgwin-Wright House,** and the **Zebulon Latimer House** (save with a three-house ticket). After lunch, walk the

Nags Head, North Carolina

the USS *North Carolina* in Wilmington

decks of the **USS *North Carolina.*** Tonight have a quality meal downtown at any one of the fine eateries on and around **Water Street.**

DAY 5

After breakfast at your B&B, head out to the ocean for some fun at **Wrightsville Beach.** In the afternoon head south toward **Myrtle Beach.** Stop for fried seafood along the way at **Calabash,** on the border between North and South Carolina. Alternately, you could continue on to Myrtle Beach for a delightfully cheesy, utensil-free dinner show at Medieval Times at **Broadway at the Beach.**

South Carolina Coast

DAY 6

Today is your big **Myrtle Beach** day. Claim your patch of sand along the miles of beaches in the morning, and after lunch visit **Ripley's Aquarium,** shop at **Barefoot Landing,** or have a round of miniature golf. Tonight enjoy some down-home entertainment by catching a show at the **Carolina Opry,** quaffing an adult

beverage or two at **The Bowery,** or perhaps learning how to do the Shag at **Ocean Drive Beach.**

DAY 7

Work your way southward with a stop at **Brookgreen Gardens** on the Grand Strand, having lunch at the waterfront in nearby **Georgetown.** This afternoon visit gorgeous **Hampton Plantation,** then it's down to **Charleston.** After checking into your room at the **Andrew Pinckney Inn,** walk the **French Quarter,** including looks at St. Philip's Episcopal Church and the French Huguenot Church. Enjoy a classic Charleston dinner at one of any number of amazing restaurants nearby, such as **Peninsula Grill** or **Husk.**

DAY 8

This full day in Charleston includes some shopping on **King Street** and a walk along the **Battery** and nearby **Rainbow Row** for a snapshot of these photogenic mansions. For an afternoon historical road trip, cross the Cooper

Best Beaches

Hunting Island State Park

Best Scenery
- **Cape Hatteras National Seashore** (The Outer Banks)
- **Sullivan's Island** (Charleston)
- **Hunting Island State Park** (South Carolina Lowcountry)

Best for Families
- **Wrightsville Beach** (Wilmington and Cape Fear)
- **Kure Beach** (Wilmington and Cape Fear)
- **Myrtle Beach** (Myrtle Beach and the Grand Strand)
- **Isle of Palms** (Charleston)
- **Hilton Head Island** (South Carolina Lowcountry)

Best for Water Sports
- **Nags Head** (The Outer Banks)
- **Myrtle Beach** (Myrtle Beach and the Grand Strand)
- **Hilton Head Island** (South Carolina Lowcountry)

Best for Solitude
- **Cape Hatteras National Seashore** (The Outer Banks)
- **Ocracoke Island** (The Outer Banks)
- **Topsail Beach** (Wilmington and Cape Fear)

Most Local Character
- **Carolina Beach State Park** (Wilmington and Cape Fear)
- **Edisto Beach State Park** (Charleston)
- **Folly Beach** (Charleston)

Georgetown's waterfront

River to Mount Pleasant, and visit **Boone Hall Plantation** and the nearby **Charles Pinckney Historical Site.** For more recent history, visit the **Patriots Point Naval and Maritime Museum.** Tonight eat and drink in style in the **Upper King area.**

DAY 9

You have a full array of choices for this full day in Charleston, including a ferry ride to **Fort Sumter,** a jaunt across the Ashley River to **Kiawah Island.** If it's a weekend, you can head up to North Charleston to see the Confederate submarine **CSS *Hunley*** at the repurposed Charleston Navy Yard.

DAY 10

Finish your tour by spending the morning in historic **Bluffton** on the relaxing May River, browsing the art galleries. Then jaunt down to **Hilton Head Island** to relax on the beach, with a visit to **Sea Pines Forest Preserve** and **Harbour Town.**

Marine Morsels

The Coastal Carolinas are awash, literally, in seafood. Here are some epicurean highlights for the seafood lover.

MAY RIVER OYSTERS

The legendary freshness and taste of May River oysters are available right off the docks in the South Carolina Lowcountry at the **Bluffton Oyster Company** or in area seafood restaurants.

LOWCOUNTRY SIGNATURES

The Lowcountry's two signature dishes, **shrimp & grits** and **she crab soup,** are both available in delicious abundance in the Charleston area. Try **Poogan's Porch** for shrimp & grits and **Hyman's Seafood** north of town for she crab soup.

CALABASH SEAFOOD

The seaside North Carolina town of **Calabash,** just north of the state line with South Carolina, has given its name to an entire genre of seafood. Enjoy these fried delectables at one of about a dozen Calabash restaurants in the town itself, including **Calabash Seafood Hut** and **Dockside Seafood,** or in Myrtle Beach, **Original Benjamin's.**

FRIED HERRING

If the idea of fried herring sounds a bit weird, head straight to the **Cypress Grill** in Jamesville, North Carolina, east of Williamston in the Albemarle or Inner Banks region (Feb.-Apr.), and see how it's done. You can eat every part of the fish except for the backbone, and it's all crispy and delicious.

Charleston's French Quarter

Coastal Carolinas for Couples

With lovely beaches, charming cities, and evocative historic districts, the Carolina coast offers up some ideal spots for a couples' getaway, whatever your romantic style.

Outdoor Romance

Hunting Island is far more than a state park, it is also a state of mind, with beautiful, windswept beaches and an awesome view from the top of the lighthouse. Outdoor activities include kayaking the inlet where parts of *Forrest Gump* were filmed and bird-watching for loons, herons, egrets, and more. Share a tentsite, or hole up in one of the cabins (there's a minimum week-long stay in high season).

Although Myrtle Beach proper isn't necessarily one's first thought when one thinks of romance, **Huntington Beach State Park** boasts a great stretch of beach, several nature trails, and a fanciful "castle" mansion and grounds. Camp at the park, then go right across the highway to **Brookgreen Gardens,** America's largest collection of outdoor sculpture, which is perfect for strolls through the various nooks and crannies on the sprawling, verdant grounds.

City Romance

Charleston is one of the most romantic cities in the world, so you really can't go wrong there. Although it's not in the center of town, one of the most romantic spots in Charleston is **Middleton Place** and its magnificent gardens. Couples can even stay on the grounds, at the **Inn at Middleton Place,** in a room with floor-to-ceiling windows overlooking the gardens and the Ashley River.

For a little bit of Paris in the South, try the atmospheric **French Quarter.** Take a carriage ride or just enjoy the intimate streetscape. More social, young-at-heart couples will want to head to the hip **Upper King** area—stop at **39 Rue de Jean** for drinks and food.

Carolina Lighthouses

Often treacherous for sailors due to its geography and susceptibility to storms, the Carolina coast is chock-a-block with historic lighthouses. Generally speaking, most have public visiting hours, including "climbing" availability, from late spring to early fall. Sometimes the grounds remain open when the lighthouses are closed to the public. It's always a good idea to call ahead.

NORTH CAROLINA

- **Currituck Beach Lighthouse:** Still active, open to the public for climbing Easter-November.
- **Bodie Island Lighthouse:** Still active, closed to the public. Keeper's building is open to the public.
- **Cape Hatteras Lighthouse:** Still active, open to the public for climbing the third Friday in April until Columbus Day. Gorgeous view.
- **Ocracoke Lighthouse:** Still active, closed to the public. Grounds are open to the public.
- **Cape Lookout Lighthouse:** Still active, closed to the public. Keeper's quarters and grounds are open to the public.
- **Bald Head Island Lighthouse:** Inactive, open to the public year-round. State's oldest light.

SOUTH CAROLINA

- **Georgetown Lighthouse:** Still active, closed to the public.
- **Morris Island Lighthouse:** Inactive, closed to the public. You can get a great view of it from the north end of Folly Island.
- **Hunting Island Lighthouse:** Inactive, open to the public year-round for climbing. It's located within a popular state park and offers a stunning view.
- **Harbour Town Lighthouse:** Technically not a real lighthouse at all, but a tourist attraction within Sea Pines Plantation. Open to the public year-round for climbing.

the spiral staircase of Currituck Beach Lighthouse

Wilmington's Graystone Inn

Equal parts evocative antebellum seaport and trendy college town, **Wilmington** is also a great choice for a romantic trip. Choose from an abundance of B&Bs, like the **Graystone Inn,** and spend a weekend soaking in the city's beautiful 19th-century architecture and well-restored waterfront.

Historical Romance

New Bern is a handy little getaway for those who like strolling through a large and tastefully restored historic district.

For those seeking a smaller, more poignant historic town, try **Beaufort,** North Carolina, which has a palpable vestige of its very old seaport past. You can rent a houseboat for the weekend and spend the entire time floating on the water. Or on land, you can stroll through the Spanish moss and live oaks in the beautiful **Old Burying Ground.**

Just Us

Of course to really get away from it all—and I mean just about *all*—head to the Outer Banks of North Carolina and get on a ferry to windswept, sparsely populated **Ocracoke Island.**

If that seems like too much, you can drive to **Cape Hatteras National Seashore,** which also offers a sense of solitude.

a hiking trail on Ocracoke Island

African American Heritage

The life and contribution of the coastal Carolinas' African American population is a testament to resilience, resourcefulness, and authentic culture. Here are the key sights in the region: You can see them all in a five- or six-day road trip with stays in Wilmington, Charleston, and Beaufort, South Carolina, or combine them with other sights when you're headed to just one area.

WILMINGTON

- **Bellamy Mansion:** This historic mansion features extensive interpretive programming on African American history, as well as one of the few intact slave quarters in the United States.

- **Louise Wells Cameron Art Museum:** At this nationally renowned museum, you'll find artwork of notable regional African American artists.

GEORGETOWN

- **Rice Museum:** This museum has several exhibits on the contributions of African Americans in building the rice culture of the Lowcountry and the way they lived.

CHARLESTON

- **Old Slave Mart Museum:** This structure that once held an indoor slave market today re-creates what happened during those auctions and traces the history of the slave trade.

- **Old City Market:** On land donated to the city with the stipulation that no slaves were ever to be sold here, the City Market was once and still is a place for African American vendors to ply their wares.

- **Avery Research Center for African American History and Culture:** Those of an academic bent can visit this research center at the College of Charleston and view exhibits that sample from its permanent archives. While on this gorgeous campus, don't miss a visit to the Cistern area in front of historic Randolph Hall, where Barack Obama spoke before a large crowd during the 2008 presidential campaign.

- **Philip Simmons Garden:** View the wrought-iron art of Charleston's most beloved artisan in the garden of St. John's Reformed Episcopal Church.

- **Drayton Hall Plantation:** At this authentically preserved plantation building in West Ashley, you can take a tour and visit the old African American cemetery on the grounds.

- **Boone Hall Plantation:** Visit this former cotton plantation and still-active agriculture facility to see the excellent restored slave quarters and the well-done interpretive exhibits. While on Mount Pleasant don't miss the sweetgrass basket-maker stands all along Highway 17.

BEAUFORT, SOUTH CAROLINA

- **Robert Smalls House:** View the home of the African American Civil War hero Robert Smalls, who later served in Congress.

- **Tabernacle Baptist Church:** Robert Smalls attended this church, which today hosts a memorial sculpture of him on the grounds.

- **Beaufort National Cemetery:** This burial ground contains a memorial to African American Civil War troops.

THE LOWCOUNTRY

- **Penn Center:** Located on St. Helena Island, this is a key research and cultural site in the study of the Gullah culture and people.

- **Daufuskie Island:** The Historic District here is where Pat Conroy taught African American children at the still-standing Mary Field School.

- **Tuskegee Airmen Memorial:** Located inland in Walterboro, this monument is dedicated to the African American fighter pilots who trained here during World War II.

- **Union Cemetery:** This small but evocative cemetery on Hilton Head Island serves as the final resting ground of several soldiers of the Civil War Colored Infantry.

Mattamuskeet National Wildlife Refuge

Adventures in Nature

You could devote a lifetime to experiencing the diverse and evocative ecosystems of the Carolina coast. Here's a week-long trip covering the highlights.

Day 1

Begin up in the **Great Dismal Swamp** of North Carolina, where you'll spend the morning kayaking amid this anything-but-dismal ecosystem. Then head down to **Nags Head** on the Outer Banks, where you can stay in a beachfront motel for the night. If you have a four-wheel drive, on the way, you can drive onto the beach near **Corolla** and see the fabled herd of wild horses there.

Day 2

Spend the morning hang-gliding off the huge sand dune of **Jockey's Ridge State Park,** or head down to **Pea Island National Wildlife Refuge** on Hatteras Island for some bird-watching. This afternoon on your way down to Beaufort, North Carolina, stop at **Mattamuskeet National Wildlife Refuge** for some more bird-watching on this important flyway.

Day 3

Today in Beaufort you begin with a ferry ride to **Harkers Island** and a tour of **Cape Lookout National Seashore,** courtesy of Coastal Ecology Tours, where you'll enjoy the protected scenery and habitat. This afternoon visit the **North Carolina Aquarium** in back in Beaufort, where you'll spend one more night.

Day 4

Today you get up bright and early to head down the South Carolina coast to the blackwater **Edisto River,** where you'll take a waterborne tour with **Carolina Heritage Outfitters,** based northeast of Beaufort, South Carolina, and spend the night in a tree house upriver.

Day 5

This morning you paddle back down the Edisto River to your vehicle.

Planning Your Trip

Where to Go

The Outer Banks and Coastal Sounds

Probably the most **culturally unique** area in this guide, the **Outer Banks** of North Carolina still harbor charming pockets of a centuries-old seafaring tradition all along their wave- and wind-battered **beach strands.** The nearby **Coastal Sounds** provide a relaxing, sheltered counterpart to the Outer Banks' heavy traffic during the high season.

Wilmington and Cape Fear

The northernmost outpost of the **antebellum rice plantation** culture, classy little **Wilmington** has been featured in many **motion pictures** due to its nostalgically scenic character. The surrounding Cape Fear region features

several **beautiful, accessible beaches** for family enjoyment.

Myrtle Beach and the Grand Strand

The 60-mile Grand Strand focuses on the resort activity of **Myrtle Beach** and the adjacent, faster-growing North Myrtle Beach. Down the strand are the more peaceful areas of **Pawleys Island** and **Murrells Inlet,** with **historic Georgetown** anchoring the bottom portion of the long, skinny peninsula.

Charleston

One of America's oldest cities and an early national center of **arts and culture,** Charleston's legendary taste for the high life is matched by its

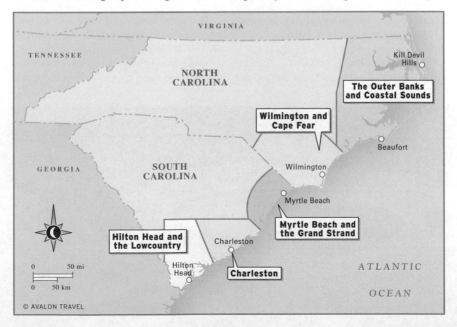

forward-thinking outlook. The birthplace of the **Civil War** is not just a city of museums resting on its historic laurels; the "Holy City" is now a **vibrant, creative hub** of the New South.

Hilton Head and the Lowcountry

The Lowcountry's **mossy, laid-back pace** belies its former status as the heart of American plantation culture and the original cradle of secession. Today it is a mix of **history** (Beaufort and Bluffton), **natural beauty** (the ACE Basin), **resort development** (Hilton Head), **military bases** (Parris Island), and **relaxed beaches** (Edisto and Hunting Islands).

When to Go

You can't go wrong hitting the Carolina coast in the **spring,** when the azaleas are in bloom and there's still a little dryness in the air. It is the absolute best time to visit Charleston and the Lowcountry. While a spring visit to the Grand Strand will avoid the crowds, the heat, and the jacked-up summer hotel prices, water temperatures will still be quite chilly at this time—equally so for the North Carolina Outer Banks.

Memorial Day weekend is a good time to visit anywhere in the coastal Carolinas; however, the beaches will be jammed. Despite Myrtle Beach's efforts to discourage big biker rallies during this period, there is still likely to be plenty of biker activity, which is harmless but can be intrusive.

Summer gets a bad rap in the South. The truly oppressive heat doesn't come until August, and the coast's sea breeze makes it much more endurable than sweltering inland areas. Late summer in the coastal Carolinas, however, means two things: humidity and hurricanes. Not until well after Labor Day will you be reasonably assured that a gathering storm will not spoil your vacation plans. To me, this is the least recommended time to visit.

September right after Labor Day is a perfect time to hit Myrtle Beach and the Grand Strand—lodging prices are cut dramatically and the crowds are much thinner, but the beach weather remains ideal.

My own favorite time to travel up and down the coast is **late October/early November,** when the kids are back in school, crowds are down, the weather is wonderful, prices are low, but there are still plenty of places open for business.

azaleas blooming in Charleston

The Outer Banks and Coastal Sounds

Look for ★ to find recommended sights, activities, dining, and lodging.

Highlights

★ **Wright Brothers National Memorial:** Visit this historic site for a fun, educational, and ultimately stirring chronicle of one of the greatest achievements in history—powered flight (page 31).

★ **Jockey's Ridge State Park:** The largest sand dune in the eastern United States is a great place to relax, enjoy the view, or fly a kite (page 32).

★ **Fort Raleigh National Historic Site:** The mysterious first chapter of English settlement in the New World unfolded here, at the site of the Lost Colony, in the 1580s (page 37).

★ **Ocracoke Island:** On this remote island, you'll find a historic village that houses one of America's most unique local communities, as well as some serious water sports and walking opportunities (page 45).

★ **Cape Lookout National Seashore:** More than 50 miles of coastline along four barrier islands are home to wild horses, dolphins, and turtle nests (page 47).

★ **North Carolina Maritime Museum:** North Carolina's seafaring heritage is represented in fascinating exhibits and activities at this great museum (page 50).

★ **Beaufort's Old Burying Ground:** In addition to being the final resting place of the "Little Girl Buried in a Barrel of Rum," this little churchyard has one of the prettiest cemeteries in the South (page 51).

★ **North Carolina Aquarium:** Sharks, jellyfish, and a myriad of other sea creatures show

their true beauty in these underwater habitats (page 55).

★ **The Great Dismal Swamp:** This natural wonder straddling the Virginia–North Carolina line is an amazing place for canoeing, kayaking, bird-watching, and sightseeing (page 56).

★ **Tryon Palace:** The splendid and, in its day, controversial seat of colonial government in North Carolina is reconstructed in New Bern's historic district (page 61).

T he Outer Banks are like a great seine net set along the northeastern corner of North Carolina, holding the Sounds and inner coast apart from the open ocean, yet shimmying obligingly with the forces of water and wind.

The Outer Banks can be—and on many occasions have been—profoundly transformed by a single storm. A powerful hurricane can fill in a centuries-old inlet in one night, and open a new channel wherever it pleases. As recently as 2003, Hatteras Island was cut in half (by Hurricane Isabel), though the channel has since been artificially filled. This evanescent landscape poses challenges to the life that it supports, and creates adaptable and hardy plants, animals, and people.

The Sounds are often overlooked by travelers, but they are an enormously important part of the state and the region. Collectively known as the Albemarle-Pamlico Estuary, North Carolina's Sounds—Albemarle, Pamlico, Core, Croatan, Roanoke, and Currituck—form the second-largest estuarine system in the country after the Chesapeake Bay.

Sheltered from the Atlantic, the Inner Banks are much more accommodating, ecologically speaking, than the Outer Banks. Wetlands along the Sounds invite migratory birds by the hundreds of thousands to shelter and rest, while pocosins (a special kind of bog found in the region) and maritime forests have nurtured a great variety of life for eons. Here is where North Carolina's oldest towns—Bath, New Bern, and Edenton—set down roots, from which the rest of the state grew and bloomed.

You may hear folks in North Carolina refer to any point on the coast, be it Wilmington or Nags Head, as "Down East." In the most authentic, local usage of the term, Down East really refers to northeastern Carteret County, to the islands and marsh towns in a confined region along the banks of Core Sound, north of Beaufort.

PLANNING YOUR TIME

The standard beach-season rules apply to the coastal areas covered in this chapter. Lodging

---

Previous: Outer Banks beach; Tryon Palace in New Bern. **Above:** Wright Brothers National Memorial.

The Outer Banks and Coastal Sounds

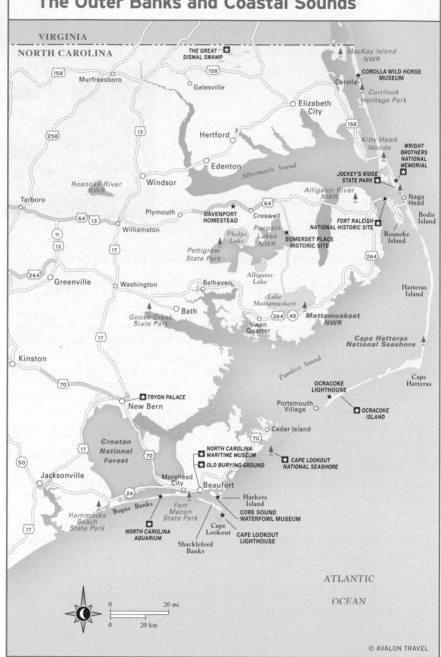

VIRGINIA

NORTH CAROLINA

THE GREAT DISMAL SWAMP

MacKay Island NWR

COROLLA WILD HORSE MUSEUM

158 Murfreesboro

158

Gatesville

Corolla

Currituck Heritage Park

Elizabeth City

158

258

13

Hertford

Kitty Hawk Woods

WRIGHT BROTHERS NATIONAL MEMORIAL

Edenton

Albermarle Sound

JOCKEY'S RIDGE STATE PARK

Roanoke River NWR

Windsor

Alligator River NWR

Nags Head

Tarboro

64

Plymouth

DAVENPORT HOMESTEAD

Creswell

64

FORT RALEIGH NATIONAL HISTORIC SITE

Bodie Island

64 13

Williamston

11

13

17

Phelps Lake

Pocosin Lakes NWR

SOMERSET PLACE HISTORIC SITE

Roanoke Island

Pettigrew State Park

264

264

Greenville

Washington

Belhaven

Alligator Lake

Hatteras Island

Bath

Lake Mattamuskeet

Goose Creek State Park

264 45 Mattamuskeet NWR

17

Swan Quarter

Cape Hatteras National Seashore

Kinston

Pamlico Sound

70

TRYON PALACE

New Bern

OCRACOKE LIGHTHOUSE

Portsmouth Village

Cape Hatteras

OCRACOKE ISLAND

Cedar Island

Croatan National Forest

70

70

NORTH CAROLINA MARITIME MUSEUM

OLD BURYING GROUND

CAPE LOOKOUT NATIONAL SEASHORE

50

Jacksonville

Morehead City

Beaufort

Harkers Island

24

Fort Macon State Park

CORE SOUND WATERFOWL MUSEUM

Hammocks Beach State Park

Bogue Banks

NORTH CAROLINA AQUARIUM

Cape Lookout

Shackleford Banks

CAPE LOOKOUT LIGHTHOUSE

17

ATLANTIC

OCEAN

0   20 mi

0   20 km

© AVALON TRAVEL

prices go up dramatically between Memorial Day and Labor Day, and though you might score a rock-bottom price if you visit on a mild weekend off-season, you might also find that some of the destinations you'd like to visit are closed.

Coastal North Carolina is beautiful four seasons of the year, and for many people fall and winter are favorite times to visit. These are wonderful times for canoeing and kayaking on eastern North Carolina's rivers, creeks, and swamps.

Late summer and early autumn are hurricane season all through the Southeast. Hurricane paths are unpredictable, so if you're planning a week on the beach and know that a hurricane is hovering over Cuba, it won't necessarily hit North Carolina, although the central Carolina coast is always an odds-on favorite for landfall.

INFORMATION AND SERVICES

The **Aycock Brown Welcome Center** (milepost 1.5, U.S. 158, 877/629-4386, www.outerbanks.org, Dec.-Feb. daily 9am-5pm, Mar.-May and Sept.-Nov. daily 9am-5:30pm, June-Aug. daily 9am-6pm) at Kitty Hawk, the **Outer Banks Welcome Center** (1 Visitors Center Circle, Manteo), and the **Cape Hatteras National Seashore Visitors Center** (Cape Hatteras Lighthouse, Memorial Day-Labor Day daily 9am-6pm, Labor Day-Memorial Day daily 9am-5pm) on Ocracoke are all clearinghouses for regional travel information. The **Outer Banks Visitors Bureau** (www.outerbanks.org) can be reached directly at 877/629-4386. Extensive travel information is also available from the **Crystal Coast Tourism Authority** (3409 Arendell St., Morehead City, 877/206-0929, www.crystalcoastnc.org).

Nags Head and Vicinity

The Outer Banks comprise a long sandbar, constantly eroding and amassing, slip-sliding into new configurations with every storm. The wind is the invisible player in this process, the man behind the curtain giving orders to the water and the sand. The enormous dune known as Jockey's Ridge was a landmark to early mariners, visible from miles out to sea.

According to legend, Nags Head was a sinister place of peril to those seafarers. Islanders, it's said, would walk a nag or mule, carrying a lantern around its neck, slowly back and forth along the beach, trying to lure ships into the shallows where they might founder or wreck, making their cargo easy pickings for the land pirates.

SIGHTS
★ Wright Brothers National Memorial

Although they are remembered for a 12-second flight on a December morning in 1903, Wilbur and Orville Wright actually spent more than three years coming and going between their home in Dayton, Ohio, and Kitty Hawk, North Carolina. As they tested their gliders on Kill Devil Hill, the tallest sand dune on the Outer Banks, the Wright brothers were helped by many locals, who fed and housed them, built hangars, and assisted with countless practicalities that helped make the brothers' experiment a success. On the morning of December 17, 1903, several local people were present to help that famous first powered flight get off the ground. That flight is honored at the **Wright Brothers National Memorial** (milepost 7.5, U.S. 158, Kill Devil Hills, 252/441-7430, www.nps.gov/wrbr, park year-round daily, visitors center June-Aug. daily 9am-6pm, Sept.-May daily 9am-5pm, free). At the visitors center, replica gliders are on display, along with artifacts from the original gliders and changing displays sponsored by NASA. You can also climb Kill Devil Hill to get a glimpse of what that first aviator saw.

marking the historic first flight of the Wright Brothers

★ Jockey's Ridge State Park

Jockey's Ridge State Park (Carolista Dr., off milepost 12, U.S. 158, Nags Head, 252/441-7132, www.jockeysridgestatepark.com, Nov.-Feb. daily 8am-6pm, Mar. and Oct. daily 8am-7pm, Apr.-May and Sept. daily 8am-8pm, June-Aug. daily 8am-9pm) contains 420 acres of a strange and amazing environment, the largest active sand dune system in the eastern United States. Ever-changing, this ocean-side desert is maintained by the constant action of the northeast and southwest winds. Visitors can walk on and among the dunes. It's a famously great place to fly kites, go sand-boarding, and hang glide (hang gliding requires a valid USHGA rating and a permit supplied by the park office).

Nags Head Woods Ecological Preserve

Bordering Jockey's Ridge is another unique natural area, The Nature Conservancy's **Nags Head Woods Ecological Preserve** (701 W. Ocean Acres Dr., about 1 mile from milepost 9.5, U.S. 158, 252/441-2525, www.nature.org, daily dawn-dusk). Nags Head Woods is over 1,000 acres of deciduous maritime forest, dunes, wetlands, and interdune ponds. More than 50 species of birds nest here in season, including ruby-throated hummingbirds, green herons, and red-shouldered hawks, and it is also home to a host of other animals and unusual plants.

Kitty Hawk Woods

Slightly smaller but no less important is The Nature Conservancy's **Kitty Hawk Woods** (south of U.S. 158 at Kitty Hawk, trail access from Woods Rd. and Birch Lane, off Treasure St., 252/261-8891, www.nature.org, daily dawn-dusk). These maritime forests harbor the unusual species of flora and fauna of the maritime swale ecosystem, a swampy forest sheltered between coastal ridges. Kitty Hawk Woods is open to the public for hiking and birding, and can be explored from the water as well. A canoe and kayak put-in is next to the parking lot of **Kitty Hawk Kayaks** (6150 N. Croatan Rd./U.S. 158, 252/261-0145, www.khkss.com).

Currituck Heritage Park

The shore of Currituck Sound is an unexpected place to find the art deco home of a 1920s industrial magnate. The **Whalehead Club** (1100 Club Rd., off milepost 11, Hwy. 12, 252/453-9040, www.whaleheadclub.com, visitors center 11am-5pm daily, standard

Nags Head and Vicinity

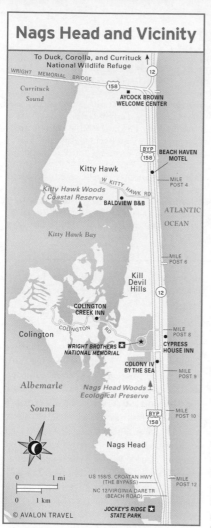

To Duck, Corolla, and Currituck
National Wildlife Refuge
WRIGHT MEMORIAL BRIDGE
12
158
Currituck
Sound
AYCOCK BROWN
WELCOME CENTER
BYP 158 BEACH HAVEN
MOTEL
Kitty Hawk
W KITTY HAWK RD
MILE
POST 4
Kitty Hawk Woods
Coastal Reserve
BALDVIEW B&B
ATLANTIC
OCEAN
Kitty Hawk Bay
MILE
POST 6
Kill
Devil
Hills
12
COLINGTON
CREEK INN
COLINGTON RD
MILE
POST 8
Colington
CYPRESS
HOUSE INN
WRIGHT BROTHERS
NATIONAL MEMORIAL
COLONY IV
BY THE SEA
MILE
POST 9
Albemarle
Nags Head Woods
Ecological Preserve
Sound
BYP 158
MILE
POST 10
Nags Head
0   1 mi
US 158/S. CROATAN HWY
(THE BYPASS)
MILE
POST 12
NC 12/VIRGINIA DARE TR
(BEACH ROAD)
0   1 km
JOCKEY'S RIDGE
STATE PARK
© AVALON TRAVEL

Sound, the center also has a huge collection of antique decoys—an important folk tradition of the Carolina coast.

The 1875 **Currituck Beach Lighthouse** (Currituck Heritage Park, 252/453-4939, Apr.-Nov. daily 9am-5pm, closed in rough weather, $8, free under age 7) stands on the other side of the Center for Wildlife Education. It is one of the few historic lighthouses that visitors can climb. The 214-step spiral staircase leads to the huge Fresnel lens and a panoramic view of Currituck Sound.

Corolla Wild Horse Museum

In the town of Corolla, the circa-1900 Corolla Schoolhouse has been transformed into a museum honoring the wild horses of the Outer Banks. The **Corolla Wild Horse Museum** (1126 Old Schoolhouse Lane, Corolla, 252/453-8002, summer Mon.-Sat. 10am-4pm, off-season hours vary, free) tells of the history of the herd, which once roamed all over Corolla but now lives in a preserve north of the town.

ENTERTAINMENT AND EVENTS

The **Outer Banks Brewing Station** (milepost 8.5, Croatan Hwy./U.S. 158, Kill Devil Hills, 252/449-2739, www.obbrewing.com) was founded in the early 1990s by a group of friends who met in the Peace Corps. The brewery-restaurant they built here was designed and constructed by Outer Bankers, modeled on the design of the old lifesaving stations so important in the region's history. The pub serves several very gourmet homebrews at $4.50 for a pint, $6 for four five-ounce samplers.

Bacu Grill (Outer Banks Mall, milepost 14, U.S. 158, Nags Head, 252/480-1892), a Cuban-fusion restaurant, features live jazz and blues music, and serves good beer, wine, and snacks into the wee hours of the morning. **Kelly's Outer Banks Restaurant and Tavern** (milepost 10.5. U.S. 158, Nags Head, 252/441-4116, www.kellysrestaurant.com, Sun.-Thurs. 4:30pm-midnight, Fri.-Sat. 4:30pm-2am) is

tours 9am-4pm daily, specialty tours require 24 hours advance notice, $5-15) was built as a summer cottage by Edward Collings Knight Jr., an industrialist whose fortune was in railroads and sugar.

Next to the Whalehead Club is the **Outer Banks Center for Wildlife Education** (Currituck Heritage Park, Corolla, 252/453-0221, www.ncwildlife.org, daily 9am-5pm, free). With exhibits focusing on the native birds, fish, and other creatures of Currituck

Pronunciation Primer

The Outer Banks are a garland of peculiar names, as well as names that look straightforward but are in fact pronounced in unexpectedly quirky ways. If you make reference publicly to the town of **Corolla,** and pronounce it like the Toyota model, you'll be recognized right away as someone "from off." It's pronounced "ker-AH-luh." Similarly, **Bodie Island,** site of the stripy lighthouse, is pronounced "body," as in one's earthly shell. That same pattern of pronouncing o as "ah," as in "stick out your tongue and say 'ah,'" is repeated farther down the coast at **Chicamacomico,** which comes out "chick-uh-muh-CAH-muh-co." But just to keep you on your toes, the rule doesn't apply to **Ocracoke,** which is pronounced like the Southern vegetable and Southern drink: "OH-kruh-coke."

Farther south along the banks is the town of **Rodanthe,** which has an elongated last syllable, "ro-DANTH-ee." On Roanoke Island, **Manteo** calls out for a Spanish emphasis, but is in fact front-loaded, like so many Carolina words and names. It's pronounced "MAN-tee-oh" or "MANNY-oh." Next door is the town of **Wanchese.** This sounds like a pallid dairy product, "WAN-cheese." Inland, the **Cashie River** is pronounced "cuh-SHY," **Bertie County** is "ber-TEE," and **Chowan County** is "chuh-WON."

also a good bet for live music and has a long wine list with some lovely vintages. **Lucky 12 Tavern** (3308 S. Virginia Dare Tr., Nags Head, 252/255-5825, www.lucky12tavern.com, daily 11:30am-2am) is a traditional sports bar with TVs, foosball, and New York-style pizza.

SPORTS AND RECREATION
Diving
The **Outer Banks Dive Center** (3917 S. Croatan Hwy., 252/449-8349, www.obxdive. com) offers instruction and guided tours of wrecks off the coast of the Outer Banks. Guided wreck dives are only available April-November. All levels of divers are welcome.

Hiking and Touring
The **Currituck Banks National Estuarine Preserve** (Hwy. 12, 252/261-8891, www.nc-coastalreserve.net) protects nearly 1,000 acres of woods and water extending into Currituck Sound. A 0.3-mile boardwalk runs from the parking lot to the sound, and a primitive trail runs from the parking lot 1.5 miles through the maritime forest.

Back Country Outfitters and Guides (107-C Corolla Light Town Center, Corolla, 252/453-0877, http://outerbankstours.com) leads a variety of tours in the Corolla region,

including Segway beach tours, wild horse-watching trips, kayaking, and other off-road tours.

Surfing
The North Carolina coast has a strong surfing culture, not to mention strong waves, making this a top destination for experienced surfers and those who would like to learn. **Island Revolution Surf Co. and Skatepark** (Corolla Light Town Center, 252/453-9484, www.islandrevolution.com, must be over age 8 and a good swimmer, group lessons $60 pp, private lessons $75) offers private and one-on-one surfing lessons as well as board rentals. So does **Ocean Atlantic Rentals** (Corolla Light Town Center, 252/453-2440, www.oar-nc.com, group lessons $50 pp, private lessons $75, couples $120, must know how to swim), which also has locations in Duck, Nags Head, and Avon, and **Corolla Surf Shop** (several locations, 252/453-9283, www.corollasurf-shop.com, age 9 and up).

Kayaking
The Outer Banks combine two very different possible kayaking experiences—the challenge of ocean kayaking and the leisurely drifting zones of the salt marshes and back creeks. **Kitty Hawk Sports** (798 Sunset Blvd.,

252/453-6900, www.kittyhawksports.com) is an old and established outdoors outfitter that leads kayaking and other expeditions. Another good bet is **Kitty Hawk Kayaks** (6150 N. Croatan Hwy., Kitty Hawk, 866/702-5061, www.khkss.com), which teaches kayaking and canoeing, rents equipment for paddling and surfing, and, in cooperation with The Nature Conservancy, leads tours, including overnight expeditions, through gorgeous waterways in pristine habitats.

Kitty Hawk Kites (877/359-8447, www.kittyhawk.com), which *National Geographic Adventure* magazine calls one of the "Best Adventure Travel Companies on Earth," has locations throughout the Outer Banks, including at Corolla.

Coastal Kayak (make reservations at North Beach Outfitters, 1240 Duck Rd., Duck, 252/261-6262, www.coastalkayak.org) offers tours throughout the northern Outer Banks, including guided trips through the Alligator River National Wildlife Refuge and the Pea Island National Wildlife Refuge, as well as the Pine Island Audubon Sanctuary and Kitty Hawk Woods. Tours last 2 to 3.5 hours and cost $35-50.

FOOD

Sam & Omie's (7728 S. Virginia Dare Tr., Nags Head, 252/441-7366, www.samandomies.net, Mar.-mid-Dec. daily 7am-10pm, $10-25) was opened during the summer of 1937, a place for charter fishing customers and guides to catch a spot of breakfast before setting sail. It still serves breakfast, with lots of options in the eggs and hotcakes department, including a few specialties like crab and eggs Benedict. It also has a dinner menu starring seasonal steamed and fried oysters, Delmonico steaks, and barbecue.

Tale of the Whale (7575 S. Virginia Dare Tr., Nags Head, 252/441-7332, www.taleofthewhalenagshead.com, spring-fall daily 4pm-9pm, closed winter, $15-50) sits at a beautiful location, at the very edge of the water with a pier jutting into Roanoke Sound. There's outdoor music from a pier-side gazebo and a dining room with such a great view of the water that it feels like the inside of a ship—but the real draw is the incredibly extensive menu of seafood, steak, and pasta specials. They also have an imaginative cocktail menu.

Grits Grill and Bakery (5000 S. Croatan Hwy., Nags Head, 252/449-2888, daily 6am-3pm, $7-12) is a favorite for breakfast, famous for its biscuits, Krispy Kreme doughnuts, eggs, and, of course, grits.

The ★ **Blue Point** (1240 Duck Rd., Duck, 252/261-8090, www.goodfoodgoodwine.com, lunch Tues.-Sun.11:30am-2:30pm, dinner daily 5pm-9:30pm, closed Mon. in winter, $20-35) has a nouveau Southern menu, with staples like catfish and trout done up in creative ways. Among the specialties, fresh Carolina shrimp is presented on "barley risotto," with broccolini, wine-soaked raisins, and lemon arugula pesto. After-dinner drinks (among them espresso martinis and special dessert wines) complement an amazing wine list that is, if anything, even more impressive than the menu. Reservations are very necessary.

Owens' Restaurant (milepost 16.5, Beach Rd., Nags Head, 252/441-7309, www.owensrestaurant.com, daily 5pm-9pm, $12-25) has been in operation at Nags Head for more than 60 years, and in addition to its good seafood menu, visitors enjoy looking over the owners' collection of historical artifacts from Outer Banks maritime life. **Blue Moon Beach Grill** (4104 S. Virginia Dare Tr., Nags Head, 252/261-2583, www.bluemoonbeachgrill.com, daily 11:30am-9pm, $12-25) is a local favorite known for its seafood dishes, and it's also a popular place to grab a draft beer after work. **Tortuga's Lie** (milepost 11.5, U.S. 158/Beach Rd., 252/441-7299, www.tortugaslie.com, Sun.-Thurs. 11:30am-9:30pm, Fri.-Sat. 11:30am-10pm, $10-20) has a good and varied menu specializing in seafood (some of it local) with Caribbean-inspired preparations, with some good vegetarian options.

For casual and on-the-go chow options at Nags Head, try **Maxximuss Pizza** (5205 S. Croatan Hwy., Nags Head, 252/441-2377,

Sun.-Thurs. noon-9pm, Fri.-Sat. noon-11pm, $12-20), which specializes in calzones, subs, and panini, in addition to pizza; **Yellow Submarine** (milepost 14, U.S. 158 Bypass, Nags Head, 252/441-3511, May-Sept. Mon.-Sat. 11am-9pm, Sun. noon-9pm, Mar.-Apr., Oct.-Nov. Tues.-Sat. 11:30am-8pm, Sun. 1pm-8pm, $7-16), a super-casual sub and pizza shop; or **Majik Beanz** (4104 S. Virginia Dare Tr., Nags Head, 252/255-2700, Sun.-Wed. 7am-3pm, Thurs.-Sat. 7am-10pm) for coffee and shakes.

ACCOMMODATIONS
Under $150

The ★ **First Colony Inn** (6720 Virginia Dare Tr., Nags Head, 800/368-9390, www.firstcolonyinn.com, $69-299, depending on season) is a wonderful 1932 beachfront hotel. This regional landmark has won historic preservation and landscaping awards for its 1988 renovation, which involved moving the entire building, in three pieces, three miles south of its original location. The pretty and luxurious guest rooms are surprisingly affordable.

Bed-and-breakfasts include the sound-front **Cypress Moon Inn** (1206 Harbor Ct., Kitty Hawk, 877/905-5060, www.cypressmooninn.com, age 18 and over, $200 summer, $175 spring and fall, $135 winter), with three pretty guest rooms. The **Baldview B&B** (3805 Elijah Baum Rd., Kitty Hawk, 252/255-2829, www.baldview.com, no children or pets, $125-200) is a modern residence located on a beautiful property along the sound, with four nicely appointed guest rooms and a carriage house.

The **Cypress House Inn** (milepost 8, Beach Rd., Kill Devil Hills, 800/554-2764, www.cypresshouseinn.com, $99-199, depending on season) is a very traditional coastal Carolina-style house, built in the 1940s and an easy walk to the beach. Its hurricane shutters and cypress-paneled guest rooms will give you a taste of Outer Banks life in the days before the motels and resorts.

In Kitty Hawk and Nags Head, you'll find an abundance of motels, from chains to classic 1950s mom-and-pops. The **Surf Side Hotel**

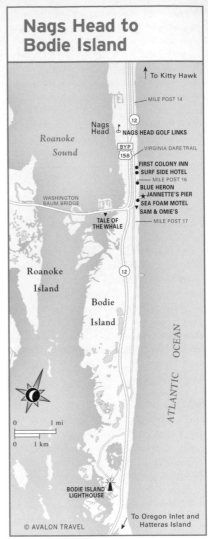

Nags Head to Bodie Island

↑ To Kitty Hawk

MILE POST 14

Roanoke Sound

Nags Head

NAGS HEAD GOLF LINKS

VIRGINIA DARE TRAIL

FIRST COLONY INN
SURF SIDE HOTEL
MILE POST 16
BLUE HERON
JANNETTE'S PIER
SEA FOAM MOTEL
SAM & OMIE'S

WASHINGTON BAUM BRIDGE

TALE OF THE WHALE

MILE POST 17

Roanoke Island

Bodie Island

ATLANTIC OCEAN

0   1 mi

0   1 km

BODIE ISLAND LIGHTHOUSE

To Oregon Inlet and Hatteras Island

© AVALON TRAVEL

(6701 Virginia Dare Tr., Nags Head, www.surfsideobx.com, 800/552-7873, from $55 off-season, from $165 high season) is a favorite for simple and comfortable accommodations, with standard rooms and efficiencies in a location right on the dunes. All guest rooms at the **Blue Heron** (6811 Virginia Dare Tr., Nags Head, 252/441-7447, www.blueheronnc.com, from $50 off-season, from $130 high season) face the ocean. The Blue Heron has a heated indoor pool as a consolation on rainy days. Super-affordable is the **Sea Foam Motel** (7111 Virginia Dare Tr., Nags Head, 252/441-7320, www.outer-banks.nc.us, from $62 off-season, from $110 high season), an old-timer with a lot of retro appeal. Other good choices in the area include the **Colony IV by the Sea** (405 S. Virginia Tr., Kill Devil Hills, 252/441-5581, www.motelbythesea.com, $68-163, depending on season) and **Beach Haven Motel** (milepost 4, Ocean Rd., Kitty Hawk, 888/559-0506, www.beachhavenmotel.com, from $65 off-season, from $105 high season).

$150-300

The **Colington Creek Inn** (1293 Colington Rd., Kill Devil Hills, 252/449-4124, www.colingtoncreekinn.com, no children or pets, $168-198, depending on season) is a large outfit with a great view of the sound and its namesake creek.

The **Sanderling Resort and Spa** (1461 Duck Rd., near Duck, 877/650-4812, www.thesanderling.com, $130-450) is a conventional full-size resort, with three lodges, a spa, and three restaurants that include the Lifesaving Station, housed in an 1899 maritime rescue station. There are various sports and recreational rental options.

TRANSPORTATION

The closest major airport to this region is the **Norfolk International Airport** (ORF, 2200 Norview Ave., Norfolk, VA, 757/857-3351, www.norfolkairport.com), approximately one hour's drive from the northern Outer Banks. **Raleigh-Durham International Airport** (RDU, 2600 W. Terminal Blvd., Morrisville, NC, 919/840-2123, www.rdu.com) is 3 to 5 hours' drive from most Outer Banks destinations.

Only two bridges exist between the mainland and the northern Outer Banks. U.S. 64/264 crosses over Roanoke Island to Whalebone, just south of Nags Head. Not too far north of there, U.S. 158 crosses from Point Harbor to Southern Shores. Highway 12 is the main road all along the northern Outer Banks.

Roanoke Island

Roanoke Island was the site of the Lost Colony, one of the strangest mysteries in all of American history. Its sheltered location—nestled between the Albemarle, Roanoke, and Croatan Sounds, and protected from the ocean by Bodie Island—made Roanoke Island a welcoming spot for that party of ocean-weary English people in the 1580s. Unhappily, they lacked the ability to make one of the bed-and-breakfast inns in Manteo or Wanchese their home base. Instead they cast their lots in the wilderness, and what befell them may never be known.

At the northern end of Roanoke Island is the town of Manteo and the Fort Raleigh National Historic Site. This is where most of the attractions and visitor services are concentrated. At the southern end is Wanchese, where some of Dare County's oldest families carry on their ancestral trades of fishing and boatbuilding.

★ FORT RALEIGH NATIONAL HISTORIC SITE

Fort Raleigh National Historic Site (1401 National Park Dr., Manteo, 252/473-5772, www.nps.gov/fora, park daily dawn-dusk except Christmas Day, visitors center Sept.-May daily 9am-5pm, June-Aug. daily 9am-6pm, park admission free, admission charged for Elizabethan Gardens and *The Lost Colony*) covers much of the original site of the first English settlement in the New World. Some of the earthworks associated with the original 1580s fort remain and have been preserved.

Roanoke Island

© AVALON TRAVEL

The visitors center displays some of the artifacts discovered during this restoration effort. Two nature trails in the park explore the island's natural landscape and the location of a Civil War battle.

Within the National Historic Site, two of Manteo's most famous attractions operate autonomously. About 60 years ago, Manteo's **Elizabethan Gardens** (252/473-3234, www.elizabethangardens.org, hours vary, $9 adults, $6 children) was conceived by the Garden Club of North Carolina as a memorial to the settlers of Roanoke Island. Much of the beautifully landscaped park re-creates the horticulture of the colonists' native England in the 16th century.

Also within the park boundaries is the Waterside Theater. North Carolina has a long history of outdoor drama celebrating regional heritage, and the best known of the many productions across the state is Roanoke Island's *The Lost Colony* (Fort Raleigh National Historic Site, Roanoke, 252/473-3414, www.thelostcolony.org, $30 adults, $28 seniors, $10 children). Chapel Hill playwright Paul Green was commissioned to write the drama in 1937 to celebrate the 350th anniversary of Virginia Dare's birth. What was expected to be a single-season production has returned almost every year for over 80 years, interrupted only occasionally for emergencies such as prowling German U-boats.

OTHER SIGHTS

The **North Carolina Maritime Museum** (104 Fernando St., Manteo, 252/475-1750, www.obxmaritime.org, hours vary, free), whose mother venue is located in Beaufort, operates a branch here on Roanoke Island. In addition to the many traditional Outer Banks working watercraft on display, the museum holds boatbuilding and handling courses at its George Washington Creef Boathouse. Visitors not enrolled in classes can still come in and watch traditional boatbuilders at work in the shop.

The **North Carolina Aquarium on Roanoke Island** (374 Airport Rd., 3 miles north of Manteo, 866/332-3475, www.ncaquariums.com, daily 9am-5pm, $10.95 adults, $8.95 children) is one of three state aquariums on the North Carolina coast. It's a great place to visit and see all sorts of marine fauna: sharks and other less ferocious fish, crustaceans, octopuses, turtles, and more. Like its sister aquariums, it's also a research station where marine biologists track and work to conserve the native creatures of the coast.

Roanoke Island Festival Park (1 Festival Park, Manteo, 252/475-1500, www.roanokeisland.com, Feb. 19-Mar. and Nov.-Dec. daily 9am-5pm, Apr.-Oct. daily 9am-6pm, $8 adults, $5 ages 6-17, free under age 6) is a state-operated living history site. The highlight is the *Elizabeth II,* a reconstruction of a 16th-century ship like the ones that brought Walter Raleigh's colonists to the New World. There is also a museum, a reconstructed settlement site, and several other places where costumed interpreters will tell you about daily life in the Roanoke colony.

TOURS

The **Downeast Rover** (sails from Manteo waterfront, 252/473-4866, www.downeastrover.com, daytime cruises $30 adults, $15 ages 2-12, sunset cruises $40) is a reproduction 19th-century 55-foot schooner that sails from Manteo on daytime and sunset cruises. Cruises last two hours and depart three times daily at 11am, 2pm, and sunset. To see the Outer Banks from the air, your options include a World War II biplane or a closed-cockpit Cessna through **Fly the Outer Banks** (410 Airport Rd., Manteo, 252/202-7433, $38-98), or a biplane through **Barrier Island Aviation** (407 Airport Rd., 252/473-4247, www.barrierislandaviation.com, $40-150).

SHOPPING

Manteo Booksellers (105 Sir Walter Raleigh St., 252/473-1221 or 866/473-1222, www.manteobooksellers.com, daily 10am-6pm) is a great independent bookstore, specializing in Outer Banks history and nature, but with a wide selection for all tastes.

Endless Possibilities (105 Budleigh St., 252/475-1575, www.ragweavers.com, Mon.-Sat. 10am-5pm) is an unusual sort of a shop where you can buy purses, boas, rugs, and other adornments of home and body made from recycled secondhand clothes. All the profits go to support the Outer Banks Hotline Crisis Intervention and Prevention Center, a regional help line for victims of rape and

See *The Lost Colony* at Waterside Theater at Fort Raleigh National Historic Site.

The Lost Colony

On July 4, 1584, an expedition of Englishmen commissioned by Walter Raleigh dropped anchor near Hatteras Island. Within a couple of days, local Native Americans were coming and going from the English ships, scoping out trade goods and offering hospitality. They got on famously, and when the English sailed back to Europe to tell Raleigh and the queen of the land they had found, two Indian men, Manteo and Wanchese, came along as guests. It seems that Wanchese was somewhat taciturn and found London to be no great shakes, but Manteo got a kick out of everything he saw and took to the English.

In 1585 a new expedition set out for Roanoke, this time intending to settle in earnest. When they reached the Pamlico Sound, their bad luck began. Most of their store of food was soaked and ruined when seawater breached the ship, so from the moment they arrived on shore they were dependent on the goodwill of the indigenous people. Manteo and Wanchese went to Roanoke chief Wingina to discuss the plight of the English. Wanchese, a man of superior insight, tried to convince Wingina to withhold help, but Manteo pled the colonists' case convincingly, and the English were made welcome. Winter came, and the colonists, having grown fat and happy on the local people's food, were doing precious little to attain self-sufficiency. Then a silver cup disappeared from the English compound. It was posited that the thief came from a nearby village, which was promptly burned to the ground. Worried about his own people, Wingina cut off food aid, hoping the English would either starve or go away. Instead, they killed him. Three weeks later, an English supply ship arrived with reinforcements of men and material, but they found the colony deserted.

Yet another attempt was made, this time with whole families rather than gangs of rowdy single men. A young couple named Eleanor and Ananais Dare was expecting a child when they landed at Roanoke, and soon Virginia Dare was born, the first English child born in the New World. Relations with the Native Americans grew worse, though, when the Roanoke people, now under the leadership of Wanchese, were unwilling to aid a new wave of colonists. Manteo, still a friend, tried to enlist the help of his kinfolk, but they were facing lean times as well. John White, leader of the expedition and grandfather of Virginia Dare, set out on what he planned would be a fast voyage back to England for supplies and food. Through no fault of his own, it was three years before he was able to return. When he did, he found no sign of the settlers, except "CRO" carved on a tree, and "CROATOAN" on a rail.

Thus began 400 years of unanswered questions and speculation that will probably never be resolved. Some believe that the English colonists were killed by the local people, others claim that they were captured and sold into slavery among Native Americans farther inland. Several communities in the South of uncertain or mixed racial heritage believe themselves to be descendants of the lost colonists, and some evidence suggests that this might in fact be possible. The answers may never be found, and for the foreseeable future, the mystery will still hang heavily over Roanoke Island and its two towns: Manteo and Wanchese.

domestic violence, as well as an HIV/AIDS information center. And if you happen to be in Manteo long enough, you can even take weaving lessons here.

FOOD

Located in the Tranquil House Inn, with a great view of Shallowbag Bay, ★ **1587** (405 Queen Elizabeth Ave., 252/473-1587, www.1587.com, June-Aug. daily 5pm-9pm, Sept.-Oct. Wed.-Sun. 5pm-9pm, Jan.-Feb. Fri.-Sat. 5pm-9pm, closed Nov.-Dec., $18-29)

is widely regarded as one of the best restaurants in this part of the state. The menu is of hearty chops and seafood, with local ingredients in season, and a full vegetarian menu is also available on request. The wine list is a mile long.

Basnight's Lone Cedar Café (Nags Head-Manteo Causeway, 252/441-5405, www. lonecedarcafe.com, spring-fall Mon.-Wed. 5pm-close, Thurs.-Sat. 11:30am-3pm and 5pm-close, Sun. 11am-close, lunch entrées $6-18, dinner entrées $18-31) is a water-view bistro that specializes in local food—oysters from Hyde and Dare Counties, fresh-caught local fish, and North Carolina chicken, pork, and vegetables. It's one of the most popular restaurants on the Outer Banks, and they don't take reservations, so be sure to arrive early.

The **Full Moon Café** (208 Queen Elizabeth St., 252/473-6666, www.thefullmooncafe.com, high season daily 11:30am-9pm, call for off-season hours, $10-30) is simple and affordable, specializing in quesadillas and enchiladas, wraps, sandwiches, a variety of seafood and chicken bakes, and quiches.

The **Magnolia Grille** (408 Queen Elizabeth St., 252/475-9787, www.roanokeisland.net, Sun.-Mon. 7am-4pm, Tues.-Sat. 7am-8pm) is a super-inexpensive place for all three meals and snacks in between. It has a great selection of breakfast omelets, burgers, salads, soups, and deli sandwiches, with nothing more than $7.

ACCOMMODATIONS
Under $150

The **Island Guesthouse** (706 U.S. 64, 252/473-2434, www.theislandmotel.com, rooms from $60 off-season, from $85 high season, cottages from $125 off-season, from $200 high season, pets welcome for a fee) offers simple and comfortable accommodations in its guesthouse, with two double beds, air-conditioning, and cable TV in each room. They also rent out three tiny, cute cottages. Another affordable option is the **Duke of Dare Motor Lodge** (100 S. U.S. 64, 252/473-2175, from $42 high season). It's a 1960s motel, not at all fancy, but a fine choice when you need an inexpensive place to lay your head.

A top hotel in Manteo is the **Tranquil House Inn** (405 Queen Elizabeth Ave., 800/458-7069, www.1587.com, $109-239). It's in a beautiful location (though it's hard not to be on this island), and downstairs is one of the best restaurants in town, 1587. The **Scarborough Inn** (524 U.S. 64, 252/473-3979, www.scarborough-inn.com, $75-125,

depending on season) is a small hotel with 12 guest rooms and great rates, the sort of old-time hotel that's hard to find these days.

Over in Wanchese, the **Wanchese Inn** (85 Jovers Lane, 252/475-1166, www.wancheseinn.com, from $69 off-season, from $129 high season) is a simple and inexpensive bed-and-breakfast. It's a nice Victorian house with modern guest rooms, and there is a boat slip and available on-site parking for a boat and trailer. The **Island House** (104 Old Wharf Rd., 866/473-5619, www.islandhouse-bb.com, $85-175) was built in the early 1900s for a local coastguardsman, with wood cut from the property and nails forged on-site. It's very comfortable and quiet, and a big country breakfast is served every day.

$150-300

The ★ **White Doe Inn** (319 Sir Walter Raleigh St., 800/473-6091, www.whitedoeinn.com, from $175 off-season, from $350 high season) is one of North Carolina's premier inns. The 1910 Queen Anne is the largest house on the island and is in the National Register of Historic Places. Guest rooms are exquisitely furnished in turn-of-the-century finery. Guests enjoy a four-course breakfast, evening sherry, espresso and cappuccino any time, and a 24-hour wine cellar. Spa services are available on-site.

The **Cameron House Inn** (300 Budleigh St., Manteo, 800/279-8178, http://cameronhouseinn.com, $130-210) is a cozy 1919 arts and crafts-style bungalow. All of the guest rooms are furnished in a lovely and understated craftsman style, but the nicest room in the house is the porch, which has an outdoor fireplace, fans, and flowery trellises.

The **Roanoke Island Inn** (305 Fernando St., 877/473-5511, www.roanokeislandinn.com, $150-200) has been in the present owner's family since the 1860s. It's a beautiful old place with a big porch that overlooks the marsh. They also rent a single cottage on a private island, five minutes away by boat, and a nice cypress-shingled bungalow in town.

Cape Hatteras National Seashore

To many Americans, Cape Hatteras is probably familiar as a name often repeated during hurricane season. Hatteras protrudes farther to the east than any part of North America, a landmark for centuries of mariners and a prime target for storms. Cape Hatteras, the "Graveyard of the Atlantic," lies near Diamond Shoals, a treacherous zone of shifting sandbars between the beach and the Gulf Stream.

In 2003 Hurricane Isabel inflicted tremendous damage and even opened a new channel right across Hatteras Island, a 2,000-foot-wide swash that was called Isabel Inlet. It separated the towns of Hatteras and Frisco, washing out a large portion of the highway that links the Outer Banks. For some weeks afterward, Hatteras residents had to live as their forebears had, riding ferries to school and to the mainland. The inlet has since been filled in and Highway 12 reconnected, but Isabel Inlet's brief reign of inconvenience highlighted the vulnerability of life on the Outer Banks.

BODIE ISLAND

The 156-foot **Bodie Island Lighthouse** (6 miles south of Whalebone Junction), whose huge Fresnel lens first beamed in 1872, was the third to guard this stretch of coast. The first light was built in the 1830s, but it leaned like the Tower of Pisa. The next stood straight but promised to be such a tempting target for the Union Navy during the Civil War that the Confederates blew it up themselves. An unfortunate flock of geese nearly put the third lighthouse out of commission soon after its first lighting, when they collided with and damaged the lens. The lighthouse is not open to the public, but the keeper's house has been converted into a **visitors center** (252/441-5711, call for hours).

The **Oregon Inlet Campground** (Hwy. 12, 877/444-6777, $20), operated by the National Park Service, offers camping behind the sand dunes, with cold showers, potable water, and restrooms.

HATTERAS ISLAND

Cape Hatteras makes a dramatic arch along the North Carolina coast, sheltering the Pamlico Sound from the ocean as if in a giant cradling arm. The cape itself is the point of the elbow, a totally exposed and vulnerable spit of land that's irresistible to hurricanes because it juts so far to the southeast. Along the Cape Hatteras National Seashore, Hatteras Island is just barely wide enough to support a series of small towns—Rodanthe, Waves, Salvo, Avon, Buxton, Frisco, and the village of Hatteras—and a great deal of dramatic scenery on all sides.

Sights

Lifesaving operations are an important part of North Carolina's maritime heritage. Corps of brave men once occupied remote stations along the coast, ready at a moment's notice to risk—and sometimes to give—their lives to save foundering sailors in the relentlessly dangerous waters off the Outer Banks. In Rodanthe, the **Chicamacomico Life Saving Station** (milepost 39.5, Hwy. 12, Rodanthe, 252/987-1552, www.chicamacomico.net, mid-Apr.-Nov. Mon.-Fri. noon-5pm, $6, $5 over age 62 and under age 17) preserves the original station building, a handsome gray-shingled 1874 structure, as well as the 1911 building that replaced it—and which now houses a museum of fascinating artifacts from maritime rescue operations.

Cape Hatteras Lighthouse (near Buxton, 252/473-2111, www.nps.gov/caha, mid-Apr.-May and Labor Day-mid Oct. daily 9am-4:30pm, June-Labor Day daily 9am-5:30pm, $8 adults, $4 children, children smaller than 3 foot 5 not permitted), at 208 feet tall, is the tallest brick lighthouse in the

Cape Hatteras Lighthouse

climbing tours run every 10 minutes starting at 9am.

Sports and Recreation

Pea Island National Wildlife Refuge

(Hwy. 12, 10 miles south of Nags Head, 252/987-2394, www.fws.gov/peaisland) occupies the northern reach of Hatteras Island. Much of the island is covered by ponds, making this an exceptional place to see migratory waterfowl. Two nature trails link some of the best bird-watching spots, and one, the 0.5-mile North Pond Wildlife Trail, is fully wheelchair accessible.

The Outer Banks owe their existence to the volatile action of the tides. The same forces that created this habitable sandbar also make this an incredible place for water sports. **Canadian Hole,** a spot in the sound between Avon and Buxton, is one of the most famous windsurfing and sailboarding places in the world, and it goes without saying that it's also perfect for kite flying. The island is extraordinarily narrow here, so it's easy to tote your board from the sound side over to the ocean for a change of scene.

As with any sport, it's important to know your own skill level and choose activities accordingly. Beginners and experts alike can

United States. It was built in 1870 to protect ships at sea from coming onto the shoals unaware. It still stands on the cape and is open for climbing during the warm months. Tickets are sold on the premises beginning at 8:15am;

Pea Island National Wildlife Refuge

benefit from the guidance of serious water sports instructors. **Real Kiteboarding** (Cape Hatteras, 866/732-5548, www.realkiteboarding.com) is the largest kiteboarding school in the world. They offer kiteboarding camps and classes for all skill levels. **Outer Banks Kiting** (Avon, 252/305-6838, www.outerbankskiting.com) also teaches lessons and two-day camps, and carries boarders out on charter excursions to find the best spots.

There are all manner of exotic ways to tour Hatteras. **Equine Adventures** (252/995-4897, www.equineadventures.com) leads two-hour horseback tours through the maritime forests and along the beaches of Cape Hatteras. With **Hatteras Parasail** (Hatteras, 252/986-2627, www.hatterasparasail.com, parasail ride $60, kayak tour $35), you can ride 400 feet in the air over the coast, or even higher with **Burrus Flightseeing Tours** (Frisco, 252/986-2679, www.hatterasislandflightseeing.com, $35-63 pp).

Food

Though the **Restaurant at the Inn on Pamlico Sound** (Hwy. 12, Buxton, 252/995-7030, www.innonpamlicosound.com, $15) is primarily for guests of the inn, if you call in advance you might be able to get a reservation for dinner even if you're staying elsewhere. The chef likes to use fresh-caught seafood, sometimes caught by the guests themselves earlier in the day. Vegetarian dishes and other special requests are served.

For breakfast, try the **Gingerbread House** (52715 Hwy. 12, Frisco, 252/995-5204), which serves great baked goods made on the premises.

Accommodations

UNDER $150

Among the lodging choices on Hatteras Island is the **Cape Hatteras Bed and Breakfast** (46223 Old Lighthouse Rd./Cape Point Way, Buxton, 800/252-3316, $119-159), which is only a few hundred feet from the ocean. Guests rave about the breakfasts.

Simpler motel accommodations include the clean, comfortable, and pet-friendly **Cape Pines Motel** (47497 Hwy. 12, Buxton, 866/456-9983, www.capepinesmotel.com, $49-159, depending on season, $20 pets); the **Outer Banks Motel** (47000 Hwy. 12, Buxton, 252/995-5601 or 800/995-1233, www.outerbanksmotel.com, $49-120), with both motel rooms and cottages; and the **Avon Motel** (Avon, 252/995-5774, www.avonmotel.com, $43-131, $10 pets), a pet-friendly motel that has been in business for more than 50 years.

$150-300

Another good choice on Hatteras Island is the very fine **Inn on Pamlico Sound** (49684 Hwy. 12, Buxton, 252/995-7030 or 866/995-7030, www.innonpamlicosound.com, $120-320, depending on season). The inn is right on the sound, with a private dock and easy waterfront access. The dozen suites are sumptuous and relaxing, many with their own decks or private porches.

CAMPING

Rodanthe Watersports and Campground (24170 Hwy. 12, 252/987-1431, www.watersportsandcampground.com) has a sound-front campground for tents and RVs under 25 feet, with water and electrical hookups and hot-water showers. Rates are $19.25 per night for two people, $4.75 for each additional adult, $3 for children and dogs, and an extra $4.75 per night for electrical hookups.

The National Park Service operates two campgrounds ($20) in this stretch of the national seashore: The **Frisco Campground** (53415 Billy Mitchell Rd., Frisco, 877/444-6777) opens in early April, and **Cape Point Campground** (46700 Lighthouse Rd., Buxton, 877/444-6777) opens in late May. At Frisco, you actually camp in the dunes, while at Cape Point, like the other National Park Service campgrounds in the area, the campsites are level and located behind the dunes. Both have cold showers, restrooms, and potable water.

Frisco Woods Campground (Hwy. 12, Frisco, 800/948-3942, www.outer-banks.com/

friscowoods, $30-90) has a full spectrum of camping options, from no-utilities tent sites and RV sites with partial or full hookups to one- and two-bedroom cabins. The campground has wireless Internet access, hot showers, and a coin laundry.

★ OCRACOKE ISLAND

Sixteen miles long, Ocracoke Island is the southernmost reach of the Cape Hatteras National Seashore. One of the most geographically isolated places in North Carolina, it's only accessible today by water and air. Regular ferry service didn't start until 1960, and it was only three years before that that Ocracokers had their first paved highway. In 1585, it was one of the first places in North America seen by Europeans, when the future lost colonists ran aground here. It may have been during the time they were waylaid at Ocracoke ("Wococon," they called it) that the

ancestors of today's wild ponies first set hoof on the Outer Banks. Theirs was not the last shipwreck at Ocracoke, and in fact, flotsam and goods that would wash up from offshore wrecks were among the sources of sustenance for generations of Ocracokers.

In the early 18th century, Ocracoke was a favorite haunt of Edward Teach, better known as the pirate Blackbeard. He lived here at times, married his 14th wife here, and died here. Teach's Hole, a spot just off the island, is where a force hired by Virginia lieutenant governor Alexander Spotswood finally cornered and killed him, dumping his decapitated body overboard (it's said to have swum around the ship seven times before going under), and sailing away with the trophy of his head on the bowsprit.

All of **Ocracoke Village,** near the southern end of the island, is in the National Register of Historic Places. While the

Ocracoke Island

To Hatteras

Pamlico Sound

Cape Hatteras National Seashore

12

SEE DETAIL

Ocracoke Island

Swan Quarter Ferry

Cedar Island-Ocracoke Ferry

Ocracoke Island

ATLANTIC

OCEAN

0   2 mi

0   2 km

Pamlico Sound

BRITISH CEMETERY

P

BRITISH CEMETERY RD

OYSTER CREEK RD

CAPTAIN'S LANDING

BACK RD

Silver Lake Harbor

AMMO DUMP RD

RIDE THE WIND SURF SHOP

EDWARDS OF OCRACOKE

SILVER LAKE RD

SCHOOL RD

OCRACOKE

PONY ISLAND MOTEL & COTTAGES

POINT RD

0   500 yds

0   500 m

12

BEACHCOMBER CAMPGROUND

© AVALON TRAVEL

historical sites of the island are distinctive, the unique thing about the island and its people is the culture that has developed here over the centuries. Ocracokers have a "brogue" all their own, similar to those of other Outer Banks communities, but so distinctive that, in the unlikely event that there were two native Ocracokers who didn't know each other already, and they happened to cross paths somewhere out in the world, they would recognize each other right away as neighbors (and probably cousins) by the cadences of their speech.

Ocracoke Lighthouse

A lighthouse has stood on Ocracoke since at least 1798, but due to constantly shifting sands, the inlet that it protected kept sneaking away. Barely 20 years after that first tower was built, almost a mile stretched between it and the water. The current **Ocracoke Lighthouse** (village of Ocracoke, 888/493-3826) was built in 1823, originally burning whale oil to power the beam. It is still in operation—the oldest operating light in North Carolina and the second oldest in the nation. Because it's on active duty, the public is not able to tour the inside, but a boardwalk nearby gives nice views.

British Cemetery

The **British Cemetery** (British Cemetery Rd.) is not, as one might suppose, a colonial burial ground but rather a vestige of World War II. During the war, the Carolina coast was lousy with German U-boats. Defending the Outer Banks became a pressing concern, and on May 11, 1942, the HMS *Bedfordshire*, a British trawler sent to aid the U.S. Navy, was torpedoed by the German *U-558*. The *Bedfordshire* sank, and all 37 men aboard died. Over the course of the next week, four bodies washed up on Ocracoke. An island family donated a burial plot, and there the four men lie today, memorialized with a plaque that bears a lovely verse by Rupert Brooke, the young poet of World War I and member of the British Navy, who died of disease on his way to the battle of Gallipoli.

Sports and Recreation

Ride the Wind Surf Shop (486 Irvin Garrish Hwy., 252/928-6311) gives individual and group surfing lessons, for adults and children, covering ocean safety and surfing etiquette in addition to board handling. A three-day surf camp ($200, or $75 per day) for kids ages 9 to 17 gives an even more in-depth tutorial. Ride the Wind also leads sunrise, sunset, and full-moon kayak tours around the marshes of Ocracoke ($35).

The **Schooner** *Windfall* (departs from Community Store Dock, Ocracoke, 252/928-7245, www.schoonerwindfall.com, tours $40), a beautiful 57-foot old-fashioned schooner, sails on three one-hour tours a day around Pamlico Sound. Passengers are allowed, and even encouraged, to try their hand at the wheel or trimming the sails.

Accommodations

The **Captain's Landing** (324 Hwy. 12, 252/928-1999, www.thecaptainslanding.com, from $200 high season, from $100 off-season), with a perch right on Silver Lake (the harbor) looking toward the lighthouse, is a modern hotel owned by a descendant of Ocracoke's oldest families. Suites have 1.5 baths, full kitchens, comfortable sleeper sofas for extra guests, and decks with beautiful views. They also have a bright, airy penthouse with two bedrooms, an office, a gourmet kitchen, and even a laundry room. The Captain's Cottage is a private two-bedroom house with great decks and its own courtyard.

The **Pony Island Motel and Cottages** (785 Irvin Garrish Hwy., 866/928-4411, www.ponyislandmotel.com, from $108 high season, from $60 off-season) has been in operation since the late 1950s and run by the same family for more than 40 years. It has regular and efficiency motel rooms as well as four cottages on the grounds. Clean guest rooms, a good location, and year-round good prices make this a top choice on the island.

Edwards of Ocracoke (226 Old Beach Rd., 800/254-1359, www.edwardsofocracoke. com, from $53 spring and fall, from $90 summer) has several cozy bungalows typical of coastal Carolina, referred to here as "vintage accommodations." The mid-20th-century vacation ambience is very pleasant, the cabins are clean and well kept, and the prices are great.

The **Island Inn** (25 Lighthouse Rd., 252/928-4351, www.ocracokeislandinn.com, from $60 off-season, from $100 high season, no children) is in the National Register of Historic Places and bills itself as the oldest operating business on the Outer Banks. It was built in 1901 and first used as an Odd Fellows Hall; during World War II it was used as a barracks. The building is made of salvaged shipwreck wood.

CAMPING

At **Ocracoke Campground** (4352 Irvin Garrish Hwy., Ocracoke, 877/444-6777, $23), campsites are right by the beach, behind the dunes. Remember to bring extra-long stakes to anchor your tent in the sand.

TRANSPORTATION

The northern part of Cape Hatteras National Seashore can be reached by car via Highway 12 south from Nags Head. Following Highway 12, you'll go through the towns of Rodanthe,

Waves, Salvo, and Avon, then around the tip of the cape to Buxton, Frisco, and Hatteras, where the highway ends. From there, you have two choices: backtrack or hop a ferry.

Ocracoke can only be reached by ferry. The **Hatteras-Ocracoke Ferry** (800/368-8949, May 13-Oct. 5 5am-midnight on the half-hour, Apr. 1-May 12 and Oct. 7-Dec. 31 5am-midnight on the hour, Jan. 1-Mar. 31 4:30am-12:30am alternating half-hours, 40 minutes, free) is the shortest route to Ocracoke. If you look at a map, Highway 12 is shown crossing from Ocracoke to Cedar Island, as if there's an impossibly long bridge over Pamlico Sound. In fact, that stretch of Highway 12 is a ferry route too. The **Cedar Island-Ocracoke Ferry** (800/856-0343, www.ncdot.org/transit/ferry, May 20-Sept. 29 7am-8pm every 90 minutes, Mar.18-May 19 and Sept. 30-Oct. 27 7am-4:30pm every 3.5 hours, Jan. 1-Mar. 17 and Oct. 28-Dec. 31 7am-4:30pm every 3.5 hours), which is a 2.25-hour ride, regular-size vehicle $15 one-way. There's also a ferry between **Ocracoke and Swan Quarter** (800/345-1665, May 20-Sept. 29 6:30am-4:30pm every 3 hours, Jan. 1-May 19 and Sept. 30-Dec. 31 7am-4:30pm every 6.5 hours, 2.5 hours, regular-size vehicle $15 one-way).

Lower Outer Banks

The southern reaches of the Outer Banks of North Carolina have some of the region's most diverse destinations. Core and Shackleford Banks lie within the Cape Lookout National Seashore, a wild maritime environment populated by plenty of wild ponies but not a single human. On the other hand, the towns of Bogue Banks—Atlantic Beach, Salter Path, Pine Knoll Shores, Indian Beach, and Emerald Isle—are classic beach towns. Both areas are great fun, Cape Lookout especially so for ecotourists and history buffs, and Bogue Banks for those looking for a day on the beach followed by

an evening chowing down on good fried seafood.

★ CAPE LOOKOUT NATIONAL SEASHORE

Cape Lookout National Seashore (office 131 Charles St., Harkers Island, 252/728-2250, www.nps.gov/calo) is an otherworldly place, with 56 miles of beach on four barrier islands, a long tape of sand so seemingly vulnerable to nature that it's hard to believe there were once several busy towns on its banks. Settled in the early 1700s, the townspeople of the south Core Banks made their living in fisheries that

Lower Outer Banks

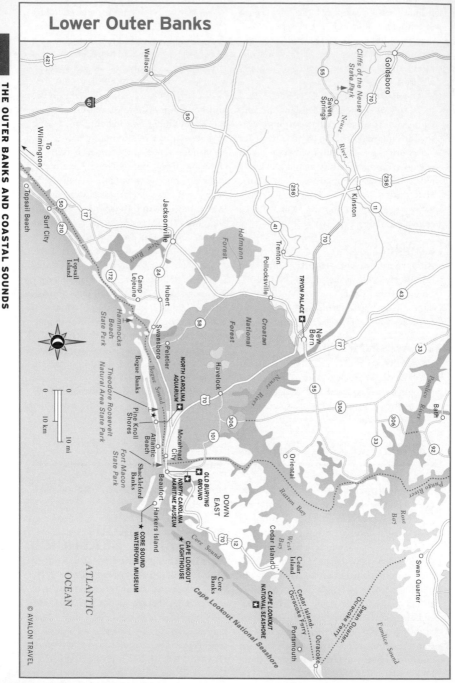

© AVALON TRAVEL

might seem brutal to today's seafood eaters—whaling and catching dolphins and sea turtles, among the more mundane species.

Wild horses roam the beaches and dunes, and dolphins frequent both the ocean and sound sides of the islands. Pets are allowed on leashes. The wild ponies on Shackleford Banks can pose a threat to dogs that get among them, and the dogs, of course, can frighten the horses, so be careful not to let them mingle.

Cape Lookout Lighthouse

By the time you arrive at the 1859 **Cape Lookout Lighthouse** (visitors center, 252/728-2250), you'll probably already have seen it portrayed on dozens of brochures, menus, business signs, and souvenirs. With its striking diamond pattern, it looks like a rattlesnake standing at attention. Because it is still a working lighthouse, visitors are allowed in on only four days each year. Visit Cape Lookout National Seashore's website (www.nps.gov/calo) for open house dates and reservation information. The allotted times fill up almost immediately.

Accommodations

Morris Marina (877/956-5688, www.cape-lookoutconcessions, $65-100) rents cabins at Great Island and Long Point. Cabins have hot and cold water, gas stoves, and furniture, but in some cases visitors must bring their own generators for lights as well as linens and utensils. Rentals are available only April-November. Book well in advance.

CAMPING

Camping is permitted within Cape Lookout National Seashore, though there are no designated campsites or services. Everything you bring must be carried back out when you leave. Campers can stay for up to 14 days.

Transportation

Except for the visitors center at Harkers Island, Cape Lookout National Seashore can only be reached by ferry. Portsmouth, at the northern end of the park, is a short ferry ride from Ocracoke, but Ocracoke is a very long ferry ride from Cedar Island. The **Cedar Island-Ocracoke Ferry** (800/856-0343, regular-size vehicle $15 one-way) is part of the state ferry system, and pets are allowed. It takes 2.25 hours to cross Pamlico Sound, but the ride is fun, and embarking from Cedar Island feels like sailing off the edge of the earth. The **Ocracoke-Portsmouth Ferry** (252/928-4361) is a passenger-only commercial route, licensed to Captain Rudy Austin. Phone to ensure a seat. There's also a vehicle and passenger ferry **from Atlantic to Long Point,** Morris Marina Kabin Kamps and Ferry Service (877/956-6568), on the North Core Banks; leashed or in-vehicle pets are allowed. Most ferries operate between April and November.

Commercial ferries cross every day **from mainland Carteret County** to the southern parts of the national seashore. There is generally a ferry route between Davis and Great Island, but service can be variable; check the Cape Lookout National Seashore website (www.nps.gov/calo) for updates.

From Harkers Island, passenger ferries to Cape Lookout Lighthouse and Shackleford Banks include Calico Jacks (252/728-3575), Harkers Island Fishing Center (252/728-3907), Local Yokel (252/728-2759), and Island Ferry Adventures (252/728-6181) at Barbour's Marina.

From Beaufort, passenger ferries include Outer Banks Ferry Service (252/728-4129), which goes to both Shackleford Banks and to Cape Lookout Lighthouse; Island Ferry Adventures (252/728-7555) and Mystery Tours (252/728-7827) run to Shackleford Banks. Morehead City's passenger-only Waterfront Ferry Service (252/726-7678) goes to Shackleford Banks as well. On-leash pets are generally allowed, but call ahead to confirm for Local Yokel, Island Ferry Adventures, and Waterfront Ferry Service.

Beaufort and Vicinity

It's an oft-cited case of the perversity of Southern speech that Beaufort, North Carolina, receives the French treatment of "eau"—so it's pronounced "BO-furt"—whereas Beaufort, South Carolina, a similar Lowcountry port town south of Charleston, is pronounced "BYEW-furt."

The third-oldest town in North Carolina, Beaufort holds its own with its elders, Bath and New Bern, in the prettiness department. The little port was once North Carolina's window on the world, a rather cosmopolitan place that sometimes received news from London or Barbados sooner than from Raleigh. The streets are crowded with beautiful old houses, many built in a double-porch, steep-roofed style that shows off the early citizenry's cultural ties to the wider Caribbean and Atlantic world.

In the late 1990s a shipwreck was found in Beaufort Inlet that is believed to be that of the *Queen Anne's Revenge*, a French slaver captured by the pirate Blackbeard in 1717 to be the flagship of his unsavory fleet. He increased its arsenal to 40 cannons, but it was nevertheless sunk in the summer of 1718. Blackbeard was killed at Ocracoke Inlet a few months later, and it took five musket balls and 40 sword wounds to finish him off. Incredibly cool artifacts from the *QAR* keep emerging from the waters of the inlet. Beaufort had been a favorite haunt of Blackbeard's, and you can find out all about him at the North Carolina Maritime Museum.

SIGHTS
★ North Carolina Maritime Museum

The **North Carolina Maritime Museum** (315 Front St., 252/728-7317, www.ah.dcr. state.nc.us/sections/maritime, Mon.-Fri. 9am-5pm, Sat. 10am-5pm, Sun. 1pm-5pm, free) is among the best museums in the state. Even if you don't think you're interested in boatbuilding or maritime history, you'll get caught up in the exhibits. Historic watercraft, reconstructions, and models of boats are on display, well presented in rich historical and cultural context.

Across the street from the museum's main

North Carolina Maritime Museum

building, perched on the dock, is the **Harvey W. Smith Watercraft Center.** For many generations, North Carolina mariners had an international reputation as expert shipbuilders, and even today, some builders continue to construct large seaworthy vessels in their own backyards. Their exceptional expertise is beautifully demonstrated by the craft in the museum and by boats still working the waters today.

★ Old Burying Ground

One of the most beautiful places in all of North Carolina, Beaufort's **Old Burying Ground** (Anne St., daily dawn-dusk) is as picturesque a cemetery as you'd ever want to be buried in. Huge old live oaks, Spanish moss, wisteria, and resurrection ferns, which unfurl and turn green after a rainstorm, give the Burying Ground an irresistibly Gothic feel. Many of the headstones reflect the maritime heritage of this town.

One of the graveyard's famous burials is the "Little Girl Buried in a Barrel of Rum." This unfortunate waif is said to have died at sea and been placed in a cask of rum to preserve her body for burial. Visitors often bring toys and trinkets to leave on her grave, which is marked by a simple wooden plank.

Beaufort Historic Site

The **Beaufort Historic Site** (130 Turner St., 252/728-5225, www.beauforthistoricsite.org, Dec.-Feb. Mon.-Sat. 10am-4pm, Mar.-Nov. Mon.-Sat. 9:30am-5pm, $8 adults, $4 children) re-creates life in late 18th- and early 19th-century Beaufort in several restored historic buildings. The 1770s "jump-and-a-half" (1.5-story) Leffers Cottage reflects middle-class life in its day. The Josiah Bell and John Manson Houses, both from the 1820s, reflect the graceful Caribbean-influenced architecture prevalent in the early days of the coastal South.

SPORTS AND RECREATION

Diving

North Carolina's coast is a surprisingly good place for diving. The **Discovery Diving Company** (414 Orange St., 252/728-2265, www.discoverydiving.com, $65-110 per excursion) leads half- and full-day diving trips to explore the reefs and dozens of fascinating shipwrecks that lie at the bottom of the sounds and ocean near Beaufort.

Cruises and Wildlife Tours

Coastal Ecology Tours (252/247-3860, www.goodfortunesails.com, prices vary)

Old Burying Ground

Blackbeard and Bonnet: The Boys of 1718

In the 18th century the Carolina coast was positively verminous with pirates. For the most part they hung out around Charleston Harbor, like a bunch of rowdies on a frat house balcony, causing headaches for passersby. Some liked to venture up the coast, however, into the inlets and sounds of North Carolina. The most famous local pirates were Blackbeard, whose real name was **Edward Teach,** and **Stede Bonnet.** They did most of their misbehaving in our waters during 1718.

Blackbeard is said never to have killed a man except in self-defense, but clearly he was so bad he didn't need to kill to make his badness known. He was a huge man with a beard that covered most of his face, and his hair is usually depicted twisted up into ferocious dreadlocks. He wore a bright red coat and festooned himself with every weapon small enough to carry; as if all that didn't make him scary enough, he liked to wear burning cannon fuses tucked under the brim of his hat. He caused trouble from the Bahamas to Virginia, taking ships, treasure, and child brides as fancy led him.

Poor Stede Bonnet. With a name like that, he should have known better than to try to make a living intimidating people. He is said to have been something of a fancy-pants, a man with wealth, education, and a nagging wife. To get away from his better half, he bought a ship, hired a crew, and set sail for a life of crime. Though never quite as tough as Blackbeard, with whom he was briefly partners, Bonnet caused enough trouble along the Southern coast that the gentry of Charleston saw to it that he was captured and hanged. Meanwhile, the Virginia nabobs had also had it with Blackbeard's interference in coastal commerce, and Lieutenant Governor Alexander Spotswood dispatched his men to kill him. This they did at Ocracoke, but it wasn't easy; even after they shot, stabbed, and beheaded Blackbeard, his body taunted them by swimming laps around the ship before finally giving up the ghost.

Blackbeard has in effect surfaced again. In 1996 a ship was found off the North Carolina coast that was identified as Blackbeard's flagship, the *Queen Anne's Revenge*. All manner of intriguing artifacts have been brought up from the ocean floor: cannons and blunderbuss parts, early hand grenades, even a penis syringe supposed to have been used by the syphilitic pirates to inject themselves with mercury. (During one standoff in Charleston Harbor, Blackbeard and his men took hostages to ransom for medical supplies. Perhaps this explains why they were so desperate.) To view artifacts and learn more about Blackbeard, Stede Bonnet, and their lowdown ways, visit the North Carolina Maritime Museum in Beaufort and in Southport, as well as the websites of the *Queen Anne's Revenge* (www.qaronline.com) and the Office of State Archaeology (www. arch.dcr.state.nc.us).

runs very special tours on the *Good Fortune* of the Cape Lookout National Seashore and other island locations in the area, as well as a variety of half-day, daylong, overnight, and short trips to snorkel, shell, kayak, and watch birds, as well as cruises to Morehead City restaurants and other educational and fun trips. Prices range from $40 per person for a 2.5-hour dolphin-watching tour to $600 per night plus meals for an off-season overnight boat rental.

Lookout Cruises (600 Front St., 252/504-7245, www.lookoutcruises.com) carries sightseers on lovely catamaran rides in the Beaufort and Core Sound region, out to Cape Lookout, and on morning dolphin-watching trips. **Island Ferry Adventures** (610 Front St., 252/728-7555, www.islandferryadventures.com, $10-15 adults, $5-8 children) runs dolphin-watching tours, trips to collect shells at Cape Lookout, and trips to see the wild ponies of Shackleford Banks. **Mystery Tours** (600 Front St., 252/728-7827 or 866/230-2628, www.mysteryboattours.com, $15-50 adults, free-$25 children, some cruises adults only) offers harbor tours and dolphin-watching trips as well as a variety of brunch, lunch, and dinner cruises and trips to wild islands where children can hunt for treasure.

Food

Among the Beaufort eateries certified by Carteret Catch as serving local seafood are the **Blue Moon Bistro** (119 Queen St., 252/728-5800, www.bluemoonbistro.biz, Tues.-Sat. 5:30pm-10pm, $17-35) and **Aqua Restaurant** (114 Middle Lane, "behind Clawsons," 252/728-7777, www.aquaexperience.com, Tues.-Sat. 5:30pm-9:30pm, $15-25).

If you're traveling with a cooler and want to buy some local seafood to take home, try the **Fishtowne Seafood Center** (100 Wellons Dr., 252/728-6644) or **Tripps Seafood** (1224 Harkers Island Rd., 252/447-7700).

★ **Beaufort Grocery** (117 Queen St., 252/728-3899, www.beaufortgrocery.com, lunch and dinner Wed.-Mon., brunch Sun., $20-36), despite its humble name, is a sophisticated little eatery. At lunch it serves salads and crusty sandwiches along with "Damn Good Gumbo" and specialty soups. In the evening the café atmosphere gives way to that of a more formal gourmet dining room. Some of the best entrées include boneless chicken breast sautéed with pecans in a hazelnut cream sauce; Thai-rubbed roast half duckling; and whole baby rack of lamb, served with garlic mashed potatoes, tortillas, and a margarita-chipotle sauce. Try the cheesecake for dessert.

The waterfront **Front Street Grill** (300 Front St., 252/728-4956, www.frontstreetgrillatstillwater.com, Tues.-Sat. lunch 11:30am-2:30pm, dinner 5:30pm-9:30pm, Sunday brunch 11:30am-2:30pm, $15-22) is popular with boaters drifting through the area, as well as diners who arrive by land. The emphasis is on seafood and fresh regional ingredients. Front Street Grill's wine list is extensive, and they have repeatedly won *Wine Spectator* magazine's Award of Excellence.

Accommodations

★ **Outer Banks Houseboats** (324 Front St., 252/728-4129, www.outerbankshouseboats.com) will rent you your own floating vacation home, sail it for you to a scenic spot, anchor it, and then come and check in on you every day during your stay. You'll have a skiff for your own use, but you may just want to lie on the deck all day and soak up the peacefulness. Rates run from $1,200 per weekend for the smaller houseboat to $3,000 per week for the luxury boat, with plenty of rental options in between.

The **Inlet Inn** (601 Front St., 800/554-5466, www.inlet-inn.com, $110-170) has one of the best locations in town, right on the water, near the docks where many of the ferry and tour boats land. If you're planning to go dolphin-watching or hop the ferry to Cape Lookout, you can get ready at a leisurely pace, and just step outside to the docks. Even in high season, rates are quite reasonable.

The **Beaufort Inn** (101 Ann St., 252/728-2600, www.beaufort-inn.com, $200-250) is a large hotel on Gallants Channel, along one side of the colonial district. It's an easy walk to the main downtown attractions, and the hotel's outdoor hot tub and balconies with great views make it tempting to stay in as well. The **Pecan Tree Inn** (116 Queen St., 800/728-7871, www.pecantree.com, $135-175) is such a grand establishment that the town threw a parade in honor of the laying of its cornerstone in 1866. The house is still splendid, as are the 5,000-square-foot gardens. Catty-corner to the Old Burying Ground is the **Langdon House Bed and Breakfast** (135 Craven St., 252/728-5499, www.langdonhouse.com, $120-185). One of the oldest buildings in town, this gorgeous house was built in the 1730s on a foundation of English ballast stones.

HARKERS ISLAND

The Core Sound region, which stretches to the east-northeast of Beaufort many miles up to the Pamlico Sound, is a region of birds and boats. Many Down Easterners also became expert decoy carvers. This art survives today, partly as art for art's sake, and also for its original purpose.

Core Sound Waterfowl Museum

The **Core Sound Waterfowl Museum** (1785 Island Rd., Harkers Island, 252/728-1500, www.coresound.com, Mon.-Sat. 10am-5pm,

Sun. 2pm-5pm, free), which occupies a beautiful modern building on Shell Point, next to the Cape Lookout National Seashore headquarters, is a community labor of love. The museum is home to exhibits crafted by members of the communities represented, depicting Down East maritime life through decoys, nets, and other tools of the trades, everyday household objects, beautiful quilts and other utilitarian folk arts, and lots of other things held dear by local people.

Food

Captain's Choice Restaurant (977 Island Rd., 252/728-7122, Fri.-Sun. 7am-9pm, Tues.-Thurs. 10am-9pm) is a great place to try traditional Down East chowder. Usually made of clams, but sometimes with other shellfish or fish, chowder in Carteret County is a point of pride. The point is the flavor of the seafood itself, which must be extremely fresh, and not hidden behind lots of milk and spices. Captain's Choice serves chowder in the old-time way—with dumplings.

MOREHEAD CITY

Giovanni da Verrazano may have been the first European to set foot in present-day Morehead City when he sailed into Bogue Inlet. It wasn't until the mid-19th century that the town actually came into being, built as the terminus of the North Carolina Railroad to connect the state's overland commerce to the sea. Morehead is also an official state port, one of the best deepwater harbors on the Atlantic Coast. This admixture of tourism and gritty commerce gives Morehead City a likeable, real-life feel missing in many coastal towns today.

Sights

Morehead City's history is on display at **The History Place** (1008 Arendell St., 252/247-7533, www.thehistoryplace.org, Tues.-Sat. 10am-4pm, free). The most striking exhibit is that of a carriage, clothes, and other items pertaining to Emeline Pigott, Morehead City's Confederate heroine. She was a busy girl all through the Civil War, working as a nurse, a

spy, and a smuggler. The day she was captured, she was carrying 30 pounds of contraband hidden in her skirts, including Union troop movement plans, a collection of gloves, several dozen skeins of silk, needles, toothbrushes, a pair of boots, and five pounds of candy.

Entertainment and Events

Seafood is a serious art in Morehead City. North Carolina's second-largest festival takes place in town every October—the enormous **North Carolina Seafood Festival** (252/726-6273, www.ncseafoodfestival.org). The city's streets shut down and over 150,000 visitors descend on the waterfront. Festivities kick off with a blessing of the fleet, followed with music, fireworks, competitions (including the flounder toss), and, of course, lots and lots of food.

If you're in the area on the right weekend in November, you'll not want to deprive yourself of the gluttonous splendor of the **Mill Creek Oyster Festival** (Mill Creek Volunteer Fire Department, 2370 Mill Creek Rd., Mill Creek, 252/247-4777). Food, and lots of it, is the focus of this event. It's a small-town fete, a benefit for the local volunteer fire department, and the meals are cooked by local experts.

Sports and Recreation

Many of this region's most important historical and natural sites are underwater. From Morehead City's **Olympus Dive Center** (713 Shepard St., 252/726-9432, www.olympusdiving.com), divers of all levels of experience can take charter trips to dozens of natural and artificial reefs that teem with fish, including the ferocious-looking but not terribly dangerous eight-foot-long sand tiger shark. There are at least as many amazing shipwrecks to choose from, including an 18th-century schooner, a luxury liner, a German U-boat, and many Allied commercial and military ships that fell victim to the U-boats that infested this coast during World War II.

Food

The **Sanitary Fish Market** (501 Evans St.,

252/247-3111, www.sanitaryfishmarket.com, daily 11:30am-9:30pm, $15-20) is probably Morehead City's best-known institution. The rather odd name reflects its 1930s origins as a seafood market that was bound by its lease and its fastidious landlord to be kept as clean as possible. Today it's a huge family seafood restaurant. Long lines in season and on weekends demonstrate its popularity. Be sure to buy a Sanitary T-shirt on the way out; it'll help you blend in everywhere else in the state.

The **Bistro-by-the-Sea** (4031 Arendell St., 252/247-2777, www.bistro-by-the-sea. com, Tues.-Thurs. 5pm-9:30pm, Fri.-Sat. 5pm-10pm, $10-25) participates in Carteret Catch, a program that brings together local fisherfolk with restaurants, fish markets, and wholesalers to ensure that fresh locally caught seafood graces the tables of Carteret County. In addition to seafood, specialties here are steak, tenderloin, and prime rib.

Captain Bill's (701 Evans St., 252/726-2166, www.captbills.com, daily 11:30am-9:30pm, $12-20) is Morehead City's oldest restaurant, founded in 1938. Try the conch stew, and be sure to visit the otters that live at the dock outside.

BOGUE BANKS

The beaches of Bogue Banks are popular with visitors, but they have a typically North Carolinian, laid-back feel, a quieter atmosphere than the fun-fun-fun neon jungles of beaches in other states. The major attractions, Fort Macon State Park and the North Carolina Aquarium at Pine Knoll Shores, are a bit more cerebral than, say, amusement parks and bikini contests. In the surfing and boating, bars and restaurants, and the beach itself, there's also a bustle of activity to keep things hopping. Bogue, by the way, rhymes with "rogue."

★ North Carolina Aquarium

The **North Carolina Aquarium at Pine Knoll Shores** (1 Roosevelt Blvd., Pine Knoll Shores, 866/294-3477, www.ncaquariums. com, Aug.-June daily 9am-5pm, July Fri.-Wed. 9am-5pm, Thurs. 9am-9pm, $10.95 adults,

$8.95 children) is one of the state's three great coastal aquariums. Here at Pine Knoll Shores, exhibit highlights include a 300,000-gallon aquarium in which sharks and other aquatic beasts go about their business in and around a replica German U-Boat (plenty of originals lie right off the coast and form homes for reef creatures); a "jellyfish gallery" (they really can be beautiful); a pair of river otters; and many other wonderful animals and habitats.

Fort Macon State Park

At the eastern tip of Atlantic Beach is **Fort Macon State Park** (2300 E. Fort Macon Rd., 252/726-3775, www.ncsparks.net/foma.html, park daily 9am-5:30pm, fort Oct.-Mar. daily 8am-6pm, Apr.-May and Sept. daily 8am-7pm, June-Aug. daily 8am-8pm, bathhouse area Nov.-Feb. daily 8am-5:30pm, Mar. and Oct. daily 8am-7pm, Apr.-May and Sept. daily 8am-8pm, June-Aug. daily 8am-9pm, bathhouse $4 adults, $3 children). The central feature of the park is Fort Macon itself, an 1820s federal fort that was a Confederate garrison for one year during the Civil War.

Food

The **Channel Marker** (718 Atlantic Beach Causeway, Atlantic Beach, 252/247-2344, daily 11am-9:30pm, $15-25) is a more upscale alternative to some of the old-timey fried seafood joints on Bogue Banks (which are also great—read on). Try the crab cakes with mango chutney, or the Greek shrimp salad. The extensive wine list stars wines from the opposite side of North Carolina, from the Biltmore Estate in Asheville.

White Swan Bar-B-Q and Chicken (2500-A W. Fort Macon Rd., Atlantic Beach, 252/726-9607, Mon.-Sat. 7am-2pm, $8) has been serving the Carolina trinity of barbecue, coleslaw, and hush puppies since 1960. They also flip a mean egg for breakfast.

The **★ Big Oak Drive-In and Bar-B-Q** (1167 Salter Path Rd., 252/247-2588, www.bi-goakdrivein.com, Fri.-Sun. 11am-3pm) is a classic beach drive-in, a little red-white-and-blue-striped building with a walk-up counter and drive-up spaces. They're best known for their shrimp burgers (large $5), a fried affair slathered with Big Oak's signature red sauce, coleslaw, and tartar sauce. Then there are the scallop burgers, oyster burgers, clam burgers, hamburgers, and barbecue—all cheap, and made for snacking on the beach.

Frost Seafood House (1300 Salter Path Rd., Salter Path, 252/247-3202, Fri.-Sun. 7am-9pm, Mon.-Thurs. 4:30pm-9:30pm, $10) began in 1954 as a gas station and quickly became the restaurant that it is today. The Frost family catches its own shrimp and buys much of its other seafood locally. Be sure to request a taste of the "ching-a-ling sauce." Yet another community institution is the **Crab Shack** (140 Shore Dr., Salter Path, 252/247-3444, daily 11am-9pm, $9-25). You'll find it behind the Methodist church in Salter Path. The restaurant was wiped out in 2005 by Hurricane Ophelia, but they have since rebuilt, rolled up their sleeves, and plunged their hands back into the cornmeal.

Accommodations

The **Atlantis Lodge** (123 Salter Path Rd., Atlantic Beach, 800/682-7057, www.atlantis-lodge.com, $70-220) is an old family-run motel. It has simple and reasonably priced efficiencies in a great beachfront location. Well-behaved pets are welcome for a per-pet, per-night fee. The **Clamdigger** (511 Salter Path Rd., Atlantic Beach, 800/338-1533, www.clamdiggerrama-dainn.com, $40-260) is another reliable choice, with all oceanfront guest rooms. Pets are not allowed. The **Windjammer** (103 Salter Path Rd., Atlantic Beach, 800/233-6466, www.wind-jammerinn.com, $50-200) is another simple, comfortable motel, with decent rates through the high season.

Transportation

A 20-minute free **passenger ferry crosses the Neuse River** between Cherry Branch (near Cherry Point) and Minesott Beach in Pamlico County every 30 minutes (800/339-9156, pets allowed).

Albemarle Sound

Referred to historically as the Albemarle, and sometimes today as the Inner Banks, the mainland portion of northeastern North Carolina is the hearth of the state's colonial history, the site of its first European towns and the earliest plantation and maritime economies.

The Great Dismal Swamp is here, a region thought of by early Carolinians and Virginians as a diseased and haunted wasteland, the sooner drained the better. They succeeded to some extent in beating back the swamp waters and vapors, but left enough for modern generations to recognize as one of the state's crown jewels.

★ THE GREAT DISMAL SWAMP

Viewed for centuries as an impediment to progress, the Great Dismal Swamp is now

recognized for the national treasure that it is, and tens of thousands of acres are protected. There are several points from which to gain access to the interior of the Dismal Swamp. A few miles south of the North Carolina-Virginia line, on U.S. 17, is the **Dismal Swamp Welcome Center** (2294 U.S. 17 N., visitors center 2356 U.S. 17 N., South Mills, 877/771-8333, www.dismalswamp.com, late May-Oct. daily 9am-5pm, Nov.-late May Tues.-Sat. 9am-5pm). Should you be arriving by water, you'll find the welcome center at mile 28 on the Intracoastal Waterway. You can tie up to the dock here and spend the night, if you wish, or wait for one of the four daily lock openings (8:30am, 11am, 1:30pm, and 3:30pm) to proceed. There are also picnic tables and grills here, and restrooms open day and night.

the Great Dismal Swamp

Another area of the swamp to explore is the **Great Dismal Swamp National Wildlife Refuge** (Suffolk, VA, 757/986-3705, www.albemarle-nc.com/gates/gdsnwr, daily dawn-dusk), which straddles the state line. Two main entrances are outside Suffolk, Virginia, off the White Marsh Road (Hwy. 642). These entrances, Washington Ditch and Jericho Lane, are open April-September daily 6:30am-8pm, October-March daily 6:30am-5pm. You may see all sorts of wildlife in the swamp—including poisonous cottonmouths, canebrake rattlers, copperheads, and possibly even black bears.

WILLIAMSTON AND VICINITY

Williamston is at the junction of U.S. 17 and U.S. 64. If you're passing through town, Williamston is a great place to stop for barbecue or a fresh seafood meal.

Sights

A little west of Williamston on U.S. 13/64 Alternate, you'll find the town of Robersonville and the **St. James Place Museum** (U.S. 64 Alt. and Outerbridge Rd., call Robersonville Public Library at 252/795-3591, by appointment, free). A Primitive Baptist church built in 1910 and restored by a local preservationist and folk art enthusiast, St. James Place is an unusual little museum that fans of Southern craft will not want to miss.

On the same highway is **East Carolina Motor Speedway** (4918 U.S. 64 Alt., 252/795-3968, www.ecmsracing.com, usually Apr.-Oct., pits open at 3pm, grandstands from 5pm), a 0.4-mile hard-surface track featuring several divisions, including late-model street stock, modified street stock, super-stock four-cylinder, and four-cylinder kids class.

Food

Come to Williamston on an empty stomach. It has an assortment of old and very traditional eateries. The ★ **Sunny Side Oyster Bar** (1102 Washington St., 252/792-3416, www.sunnysideoysterbarnc.com, Sept.-Apr. Mon.-Thurs. 5:30pm-9pm, Fri.-Sat. from 5:30pm, Sun. 5pm-8pm, $12-20) is the best known, a seasonal oyster joint open in the months with the letter *r*—that is, oyster season. It's been in business since 1935, and is a historic as well as gastronomic landmark. The Sunny Side doesn't take reservations, and it fills to capacity in no time flat, so come early.

Down the road a piece, **Martin Supply** (118 Washington St., 252/792-2123), an old general store, is a good place to buy local produce and preserves, honey, molasses, and hoop cheese. **Griffin's Quick Lunch** (204 Washington St., 252/792-0002, Mon.-Fri. 6am-8:30pm, Sat. 6am-2pm, $8) is a popular old diner with good barbecue. Back on U.S. 64, **Shaw's Barbecue** (U.S. 64 Alt., 252/792-5339, Mon.-Sat. 6am-7pm, $7-10) serves eastern Carolina-style barbecue, as well as good greasy breakfasts.

East of Williamston at the intersection of U.S. 64 and Highway 171, the small Roanoke River town of Jamesville is home to a most unusual restaurant that draws attention from all over the country (it's even been featured in the *New York Times*). The ★ **Cypress Grill** (1520 Stewart St., off U.S. 64, 252/792-4175, mid-Jan.-Apr. Mon.-Sat. 11am-8pm, $7-10) is an unprepossessing wooden shack right-smack on the river, a survivor of the days when Jamesville made its living in the herring industry, dragging the fish out of the water with horse-drawn seine nets. Herring—breaded and seriously deep-fried, not pickled or sweet—is the main dish here, though they also dress the herring up in other outfits, and serve bass, flounder, perch, oyster, catfish, and other fish too. The Cypress Grill is open from the second Thursday in January through the end of April.

EAST ON U.S. 64

The eastern stretch of U.S. 64 runs along the Albemarle Sound between Williamston and the Outer Banks. Here you'll encounter evidence of North Carolina's ancient past in the form of old-growth forests; of the recent past in a plantation with a long and complex history of slavery; and the present, in art galleries and abundant wildlife-watching and recreational opportunities.

Somerset Place Historic Site

Somerset Place Historic Site (2572 Lake Shore Rd., Creswell, 252/797-4560, www. ah.dcr.state.nc.us, Apr.-Oct. Mon.-Sat. 9am-5pm, Sun. 1pm-5pm, Nov.-Mar. Tues.-Sat. 10am-4pm, Sun. 1pm-4pm, free) was one of North Carolina's largest and most profitable plantations for the 80 years leading up to the Civil War. In the late 18th and early 19th centuries, 80 enslaved Africa-born men, women, and children were brought to Somerset to labor in the fields. The grief and spiritual disorientation they experienced, and the subsequent trials of the enslaved community that grew to include more than 300 people, are told by the historian Dorothy Spruill Redford in the amazing book *Somerset Homecoming*.

Pettigrew State Park

On the banks of Lake Phelps, **Pettigrew State Park** (2252 Lakeshore Rd., Creswell, 252/797-4475, http://ncparks.gov, day-use hours June-Aug. 8am-9pm, Mar.-May and Sept.-Oct. 8am-8pm, Nov.-Feb. 8am-6pm, free) preserves a weird ancient waterscape that's unlike anywhere else in the state. Archaeological studies reveal that there was a human presence here a staggering 10,000 years ago. Visitors to Pettigrew State Park can camp at the family campground ($15), which has drive-in sites and access to restrooms and hot showers, or at primitive group campsites (from $9).

Sports and Recreation

Palmetto-Peartree Preserve (Pot Licker Rd./Loop Rd./Hwy. 1220, east of Columbia, 252/796-0723 or 919/967-2223, www.palmettopeartree.org, daily dawn-dusk, free) is a 10,000-acre natural area, wrapped in 14 miles of shoreline along the Albemarle Sound and Little Alligator Creek. Originally established as a sanctuary for the red-cockaded woodpecker, this is a great location for bird-watching and spotting other wildlife, including alligators, wolves, bears, and bobcats; hiking, biking, and horseback riding along the old logging trails through the forest; and canoeing and kayaking.

Once the southern edge of the Great

Dismal Swamp, **Pocosin Lakes National Wildlife Refuge** (252/796-3004, www.fws.gov/pocosinlakes, daily dawn-dusk, free) is an important haven for many species of animals, including migratory waterfowl and reintroduced red wolves. The refuge headquarters is at Walter B. Jones Sr. Center for the Sounds (U.S. 64, 6 miles south of Columbia).

Also east of Columbia on U.S. 64 is the **Alligator River National Wildlife Refuge** (between Columbia and Roanoke Island, 252/473-1131, http://alligatorriver.fws.gov, daily dawn-dusk, free). This large swath of woods and pocosin represents one of the most important wildlife habitats in the state, home to over 200 species of birds.

Pamlico Sound

WASHINGTON, BATH, AND BELHAVEN

On the north side of the Pamlico River, as you head toward Mattamuskeet National Wildlife Refuge and the Outer Banks, the towns of Washington, Bath, and Belhaven offer short diversions into the nature and history of this region.

North Carolina Estuarium

The **North Carolina Estuarium** (223 E. Water St., Washington, 252/948-0000, www.partnershipforthesounds.org, Tues.-Sat. 10am-4pm, $3 adults, $2 children) is a museum about both the natural and cultural history of the Tar-Pamlico River Basin. In addition to the exhibits, which include live native animals, historical artifacts, and much more, the Estuarium operates pontoon boat tours on the Pamlico River. River roving is free, but reservations are required.

Moss House

Located in the Washington historic district, a block from the river, is the **Moss House** (129 Van Norden St., Washington, 252/975-3967, www.themosshouse.com, $110-235). This 1902 house is a cozy bed-and-breakfast with airy guest rooms and delicious breakfasts. An easy walk from the Moss House is **Bill's Hot Dogs** (109 Gladden St., Washington, 252/946-3343, daily 8:30am-5pm), a longtime local favorite for a quick snack.

Goose Creek State Park

Goose Creek State Park (2190 Camp Leach Rd., 252/923-2191, http://ncparks.gov, daily 8am-dusk, free) is on the banks of the Pamlico, where Goose Creek empties into the river. It's an exotic environment of brackish marshes, freshwater swamps, and tall pine forests, home to a variety of wildlife, including bears, a multitude of bird species, and rather many snakes. Twelve primitive campsites ($13/day), with access to toilets and water, are available year-round, including one that is disabled-accessible.

Historic Bath

North Carolina's oldest town, Bath, was chartered in 1705. For its first 70 or so years, Bath enjoyed the spotlight as one of the colony's most important centers of trade and politics—home of governors, refuge from conflicts with Native Americans, frequent host to and victim of Blackbeard. Today, almost all of Bath is designated as **Historic Bath** (252/923-3971, www.bath.nchistoricsites.org, visitors center and tours Apr.-Oct. Mon.-Sat. 9am-5pm, Sun. 1pm-5pm, Nov.-Mar. Tues.-Sat. 10am-4pm, Sun. 1pm-4pm, $2 admission for Palmer-Marsh and Bonner Houses). Important sites on the tour of the village are the 1734 St. Thomas Church, the 1751 Palmer-Marsh House, the 1790 Van Der Veer House, the 1830 Bonner House, and, from time immemorial, a set of indelible hoofprints said to have been made by the devil's own horse.

While in Bath, drop in at the **Old Town Country Kitchen** (436 Carteret St., 252/923-1840, Fri.-Sat. 7am-8:30pm, Sun.-Tues. 7am-2pm, Wed.-Thurs. 7am-8pm, $10) for some country cooking and seafood. If you decide to stay the night, try the **Inn on Bath Creek** (116 S. Main St., 252/923-9571, www.innonbathcreek.com, 2-night minimum Apr.-Nov. Fri.-Sat., $130-225). This bed-and-breakfast, built on the site of the former Buzzard Hotel, fits in nicely with the old architecture of the historic town, but because it was built in 1999, it has modern conveniences to make your stay especially comfortable.

Belhaven

The name **Belhaven Memorial Museum** (210 E. Main St., Belhaven, 252/943-6817, www.beaufort-county.com, Thurs.-Tues. 1pm-5pm, free) gives no hint as to what a very strange little institution this is. The museum houses the collection of Miss Eva—Eva Blount Way, who died in 1962 at the age of 92—surely one of the most accomplished collectors of oddities ever. Miss Eva kept among her earthly treasures a collection of pickled tumors (one weighs 10 pounds), a pickled one-eyed pig, a pickled two-headed kitten, cataracts (pickled), and three pickled human babies.

Belhaven has an especially nice inn, the **Belhaven Water Street Bed and Breakfast** (567 E. Water St., 866/338-2825, www.belhavenwaterstreetbandb.com, $85-115). The guest rooms in this 100-year-old house face Pantego Creek and have their own fireplaces and private baths as well as wireless access.

MATTAMUSKEET NATIONAL WILDLIFE REFUGE

Near the tiny town of Swan Quarter, the **Mattamuskeet National Wildlife Refuge** (Hwy. 94, between Swan Quarter and Englehard, 252/926-4021, www.fws.gov/mattamuskeet, daily dawn-dusk, free) preserves one of North Carolina's most remarkable natural features. Lake Mattamuskeet, 18 miles long by 6 miles wide, is the state's largest natural lake, and being an average of 1.5 feet deep—five feet at its deepest point—it is

Mattamuskeet National Wildlife Refuge

a most unusual environment. The hundreds of thousands of waterfowl who rest here on their seasonal rounds make this a world-famous location for bird-watching and wildlife photography.

Hiking and biking trails thread through the refuge, but camping is not permitted. Within the administration of the Mattamuskeet Refuge is the **Swan Quarter National Wildlife Refuge** (252/926-4021, www.fws.gov/swanquarter, daily dawn-dusk, free), located along the north shore of the Pamlico Sound, and mostly accessible only by water. This too is a gorgeous waterscape full of wildlife.

New Bern

New Bern was settled in 1710 by a community of Swiss and German colonists. It also became North Carolina's capital in an era symbolized by the splendor of Tryon Palace, one of the most recognizable architectural landmarks in the state. Despite the considerable traffic it draws, New Bern is still a small and enormously pleasant city.

One all-important note: how to say it. It's your choice of "NYEW-bern" or "NOO-bern"—and in some folks' accents it sounds almost like "neighbor"—but never "new-BERN."

SIGHTS
★ Tryon Palace

Tryon Palace (610 Pollock St., 252/514-4956 or 252/514-4900, www.tryonpalace. org, Mon.-Sat. 9am-5pm, Sun. 1pm-5pm, last tour 4pm, gardens summer Mon.-Sat. 9am-7pm, Sun. 1pm-7pm, shop Mon.-Sat. 9:30am-5:30pm, Sun. 1pm-5:30pm, $20 adults, $10 grades 1-12, gardens and stables only $8 adults, $3 grades 1-12) is a rather remarkable feat of historic re-creation, a from-the-ground-up reconstruction of the 1770 colonial capitol and governor's mansion.

the garden at Tryon Palace

New Bern

The original stood for a scant 25 years before burning down in 1798, and as the by-now state of North Carolina had relocated its governmental operations to Raleigh, there was no need to rebuild the New Bern estate.

The property continued, however, to live on in Carolinians' imaginations. In the early 20th century, a movement to rebuild Tryon Palace began. By the 1950s, both the funds and, incredibly, the original drawings and plans had been secured, and over a period of seven years the palace was rebuilt. When you visit, allow yourself plenty of time—a whole afternoon or even a full day.

In 2010, in honor of New Bern's 300th anniversary, Tryon Palace opened its **North Carolina History Center,** an enormous complex along the Trent River next to the Tryon Palace gardens, with galleries, a performance hall, outdoor interpretive areas, and more. You should begin your Tryon Palace adventure here.

New Bern Firemen's Museum

The **New Bern Firemen's Museum** (408 Hancock St., 252/636-4087, www.newbernmuseums.com, Mon.-Sat. 10am-4pm, $5 adults, $2.50 children) is a fun little museum—an idyll for the gearhead with an antiquarian bent. The museum houses a collection of 19th- and early 20th-century fire wagons and trucks, and chronicles the lively and contentious history of firefighting in New Bern.

Attmore-Oliver House

The beautiful 1790 **Attmore-Oliver House** (510 Pollock St., 252/638-8558, www.newbernhistorical.org, call for hours and tour schedule, $4 adults, free for students) is a nice historic house museum, with exhibits about New Bern's very significant Civil War history. It's also the headquarters of the New Bern Historical Society.

Birthplace of Pepsi-Cola

We often think of Coca-Cola as the quintessential Southern drink, but it was here in New Bern that Caleb Bradham, a drugstore owner, put together what he called Brad's Drink—later Pepsi-Cola. Pepsi-Cola Bottling Company operates a soda fountain and gift shop at the location of Bradham's pharmacy, called the **Birthplace of Pepsi**

(256 Middle St., 252/636-5898, www.pepsistore.com).

ENTERTAINMENT AND EVENTS

New Bern's historic Harvey Mansion has a cozy old-fashioned pub in its cellar, the **1797 Steamer Bar** (221 S. Front St., 252/635-3232). As one would gather from its name, the pub serves steamed seafood and other light fare. **Captain Ratty's Seafood Restaurant** (202-206 Middle St., 252/633-2088 or 800/633-5292, www.captainrattys. com) also has a bar that's a popular gathering spot for locals and visitors alike.

SHOPPING

New Bern is a great place to shop for antiques. The majority of the shops are on the 220-240 blocks of Middle Street. There are also periodic antiques shows (and even a salvaged antique architectural hardware show) at the New Bern Convention Center. See www.visitnewbern.com for details.

Tryon Palace is a fun shopping spot for history buffs and home-and-garden fanciers.

the Birthplace of Pepsi-Cola

The historical site's **Museum Shop** (Jones House, Eden St. and Pollock St., 252/514-4932, Mon.-Sat. 9:30am-5:30pm, Sun. 1pm-5:30pm) has a nice variety of books about history and architecture as well as handicrafts and children's toy and games. The **Garden Shop** (610 Pollock St., 252/514-4932, Mon.-Sat. 10am-5pm, Sun. 1pm-5pm) sells special bulbs and plants, when in season, grown in Tryon Palace's own greenhouse.

SPORTS AND RECREATION

At New Bern's Sheraton Marina, **Barnacle Bob's Boat and Jet Ski Rentals** (100 Middle St., Dock F, 252/634-4100, www.boatandjetskinewbern.com, daily 9am-7pm) rents one- and two-person Jet Skis ($65 per hour, half-hour $45) and 6- to 8-person pontoon boats ($65 per hour, 4 hours $220, 8 hours $420).

FOOD

Down-home food choices include the **Country Biscuit Restaurant** (809 Broad St., 252/638-5151, Mon.-Tues. 5am-2pm, Wed.-Fri. 5am-2pm and 4pm-9pm, Sat. 5am-9pm, $7-12), which is open for breakfast, and is popular for, not surprisingly, its biscuits. **Moore's Olde Tyme Barbeque** (3711 U.S. 17 S./Martin Luther King Jr. Blvd., 252/638-3937, www.mooresbarbeque.com, Mon.-Sat. 10am-8pm, $6-9) is a family business, in operation (at a series of different locations) since 1945.

ACCOMMODATIONS

The ★ **Aerie Bed and Breakfast** (509 Pollock St., 800/849-5553, www.aeriebedandbreakfast.com, $119-169) is the current incarnation of the 1880s Street-Ward residence. Its seven luxurious guest rooms are done up in Victorian furniture and earthtone fabrics reflecting the house's earliest era. There is a lovely courtyard for guests to enjoy, and the inn is only one short block from Tryon Palace.

Also on Pollock Street, a few blocks away, are the **Harmony House Inn** (215 Pollock St., 800/636-3113, www.harmonyhouseinn.com, $99-175), the **Howard House Bed and Breakfast** (207 Pollock St., 252/514-6709, www.howardhousebnb.com, $89-149), and the **Meadows Inn** (212 Pollock St., 877/551-1776, www.meadowsinn-nc.com, $106-166). All three are appealing 19th-century houses decorated in the classic bed-and-breakfast style, and within easy walking distance to Tryon Palace and downtown.

Wilmington and Cape Fear

Look for ★ to find recommended
sights, activities, dining, and lodging.

Highlights

★ **Wilmington's Historic District:** North Carolina's largest historic district is a gorgeous collection of antebellum and late Victorian buildings (page 71).

★ **Wrightsville Beach:** Few other beaches in the state can compare with Wrightsville for its pretty strand, easy public access, clear waters, and overall beauty (page 72).

★ **USS *North Carolina:*** Take a tour of this enormous World War II battleship, permanently berthed on the Cape Fear River (page 73).

★ **Hammocks Beach State Park:** Accessible only by boat, one of the wildest and least disturbed Atlantic beaches is a popular stopover for migrating waterfowl and turtles (page 81).

★ **Museum of the Native American Resource Center:** This small but high-quality museum in Pembroke highlights the culture and artifacts of the local Lumbee people (page 89).

★ **Lake Waccamaw State Park:** The central feature of this scenic area is a Carolina bay, a unique geographical feature with a diverse surrounding ecosystem (page 90).

Cape Fear is part of the Caribbean culture that stretches up through the south Atlantic coast of North America—a world that reflects English, Spanish, and French adaptation to the tropics and, above all, the profound, trans-

formative influence of African cultures brought to the New World by enslaved people. Wilmington is part of the sorority that includes Havana, Caracas, Port au Prince, Santo Domingo, New Orleans, Savannah, and Charleston. All exhibit the richness of Afro-Caribbean culture in their architecture, cuisine, folklore, and speech.

The area between Wilmington and Lumberton in the state's southeast corner is a strange, exotic waterscape (more so than a landscape) of seductively eerie swamps and backwaters. In this little band of coastal counties straddling the state line, within a 100-mile radius of Wilmington, is the native habitat—the only one in the world—of the Venus flytrap, a ferocious little plant of rather ghastly beauty. It somehow seems like an appropriate mascot for these weird backwaters.

The greatest draw to this region, even more than colonial cobblestones and carnivorous plants, are the beaches of Brunswick,

New Hanover, Pender, and Onslow Counties. Some of them, like Wrightsville and Topsail, are well known, and others remain comparatively secluded barrier island strands. In some ways the "Brunswick Islands," as visitors bureaus designate them, can be thought of as the northern edge of the famous Grand Strand area around Myrtle Beach, South Carolina.

HISTORY

The Cape Fear River, deep and wide, caught the attention of European explorers as early as 1524, when Giovanni de Verrazano drifted by, and two years later, when Lucas Vásquez de Ayllón and his men (including, possibly, the first enslaved Africans brought to the present-day United States) walked around before proceeding to their appointment for shipwreck near Winyah Bay in South Carolina. Almost 150 years later, William Hilton and explorers from the Massachusetts Bay Colony visited. They were either unimpressed with what

---

Previous: downtown Wilmington; the Wilmington waterfront. **Above:** fountain in Airlie Gardens.

Wilmington and Cape Fear

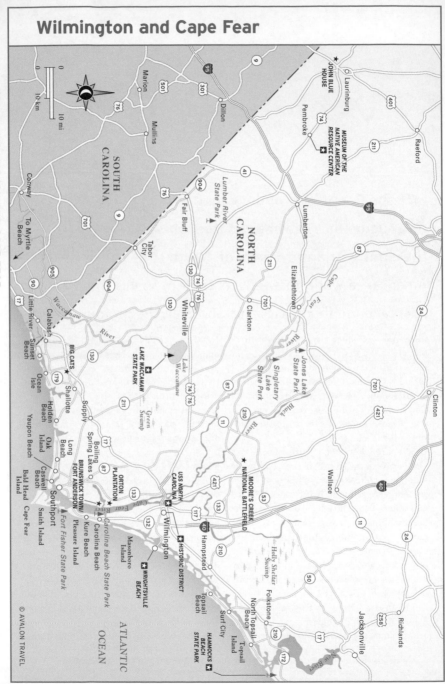

© AVALON TRAVEL

they saw or knew they'd found a really good thing and wanted to discourage rival claims, because they left right away and posted a sign at the tip of the cape to the effect of, "Don't bother; the land's no good."

It wasn't until 1726 that European settlement took hold, when Maurice Moore claimed the banks of the river on behalf of a group of allied families holding a patent to the area. Moore platted Brunswick Town, and his brother Roger established his own personal domain at Orton. Brunswick was briefly an important port, but it was soon eclipsed by Wilmington, a new settlement up the river established by an upstart group. By the time of the Revolution, it was Wilmington that dominated trade along the river.

During the Civil War, Wilmington's port was a swarming hive of blockade-runners. Its fall to the Union at the late date of January 1865 was a severe blow to the sinking Confederacy. Commerce allowed the city to weather the Civil War and Reconstruction, and it continued to grow and flourish.

In the late 20th and early 21st centuries, southeastern North Carolina has gained prominence as a military center. Fort Bragg, in Fayetteville, is one of the country's largest army installations. Nearby Pope Air Force Base is the home of the 43rd Airlift Wing, and at Jacksonville, the U.S. Marine Corps' II Expeditionary Force, among other divisions, is stationed at Camp Lejeune.

PLANNING YOUR TIME

Wilmington is an easy drive from pretty much anywhere in this region, giving ready access to the beaches to the north and south. It's so full of sights and activities that you'll probably want to stay here, and give yourself a day or more just to explore the city. If you're planning on visiting the beaches south of Wilmington, you might also want to consider staying in Myrtle Beach, South Carolina, about 20 minutes' drive (with no traffic—in high season it's a very different story) on U.S. 17 from the state line. Farther inland, you'll find plenty of motels around Fayetteville and Lumberton, which are also a reasonable distance from Raleigh to make day trips.

INFORMATION AND SERVICES

The several area hospitals include two in Wilmington, **Cape Fear Hospital** (5301 Wrightsville Ave., 910/452-8100, www.nhhn. org) and the **New Hanover Regional Medical Center** (2132 S. 17th St., 910/343-7000, www.nhhn.org); two in Brunswick County, **Brunswick Community Hospital** (1 Medical Center Dr., Supply, 910/755-8121, www.brunswickcommunityhospital.com) and **Dosher Memorial Hospital** (924 N. Howe St., Southport, 910/457-3800, www. dosher.org); two in Onslow County, **Onslow Memorial Hospital** (317 Western Blvd., Jacksonville, 910/577-2345, www.onslow-memorial.org) and the **Naval Hospital at Camp Lejeune** (100 Brewster Blvd., Camp Lejeune, 910/451-1113); and Fayetteville's **Cape Fear Valley Medical System** (1638 Owen Dr., Fayetteville, 910/609-4000, www. capefearvalley.com). Myrtle Beach's **Grand Strand Regional Medical Center** (809 82nd Pkwy., Myrtle Beach, SC, 843/692-1000, www.grandstrandmed.com) is not too far from the southernmost Brunswick communities. In an emergency, of course, calling 911 is the safest bet.

Extensive travel and visitor information is available from local convention and visitors bureaus: the **Wilmington/Cape Fear Coast CVB** (23 N. 3rd St., Wilmington, 877/406-2356, www.cape-fear.nc.us, Mon.-Fri. 8:30am-5pm, Sat. 9am-4pm, Sun. 1pm-4pm), and the **Brunswick County Chamber of Commerce** (4948 Main St., Shallotte, 800/426-6644, www.brunswickcountychamber.org, Mon.-Fri. 8:30am-5pm).

Wilmington

In many cities, economic slumps have an unexpected benefit: historic preservation. With Wilmington's growth at a standstill for much of the 20th century, there was no need to replace the city's old buildings and neighborhoods. As a result, downtown Wilmington has remained a vast museum of beautiful architecture from its early days, and that historical appeal accounts for much of its popularity today as a destination.

Hollywood noticed the little city a couple of decades ago, and for a while Wilmington was one of the largest film and TV production sites east of Los Angeles. *Sleepy Hollow, Homeland,* and *Eastbound & Down* are just some of the recent series to have filmed here, and noteworthy movies filmed at least partly in Wilmington include *Forrest Gump, Iron Man 3, The Conjuring,* and many more (though not, ironically, either version of *Cape Fear*).

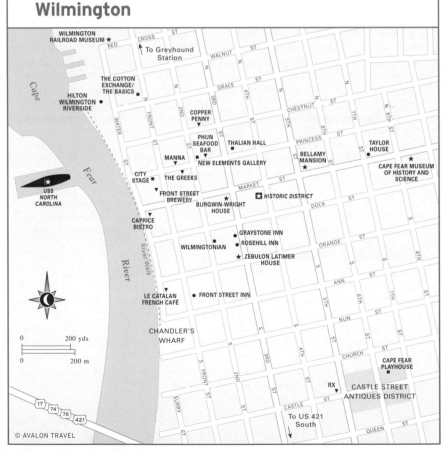

That said, North Carolina's state film industry tax incentives—once the most generous in the country—fell victim to politics and budget-slashing, with most of the work heading to Atlanta. There's no longer a film crew on every corner in Wilmington, but the evocative settings and sultry mood do remain. In addition to downtown's antebellum appeal, the long and well-done Riverwalk along the Cape Fear River is a nice place to stroll.

SIGHTS
★ Historic District

Wilmington is to 19th-century architecture what Asheville is to that of the early 20th century. Having been the state's most populous city until around 1910, when Charlotte and its Piedmont neighbors left the old port city in their wake, Wilmington's downtown reflects its glory days of commerce and high society. This is North Carolina's largest 19th-century historic district, a gorgeous collection of antebellum and late Victorian town houses and commercial buildings, including many beautiful Southern iterations of the Italianate craze that preceded the Civil War.

The **Bellamy Mansion** (503 Market St., 910/251-3700, www.bellamymansion.org, tours hourly Tues.-Sat. 10am-5pm, Sun. 1pm-5pm, $12 adults, $6 under age 12) is a spectacular example of Wilmington's late-antebellum Italianate mansions. This enormous white porticoed house ranks among the loveliest Southern city houses of its era. Built by planter Dr. John Bellamy just before the outbreak of the Civil War, the house was commandeered by the Yankees after the fall of Fort Fisher, and a trip to Washington DC and a pardon granted personally by President Andrew Johnson, a fellow North Carolinian, were required before Bellamy could pry his home out of government hands. In addition to the mansion, another highly significant building stands on the property: the slave quarters. This confined but rather handsome two-story brick building is one of the few surviving examples in the country of urban slave dwellings. Extensive renovations are underway to restore the quarters to their early appearance.

The **Burgwin-Wright House** (224 Market St., 910/762-0570, www.burgwinwrighthouse. com, tours Tues.-Sat. 10am-4pm, $12 adults, $6 under age 12) has an oddly similar history to that of the Bellamy Mansion, despite being nearly a century older. John Burgwin (the emphasis is on the second syllable), a planter and the treasurer of the North Carolina colony, built the house in 1770 on top of the city's

the Bellamy Mansion

early jail. Soon thereafter, Wilmington became a theater of war, and the enemy, as was so often the case, took over the finest dwelling in town as its headquarters. In this case, the occupier, who had a particularly fine eye for rebel digs, was General Cornwallis, then on the last leg of his campaign before falling into George Washington's trap. The Burgwin-Wright House, like the Bellamy Mansion, is a vision of white-columned porticoes shaded by ancient magnolias, but the architectural style is a less ostentatious, though no less beautiful, 18th-century form, the mark of the wealthy merchant and planter class in the colonial South Atlantic and Caribbean world. Seven terraced sections of garden surround the house; they are filled with native plants and many original landscape features, making an intoxicating setting for an early spring stroll.

Yet another beautiful home in the historic district is the **Zebulon Latimer House** (126 S. 3rd St., 910/762-0492, www.latimer-house.org, Mon.-Sat. 10am-3pm, $12 adults, $6 children). The Latimer House is several years older than the Bellamy Mansion, but in its day was a little more fashion-forward, architecturally speaking. Latimer, a merchant from Connecticut, preferred a more urban expression of the Italianate style, a blocky, flat-roofed design with cast-iron cornices and other details that hint at the coming decades of Victorian aesthetics. Also located on the grounds is a very interesting two-story brick slave dwelling. The Latimer House is the headquarters of the Lower Cape Fear Historical Society, whose archive of regional history is important to genealogists and preservationists.

If you'd like to visit the Bellamy Mansion, Latimer House, and Burgwin-Wright House, be sure to buy a **three-house ticket** at the first house you visit. For $28, it will save you several bucks over what you'd pay were you to buy a ticket at each stop.

★ Wrightsville Beach

Wrightsville Beach, just outside of Wilmington, is easily one of the nicest beaches in the coastal Carolinas, which is a linear kingdom of beautiful strands. The beach is wide and easily accessible, visitor- and family-friendly, and simply beautiful. The water at Wrightsville often seems to be a brighter blue than one is accustomed to seeing this far north on the Atlantic coast, lending the feeling of a tropical beach. Wrightsville enjoys warm summertime water temperatures, a very wide strand, and lots of lodging and rental choices along the beach. Numerous public beach access points line Lumina Avenue, searchable at www.townofwrightsvillebeach.com; some are wheelchair accessible and some have showers or restrooms. The largest public parking lot, with 99 spaces, is at Beach Access No. 4 (2398 Lumina Ave.); No. 36 (650 Lumina Ave.) also has a large lot. They all fill up on busy days, but if you press on from one access point to the next, you'll eventually find a spot.

Historic Sights Around Wilmington

MOORE'S CREEK NATIONAL BATTLEFIELD

Not surprisingly, given their importance as a maritime center, the environs of Wilmington have seen much military action over the last 300 years. About 20 miles northwest of Wilmington, outside the town of Currie, near Burgaw, is **Moore's Creek National Battlefield** (40 Patriots Hall Dr., Currie, 910/283-5591, www.nps.gov/mocr, daily 9am-5pm except Thanksgiving Day, Dec. 25, and Jan. 1). The site commemorates the brief and bloody skirmish of February 1776 in which a Loyalist band of Scottish highlanders, kilted and piping, clashed with Patriot colonists. An important moment in the American Revolution, it was also noteworthy as the last major broadsword charge in Scottish history, led by the last Scottish clan army. The scenic "colonial garden" at Moore's Creek experienced significant damage in the flooding of 2016, but most of that has been mitigated and restored and the garden is back to normal.

★ USS *NORTH CAROLINA*

Docked in the Cape Fear River, across from the Wilmington waterfront at Eagles Island, is the startling gray colossus of the battleship **USS *North Carolina*** (Eagles Island, 910/251-5797, www.battleshipnc.com, Memorial Day-Labor Day daily 8am-8pm, Labor Day-Memorial Day daily 8am-5pm, $12 adults, $6 under age 13). This decommissioned World War II warship, which saw service at Guadalcanal, Iwo Jima, and many other important events in the Pacific theater, is a floating monument to the nearly 10,000 North Carolinians who died in World War II as well as a museum of what life was like in a floating metal city.

Tours are self-guided and include nine decks, the gun turrets and the bridge, crew quarters, the sick deck, and the Roll of Honor display of the names of North Carolina's war dead. Allow at least two hours to see it all. Visitors prone to claustrophobia might want to stay above deck; the passageways and quarters below are close, dark, and very deep. From the heart of the ship it can take quite a while to get back out, and on a busy day the crowds can make the space seem even more constricted. (Just imagine how it would have felt to be on this ship in the middle of the Pacific, with nearly 2,000 other sailors aboard.)

The battleship is also one of North Carolina's most famous haunted houses, as it were—allegedly home to several ghosts who have been seen and heard on many occasions. The ship has been featured on the Syfy Channel and on ghost-hunting television shows. Visit www.hauntednc.com to hear some chilling unexplained voices caught on tape.

OAKDALE CEMETERY

In the mid-19th century, as Wilmington was bursting at the seams with new residents, the city's old cemeteries were becoming overcrowded with former residents. **Oakdale Cemetery** (520 N. 15th St., 910/762-5682, www.oakdalecemetery.org, daily 8am-5pm) was founded some distance from downtown to ease the subterranean traffic jam. It was designed in the parklike style of graveyards popular at the time, and soon filled up with splendid funerary art—weeping angels, obelisks, willows—to set off the natural beauty of the place. (Oakdale's website has a primer on Victorian grave art symbolism.) It's a fascinating place for a quiet stroll.

the USS *North Carolina*

Anoles of Carolina

A little anole pauses on a downspout.

During your visit to the Wilmington area, you'll almost certainly see anoles. These are the tiny green lizards that skitter up and down trees and along railings—impossibly fast, beady-eyed little emerald beasts. Sometimes called "chameleons" by the locals, anoles can change color to camouflage themselves against their backgrounds. They also like to puff out their crescent-shaped dewlaps, the little scarlet pouches under their chins, when they're courting, fighting, or otherwise advertising their importance.

Museums

CAPE FEAR MUSEUM OF HISTORY AND SCIENCE

The **Cape Fear Museum of History and Science** (814 Market St., 910/798-4370, www.capefearmuseum.com, Tues.-Sat. 9am-5pm, Sun. 1pm-5pm, $8 adults, $7 students and seniors, $5 ages 3-17) has exhibits about the ecology of the Cape Fear region and its human history. Special treats are exhibits about giant indigenous life forms, including the prehistoric ground sloth and Michael Jordan.

LOUISE WELLS CAMERON ART MUSEUM

The **Louise Wells Cameron Art Museum** (3201 S. 17th St., 910/395-5999, www.cameronartmuseum.com, Tues.-Wed. and Fri.-Sun. 10am-5pm, Thurs. 10am-8pm, $10 adults, $8 students), or "the CAM," is one of the major art museums in North Carolina, a very modern gallery with a good permanent collection of art in many media, with a special emphasis on North Carolina artists. Masters represented include Mary Cassatt and Utagawa Hiroshige. Special exhibits change throughout the year.

WILMINGTON RAILROAD MUSEUM

The **Wilmington Railroad Museum** (505 Nutt St., 910/763-2634, www.wilmingtonrailroadmuseum.org, Apr.-Oct. Mon.-Sat. 10am-5pm, Sun. 1pm-5pm, Oct.-April. Mon.-Sat. 10am-4pm, $9.50 adults, $8.50 seniors and military, $5.50 ages 2-12) explores a crucial but now largely forgotten part of this city's history: its role as a railroad town. In 1840, Wilmington became the terminus for the world's longest continuous rail line, the Wilmington and Weldon Railroad. The

Atlantic Coast Line Railroad (into which the W&W merged around 1900) kept its head-quarters at Wilmington until the 1960s, when it moved its offices, employees, and a devas-tatingly large portion of the city's economy to Florida. All manner of railroad artifacts are on display in this great little museum, from timetables to locomotives.

Gardens and Parks
AIRLIE GARDENS
Airlie Gardens (300 Airlie Rd., 910/798-7700, www.airliegardens.org, Mar. 20-Dec. daily 9am-5pm, longer hours Apr.-May, $9 adults, $3 ages 4-12, no pets) is most famous for its countless azaleas, but this 100-year-old formal garden park has many remarkable features, including an oak tree believed to be nearly 500 years old, and the Minnie Evans Sculpture Garden and Bottle Chapel. Evans, a visionary African American artist whose mys-tical work is among the most prized "outsider art," was the gatekeeper here for 25 of her 95 years. Golf cart tours are available with 48 hours' notice for visitors who are not mobile enough to walk the gardens.

HALYBURTON PARK
A more natural landscape for hiking and biking is **Halyburton Park** (4099 S. 17th St., 910/341-7800, www.halyburtonpark.com, park daily dawn-dusk, nature center Tues.-Sat. 9am-5pm). The 58 acres of parkland, en-circled by a 1.3-mile wheelchair-accessible trail and crisscrossed by interior trails, give a beautiful glimpse of the environment of sand-hills, Carolina bays (elliptical, often boggy de-pressions), and longleaf pine and oak forest that used to make up so much of this area.

ENTERTAINMENT AND EVENTS
Performing Arts
Thalian Hall (310 Chestnut St., 800/523-2820, www.thalianhall.com) was built in the mid-1850s and today is the last standing theater designed by the prominent architect John Montague Trimble. It is still a major arts venue in the region, hosting performances of classical, jazz, bluegrass, and all sorts of other music. Its resident theater company is the **Thalian Association** (910/251-1788, www.thalian.org), which traces its roots back to 1788 and has been named the official com-munity theater company of North Carolina. Wilmington City Hall is located contiguously within the building.

Often staging shows at Thalian Hall is **Big Dawg Productions** (http://bigdawgproduc-tions.org). They put on a variety of plays and musicals of all genres throughout the year and host the **New Play Festival** of first-time productions by authors under age 18. Another Thalian company for nearly 25 years, the **Opera House Theatre Company** (910/762-4234, www.operahousetheatrecompany.net) has produced one varied season after another of big-name musicals and dramas, as well as the work of North Carolinian and Southern playwrights.

Also working in the Thalian is the criti-cally acclaimed **Red Barn Studio Theatre** (1122 S. 3rd St., 910/762-0955, www.redbarn-studiotheatre.com). Actress Linda Lavin of *Alice* fame and her husband, Steve Bakunas, lived in Wilmington up until a few years ago and founded Red Barn while there.

Festivals
Wilmington's best-known annual event is the **Azalea Festival** (910/794-4650, www.ncazaleafestival.org), which takes place in early April at venues throughout the city. It centers on the home and garden tours of Wilmington's most beautiful—and, at this time of year, azalea-festooned—historic sites. There is a dizzying slate of events, including a parade, a circus, gospel concerts, shag and step competitions, and even boxing matches. And like any self-respecting Southern town, it crowns royalty—in this case, the North Carolina Azalea Festival Queen as well as the Queen's Court. The Azalea Festival draws over 300,000 visitors, so book your accom-modations well in advance. If you're travel-ing through the area in early April but aren't

Greater Wilmington

GOVERNORS RD
DAWS CREEK RD
Town Creek
OCEAN HWY E
CAPE FEAR NATIONAL AT BRUNSWICK FOREST
LANVALE RD
OLD FAYETTEVILLE RD
VILLAGE RD
OLD MILL RD
74
17
MT MISERY RD
CEDAR HILL RD
Cape Fear River
Lake Sutton
421
NE Cape Fear River
140

RIVER RD SE
RIVER RD SE
Cape Fear River
RIVER RD
DUKE'S OLD SOUTH BBQ
Wilmington
SEE "WILMINGTON" MAP
HISTORIC DISTRICT
OAKDALE CEMETERY
PRINCESS PL DR
CASTLE HAYNE RD
BLUE CLAY RD
WILMINGTON INTERNATIONAL AIRPORT
KERR AVE
133
421
INDEPENDENCE BLVD
CAROLINA BEACH RD
SHIPYARD BLVD
16TH ST
17TH ST
11TH ST
MARKET ST
3RD ST
N 23RD ST
M.L.K. JR. PKWY
South Creek
CAPE FEAR ANTIQUE CENTER
INDOCHINE THE IVY COTTAGE
JAMESON INN
SANDERS DR
COASTAL K-9 BAKERY
17TH ST
COLLEGE RD
132
REGIONAL MEDICAL CENTER
117
LOUISE WELLS CAMERON ART MUSEUM
Halyburton Park
COLLEGE RD
TEN PIN ALLEY
HOLIDAY INN
EASTWOOD DR
GORDON RD
132
COLLEGE RD
40
MYRTLE GROVE RD
MORICIA TRAIL
MASONBORO LOOP
OLEANDER DR
GREENVILLE LOOP RD
UNIVERSITY OF NORTH CAROLINA AT WILMINGTON
WRIGHTSVILLE GRILLE
MILITARY CUTTOFF RD
17
SIDBURY RD
140

Intracoastal Waterway
Masonboro Island Coastal Reserve
Masonboro Island
AIRLIE GARDENS
WB SURF CAMP
BLOCKADE RUNNER BEACH RESORT
OCEANIC
WRIGHTSVILLE BEACH
FISH HOUSE GRILL/ DOCKSIDE
LUMINA AVE
MARKET ST
Intracoastal Waterway
BEACH RD
PORTERS NECK RD
SCOTTS HILL LOOP RD
17

0 2 km
0 2 mi

ATLANTIC OCEAN

© AVALON TRAVEL

coming to the festival, be forewarned, this will be one crowded town.

Although Wilmington has become a magnet for Hollywood film production, there's also a passion here for independent films. Over the course of 20 years, November's **Cucalorus Film Festival** (910/343-5995, www.cucalorus.org) has become an important festival that draws viewers and filmmakers from around the world. Roughly 100 films are screened during each year's festival, which takes place at Thalian Hall and at the small Jengo's Playhouse (815 Princess St.), where the Cucalorus Foundation also holds regular screenings throughout the year.

Nightlife

Front Street Brewery (9 N. Front St., 910/251-1935, http://frontstreetbrewery.com, Mon.-Wed. 11:30am-midnight, Thurs.-Sat. 11:30am-2am, Sun. 11:30am-10pm, late-night menu from 10:30pm) serves lunch and dinner, but what is most special is their menu of beers brewed on-site. They serve their own pilsner, IPA, and lager, Scottish and Belgian ales, and their specialty River City Raspberry Wheat ale. The space has an attractive dark-paneled saloon decor, and plenty of seating areas to choose from. Brewery tours are 3pm-5pm daily.

Billing itself as Wilmington's oldest bar, **Barbary Coast** (116 S. Front St., 910/762-8996, Mon.-Sat. 11am-2am) is a short walk from Front Street Brewery. It sports more of a classic dive bar atmosphere and is frequented by many locals. Enjoy craft beer on tap, a game of pool, and an old-fashioned jukebox.

SHOPPING
Shopping Centers
The buildings of **The Cotton Exchange** (Front St. and Grace St., 910/343-9896, www.shopcottonexchange.com) have housed all manner of businesses in over 150 years of continuous occupation: a flour and hominy mill, a Chinese laundry, a peanut cleaning operation (really), a "mariner's saloon" (we'll say no more about that), and, of course, a cotton

exchange. Today, they're home to dozens of boutiques, restaurants, and lovely little specialty shops selling kites, beads, and spices.

Antiques and Consignment Stores

Along Castle Street, at the southern edge of the historic district, there is a growing district of antiques shops, all within two or three blocks of each other. **Castle Keep Antiques** (507 Castle St., 910/343-6046) occupies an old church building and has an absorbingly varied selection, with a more rural bent than the surrounding shops. Also be sure to stop in at **New Castle Antiques Center** (606 Castle St., 910/341-7228) and **Maggy's Antiques** (511 Castle St., 910/343-5200).

In the riverfront area, **Antiques of Old Wilmington** (25 S. Front St., 910/763-5188) and **Silk Road Antiques** (103 S. Front St., 910/343-1718) are within an easy walk of many restaurants and each other. On Market Street headed away from downtown is **Cape Fear Antique Center** (1606 Market St., 910/763-1837, www.capefearantiquecenter.com), which carries fancy vintage home furnishings, from bedroom and dining room furniture to desks and armoires in beautiful tones of wood, as well as a nice selection of antique jewelry.

Books

Wilmington has quite a few nice bookstores, both retail and used. **McAllister & Solomon** (4402-1 Wrightsville Ave., 910/350-0189, www.mcallisterandsolomon.com) stocks over 20,000 used and rare books, a great treat for collectors to explore. **Two Sisters Bookery** (318 Nutt St., Cotton Exchange, 910/762-4444, Mon.-Sat. 10am-6pm, Sun. noon-6pm) is a nice little independent bookseller at the Cotton Exchange, with an inventory covering all genres and subject matters, and a calendar full of readings by favorite authors. Also excellent is **Pomegranate Books** (4418 Park Ave., 910/452-1107, www.pombooks.net, Mon.-Sat. 10am-6pm), which has a progressive bent and a wide selection of good reads.

Art Galleries

Perhaps the most interesting arts experience in town is the "gallerium" **Expo 216** (216 Front St., 910/769-3899, www.expo216.com, Wed.-Sun. noon-6pm), a nonprofit museum/gallery in a 5,000-square-foot space downtown. Its theme-driven exhibits tend to focus on topical issues such as the environment, and it also features the work of regional artists for purchase.

New Elements Gallery (201 Princess St., 910/343-8997, www.newelementsgallery.com, Tues.-Sat. 11am-5:30pm) has been a leading institution in Wilmington's art scene since 1985. Featuring contemporary art in a wide variety of styles and media, New Elements has a special focus on artists from North Carolina and the wider Southeast.

Music

Finkelstein Music (6 S. Front St., 910/762-5662, www.finkelsteins.com) is a family business that has been at this site, a great old commercial building on a busy downtown corner, for over 100 years. It began as a dry goods store but gradually evolved into today's music store, which carries a great selection of guitars, electric basses, and percussion.

For Dogs

Coastal K-9 Bakery (5905 Carolina Beach Rd., Ste. 9, 866/794-4014, www.coastalk9bakery.com, Mon.-Sat. 10am-6pm, Sun. 1pm-5pm) sells fresh-baked gourmet dog treats, including various organic and hypoallergenic goodies, Carolina barbecue biscuits, liver brownies, and even vegetarian bacon bits.

SPORTS AND RECREATION

Masonboro Island

A 30-minute boat ride from Wrightsville Beach is Masonboro Island, an undeveloped barrier island that is a favorite spot for birding, shelling, and camping. **Wrightsville Beach Scenic Tours** (910/200-4002, www.wrightsvillebeachscenictours.com) operates the Wrightsville Water Taxi, which docks

across the street from the Blockade Runner Hotel (275 Waynick Blvd.) and offers daily shuttle service ($20 round-trip) to the island in high season. The boat leaves the dock Monday-Saturday at 9am and returns at 3pm. Call ahead for reservations.

Surfing

Wrightsville Beach is a very popular destination for East Coast surfers and is home to several surfing schools. **Surf Camp** (530 Causeway Dr., 866/844-7873, www.wbsurfcamp.com) is probably the area's largest surfing instruction provider. They teach a staggering number of multiday camps; one-day courses; kids-only, teenagers-only, women-only, and whole-family offerings; and classes in safety as well as technique. **Crystal South Surf Camp** (Public Access No. 39, on the beach, 910/395-4431, www.crystalsouthsurfcamp.com) is a family-run operation that gives group and individual five-day instruction for all ages.

Spectator Sports

The **Wilmington Sharks** (910/343-5621, www.wilmingtonsharks.com, box seats $8, general admission $5), a Coastal Plains League baseball team, play at Legion Stadium (2149 Carolina Beach Rd.). This is college summer league ball, so they play with real wooden bats unlike in NCAA-administered play.

FOOD

Continental

★ **Caprice Bistro** (10 Market St., 910/815-0810, www.capricebistro.com, Sun.-Thurs. 5pm-10pm, Fri.-Sat. 5pm-midnight, bar until 2am, $13-22) is an absolutely wonderful little café and bar hosted by Thierry and Patricia Moity. The French cuisine here is delicious and the wine list is extensive. This is one of the best restaurants in town and well worth a visit.

Le Catalan French Café (224 S. Water St., 910/815-0200, www.lecatalan.com, fall-spring lunch and dinner Tues.-Sat. from 11:30am, summer Tues.-Sun. from 11:30am, $10-20) couldn't have a nicer location, on the

Riverwalk in the old downtown. They serve wonderful classic French food—quiches and *feuilletés,* beef bourguignon on winter Fridays, and a chocolate mousse for which they are famous. Their greatest draw, though, is the wine list (and the attached wine store). The proprietor, Pierre Penegre, is a Cordon Bleu-certified oenologist, and is frequently on hand to make recommendations.

Seafood

Wrightsville Beach's **Bridge Tender** (1414 Airlie Rd., Wilmington, 910/256-4519, www.thebridgetender.com, lunch daily 11:30am-2pm, dinner daily from 5pm, $20-35) has been in business for over 30 years and is an icon of the local restaurant scene. The atmosphere is simple and elegant, with a dockside view. Entrées focus on seafood and Angus beef, with an extensive à la carte menu from which you can create delicious combinations of your favorite seafood and the Bridge Tender's special sauces. A sushi menu rounds out the appetizers, and a long wine list complements everything.

When you see a restaurant set in a really beautiful location, you dearly hope the food is as good as the view. Such is the case at Wrightsville's **Oceanic** (703 S. Lumina, Wrightsville Beach, 910/256-5551, www.oceanicrestaurant.com, Mon.-Sat. 11am-11pm, Sun. 10am-10pm, $10-27). The Wilmington *Star-News* has repeatedly voted it the Best Seafood Restaurant in Wilmington, and it receives similar word-of-mouth accolades right and left. It occupies a big old house right on the beach, with a wraparound porch and a pier. For an extra-special experience, ask for a table on the pier.

Southern and Barbecue

Right downtown at the Cotton Exchange, facing Front Street, is **The Basics** (319 Front St., 910/343-1050, www.thebasicswilmington.com, breakfast Mon.-Fri. 8am-11am, lunch Mon.-Fri. 11am-4pm, dinner daily from 5pm, brunch Sat.-Sun. 11am-4pm, $10-18). In a streamlined, simple setting, The Basics serves comfort food classics, Southern-style. Be sure to try the Coca-Cola cake, a surprisingly delicious Southern delicacy. An ambitious renovation was particularly tasteful and well-done.

In business since 1984, ★ **Jackson's Big Oak Barbecue** (920 S. Kerr Ave., 910/799-1581, http://jacksonsbigoak.com, Mon.-Sat. 10:30am-8:45pm, under $8) is an old favorite. Their motto is, "We ain't fancy, but we sure

Le Catalan French Café

are good." Good old vinegary eastern North Carolina-style pork barbecue is the main item, though you can pick from Brunswick stew, fried chicken, and a mess of country vegetables. You'll get hush puppies and corn sticks at the table, but it will be worth your while not to fill up too fast—the cobblers and banana pudding are great.

Eclectic American

Flaming Amy's Burrito Barn (4002 Oleander Dr., 910/799-2919, www.flamingamysburritobarn.com, daily 11am-10pm) is, in their own words, "Hot, fast, cheap, and easy." They have a long menu with 20 specialty burritos (Greek, Philly steak, Thai), eight fresh salsas, and bottled and on-tap beers. It's very inexpensive—you can eat well for under $10, drinks included. Frequent special promotions include Tattoo Tuesdays; if you show the cashier your tattoo (come on, we all know you've got one), you can take 10 percent off your meal.

Boca Bay (2025 Eastwood Rd., 910/256-1887, www.bocabayrestaurant.com, Mon.-Thurs. 5pm-10pm, Fri.-Sat. 5pm-11pm, brunch Sun. 9am-2pm, entrées $11-20) serves a tapas-style menu of sushi, stir-fries, and heartier entrées, all very tasty. Vegetarian options are fairly limited, but you can cobble together a meal of tapas, salad, and sides.

Asian

Indochine, A Far East Café (7 Wayne Dr., at Market St., 910/251-9229, www.indochinewilmington.com, lunch Tues.-Thurs. 11am-2pm, Sat. 11am-3pm, dinner daily 5pm-10pm, $10-15) specializes in Thai and Vietnamese cuisine, has an extensive vegetarian menu, and has plenty of options for nonvegetarians as well. This restaurant is not downtown, but some distance out on Market Street; it's worth the drive. Try the vegetarian samosa egg rolls as an appetizer.

★ **Double Happiness** (4403 Wrightsville Ave., 910/313-1088, www.chinesedoublehappiness.com, daily lunch and dinner, $12-18) is a popular Chinese and Malaysian restaurant

known for serving traditional dishes that are a refreshing departure from the standard canon of American Chinese restaurants. The setting is original too, without, as one local food critic wrote, "a buffet or glamour food photos over a hospital-white take-out counter." You can choose between regular booths and traditional floor seating. If you're lucky, you might be present when the chef decides to send around rice balls, a sweet dessert snack, for everyone on the house.

Coffee

Port City Java (21 N. Front St., 910/762-5282, Sun.-Thurs. 6:30am-10pm, Fri.-Sat. 6:30am-midnight) is my favorite coffeehouse in town. The java is great and the baristas very friendly, and the warm, wooden interior is conducive to relaxation.

ACCOMMODATIONS
Under $150

Affordable options are plentiful, especially on Market Street a couple of miles from downtown. Wilmington's **Holiday Inn** (5032 Market St., 866/553-0169, www.wilmingtonhi.com, $65-135) is clean and comfortable, and just a few minutes' drive from the historic district. Nearby is the **Jameson Inn** (5102 Dunlea Ct., 910/452-9828, www.jamesoninns.com, from $65), another fine choice. The Jameson Inn is a little hard to find, hidden behind other buildings. From Market Street, turn onto New Centre Drive and look for the sign across the street from Target.

$150-300

Wilmington overflows with historic bed-and-breakfasts. ★ **Front Street Inn** (215 S. Front St., 800/336-8184, www.frontstreetinn.com, $139-239) is a tiny boutique hotel in the historic district, one block from the Cape Fear River and easy walking distance from the restaurants and shops at Market and Front Streets. The inn occupies the old Salvation Army of the Carolinas building, an attractive brick city building with arched windows and bright, airy guest rooms. For comfortable and classy lodging in the heart of the historic district, the Front Street Inn is a best bet.

The **Wilmingtonian** (101 S. 2nd St., 910/343-1800, www.thewilmingtonian.com, $87-325) is a complex of five buildings, four of which are renovated historic structures, from the 1841 De Rosset House to a 1950s convent. The De Rosset House is an utterly fabulous Italianate mansion, one of the most recognizable buildings in Wilmington. For $325 ($250 off-season), you can stay in the Cupola Suite, a spectacular aerie with a panoramic view of the port. The **Rosehill Inn** (114 S. 3rd St., 800/815-0250, www.rosehill.com, $90-200) occupies a pretty 1848 residence three blocks from the river. The flowery high-B&B-style decor suits the house well, making for elegant but comfy quarters. The **Taylor House** (14 N. 7th St., 800/382-9982, www.taylorhousebb.com, $125-140) is an absolutely lovely 1905 home—rather subdued in design when compared to some of the architectural manifestos nearby, but in a very attractive way. The pretty, sunny guest rooms promise relaxation. The famous ★ **Graystone Inn** (100 S. 3rd St., 888/763-4773, www.graystoneinn.com, $159-379) was built in the same year as the Taylor House, but its builder, the widow Elizabeth Bridgers, had a very different aesthetic. The splendor of the palace first known as the Bridgers House reflects the fortune of Mrs. Bridgers's late husband, a former Confederate congressman and one of the most influential figures in Wilmington's days as a railroad center.

These are by no means the only excellent bed-and-breakfast inns in Wilmington; the city is full of them. Check with the **Wilmington and Beaches Convention and Visitors Bureau** (www.wilmingtonandbeaches.com) for comprehensive listings.

A plush place to stay in the downtown area is the **Hilton Wilmington Riverside** (301 N. Water St., 888/324-8170, www.wilmingtonhilton.com, $180-200). Located right on the river, many of the guest rooms have a great view. The shops, restaurants, and galleries of the riverfront are right outside the front door,

making this a great place to stay if you're planning to enjoy Wilmington's downtown.

NORTH OF WILMINGTON
Topsail Island

In the manner of an old salt, Topsail is pronounced "Tops'l." The three towns on Topsail Island—Topsail Beach, North Topsail Beach, and Surf City—are popular beach communities. They're less commercial than some of their counterparts elsewhere along the coast, but still destinations for throngs of visitors in the summer months. A swing bridge gives access to the island at Surf City (the bridge opens around the beginning of each hour, so expect backups), and there is a high bridge between Sneads Ferry and North Topsail.

At Topsail Beach is the **Missiles and More Museum** (720 Channel Ave., 910/328-8663, www.missilesandmoremuseum.org, Memorial Day-Labor Day Mon.-Sat. 2pm-5pm, Labor Day-Memorial Day Mon.-Fri. 2pm-5pm, free). This little museum commemorates a rather peculiar chapter in the island's history: when it was used by the U.S. government for a project called Operation Bumblebee. During Operation Bumblebee, Topsail was a proving ground for missiles, and the work done here led to major advancements in missile technology and the development of a precursor of the ram jet engine used later in supersonic jet design. Exhibits include real warheads left over from the tests. Especially interesting to lovers of projectiles will be the 1940s color film of missile firings here at Topsail.

★ Hammocks Beach State Park

At the very appealing little fishing town of Swansboro, you'll find the mainland side of **Hammocks Beach State Park** (1572 Hammocks Beach Rd., 910/326-4881, http://ncparks.gov, Sept.-May daily 8am-6pm, June-Aug. daily 8am-7pm, free). Most of the park lies on the other side of a maze of marshes, on Bear and Huggins Islands. These wild, undeveloped islands are important havens for migratory waterfowl and nesting logger-head sea turtles. Bear Island is 3.5 miles long and less than a mile wide, surrounded by the Atlantic Ocean, Intracoastal Waterway, Bogue and Bear Inlets, and wild salt marshes. A great place to swim, Bear Island has a bathhouse complex with a snack bar, restrooms, and outdoor showers. Huggins Island is the smaller of the two, and is covered in ecologically significant maritime forest and lowland marshes. Two paddle trails, one just over 2.5 miles and the other 6 miles, weave through the marshes that surround the islands.

Camping is permitted on Bear Island, in reserved and first-come sites near the beach and inlet, with restrooms and showers available nearby.

A private boat or **passenger ferry** (910/326-4881, $5 adults, $3 seniors and children) are the only ways to reach the islands. The ferry's schedule varies by days of the week and season: in May and September Wednesday-Saturday and in April and October Friday-Saturday, the ferry departs from the mainland every half hour 9:30am-4:30pm, and departs from Bear Island every hour 10am-5pm. Memorial Day-Labor Day Monday-Tuesday, it departs from the mainland every hour 9:30am-5:30pm, and departs from the island every hour 10am-6pm; Wednesday-Sunday it departs from the mainland every half hour 9:30am-5:30pm, and departs from the island every half hour 10am-6pm.

TRANSPORTATION

Wilmington is the eastern terminus of I-40, more than 300 miles east of Asheville, approximately 120 miles east of Raleigh. The Cape Fear region is also crossed by a major north-south route, U.S. 17, the old Kings Highway of colonial times. Wilmington is roughly equidistant along U.S. 17 between Jacksonville to the north and Myrtle Beach, South Carolina, to the south; both cities are about an hour away.

Wilmington International Airport (ILM, 1740 Airport Blvd., 910/341-4125, www.flyilm.com) serves the region with flights to East Coast cities. For a wider selection of routes, it may be worthwhile to fly into Myrtle Beach or Raleigh and rent a car. If driving to Wilmington from the Myrtle Beach airport, add another 30-60 minutes to get through Myrtle Beach traffic, particularly in summer, as the airport there is on the southern edge of town. If driving from Raleigh-Durham International Airport, figure on the trip taking at least 2.5 hours. There is no passenger train service to Wilmington.

Wave Transit (910/343-0106, www.wavetransit.com), Wilmington's public transportation system, operates buses throughout the metropolitan area and trolleys in the historic district. They run a free downtown trolley that can take you to most areas of interest. Otherwise fares are $2 round-trip.

The Southern Coast

From the beaches of Brunswick and New Hanover County to the swampy, subtropical fringes of land behind the dunes, this little corner of the state is one of the most beautiful parts of North Carolina.

There are a string of beaches here, starting with Carolina Beach and Kure, just south of Wilmington, and descending through the "Brunswick Islands," as designated in tourist

literature. Most of these beaches are low-key, quiet family beaches, largely lined with residential and rental properties. They're crowded in the summertime, of course, but are still much more laid back than Myrtle Beach, over the state line to the south, and even Wrightsville and some of the "Crystal Coast" beaches.

You'll see some distinctive wildlife here.

The first you'll notice, more likely than not, is the ubiquitous green anole (called "chameleons" by many locals). These tiny lizards, normally a bright lime green, but able to fade to brown when camouflage is called for, are everywhere—skittering up porch columns and along balcony railings, peering at you around corners, hiding between the fronds of palmetto trees. The males put on a big show by puffing out their strawberry-colored dewlaps.

This is also the part of the state where the greatest populations of alligators live. Alligators are nonchalant creatures that rarely appear better than comatose, but they are genuinely deadly if crossed. All along river and creek banks, bays, and swamps, you'll see their scaly hulks basking motionless in the sun. Keep small children and pets well clear of anywhere a gator might lurk.

In certain highly specialized environments—mainly in and around Carolina bays that offer both moistness and nutrient-poor soil—the Venus flytrap and other carnivorous plants thrive. To the average fly, these are more threatening than an alligator any day. The flytrap and some of its cousins are endangered, but in this region—and nowhere else in the world—you'll have plenty of opportunities to see them growing and gorging.

KURE BEACH

Kure is a two-syllable name: pronounced "KYU-ree" (as in Marie Curie, not "curry"). This is a small beach community, not an extravaganza of neon lights and shark-doored towel shops. Most of the buildings on the island are houses, both rental houses for vacationers and the homes of Kure Beach's year-round residents. The beach itself, like all North Carolina ocean beaches, is public.

Carolina Beach State Park

Just to the north of Kure is **Carolina Beach State Park** (1010 State Park Rd., off U.S. 421, Carolina Beach, 910/458-8206, http://ncparks. gov, Mar.-Apr. and Sept.-Oct. 8am-8pm, May-Aug. 8am-10pm, Nov.-Feb. 8am-6pm, free). Of all the state parks in the coastal region, this may be the one with the greatest ecological diversity. Within its boundaries are coastal pine and oak forests, pocosins between the dunes, saltwater marshes, a 50-foot sand dune, and lime-sink ponds; of the lime-sink ponds, one is a deep cypress swamp, one is a natural garden of water lilies, and one an ephemeral pond that dries into a swampy field every year, an ideal home for the many carnivorous plants that live here. You'll see Venus flytraps and their ferocious cousins, but resist the urge to dig or pick them, or to tempt them with your fingertips. Sort of like stinging insects that die after delivering their payload, the flytraps' traps can wither and fall off once they're sprung.

The park has 83 drive-to and walk-in campsites ($20), each with a grill and a picnic table. Two are wheelchair accessible. Restrooms and hot showers are nearby.

Fort Fisher State Park

At the southern end of Kure Beach is **Fort Fisher State Park** (1000 Loggerhead Rd., off U.S. 421, 910/458-5798, http://ncparks. gov, June-Aug. daily 8am-9pm, Mar.-May and Sept.-Oct. daily 8am-8pm, Nov.-Feb. daily 8am-6pm, free). Fort Fisher has six miles of beautiful beach, a less crowded and commercial alternative to the other beaches of the area. A lifeguard is on duty Memorial Day-Labor Day daily 10am-5:45pm. The park also includes a 1.1-mile hiking trail that winds through marshes and along the sound, ending at an observation deck where visitors can watch wildlife.

This is also a significant historic site. Fort Fisher was a Civil War earthwork stronghold designed to withstand massive assault. Modeled in part on the Crimean War's Tower of Malakoff, Fort Fisher's construction was an epic saga in itself, as hundreds of Confederate soldiers, enslaved African Americans, and conscripted indigenous Lumbee people were brought in to build what became the Confederacy's largest fort. After the fall of Norfolk in 1862, Wilmington became the most important open port in the South, a vital harbor for blockade-runners and military vessels. Fisher held until nearly the end of the war. On December 24, 1864, U.S. general Benjamin "the Beast" Butler attacked the fort with 1,000 soldiers but was repulsed. A few weeks later, in January 1865, Fort Fisher was finally taken, but it required a Yankee force of 9,000 soldiers and 56 ships in what was to be the largest amphibious assault until World War II. Without its defenses at Fort Fisher, Wilmington soon fell, hastening the end of the war, which came only three months later. Thanks to the final assault by the Union forces and 150 subsequent years of winds, tides, and hurricanes, not a great deal of the massive earthworks survives. But the remains of this vitally important Civil War site are preserved in an oddly peaceful and pretty seaside park, which contains a restored gun emplacement and a visitors center with interpretive exhibits.

Also at Fort Fisher is a branch of the **North Carolina Aquarium** (910/458-8257, daily 9am-5pm, $10.95 adults, $9.95 seniors, $8.95 ages 3-12). Like its sisters at Roanoke and Pine Knoll Shores, this is a beautiful aquarium that specializes in the native marine life of the North Carolina waters. It's also a center for marine biology and conservation efforts, assisting in the rescue and rehabilitation of sea turtles, marine mammals, freshwater reptiles, and other creatures of the coast. While at the aquarium, be sure to visit the albino alligator.

Accommodations

The beaches of the Carolinas used to be lined with boardinghouses, the old-time choice in lodging for generations of middle-class travelers. They were sort of a precursor to today's bed-and-breakfasts, cozy family homes where visitors dined together with the hosts and were treated not so much like customers as houseguests—which is just what they were. Hurricane Hazel razed countless guesthouses when it pummeled the coast in 1954, ushering in the next epoch, that of the family motel. The **Beacon House** (715 Carolina Beach Ave. N., 877/232-2666, www.beaconhouseinnb-b.

com, from $150 high season, breakfast not included, some pets permitted in cottages with an extra fee) at Carolina Beach, just north of Kure, is a rare survivor from that era. The early-1950s boardinghouse has the typical upstairs and downstairs porches and dark wood paneling indoors. (Nearby cottages are also rented by the Beacon House.) The price is much higher than it was in those days, but you'll be treated to a lodging experience from a long-gone era.

BALD HEAD ISLAND

Bald Head Island, an exclusive community where golf carts are the only traffic, is a two-mile, 20-minute ferry ride from Southport. More than 80 percent of the island is designated as a nature preserve, and at the southern tip stands "Old Baldy," the oldest lighthouse in North Carolina.

Sights

The **Bald Head Island Lighthouse** (910/457-5003, www.oldbaldy.org, spring-fall Tues.-Sat. 10am-4pm, Sun. 11am-4pm, call for winter hours, $6 adults, $3 children) was built in 1818, replacing an even earlier tower that was completed in 1795. Despite being the newcomer at Bald Head, the 109-foot lighthouse is the oldest such structure surviving in North Carolina. A visit to the lighthouse includes a stop next door at the **Smith Island Museum,** housed in the lighthouse keeper's home. The development of Smith Island (of which Bald Head is the terminus) allowed almost 17,000 acres to be set aside as an ecological preserve. The Old Baldy Foundation leads **historical tours** (910/457-5003, Tues.-Sat. 10:30am, $57, includes round-trip ferry) of Bald Head, departing from Island Ferry Landing, a short walk from the lighthouse.

Food

At Carolina Beach the **Shuckin' Shack** (6 N. Lake Park Blvd., 910/458-7380, www.theshuckinshack.com, Mon.-Sat. 11am-midnight, Sun. noon-midnight, $7-25) is a friendly little oyster bar that serves fresh local seafood, and oysters by the bucket. After a meal at the Shuckin' Shack, stop by **Britt's Donuts** (11 Boardwalk, 910/707-0755, Mon.-Thurs. and Sat.-Sun. 8:30am-10:30pm, Fri. 4pm-midnight, closed Oct.-Feb.). Britt's has been famous for its homemade doughnuts since opening its doors in 1939. Note they are very seasonal and close in the colder months.

SOUTHPORT

One of North Carolina's prettiest towns, Southport is an 18th-century river hamlet whose port was overtaken in importance by Wilmington's—and hence it has remained small and quiet. It was the Brunswick County seat until the late 1970s, when that job was outsourced to Bolivia (Bolivia, North Carolina, that is). It's a wonderfully charming place, with block upon block of beautiful historic houses and public buildings. The old cemetery is a gorgeous spot, and in it you'll find many tombstones that bear witness to the town's seafaring history—epitaphs for sea captains who died while visiting Smithville

the Bald Head Island Lighthouse

(Southport's original name), and stones carved with pictures of ships on rolling waves.

Sights

The **North Carolina Maritime Museum at Southport** (204 E. Moore St., 910/457-0003, www.ncmaritime.org, Tues.-Sat. 9am-5pm, $2 adults, $1 over age 62, free under age 16) is a small branch of the Maritime Museum at Beaufort, where you can learn about the seafaring history of the Carolina coast. Among the many topics of interest here is the life of pirate Stede Bonnet, whose surname belies his infamous life of crime. Bonnet, who spent much time in the Southport area, was by turns the pillaging buddy and bitter rival of Blackbeard. Other cool displays in the museum include a section of a 2,000-year-old, 54-inch-long Indian canoe, and the eight-foot jawbone of a whale.

Events

Southport hosts the state's best-known **Fourth of July Celebration** (910/457-6964, www.nc4thofjuly.com), attended each year by up to 50,000 people. (That's approximately 20 times the normal population of the town.) In addition to the requisite fireworks, food, and music, the festival features a special tribute to veterans, a flag retirement ceremony (that is, folks bring their old and worn-out flags), and a naturalization ceremony for new Americans.

Food

The ★ **Yacht Basin Provision Company** (130 Yacht Basin St., 910/457-0654, www.provisioncompany.com, Sun.-Thurs. 11am-4pm, Fri.-Sat. 11am-9pm, $10-20) is a Southport seafood joint with a super-casual atmosphere. Customers place their orders at the counter and serve themselves drinks (on the honor system), then seat themselves dockside to await the arrival of their chow. Most popular here are the conch fritters and grouper salad sandwich, but anything you order will be good.

Accommodations

Lois Jane's Riverview Inn (106 W. Bay St., 800/457-1152, www.loisjanes.com, $93-143, depending on season) is a Victorian waterfront home built by the innkeeper's grandfather. The guest rooms are comfortably furnished, bright and not froufrou, and a two-suite cottage behind the inn has its own kitchen and separate entrance. The front porch of the inn has a wonderful view of the harbor. Another affordable option is the **Inn at River Oaks** (512 N. Howe St., 910/457-1100, www.theinnatriveroaks.com, $65-135), a motel-style inn with very simple suites. The **Island Resort and Inn** (500 Ocean Dr., Oak Island, 910/278-5644, www.islandresortandinn.com, $75-190, depending on season) is a beachfront property with standard motel rooms and one- and two-bedroom apartment suites.

OCEAN ISLE

Ocean Isle is the next-to-most-southerly beach in North Carolina, separated from South Carolina only by Bird Island and the town of Calabash. In October, Ocean Isle is the site of the **North Carolina Oyster Festival** (www.brunswickcountychamber.org), a huge event that's been happening for nearly 30 years. In addition to an oyster stew cook-off, surfing competition, and entertainment, this event features the North Carolina Oyster Shucking Competition. In the not-that-long-ago days when North Carolina's seafood industry was ascendant, workers—most often African American women—lined up on either side of long work tables in countless oyster houses along the coast and the creeks, and opened and cut out thousands of oysters a day. A complex occupational culture was at work in those rooms, one with its own vocabulary, stories, and songs. The speed at which these women worked was a source of collective and individual pride, and the fastest shuckers enjoyed quite a bit of prestige among their colleagues. The state shucking championship is the time when some of the best shuckers prove that

although North Carolina may have changed around them, they haven't missed a beat.

SOUTH ALONG U.S. 17

U.S. 17 is an old colonial road—in fact, its original name, still used in some stretches, is the Kings Highway. George Washington passed this way on his 1791 tour of the South, staying with the prominent planters of this area and leaving in his wake the legends about where he laid his head for an evening. Today, the Kings Highway, following roughly its original course, is still the main thoroughfare through Brunswick County into South Carolina.

Brunswick Town and Fort Anderson

Near Orton is the **Brunswick Town/Fort Anderson State Historic Site** (8884 St. Philip's Rd. SE, Winnabow, 910/371-6613, www.ah.dcr.state.nc.us, Tues.-Sat. 9am-5pm, free), the site of what was a bustling little port town in the early and mid-1700s. In its brief life, Brunswick saw quite a bit of action. It was attacked in 1748 by a Spanish ship that, to residents' delight, blew up in the river. (One of that ship's cannons was dragged out of the river about 20 years ago and is on display here.) In 1765, the town's refusal to observe royal tax stamps was a successful precursor to the Boston Tea Party eight years later. But by the end of the Revolutionary War, Brunswick Town was completely gone, burned by the British and having been made obsolete anyway by the growth of Wilmington. Today, nothing remains of the colonial port except for the lovely ruins of the 1754 **St. Philip's Anglican Church** and some building foundations uncovered by archaeologists. During the Civil War, Fort Anderson, sand earthworks that were part of the crucial defenses of the Cape Fear, was built on this site, protecting the blockade-runners who came and went from Wilmington. A visitors center at the historic site tells the story of this surprisingly significant stretch of riverbank, and the grounds, with the town's foundations exposed and interpreted, are an intriguing vestige of a forgotten community.

Nature Preserves

The Nature Conservancy's **Green Swamp Preserve** (Hwy. 211, 5.5 miles north of Supply, 910/395-5000, www.nature.org, daily dawn-dusk, free) contains nearly 16,000 acres of some of North Carolina's most precious coastal ecosystems, the longleaf pine savanna and evergreen shrub pocosin. Hiking is allowed in the preserve, but the paths are primitive. It's important to stay on the trails and not explore in the wilds because this is an intensely fragile ecosystem. In this preserve are communities of rare carnivorous plants, including the monstrous little pink-mawed Venus flytrap, four kinds of pitcher plant, and sticky-fingered sundew. It's also a habitat for the rare red-cockaded woodpecker, which is partial to diseased old-growth longleaf pines as a place to call home.

The Nature Conservancy maintains another nature preserve nearby, the **Boiling Spring Lakes Preserve** (off Hwy. 87, Boiling Spring Lakes, trail begins at community center, 910/395-5000, www.nature.org, daily dawn-dusk, free), with a trail that begins at the Boiling Spring Lakes Community Center. Brunswick County contains the state's greatest concentration of rare plant species, and the most diverse plant communities anywhere on the East Coast north of Florida. This preserve is owned by the Plant Conservation Program and includes over half the acreage of the town of Boiling Spring Lakes. The ecosystem comprises Carolina bays, pocosins, and longleaf pine forests. Like the Green Swamp Preserve, many of the species here are dependent on periodic fires to propagate and survive. The Nature Conservancy does controlled burning at both sites to maintain this rare habitat.

Calabash and Vicinity

The once tiny fishing village of Calabash, just north of the South Carolina line, was founded in the early 18th century as Pea Landing, a shipping point for the bounteous local peanut crop. Calabashes, a kind of gourd, were used as dippers in the town supply of drinking water, and when the settlement was renamed in 1873, it was supposedly for that reason that it became Calabash.

In the early 1940s, a style of restaurant seafood was developed here that involves deep-frying lightly battered fish and shellfish. As the style caught on and more restaurants were built, the term "Calabash-style seafood" was born. Jimmy Durante was fond of dining in Calabash, and some people claim that it was in tribute to the food here that he signed off his shows by saying, "Good night, Mrs. Calabash, wherever you are." Though Calabash seafood is now advertised at restaurants all over the country, this little town has more than enough restaurants of its own to handle the yearly onslaught of visitors in search of an authentic Calabash meal. Local favorite spots for seafood are the **Calabash Seafood Hut** (1125 River Rd., 910/579-6723, daily 11am-9pm, $10-28) and, right on the docks, **Dockside Seafood House** (9955 Nance St. SW, 910/579-6775, daily 4pm-9pm, $9-17).

Indigo Farms (1542 Hickman Rd. NW, 910/287-6794, www.indigofarmsmarket.com, Mon.-Sat. 8:30am-5:30pm, longer hours in warm months), three miles north of the South Carolina line in Calabash, is a superb farm market, selling all manner of produce, preserves, and baked goods. It also has corn mazes and farm activities in the fall, and is a training site for porcine contestants in the prestigious local NASPIG races.

Sunset Beach, the southernmost of the Brunswick County beaches, is a wonderfully small-time place, a cozy town that until 2008 could only be reached via a one-lane pontoon bridge. One of the area's most popular restaurants is located just on the inland side of the bridge to Sunset Beach: **Twin Lakes Seafood Restaurant** (102 Sunset Blvd., 910/579-6373, http://twinlakesseafood.com, daily 4:30pm-9:30pm, closed Nov.-Feb., $10-30) was built almost 40 years ago by Clarice and Ronnie Holden, both natives of the area. Clarice was born into a cooking family, the daughter of one of the founders of the Calabash restaurant tradition. Twin Lakes serves fresh locally caught seafood, a rarity in this time and place. In high season and on weekends, expect long lines.

TRANSPORTATION

The Brunswick County beaches, including Holden, Ocean Isle, and Sunset, are an easy drive from Wilmington on U.S. 17. The beaches and islands along the cape, due south of Wilmington, are not as close to U.S. 17. They can be reached by taking U.S. 76 south from Wilmington, or by ferry from Southport. The **Southport-Fort Fisher Ferry** (800/293-3779 or 800/368-8969) is popular as a sightseeing jaunt as well as a means simply to get across the river. It's a 30-minute crossing; most departures are 45 minutes apart, from Southport in summer daily 5:30am-7:45pm, winter daily 5:30am-6:15pm, and leaving Fort Fisher in summer daily 6:15am-8:30pm, winter daily 6:15am-7pm. For most vehicles the fare is $5, but if you're driving a rig that's more than 20 feet long, boat trailers and the like included, the price can be as high as $15. It's $1 for pedestrians, $2 for bicyclists, and $3 for motorcyclists. Pets are permitted if leashed or in a vehicle, and there are restrooms on all ferries.

Points Inland from Wilmington

Moving inland from the Wilmington area, you first pass through a lush world of wetlands distinguished by the peculiar Carolina bays. Not necessarily bodies of water, as the name would suggest, the bays are actually ovoid depressions in the earth, of unknown and much debated origin. They are often water-filled, but by definition are fed by rainwater rather than creeks or groundwater. They create unique environments and are often surrounded by bay laurels (hence the name), and are guarded by a variety of carnivorous plants.

The next zone, bounded by the Waccamaw and Lumber Rivers, is largely farmland and small towns. This was for generations prime tobacco country, and that heritage is still very much evident in towns like Whiteville, where old tobacco warehouses line the railroad tracks. Culturally, this area—mostly in Columbus County, extending some distance into Robeson to the west and Brunswick to the east—is congruous with the three counties in South Carolina with which it shares a border—Horry, Marion, and Dillon.

The area around the Lumber River, especially in Robeson County, is the home of the indigenous Lumbee people, who have an amazing heritage of devotion to faith and family and steadfast resistance to oppression. If you turn on the radio while driving through this area, you'll likely find Lumbee gospel programming and get a sense of the cadences of Lumbee English.

At the edge of the region is Fayetteville. From its early days as the center of Cape Fear Scottish settlement to its current role as one of the most important military communities in the United States, Fayetteville has always been a significant North Carolina city.

ALONG U.S. 74

A little way inland from Calabash, the countryside is threaded by the Waccamaw River, a gorgeous, dark channel full of cypress knees and dangerous reptiles. (The name is pronounced "WAW-cuh-MAW," with slightly more emphasis on the first syllable than the third.) It winds its way down from Lake Waccamaw through a swampy little portion of North Carolina, crossing Horry County, South Carolina (unofficial motto: "The *H* is silent"), before joining the Pee Dee and Lumber Rivers to flow into Winyah Bay at the colonial port of Georgetown. Through

The Legend of Henry Berry Lowry

In some places, the Civil War didn't end the day General Lee surrendered, but smoldered on in terrible local violence. One such place was the indigenous Lumbee community of Robeson County, in the days of the famous Lowry Band.

Then as now, Lowry (also spelled Lowrie) was a prominent surname among the Lumbee people. During the Civil War, Allen Lowry led a band of men who hid out in the swamps, eluding conscription into the backbreaking corps of semi-slave labor that was forced to build earthworks to defend Wilmington. When the war ended, violence against the Lumbees continued, and the Lowry Band retaliated, attacking the plantations of their wartime pursuers. Allen Lowry and his oldest son were captured in 1865 and executed. Henry Berry Lowry, the youngest son, inherited the mantle of leadership.

For the next several years, long after the end of the Civil War, the Lowry Band was pursued relentlessly. Arrested and imprisoned, Lowry and his men escaped from prison in Lumberton and Wilmington. Between 1868 and 1872, the state and federal governments tried various ways to apprehend them—putting a bounty on Lowry's head, even sending in a federal artillery battalion. After an 11-month campaign of unsuccessful pursuit, the federal soldiers gave up. Soon afterward, the Lowry Band emerged from the swamps, raided Lumberton, and made off with a large amount of money. This was the end of the road for the Lowry Band, however, and one by one its members were killed in 1872—except, perhaps, Henry Berry. It's unknown whether he died, went back into hiding, or left the area altogether. As befits a legend, he seems simply to have disappeared.

Henry Berry Lowry is a source of fierce pride to modern Lumbee people, a symbol of the community's resistance and resilience. Every summer, members of the Lumbee community perform in the long-running outdoor drama *Strike at the Wind,* which tells the story of the Lowry Band. Another vivid retelling of the story is the 2001 novel *Nowhere Else on Earth* by Josephine Humphreys.

Henry Berry Lowry

the little toenail of North Carolina that the Waccamaw crosses, it parallels the much longer Lumber River, surrounding the very rural Columbus County and part of Robeson County in an environment of deep subtropical wetlands.

Sights

★ MUSEUM OF THE NATIVE AMERICAN RESOURCE CENTER

Pembroke is the town around which much of the indigenous Lumbee community revolves, and at the center of life here is the University of North Carolina at Pembroke (UNCP). Founded in 1887 as the Indian Normal School, UNCP's population is now only about one-quarter Native American, but it's still an important site in the history of North Carolina's indigenous people. The **Museum of the Native American Resource Center** (Old Main, UNCP, 910/521-6282, www.uncp.edu, Mon.-Sat. 8am-5pm, free) is on campus, occupying Old Main, a 1923 building that's a source of pride for the Pembroke community. The Resource Center has a small but very good collection of historical artifacts and contemporary art by Native Americans from across the country.

JOHN BLUE HOUSE

Laurinburg's **John Blue House** (13040 X-way Rd., Laurinburg, 910/276-2495, www. johnbluecottonfestival.com, Tues.-Sat. 10am-noon and 1pm-4pm, free) is a spectacle of Victorian design, a polygonal house built entirely of heart pine harvested from the surrounding property and done up like a wedding cake with endless decorative devices. John Blue, the builder and original owner, was an inventor of machinery used in the processing of cotton. A pre-Civil War cotton gin stands on the property and is used for educational demonstrations throughout the year. This is the site of the **John Blue Cotton Festival,** an October event that showcases not only the ingenuity of the home's famous resident and the process of ginning cotton, but also lots of local and regional musicians and other artists.

Sports and Recreation

Several beautiful state parks line the Waccamaw and Lumber Rivers.

Yogi Bear's Jellystone Park (626 Richard Wright Rd., 877/668-8586, www. taborcityjellystone.com, $30 tents, $120 cabins), formerly known as Daddy Joe's, is a popular campground with RV and tent spaces, rental cabins, and yurts. The facilities are clean and well maintained, and there are tons of children's activities on-site. Some of the camping is in wooded areas, but for the most part expect direct sun and plan accordingly.

In Fair Bluff is **River Bend Outfitters** (1206 Main St., 910/649-5998, www.whitevillenc.com/rbo), a canoe and kayak company that specializes in paddling and camping trips along the beautiful blackwater Lumber River.

★ LAKE WACCAMAW STATE PARK

Lake Waccamaw State Park (1866 State Park Dr., Lake Waccamaw, 910/646-4748, http://ncparks.gov, office daily 8am-5pm, park Nov.-Apr. daily 8am-6pm, Mar.-May and Sept.-Oct. daily 8am-8pm, June-Aug. daily 8am-9pm, free) encompasses the 9,000-acre Lake Waccamaw. The lake is technically a Carolina bay, a mysterious geological feature of this region. Carolina bays are large, oval depressions in the ground, many of which are boggy and filled with water, but which are actually named for the bay trees that typically grow in and around them. Lake Waccamaw has geological and hydrological characteristics that make it unique even within the odd category of Carolina bays. Because of its proximity to a large limestone deposit, the water is more neutral than its usually very acidic cousins and so supports a greater diversity of life. There are several aquatic creatures that live only here, with great names like the Waccamaw fatmucket and silverside (a mollusk and a fish, respectively). The park draws many boaters and paddlers, naturally, although the only available launches are outside the park. Primitive campsites are available in the park.

JONES LAKE STATE PARK

North of Whiteville on U.S. 701 is Elizabethtown, location of **Jones Lake State Park** (4117 Hwy. 242, Elizabethtown, 910/588-4550, http://ncparks.gov, office Mon.-Fri. 8am-5pm, park Nov.-Feb. daily 8am-6pm, Mar.-May and Sept.-Oct. daily 8am-8pm, June-Aug. daily 8am-9pm). Visitors can go boating on Jones Lake, either in their own craft (no motors over 10 hp), or in canoes or paddleboats rented from the park ($5 per hour, $3 each additional hour). The lake is also great for swimming Memorial Day-Labor Day, with shallow, cool water and a sandy beach. There is a concession stand and a bathhouse at the beach. Camping is available in a wooded area, with drinking water and restrooms nearby. Visit the park's website for the rather complicated pricing system.

SINGLETARY LAKE STATE PARK

Singletary Lake State Park (6707 Hwy. 53 E., Kelly, 910/669-2928, http://ncparks. gov, daily 8am-5pm, free), north of Lake

Waccamaw in Kelly, centers on one of the largest of the Carolina bays, the 572-acre Singletary Lake, which lies within the Bladen Lakes State Forest. There is no individual camping allowed, although there are facilities for large groups—including the entrancingly named Camp Ipecac—which date from the Civilian Conservation Corps (CCC) era. There is a nice one-mile hiking trail, the CCC-Carolina Bay Loop Trail, and a 500-foot pier extending over the bay. Some of the cypress trees here are estimated to have been saplings when the first English colonists set foot on Roanoke Island.

LUMBER RIVER STATE PARK

Lumber River State Park (2819 Princess Ann Rd., Orrum, 910/628-4564, http://ncparks.gov, Nov.-Feb. 8am-6pm, Mar.-May and Sept.-Oct. 8am-8pm, June-Aug. 8am-9pm, free) has 115 miles of waterways, with numerous put-ins for canoes and kayaks. The river, referred to as the Lumber or Lumbee River, or, in areas farther upstream, Drowning Creek, traverses both the coastal plain region and the eastern edge of the sandhills. Camping is available at unimproved walk-in and canoe-in sites.

Food

If you pass through Tabor City, don't neglect to have a meal at the ★ **Todd House** (102 Live Oak St., 910/653-3778, www.todd-house.com, Mon.-Fri. 11am-8pm, Sun. 11am-3pm, $12), which has been serving fine country cooking since 1923. The Todds are one of the oldest families in the area along the state line, and the first in the restaurant business was Mary Todd, who took to cooking meals for visiting tobacco buyers. Through her daughter's time, and a couple of subsequent owners, the Todd House has continued to serve famously good barbecue, fried chicken, and other down-home specialties. The wonderful pies are available for purchase, so pick one up for the road.

There's a take-out counter in Whiteville

that chowhounds will drive an hour out of their way to reach because it's said to have the best burgers around. Next to the railroad tracks, **Ward's Grill** (706 S. Madison St., 910/642-2004, Mon.-Tues. and Thurs. 7am-2pm, Wed. 7am-1pm, 1st two Sat. of the month 7am-noon, $8) has no seating, just a walk-up counter. Its burgers are famous, as are its chili dogs.

In Lumberton, try **Fuller's Old-Fashion BBQ** (3201 Roberts Ave., Lumberton, 910/738-8694, www.fullersbbq.com, Mon.-Sat. 11am-9pm, Sun. 11am-4pm, lunch buffet $7, dinner buffet $9.50). Fuller's has a great reputation for its barbecue, but it also makes all sorts of country specialties like chicken gizzards and chitterlings, and a special 12-layer cake.

Transportation

This section of southeastern North Carolina is bisected by I-95, the largest highway on the East Coast. I-95 passes just outside both Fayetteville and Lumberton. Major east-west routes include U.S. 74, which crosses the Cape Fear at Wilmington and proceeds through Lake Waccamaw and Whiteville to pass just south of Lumberton and Pembroke, going to Laurinburg. Highway 87 goes through Elizabethtown, where you can choose to branch off onto Highway 211 to Lumberton, or bear north on Highway 87 to Fayetteville.

FAYETTEVILLE

Fayetteville is North Carolina's sixth-largest city, and in its own quiet way has always been one of the state's most powerful engines of growth and change. In the early 1700s it became a hub for settlement by Scottish immigrants, who helped build it into a major commercial center. From the 1818 initiation of steamboat travel between Fayetteville and Wilmington along the Cape Fear—initially a voyage of six days!—to the building of the Plank Road, a huge boon to intrastate commerce, Fayetteville was well connected to commercial resources all through the Carolinas.

At a national level, Fayetteville serves as the location of the largest single U.S. Army base in existence. Fort Bragg is the home of the XVIII Airborne Corps, the 82nd Airborne, the Delta Force, and the John F. Kennedy Special Warfare Center and School. As such, it's also the home of many widows and children of soldiers who have died in Iraq and Afghanistan. Within Fort Bragg is Pope Field, formerly Pope Air Force Base, which provides air support for the Fort's varied missions.

Sights

The **Museum of the Cape Fear Regional Complex** (801 Arsenal Ave., 910/486-1330, www.ncdcr.gov/ncmcf, Tues.-Sat. 10am-5pm, Sun. 1pm-5pm, free) has three components, each telling different stories of Fayetteville's history. The museum itself has exhibits on the history and prehistory of the region, including its vital role in developing transportation in the state, as well as its centrality as a military center. There is an 1897 house museum, the Poe House, which belonged to Edgar Allen Poe—not Edgar Allan, the writer, but Edgar Allen, a brickyard owner. The third section is the 4.5-acre Arsenal Park, site of a federal arms magazine built in 1836, claimed by the Confederacy in 1861, and destroyed by General Sherman in 1865.

The **Airborne and Special Operations Museum** (100 Bragg Blvd., 910/643-2766, www.asomf.org, Tues.-Sat. 10am-5pm, Sun. noon-5pm, free) is an impressive facility that presents the history of special operations paratroopers, from the first jump in 1940 to the divisions' present-day roles abroad in peacekeeping missions and war. In the museum's theater you can watch an amazing film of what it looks like when a paratrooper makes the jump, and the 24-seat Pitch, Roll, and Yaw Vista Dome Motion Simulator makes the experience even more exciting.

The **JFK Special Warfare Museum** (Bldg. D-2502, Ardennes St. and Marion St., Fort Bragg, 910/432-4272, www.jfkwebstore.

com, Tues.-Sun. 11am-4pm, ID required) tells the story of some interesting facets of the U.S. military, including Special Ops and Psychological Ops. The museum focuses on the Vietnam War era, but chronicles unconventional warfare from colonial times to present.

Going back farther in time, the **Fayetteville Independent Light Infantry Armory and Museum** (210 Burgess St., 910/433-1612, by appointment, free) displays artifacts from the history of the Light Infantry. The Fayetteville Independent Light Infantry (FILI) is still active, dedicated as North Carolina's official historic military command, a ceremonial duty. But in its active-duty days, which began in 1793, FILI had some exciting times, particularly during the Civil War. In addition to the military artifacts, this museum also exhibits a carriage in which the Marquis de Lafayette was shown around Fayetteville—the only one of the towns bearing his name that he actually visited.

The 79-acre **Cape Fear Botanical Garden** (536 N. Eastern Blvd., 910/486-0221, www.capefearbg.org, Mar.-mid-Dec. Mon.-Sat. 10am-5pm, Sun. noon-5pm, mid-Dec.-Feb. Mon.-Sat. 10am-5pm, $10 adults, $5 children) is one of the loveliest horticultural sites in North Carolina. The camellia and azalea gardens are spectacular sights in the early spring, but the variety of plantings and environments represented makes the whole park a delight. Along the banks of the Paw Paw River and Cross Creek, visitors will find dozens of garden environments, including lily gardens, hosta gardens, woods, a bog, and an 1880s farmhouse garden. Without a doubt, this is the prettiest place in Fayetteville.

Cross Creek Cemetery (North Cool Spring St. and Grove St., 800/255-8217, daily dawn-dusk) is an attractively sad spot, the resting place of many Scottish men and women who crossed the ocean to settle the Cape Fear. Though all kinds of people were buried here over the years, it is the oldest section that is most poignant, where one stone after another commemorates Mr. or Mrs. Mac-So-and-So, Late of Glasgow or Perth, Merchant in This Town.

Entertainment and Events

The **Cameo Theatre** (225 Hay St., 910/486-6633, www.cameoarthouse.com) is a cool early 20th-century movie house, originally known as the New Dixie. Today it is "Fayetteville's alternative cinematic experience," a place for independent and art-house movies.

The **Cape Fear Regional Theatre** (1209 Hay St., 910/323-4233, www.cfrt.org) began in 1962 as a tiny company with a bunch of borrowed equipment. Today it is a major regional theater with a wide reputation. Putting on several major productions each season, with a specialty in popular musicals, it draws actors and directors from around the country, but maintains its heart here in the Fayetteville arts community.

Fayetteville's late-April **Dogwood Festival** features rock, pop, and beach music bands; a dog show; a recycled art show; a "hogs and rags spring rally"; and the selection and coronation of Miss, Teen Miss, Young Miss, and Junior Miss Dogwood Festival.

Food and Accommodations

Fayetteville's dining choices tend toward highway chains, though there are some exceptions. The ★ **Hilltop House** (1240 Fort Bragg Rd., 910/484-6699, www.hilltophousenc.com, lunch Mon.-Sat. 11am-2pm, dinner Mon.-Thurs. 5pm-9pm, Fri.-Sat. 5pm-10pm, brunch Sun. 10:30am-2:30pm, $15-25) serves hearty fare in an elegant setting, has complimentary wine-tasting Tuesday evening, and has been recognized with a Wine Spectator Award for Excellence—not surprising, given that the Hilltop House has a 74-page wine list. More casual is the **Mash House** (4150 Sycamore Dairy Rd., 910/867-9223, www.themashhouse.com, Mon.-Thurs. 5pm-10pm, Fri. 5pm-11pm, Sat. noon-11pm, Sun. noon-9pm, $8-16), which has a good variety of pizzas and sandwiches as well as heavier entrées and a selection of good home-made brews.

Likewise, the city's lodging options are mostly chain motels, a multitude of which can be found at I-95's Fayetteville exits. You'll generally find a pretty reasonable deal at the old standards, but if you'd like to stay somewhere with more personality, Wilmington and Raleigh are both easily accessible.

Information and Services

Cape Fear Valley Health Services (1638 Owen Dr., 910/615-4000, www.capefearvalley.com) is a large hospital complex with acute care services, a major cardiac care program, and everything else one would expect from a major regional hospital.

The website of the **Fayetteville Area Convention and Visitors Bureau** (www.visitfayettevillenc.com) is an excellent source of visitor information for this city. You'll find the basics as well as detailed driving tours, extensive historical information, and much more.

Transportation

Fayetteville is a short hop off I-95. Fayetteville is also easily reached by Highway 24 via Jacksonville, Warsaw, and Clinton. **Fayetteville Regional Airport** (FAY, 400 Airport Rd., 910/433-1160, fly-fay.ci.fayetteville.nc.us) has daily flights to Charlotte, Atlanta, and Washington DC on Delta and US Airways. The city is served by **Amtrak** (472 Hay St., 800/872-7245, www.amtrak.com, daily 10am-5:45pm and 10pm-5:45am) via the regional *Palmetto* and the New York-Miami *Silver Meteor* lines.

Myrtle Beach and the Grand Strand

The West has Las Vegas, Florida has Orlando, and South Carolina has Myrtle Beach.

There's no Bellagio Resort or Magic Kingdom here, but Myrtle Beach remains the number one travel destination in the state, with even more visitors than Charleston. Unlike Charleston, you'll find little history here. With several theme parks, 100 golf courses, 50 miniature golf courses, over 2,000 restaurants—not to mention miles of beautiful shoreline—Myrtle Beach is built for all-out vacation enjoyment. The hot, hazy height of the summer marks the busy season on the Strand, when its long main drag, Kings Highway (aka Business U.S. 17), is packed full of families eager for more swimming, more shopping, more eating, and just plain more.

While to many people the name Myrtle Beach conjures an image of tacky, downscale people doing tacky, downscale things, that's an outmoded stereotype. Tacky is certainly still in vogue here, but an influx of higher-quality development, both in accommodations and entertainment value, has lifted the bar significantly. Rather than slumming in a beat-up motel, quaffing PBR on the beach, and loading up on $2 T-shirts like in the "good old days," a typical Myrtle Beach vacation now involves a stay in a large condo apartment with flat-screen TVs, a full kitchen, and a sumptuous palmetto-lined pool; dining at the House of Blues; having drinks at the Hard Rock Café; stops at high-profile attractions like Ripley's Aquarium; and shopping at trendy retailers like Anthropologie and Abercrombie & Fitch.

The Grand Strand on which Myrtle Beach sits—a long, sandy peninsula stretching 60 miles from Winyah Bay to the North Carolina border—has been a vacation playground for generations of South Carolinians. Unlike Hilton Head, where New York and Midwestern accents are more common than Lowcountry drawls, Myrtle Beach and the Grand Strand remain largely homegrown passions, with many visitors living within a few hours' drive. Despite the steady increase of money and high-dollar development in the area, its strongly regional nature works to your advantage in that prices are generally lower than in Vegas or Orlando.

To the south of Myrtle proper lies the understated, affluent, and relaxing Pawleys Island, with nearby Murrells Inlet and its

Previous: family fun at Myrtle Beach; Ripley's Aquarium at Broadway at the Beach. **Above:** lounging chairs on Myrtle Beach.

Highlights

★ **Broadway at the Beach:** You'll find good cheesy fun along with tons of interesting shops, theme restaurants, and, of course, miniature golf (page 100).

★ **Barefoot Landing:** This commercial hub is North Myrtle Beach's answer to Broadway at the Beach, with the Alabama Theatre and the House of Blues nearby (page 102).

★ **Ocean Drive Beach:** The still-beating, still-shuffling heart of the Grand Strand is also the center of shag dancing culture (page 104).

★ **Carolina Opry:** This popular show offers corny but high quality family entertainment in an intimate, friendly setting (page 106).

★ **Brookgreen Gardens:** Enjoy the country's largest collection of outdoor sculptures, set amid a fine collection of formal gardens (page 126).

★ **Huntington Beach State Park:** The scenic beach combines with one-of-a-kind Atalaya Castle to make a unique getaway (page 126).

★ **Hampton Plantation:** This historic Georgian mansion on the scenic Wambaw Creek inspired a South Carolina poet laureate to give it to the state for posterity (page 132).

Myrtle Beach and the Grand Strand

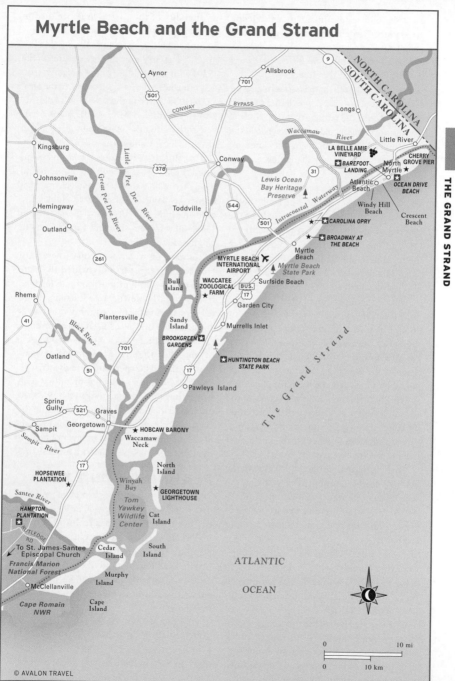

Aynor

Allsprook

9

NORTH CAROLINA
SOUTH CAROLINA

701

501

CONWAY   BYPASS

Longs

Waccamaw   River   Little River

Kingsburg

Little

LA BELLE AMIE VINEYARD
BAREFOOT LANDING   North
Myrtle   CHERRY GROVE PIER

378

Conway

31

OCEAN DRIVE BEACH

Johnsonville

Great Pee Dee River

Pee Dee River

Lewis Ocean Bay Heritage Preserve

Atlantic Beach

Hemingway

Toddville

544

Windy Hill Beach

Crescent Beach

Outland

501

Intracoastal Waterway

CAROLINA OPRY

261

BROADWAY AT THE BEACH

Myrtle Beach

MYRTLE BEACH INTERNATIONAL AIRPORT

Myrtle Beach State Park

Rhems

Bull Island

WACCATEE ZOOLOGICAL FARM

BUS.
17

Surfside Beach

41

Black River

Plantersville

Sandy Island

Garden City

Murrells Inlet

Oatland

701

BROOKGREEN GARDENS

The Grand Strand

51

17

HUNTINGTON BEACH STATE PARK

Spring Gully

521

Graves

Pawleys Island

Sampit

Georgetown

HOBCAW BARONY

Sampit River

Waccamaw Neck

17

North Island

HOPSEWEE PLANTATION

Winyah Bay

GEORGETOWN LIGHTHOUSE

Santee River

HAMPTON PLANTATION

Tom Yawkey Wildlife Center

Cat Island

RUTLEDGE RD

To St. James-Santee Episcopal Church

Cedar Island

South Island

ATLANTIC

Francis Marion National Forest

Murphy Island

OCEAN

McClellanville

Cape Romain NWR

Cape Island

0   10 mi

0   10 km

© AVALON TRAVEL

great seafood restaurants. Unique, eclectic Brookgreen Gardens hosts the largest collection of outdoor sculpture in the country, with one-of-a-kind Huntington Beach State Park literally right across the street.

Even farther south, in the northern quarter of the Lowcountry proper, you'll find a totally different scene: the remnants of the Carolina rice culture in quaint old Georgetown, and the haunting antebellum mansions at Hampton Plantation and Hopsewee Plantation.

HISTORY

The Grand Strand was once the happy hunting and shellfish-gathering grounds of the Waccamaw people, whose legacy is still felt today in the name of the dominant river in the region and the Strand's main drag itself, Kings Highway, which is actually built on an old Native American trail.

The southern portion of the Strand, especially Georgetown and Pawleys Island, rapidly became home to a number of rice plantations soon after the area was colonized. However, the area now known as Myrtle Beach didn't share in the wealth because its soil and topography weren't conducive to the plantation system. Indeed, the northern portion of the Grand Strand was largely uninhabited during colonial times, and hurricane damage prevented much development through the first half of the 19th century.

That changed after the Civil War with the boom of nearby Conway to the west, now the seat of Horry County (pronounced "OR-ee"). As Conway's lumber and export economy grew, a railroad spur was built to bring in lumber from the coast, much of which was owned by a single firm, the Conway Lumber Company. Lumber company employees began using the rail lines to take vacation time on the Strand, in effect becoming the first of millions of tourists to the area.

In the second half of the 19th century, Civil War veteran Franklin G. Burroughs, of the Burroughs and Collins Company, which supplied lumber and turpentine to Conway business interests, sought to expand the tourism profitability of the coastal area. He died in 1897, but his heirs continued his dream, inaugurated by the opening of the Seaside Inn in 1901. The first bona fide resort came in the 1920s with the building of the Arcady resort, which included the first golf course in the area.

In 1938 Burroughs's widow, Adeline, known locally as "Miss Addie," was credited with giving the town its modern name, after the locally abundant wax myrtle shrub. During this time, locals on the Strand originated the shagging subculture, built around the dance of the same name and celebrated at numerous pavilions and "beach clubs." The building of Myrtle Beach Air Force Base in 1940—now closed—brought further growth and jobs to the area.

Tourism, especially, grew apace here until Hurricane Hazel virtually wiped the slate clean in 1954. In typical Carolinian fashion, residents and landowners made lemonade out of lemons, using the hurricane's devastation as an excuse to build even bigger resort developments, including a plethora of golf courses.

Since then, the Strand has grown to encompass about 250,000 permanent residents, with about 10 million visitors on top of that each year. A huge influx of money in the 1990s led to a higher-dollar form of development on the coast, sadly leading to the demolition of many of the old beach pavilions in favor of new attractions and massive condo high-rises.

PLANNING YOUR TIME

The most important thing to remember is that the Grand Strand is *long*—60 miles from one end to the other. This has real-world effects that must be taken into account. For example, while the separate municipality of North Myrtle Beach may sound like it is right next door to Myrtle Beach proper, getting from one to the other can take half an hour even in light traffic.

Due to this geographical stretching, as well as to all the attractions, it is impossible to cover this area in a single day, and even two days is a ridiculously short amount of time. That's probably the main reason many folks indulge in a weekly rental. Not only does it give you enough time to see everything, but it enables you to relax, slow down, and enjoy the beaches and the general laid-back attitude.

In May, Memorial Day weekend and Bike Week have traditionally signaled the beginning of the tourism season in Myrtle Beach. The busy season exactly corresponds with the hottest months of the year, July and August. This is when crowds are at their peak, restaurants are most crowded, and the two spurs of U.S. 17 are at their most gridlocked.

Springtime in Myrtle Beach is quite nice, but keep in mind that water temperatures are still chilly through April. There is almost always one last cold snap in March that augurs the spring.

Personally, I recommend hitting Myrtle Beach just as the busy season wanes, right after Labor Day. Rooms are significantly cheaper, but most everything is still fully open and adequately staffed, with the added benefit of the biggest crush of visitors being absent. Similarly, for some really inexpensive room rates, try to hit town in late February.

Winter on the Grand Strand is very slow, as befitting this very seasonal locale. Many restaurants, especially down the Strand near Murrells Inlet, close entirely through February.

ORIENTATION

This part of the Strand comprises several municipalities, from Surfside Beach to the south up to Little River near the North Carolina border, but for all intents and purposes it's one big place all its own. As a general rule, development (read: money) is moving more quickly to the North Myrtle Beach area rather than the older Myrtle Beach proper to the south.

North Myrtle is actually a recent aggregation of several historic beachfront communities: Windy Hill, Crescent Beach, Cherry Grove, and Ocean Drive. You'll see numerous signs announcing the entrance or exit into or out of these communities, but keep in mind you're still technically in North Myrtle Beach.

The **Grand Strand grid** is based on a system of east-west avenues beginning just north of Myrtle Beach State Park. Confusingly, these are separated into "North" and "South" avenues. Perhaps even more confusing, North Myrtle Beach also uses its own distinct north-and-south avenue system, also for roads running east-west. Got it?

It goes like this: Myrtle Beach starts with 29th Avenue South at the Myrtle Beach International Airport and goes up to 1st Avenue South just past Family Kingdom Amusement Park. From here, the avenues are labeled as "North" from 1st Avenue North up to 82nd Avenue North, which concludes Myrtle Beach proper. North Myrtle Beach begins at 48th Avenue South near Barefoot Landing and goes up to Main Street (the center of the shag culture). It continues with 1st Avenue North, goes up to 24th Avenue North (Cherry Grove Beach), and finally concludes at 61st Avenue North, near the North Carolina state line.

Sights

★ BROADWAY AT THE BEACH

Love it or hate it, **Broadway at the Beach** (1325 Celebrity Circle, 800/386-4662, www.broadwayatthebeach.com, summer daily 10am-11pm, winter daily 10am-6pm), between 21st and 29th Avenues, is one of Myrtle's biggest and flashiest attractions—which is saying a lot. Opened in the late 1990s and expanded significantly since then, this collection of three hotels, over two dozen restaurants, about 50 shops, and a dozen kid-oriented activities sprawls over 350 acres with several other major attractions, restaurants, and clubs (such as the Hard Rock Café) on its periphery.

Just like the Magic Kingdom that many of Myrtle's attractions seek to emulate, Broadway at the Beach has at its center a large lagoon, around which everything else is situated. Needless to say, there's also a massive parking lot. Activity goes on all day and well into the wee hours, with the weekly Tuesday-night fireworks a big draw. While there's plenty to do, what with the great shops, tasty treats, and piped-in music following you everywhere, it's also fun just to walk around.

The biggest attraction at Broadway—and it's really big—is **Wonderworks** (1313 Celebrity Circle, 843/626-9962, www.wonderworksonline.com, Sun.-Thurs. 10am-8pm, Fri.-Sat. 10am-9pm, $23 adults, $15 children). You can't miss it—look for the thing that looks exactly like a massive, crumbling, upside-down creepy mansion. Inside you'll find a wide and quite varied assortment of interactive experiences designed to let you know what it's like to be upside down, or on a bed of nails, or in a hurricane, or freezing after the *Titanic* sank, and things of that nature. Think Ripley's Believe It or Not updated for a modern age, complete with laser tag.

Adjacent to the main Wonderworks building is the **Soar and Explore Zipline and Ropes Course** (daily noon-dusk, hours vary seasonally, zip line $19.95, ropes course $11.99, combo $26.99), where you can strap in and zip 1,000 feet overwater across the large lagoon around which Broadway at the Beach is constructed.

Medieval Times (2904 Fantasy Way, 843/236-4635, www.medievaltimes.com, $51 adults, $31 ages 3-12, free under age 3) is a combination dinner theater and medieval tournament reenactment. If the ticket prices sound high, keep in mind you're getting a three-course meal and a professional show done largely on horseback. Ask around for coupons to get a discount.

Now that almost all of the old-fashioned amusement parks at Myrtle Beach are gone, victims of "modernization," you can find a

Wonderworks is an upside-down mansion!

facsimile of sorts at **Pavilion Nostalgia Park** (843/913-9400, www.pavilionnostalgiapark.com, summer daily 11am-11pm, hours vary in other seasons, rides $3 each), which seeks to simulate the days of Myrtle gone by.

Of course, nowhere in Myrtle is really complete without miniature golf, and Broadway at the Beach's version is **Dragon's Lair Fantasy Golf** (1197 Celebrity Circle, 843/913-9301, $9), with two medieval-themed 18-hole courses boasting a fire-breathing dragon.

Ripley's Aquarium

If you've been to Boston's New England Aquarium, don't expect something similar at **Ripley's Aquarium** (1110 Celebrity Circle, 800/734-8888, www.ripleysaquarium.com, Sun.-Thurs. 9am-9pm, Fri.-Sat. 9am-10pm, $22 adults, $11 ages 6-11, $4 ages 2-5, free under age 2) at Broadway at the Beach. This is a smaller but quite delightful aquarium built primarily for entertainment purposes rather than education. Calming music plays throughout, and a moving sidewalk takes you around and under a huge main tank filled with various marine creatures. There's even the requisite stingray-petting touch tank.

You might see the garish billboards for the aquarium up and down U.S. 17, featuring massive sharks baring rows of scary teeth. But don't expect an over-the-top shark exhibit—the truth is that most of the sharks in the aquarium are smaller and much more peaceful.

Broadway Grand Prix

Just outside Broadway at the Beach you'll find the **Broadway Grand Prix** (1820 21st Ave. N., 843/839-4080, www.broadwaygrandprix.com, summer daily 10am-midnight, shorter hours in other seasons, from $20), where can you speed around in little go-karts on your choice of seven tracks, organized according to speed, age, and skill level. This being Myrtle Beach, there's other family-oriented entertainment offered here, including a rock-climbing wall and, of course, miniature golf.

Myrtle Waves Water Park

Billed as South Carolina's largest water park, **Myrtle Waves Water Park** (U.S. 17 Bypass and 10th Ave. N., 843/913-9260, www.myrtle-waves.com, May-Labor Day 10am-dusk, $25 ages 7 and over, $23 ages 3-6, free under age 3) is right across the street from Broadway at the Beach, covers 20 acres, and features all kinds of safe, fun "rides," such as the Ocean in Motion Wave Pool, the Layzee River, and the Saturation Station, where a huge water volcano absolutely soaks everybody in proximity every five minutes or so. That's just to name a few.

As you would expect, there are plenty of lifeguards on hand at all the rides. Food is plentiful if unremarkable, and there are shaded areas for the less adventurous to chill while the kids splash around. With one admission price covering all rides all day, this is one of the better deals in Myrtle Beach, which has more than its share of confusingly (and occasionally exorbitantly) priced attractions.

MYRTLE BEACH BOARDWALK AND PROMENADE

The **Boardwalk** (www.visitmyrtlebeach. com, daily 24 hours, free) is the new pride of old Myrtle, greatly improving civic life and morale. The fun, meandering 1.2-mile jaunt from the 2nd Avenue Pier to the 14th Avenue Pier is built in three distinct sections, not only leading you through the commercial areas of the waterfront, but also allowing easy pedestrian beach access. One section provides a nice peaceful walking experience amid the dunes.

Skywheel

You can't miss spotting the **Skywheel** (1110 N. Ocean Blvd., 843/839-9200, http://myrtle-beachskywheel.com, summer daily noon-midnight, $13 adults, $9 children), a huge Ferris wheel dominating the skyline at the Boardwalk. The cars are family-size and fully enclosed, and offer a great view of the ocean and surrounding area during the approximately 10-minute, three-rotation trip.

★ BAREFOOT LANDING

Before the arrival of Broadway at the Beach, the Strand's original high-concept retail and dining complex was **Barefoot Landing** (4898 U.S. 17 S., 843/272-8349, www.bflanding.com, hours vary). It's less flashy on the surface and certainly more tasteful, but just as commercial.

The centerpiece of the two-decade-old entertainment and shopping complex is **The Alabama Theatre** (4750 U.S. 17 S., 843/272-5758, www.alabama-theatre.com, ticket prices vary), a project of the famed country-and-western band of the same name, who despite their eponymous roots actually got their start gigging in juke joints in the Grand Strand. A stone's throw away is the **House of Blues** (4640 U.S. 17 S., 843/272-3000, www.hob.com, ticket prices vary), bringing in name acts on an almost nightly basis as well as diners to its excellent restaurant. On some nights you can pose for a picture with a real live tiger cub on your lap at **T.I.G.E.R.S. Preservation Station** (843/361-4552, www.tigerfriends.com, hours vary, free). Shopping is mostly the name of the game here, though.

Alligator Adventure

One of the most popular attractions within Barefoot Landing is **Alligator Adventure** (843/361-0789, www.alligatoradventure.com, daily 9am-7pm, $21.99 adults, $16.99 ages 4-12, free under age 4). They have hundreds of alligators, yes, but also plenty of turtles, tortoises, snakes, and birds. The otters are a big hit as well. The highlight, though, comes during the daily alligator feedings, when you get a chance to see the real power and barely controlled aggression of these magnificent indigenous beasts. Keep in mind that due to the cold-blooded reptiles' dormant winter nature, the feedings are not held in the colder months.

CHILDREN'S MUSEUM OF SOUTH CAROLINA

A less-expensive form of entertainment with an added educational component at Myrtle is the **Children's Museum of South Carolina**

(2501 N. Kings Hwy., 843/946-9469, www. cmsckids.org, summer Mon.-Sat. 9am-5pm, Sun. noon-5pm, $8). This facility tries hard to compete with the splashier attractions in town but still manages to keep a reasonably strong educational focus with programs like "Crime Lab Chemistry," "World of Art," and "Space Adventures."

FAMILY KINGDOM AMUSEMENT AND WATER PARK

For a taste of old-time beachfront amusement park fun, try the **Family Kingdom** (300 4th Ave. S., 843/626-3471, www.family-kingdom. com, free admission, cost of rides varies) overlooking the Atlantic Ocean. It boasts several good old-school rides, such as the Sling Shot, the Yo-Yo, and everyone's favorite, the wooden Swamp Fox roller coaster with a crazy 110-foot free fall. The attached water park, though not a match to the one at Broadway at the Beach, is a lot of fun, with the requisite slides and a long "lazy river" floating ride.

There is no admission charge—you pay by the ride (although all-inclusive wristbands are available starting at $27). This means parents and grandparents without the stomach for the rides don't have to pay through the nose just to chauffeur the little ones who do.

RIPLEY'S BELIEVE IT OR NOT!

Distinct in all but name from Ripley's Aquarium at Broadway at the Beach, this combo attraction down in the older area of Myrtle Beach—but very close to the brand-new Boardwalk—features several separate, though more or less adjacent, offerings from the venerable Ripley's franchise.

The **Ripley's Believe It or Not! Odditorium** (901 N. Ocean Blvd., 843/448-2331, www.ripleys.com, Sun.-Thurs. 10am-10pm, Fri.-Sat. 10am-11pm, $15 adults, $10 ages 6-11, free under age 6) is a repository of strange artifacts from around the world, updated with video and computer graphics for the new generation. It's fun and easy and takes no more than a half hour.

Ripley's Haunted Adventure (915 N. Ocean Blvd., 843/448-2331, www.ripleys.com, Sun.-Thurs. noon-10pm, Fri.-Sat. noon-11pm, $15 adults, $10 ages 6-11, free under age 6) is a sort of scaled-down version of Disney's famous Haunted House ride, with live actors scaring you through three floors.

SIGHTS

THE GRAND STRAND

Ripley's Believe It or Not!

Ripley's Moving Theater (917 N. Ocean Blvd., 843/448-2331, www.ripleys.com, Sun.-Thurs. 10am-10pm, Fri.-Sat. 10am-11pm, $15 adults, $10 ages 6-11, free under age 6) is a combined ride and movie theater featuring two motion-oriented films screened on a self-contained human conveyor belt, with a sort of kinetic IMAX effect.

★ OCEAN DRIVE BEACH

Less an actual place than a state of mind, the "OD" up in North Myrtle Beach is notable for its role in spawning one of America's great musical genres, beach music. Don't confuse beach music with the Beach Boys or Dick Dale—that's surf music. Beach music, simply put, is music to dance the shag to. Think the Drifters, the Platters, and the Swingin' Medallions.

To experience the OD, go to the intersection of Ocean Boulevard and Main Street and take in the vibe. There's still major shag action going on up here, specifically at several clubs specializing in the genre. If you don't want to shag, don't worry—this is still a charming, laid-back area that's a lot of fun simply to stroll around and enjoy a hot dog or ice cream cone.

CHERRY GROVE PIER

One of the few grand old pavilions left on the Southeast coast, North Myrtle's **Cherry Grove Pier** (3500 N. Ocean Blvd., 843/249-1625, www.cherrygrovepier.com, Sun.-Thurs. 6am-midnight, Fri.-Sat. 6am-2am, free) was built in the 1950s. Despite renovations in the late 1990s, it still retains that nostalgic feel, with anglers casting into the waters and kids eating ice cream cones. There's a neat two-story observation deck, and on a clear day you can see North Carolina.

Unusually, this is a privately owned pier. It's particularly popular with anglers, who have their state licensing needs covered by the pier. Get bait or rent a fishing rod ($20 per day plus refundable $50 deposit) at the **Tackle and Gift Shop** (843/249-1625). They'll also sell you a crab net to cast off the pier ($6, licenses and permits included).

TOURS

The number of tours offered in Myrtle Beach is nothing compared to Charleston, this being much more of a "doing" place than a "seeing" place. The most fun and comprehensive tour in the area is **Coastal Safari Jeep Tours** (843/497-5330, www.carolinasafari.com, $38 adults, $20 children), which takes you on a guided tour in a super-size Jeep (holding 12-14 people). You'll go well off the commercial path to see such sights on the Waccamaw Neck as old plantations, Civil War sites, and slave cabins, as well as hear lots of ghost stories. They'll pick you up at most area hotels.

Entertainment and Events

NIGHTLIFE

Any discussion of Myrtle Beach nightlife must begin with a nod to **The Bowery** (110 9th Ave. N., 843/626-3445, www.thebowerybar.com, daily 11am-2am), a country-and-western and Southern-rock spot right off the beach, which has survived several hurricanes since opening in 1944. Its roadhouse-style decor hasn't changed a whole lot since then, other than some cheesy marketing to play up its role in history as the place where the country band

Alabama got its start playing for tips in 1973 under the name Wildcountry. They were still playing gigs here when their first big single, "Tennessee River," hit the charts in 1980.

Bands usually crank up here around 9pm, and there is a nominal cover charge. There's only one type of draft beer served at The Bowery, at $2.50 per mug, and there is no real dance floor to speak of. If the proud display of Confederate flags doesn't bother you, it's usually a lot of fun. Next door is The Bowery's

The Bowery

"sister bar," **Duffy's** (110 9th Ave. N., 843/626-3445, daily 11am-2am), owned by the same folks and with a similarly down-home vibe, except without the live music.

For a more upscale if definitely less personal and unique experience, Broadway at the Beach hosts the high-profile **Hard Rock Café** (1304 Celebrity Circle, 843/946-0007, www.hardrock.com, daily 11am-midnight). This is a new location as of 2016, the previous landmark pyramid having been demolished.

You don't have to be a Parrothead to enjoy **Jimmy Buffett's Margaritaville** (1114 Celebrity Circle, 843/448-5455, www.margaritavillemyrtlebeach.com, daily 11am-midnight) at Broadway at the Beach, actually a pretty enjoyable experience considering it's a national chain. The eponymous margaritas are, of course, the beverage highlight, but they also serve Jimmy's signature LandShark Lager on tap for beer lovers.

In addition to its attached live performance space, the **House of Blues** (4640 U.S. 17 S., 843/272-3000, www.hob.com) at Barefoot Landing features a hopping bar in its dining area, situated amid a plethora of folk art reminiscent of the Mississippi Delta. Most nights feature live entertainment starting at about 10pm, with one of the best-mixed sound systems you're likely to hear.

SHAG DANCING

North Myrtle Beach is the nexus of that Carolina-based dance known as the shag. There are several clubs in town that have made a name for themselves as the unofficial "shag clubs" of South Carolina. The two main ones are **Duck's** (229 Main St., 843/249-3858, www.ducksatoceandrive.com) and **Fat Harold's** (210 Main St., 843/249-5779, www.fatharolds.com). There's also **The Pirate's Cove** (205 Main St., 843/249-8942).

Another fondly regarded spot is the **OD Pavilion** (91 S. Ocean Blvd., 843/280-0715), aka the Sunset Grill or "Pam's Palace," on the same site as the old Roberts Pavilion that was destroyed by 1954's Hurricane Hazel. Legend has it this was where the shag was born. Also in North Myrtle, the **Ocean Drive Beach Club** (98 N. Ocean Blvd., 843/249-6460), aka "the OD Lounge," inside the Ocean Drive Beach and Golf Resort, specializes in shag dancing most days after 4pm. The resort is a focal point of local shag conventions and is

The Story of the Shag

Duck's is one of the oldest shag emporiums.

In South Carolina, the shag is neither a type of rug nor what Austin Powers does in his spare time. It's a dance—a smooth, laid-back, happy dance done to that equally smooth, laid-back, happy kind of rhythm and blues called beach music (not to be confused with surf music such as the Beach Boys). The boys twirl the girls while their feet kick and slide around with a minimum of upper-body movement—the better to stay cool in the Carolina heat.

Descended from the Charleston, another indigenous Palmetto State dance, the shag originated on the Strand sometime in the 1930s, when the popular Collegiate Shag was slowed down to

even home to the **Shaggers Hall of Fame.** Also inside the Ocean Drive Resort is another popular shag club, **The Spanish Galleon** (100 N. Ocean Blvd., 843/249-1047), aka "the Galleon."

Key local shag events, which are quite well attended, include the **National Shag Dance Championships** (www.shagnationals.com, Jan.-Mar.), the **Spring Safari** (www.shagdance.com, Apr.), and the **Fall Migration** (www.shagdance.com, mid-Sept.).

SHOWS
★ Carolina Opry

Nothing can duplicate the experience of the Grand Ole Opry in Nashville, but don't snicker at Myrtle's **Carolina Opry** (8901-A Business U.S. 17, 800/843-6779, www.thecarolinaopry.com, showtimes and ticket prices vary). Since 1986 this well-respected stage show, begun by legendary promoter Calvin Gilmore, has packed 'em in at the Grand Strand. It is a hoot for country music fans and city slickers alike.

The main focus is the regular Opry show, done in the classic, freewheeling, fast-moving variety format known to generations of old-school country fans from the original Opry. Some of the humor is corny, and the brief but open displays of patriotic and faith-based music aren't necessarily for everyone. But there's no arguing the high energy and the subgenre now called the Carolina Shag. While shag scholars differ as to the exact spawning ground, there's a consensus that North Myrtle Beach's Ocean Drive, or "OD" in local patois, became the home of the modern shag sometime in the mid-1940s.

Legend has it that the real shag was born when white teenagers, "jumping the Jim Crow rope" by watching dancers at black nightclubs in the segregated South, brought those moves back to the beach and added their own twists. Indeed, while the shag has always been primarily practiced by white people, many of the leading beach music bands were (and still are) African American.

By the mid-late 1950s, the shag, often called simply "the basic" or "the fas' dance," was all the rage with the Strand's young people, who gathered at beachfront pavilions and in local juke joints called beach clubs, courting each other to the sounds of early beach music greats like the Drifters, the Clovers, and Maurice Williams and the Zodiacs. This is the time period most fondly remembered by today's shaggers, a time of penny loafers (no socks!), poodle skirts, and 45-rpm records, when the sea breeze was the only air-conditioning.

The shag is practiced today by a graying but devoted cadre of older fans, with a vanguard of younger practitioners keeping the art form alive. A coterie of North Myrtle clubs specializes in the dance, while the area hosts several large-scale gatherings of shag aficionados each year.

To immerse yourself in shag culture, head on up to Ocean Drive Beach in North Myrtle at the intersection of Ocean Boulevard and Main Street and look down at the platters in the sidewalk marking the **Shaggers Walk of Fame.** Walk a couple of blocks up to the corner of Main Street and Hillside Drive and visit the mecca of beach music stores, **Judy's House of Oldies** (300 Main St., 843/249-8649, www.judyshouseofoldies.com, Mon.-Sat. 9am-6pm). They also sell instructional DVDs.

To get a taste of the dance itself, stop by the **OD Pavilion** (91 S. Ocean Blvd., 843/280-0715), **Duck's** (229 Main St., 843/249-3858, www.ducksatoceandrive.com), or **Fat Harold's** (210 Main St., 843/249-5779, www.fatharolds.com), or visit **The Spanish Galleon** (100 N. Ocean Blvd., 843/249-1047) inside the Ocean Drive Beach Resort. If you're interested, don't be shy; shaggers are notoriously gregarious and eager to show off their stock-in-trade. It's easy to learn, it's family-friendly, and there will be no shortage of pleasant young-at-heart shaggers around who will be happy to teach you the steps.

vocal and instrumental abilities of these very professional singers, instrumentalists, and dancers, who gamely take on hits through the generations ranging from bluegrass to Motown, pop, and modern country.

The Carolina Opry augments its regular music, comedy, and dance show with a seasonal Christmas special, which is extremely popular and sells out even faster than the regular shows, often six or more months in advance.

Legends in Concert

Way down in Surfside Beach, where the big buildup on the Strand begins, you'll find *Legends in Concert* (301 Business U.S. 17, 843/238-7827, www.legendsinconcert.com, ticket prices vary), a popular rotating show of celebrity impersonators from Elvis to Barbra Streisand. As cheesy as that sounds, the resemblances can be quite uncanny, and the shows are really entertaining.

House of Blues

Besides being a great place for dinner, on the other side of the restaurant is the stage for the **House of Blues** (4640 U.S. 17 S., 843/272-3000, www.hob.com, ticket prices vary) at Barefoot Landing in North Myrtle Beach. They bring some pretty happening names in R&B, straight blues, and rock-and-roll to this fun venue dedicated to preserving old-school music and live performance, with a professional sound mix.

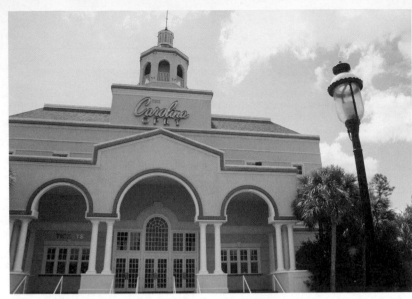

the Carolina Opry

Medieval Times

the House of Blues

Oh, come on—what's not to like about bountiful feasts, juggling jesters, skillful falconers, fetching maidens, and brave jousting knights? At **Medieval Times** (2904 Fantasy Way, 843/236-4635, www.medievaltimes.com, $51 adults, $31 under age 13) you'll get all that and more. The kitsch quotient is high at this Renaissance Faire on steroids, a live-action story line featuring plenty of stage combat, music, and a steady stream of culinary items for your enjoyment (and yes, there's a full bar for those of drinking age). The price may seem high at first glance, but keep in mind you're getting a hearty full dinner plus a two-hour stage and equestrian show.

Pirate's Voyage

Sharing a parking lot with the Carolina Opry is **Pirate's Voyage** (8901-B N. Kings Hwy., 843/497-9700, www.piratesvoyage.com, from $44.99 adults, $26.99 ages 4-11, free under age 4), one of the newer entertainment attractions to hit Myrtle Beach. Affiliated with Dolly Parton's entertainment empire—her "Dixie Stampede" originally occupied this building—Pirate's Voyage takes you on a rollicking two-hour trip into the world of buccaneers, with fighting, lost treasure, dancing, acrobatics, mermaids, and assorted high-seas drama, all with photographers on hand to document your experience . . . for a price, me hearties. Like Medieval Times, this is essentially dinner theater, with three shows a day in the high season of late summer.

The Alabama Theatre

The Alabama Theatre (4750 U.S. 17, 843/272-5758, www.alabama-theatre.com, ticket prices vary) at Barefoot Landing in North Myrtle Beach focuses on the long-running song-and-dance revue One: The Show as well as big-name acts who may be past their prime but are still able to fill seats, such as the Oak Ridge Boys, Kenny Rogers, and, of course, the eponymous troubadours Alabama, who got their big break while playing at Myrtle Beach. It's not all country, though—Motown and beach music acts like the Temptations and the Platters are often featured as well. As with the Carolina Opry, Barefoot Landing has its own Christmas special, and as with the Opry's offering, this one sells out well in advance.

Palace Theatre

The Palace Theatre (1420 Celebrity Circle, 800/905-4228, www.palacetheatremyrtlebeach.com, ticket prices vary) at Broadway at the Beach offers a variety of toned-down Vegas-style entertainment. Recent shows included tributes to the Beatles and Queen.

CINEMA

At Broadway at the Beach, there's a multiplex, Carmike's Broadway Cinema 16 (843/445-1600, www.carmike.com). Other movie theaters include the Cinemark (2100 Coastal Grand Circle, 843/839-3221, www.cinemark.com) at the Coastal Grand Mall and the massive Grand 14 at the Market Common (4002 Deville St., 843/282-0550), part of a multiuse development on a repurposed Air Force base.

FESTIVALS AND EVENTS

Interestingly, most events in Myrtle Beach don't happen during the three-month high season of June-August, mostly because it's so darn hot that all anyone wants to do is get in the water.

Winter

The Grand Strand is the birthplace of the dance called the shag, and each winter for the last 25 years the National Shag Dance Championships (2000 N. Kings Hwy., 843/497-7369, www.shagnationals.com, from $15 per night) have been the pinnacle of the art form. Beginning with preliminaries in January, contestants in five age ranges compete for a variety of awards, culminating in the finals the first week in March. The level of professionalism might amaze you—for such a lazy-looking dance, these are serious competitors.

Spring

You might not automatically associate our colder neighbor to the north with Myrtle Beach, but Canadian American Days (various venues, www.myrtlebeachinfo.com, free), or "Can Am," brings tens of thousands of visitors of both nationalities to sites all over the Strand each March to enjoy a variety of musical and cultural events. Always on top of marketing opportunities, the Myrtle Beach Chamber of Commerce makes sure this happens during Ontario's spring holidays to ensure maximum north-of-the-border attendance. While most of the events have little or nothing to do with Canada itself, this is basically a great excuse for Canucks to get some Carolina sunshine.

The Spring Games and Kite Flying Contest (843/448-7881, free) brings an exciting array of airborne craft to the Strand in front of Broadway at the Beach on an April weekend as the springtime winds peak.

Also in April is the area's second-largest shag event, the Society of Stranders Spring Safari (www.shagdance.com). Several clubs

Motorcycle Madness

Growling engines? Spinning tires? Patriotic colors? Polished chrome? Bikini car washes? Erotic bull-riding contests? That is the spectacle known as **Myrtle Beach Bike Week,** one of the largest gatherings of Harley-Davidson enthusiasts on the East Coast and one of the oldest, at about 75 years.

The event has historically happened each May on the week and weekend before Memorial Day weekend, bringing over 250,000 motorcyclists and their entourages to town for 10 days of riding, bragging, and carousing. South Carolina's lack of a helmet law is a particular draw to these freedom-cherishing motorcyclists. A few days later, on Memorial Day weekend, there's another bike rally, this one simply called Black Bike Week. Nearly as large as the regular Bike Week, the focus is on African American riders and their machines.

Contrary to stereotype, there's not much of an increase in crime during either Bike Week. Regardless, they are widely known as a particularly bad time to bring families to the area, and therein lies the controversy. Joining other municipalities around the nation in discouraging motorcycle rallies, the city of Myrtle Beach has enacted tough measures to force the bike rallies to leave town and make the area more family-friendly during that time. Most controversial among recent measures was a municipal helmet law, enforceable only within Myrtle Beach city limits, that was later struck down by the South Carolina Supreme Court. Other still-standing measures include stringent noise ordinances designed to include the roaring, rattling tailpipes of pretty much every Harley ever made. The separate municipality of North Myrtle Beach, however, has made it clear that bikers are welcome there even if they're non grata a few miles to the south.

As of now, it seems that the rallies will remain on the Strand rather than gun their collective throttle and head elsewhere, as they occasionally threaten to do when relations with local municipalities and police departments get too tense. The upshot for the nonmotorcyclist visitor? Bikers are somewhat less of a factor than in years past, and certainly local police are taking them more seriously. But the time around Memorial Day is still as crowded as ever.

in North Myrtle Beach host shag dancers from all over for a week of, well, shagging.

The biggest single event in Myrtle Beach happens in May with the **Spring Bike Rally** (various venues, www.myrtlebeachbikeweek. com, free), always known simply as "Bike Week." In this 75-year-old event, over 250,000 Harley-Davidson riders and their entourages gather to cruise around the place, admire each other's custom rides, and generally party their patooties off. While the typical Harley dude these days is getting on in years and is probably a mild-mannered store manager in regular life, young or old they all do their best to let their hair down at this festive event. Dozens of related events go on throughout the week at venues all over the Strand, from tough-man contests to "foxy boxing" matches to wet T-shirt contests. You get the picture— it's not for the politically correct or for young children.

Summer

Right after the Spring Bike Rally, on Memorial Day weekend, is the **Atlantic Beach Bikefest** (various venues), much more commonly referred to as "Black Bike Week." This event started in the 1980s and is spiritually based in Atlantic Beach, formerly the area's "black beach" during the days of segregation. It sees over 200,000 African American motorcycle enthusiasts gather in Myrtle Beach for a similar menu of partying, bikini contests, cruising, and the like. While the existence of separate events often reminds some people of the state's unfortunate history of segregation, supporters of both Bike Week and Black Bike Week insist it's not a big deal, and that bikers of either race are welcome at either event.

Kicking off with a festive parade, the 50-year-old **Sun Fun Festival** (various venues, www.grandstrandevents.com), generally held the weekend after Memorial Day weekend, signals the real beginning of the summer season with bikini contests, Jet Ski races, parades, air shows, and concerts galore.

The **City of Myrtle Beach Independence Day Celebration** (www.cityofmyrtlebeach.com, free) is held each July 4 weekend, when the largest number of visitors is in Myrtle Beach. It's fun, it's hot, there's fireworks aplenty, and boy, is it crowded.

Fall

For a week in mid-September, North Myrtle Beach hosts one of the world's largest shag dancing celebrations, the **Society of Stranders Fall Migration** (www.shagdance.com, free). Head up to the intersection of Ocean Drive and Main Street to hear the sounds of this unique genre, and party with the shaggers at various local clubs. If you don't know the steps, don't worry—instructors are usually on hand.

There's another, smaller Harley riders' rally the first week in October, the **Fall Motorcycle Rally** (various venues, www.myrtlebeachbikeweek.com, free).

Thanksgiving weekend, when the beaches are much less crowded and the hotels much cheaper, is the **South Carolina Bluegrass Festival** (2101 N. Oak St., 706/864-7203, www.aandabluegrass.com, $30 adults, $20 ages 6-13, free under age 6), a delightful and well-attended event at the Myrtle Beach Convention Center, celebrating the Appalachian music tradition. It attracts some of the biggest names in the genre.

Shopping

Shopping on the Grand Strand is strongly destination-oriented. You tend to find shops of similar price points and merchandise types clustered together in convenient locations: Upscale shops are in one place and discount and outlet stores in another. Here's a rundown of the main retail areas on the Strand with some of the standout shops.

BROADWAY AT THE BEACH

The sprawling **Broadway at the Beach** (U.S. 17 Bypass and 21st Ave. N., www.broadwayatthebeach.com, hours vary) complex has scads of stores, some of which are quite interesting and rise well beyond tourist schlock. There are maps and directories of the site available at various kiosks around the area.

One of my favorite stores is **Retroactive** (843/916-1218, www.shopretroactive.com), a shop specializing in 1970s and 1980s styles and kitsch, with some of the best (and wittiest) pop-culture T-shirts I've seen. The owners are frank about their continuing obsession with '80s hair bands. Another awesome T-shirt and trinket shop that the kids and teens will particularly enjoy is **Stupid Factory** (843/448-1100). The kids—and those with a sweet tooth—will go crazy in the aptly named **It'SUGAR** (843/916-1300, www.itsugar.com), a store dedicated to just about any kind of candy and candy-themed merchandise you can think of, from modern brands to retro favorites. If the packaged or bulk varieties don't float your boat, you can design your own massive chocolate bar. And, of course, this being Myrtle Beach, there's a **Harley Davidson** (843/293-5555) gift store with Hog-oriented merch galore.

The bottom line on Broadway at the Beach, though, is that it's made for walking around and browsing. Just bring your walking shoes—the place is huge—and keep in mind that there's not a lot of shade.

BAREFOOT LANDING

There are over 100 shops at **Barefoot Landing** (4898 U.S. 17 S., 843/272-8349, www.bflanding.com, hours vary) in North Myrtle Beach—as well as one cool old-fashioned carousel—but perhaps the most unique spot is **T.I.G.E.R.S. Preservation Station** (843/361-4552, www.tigerfriends.com, hours vary), where you get the opportunity to have your picture taken with a live tiger or lion cub. This is the fund-raising arm of a local organization for conservation of the big cats as well as gorillas and monkeys. Portraits begin at $100 to pose with a single critter and go up from there depending on the number of people you want to pose with in the shot. It's a lot of money, but this is truly a once-in-a-lifetime experience.

Relocated to the Strand from its grape yards in Chester, South Carolina, is **Carolina Vineyards Winery** (843/361-9181, www.carolinavineyards.com). Buy wine as a gift, or taste any seven of its labels for only $3.

There are magic shops, and then there are *magic shops*. **Trickmaster Magic Shop** (843/281-0705, http://trickmastermagicshop.com) is definitely the latter. Packed in this relatively small space is just about every legendary trick and trick deck known to the magician's art, along with a cool variety of magic books teaching you, in deadly serious fashion, the innermost secrets of the trade.

THE MARKET COMMON

The Market Common (4017 Deville St., www.marketcommonmb.com, hours vary) is an ambitious residential-retail mixed-use development opened for business on the site of the decommissioned Myrtle Beach Air Force Base. While its location near the Myrtle Beach International Airport means it's not exactly amid the sun-and-fun action (possibly a good thing, depending on the season), the very pedestrian-friendly development style and tasteful shops might provide a refreshing change of pace.

There are three dozen (and counting) stores, including Anthropologie, Williams-Sonoma, Copper Penny, Chico's, Brooks Brothers, Fossil, Banana Republic, Barnes & Noble, and Jake and Company ("Life Is Good"). There are plenty of restaurants, including Ultimate California Pizza and P. F. Chang's, and a large multiplex movie theater.

For those interested in how the sprawling old base was closed in the 1990s and repurposed so completely, there's interpretive signage all around the pedestrian mall and along the roadways leading to it. At The Market Common's entrance is Warbird Park, a well-done veterans memorial featuring an Air Force A-10 attack aircraft, an F-100 Super Sabre, and a Corsair II.

MALLS

The premier mall in the area is **Coastal Grand Mall** (2000 Coastal Grand Circle, 843/839-9100, www.coastalgrand.com, Mon.-Sat. 10am-9pm, Sun. noon-6pm) at the U.S. 17 Bypass and U.S. 501. It's anchored by Belk, J. C. Penney, Sears, Dillard's, and Dick's Sporting Goods.

Your basic meat-and-potatoes mall, **Myrtle Beach Mall** (10177 N. Kings Hwy., 843/272-4040, http://shopmyrtlebeachmall.com, Mon.-Sat. 10am-9pm, Sun. noon-6pm) is anchored by Belk, J. C. Penney, and Bass Pro Shops.

DISCOUNT BEACHWEAR

Literally dozens of cavernous, tacky, deep-discount T-shirt-and-towel-type places are spread up and down Kings Highway like mushrooms after a rain. The vast majority of them belong to one of several well-established chains: **Eagles Beachwear** (www.eaglesbeachwear.net), **Whales** (www.whalesnauticalgifts.com), **Wing's Beachwear** (www.wingsbeachwear.com), and **Bargain Beachwear** (www.bargainbeachwear.com). These are the kinds of places to get assorted bric-a-brac and items for your beach visit. The quality isn't that bad, and the prices are uniformly low.

OUTLET MALLS

There are two massive **Tanger Outlets** (www.tangeroutlet.com) at Myrtle Beach: **Tanger Outlet North** (10835 Kings Rd., 843/449-0491), off Kings Road/U.S. 17, and **Tanger Outlet South** (4635 Factory Stores

Blvd., 843/236-5100), off U.S. 501. Both offer over 100 factory outlet stores of almost every imaginable segment, from Fossil to Disney, OshKosh B'gosh to Timberland. Full food courts are available, and many folks easily spend an entire day here.

For years, busloads of hard-core shoppers from throughout the South have taken organized trips to the Grand Strand specifically to shop at **Waccamaw Factory Shoppes** (3071 Waccamaw Blvd., 843/236-8200). Their passion hasn't abated, as new generations of shopaholics get the fever to come here and browse the often deeply discounted offerings at row after row of outlet stores. There are actually two locations, the Factory Shoppes themselves and the nearby **Waccamaw Pottery** (3200 Pottery Dr., 843/236-6152). Bring your walking shoes (or buy some new ones at one of the many shoe stores), but don't worry about getting from one mall to the other—there's a free shuttle.

Sports and Recreation

Myrtle Beach's middle name might as well be recreation. While some of the local variety tends toward overkill—I personally loathe Jet Skis, for example—there's no denying that if it involves outdoor activity, it's probably offered here. For general info, visit www.grandstrandevents.com. For municipal recreation info, visit www.cityofmyrtlebeach.com.

ON THE WATER
Beaches
The center of activity is the Strand itself, with its miles of user-friendly beaches. They're not the most beautiful in the world, but they're nice enough, and access is certainly no problem. In Myrtle Beach and North Myrtle Beach, you'll find clearly designated public access points off Ocean Boulevard, some with parking and some without. Both municipalities run well-marked public parking lots at various points, some of which are free during the off-season.

Dog owners will be pleased to know that May 15-September 15, dogs are allowed on the beach before 9am and after 5pm. September 15-May 15, dogs are allowed on the beach at any time of day.

Restrict your swimming to within 150 feet of shore. Surfside Beach to the south is a no-smoking beach with access points at 16th Avenue North, 6th Avenue North, 3rd Avenue North, Surfside Pier, 3rd Avenue South, 4th Avenue South, 13th Avenue South, and Melody Lane.

Surfing
There's a steady, if low-key, surf scene in Myrtle Beach, despite the fact that the waves are not really that good and the sport is restricted to certain areas during the busy summer season. The rules are a little complicated.

In **Myrtle Beach proper,** surfing is only allowed April 15-September 15 daily 10am-5pm in the following zones:

• 29th Avenue South to the southern city limits
• 37th Avenue North to 47th Avenue North
• 62nd Avenue North to 68th Avenue North

82nd Avenue North to the northern city limits Up in **North Myrtle Beach,** surfers must stay in the following zones May 15-September 15 daily 9am-4pm:

• Cherry Grove Pier
• 6th Avenue North
• 13th Avenue South
• 28th Avenue South

38th Avenue South Down at **Surfside Beach,** surfing is restricted to the following zones, year-round daily 10am-5pm:

• 12th Avenue North to 14th Avenue North
• Melody Lane to 13th Avenue South

The oldest surf shop in the area, south of Myrtle Beach in Garden City Beach, is the

Village Surf Shoppe (500 Atlantic Ave., 843/651-6396, www.villagesurf.com), which has catered to the Strand's growing surf scene since 1969. Nearly as old is the **Surf City Surf Shop** (1758 U.S. 17 S., 843/272-1090; 3001 N. Kings Hwy., 843/626-5412, www.surfcitysurf-shop.com) franchise in Myrtle proper.

Diving

Diving is popular on the Strand. As with fishing, many trips depart from Little River just above North Myrtle Beach. Offshore features include many historic wrecks, including the post-Civil War wreck of the **USS *Sherman*** offshore of Little River, and artificial reefs such as the famed **"Barracuda Alley,"** teeming with marine life, off Myrtle Beach.

Coastal Scuba (1901 U.S. 17 S., 843/361-3323, www.coastalscuba.com) in North Myrtle is a large operator, offering several different dive tours.

Parasailing, Windsurfing, and Jet Skis

Ocean Watersports (405 S. Ocean Blvd., 843/445-7777, www.parasailmyrtlebeach.com) takes groups of up to six people on well-supervised, well-equipped parasailing adventures (about $50 pp), with tandem and triple flights available. Observers can go out on the boat for about $20. They also rent Jet Skis and offer "banana boat" rides ($15) in which a long—yes, banana-shaped—raft, straddled by several riders, is towed by a boat up and down the beach.

Downwind Watersports (2915 S. Ocean Blvd., 843/448-7245, www.downwindsails-myrtlebeach.com) has similar offerings, with the addition of good old-fashioned sailboat lessons and rentals ($16). Parasailing is about $65 per person for a single ride, banana boats are $16 for 20 minutes, and Jet Ski rentals are about $100 per hour.

Farther up the Strand in North Myrtle, between Cherry Grove Beach and Little River, you'll find **Thomas Outdoors Watersports** (2200 Little River Neck Rd., 843/280-2448, www.mbjetski.com), which rents kayaks in addition to Jet Skis and pontoon boats. They offer several Jet Ski tours ($75-125), including a dolphin-watching trip, as well as all-day kayak rental ($45 pp).

Fishing

Most fishing on the Strand is saltwater, with charters, most based in Little River, taking anglers well into Atlantic waters. Tuna, wahoo, mackerel, and dolphin (not the mammal!) are big in the hot months, while snapper and grouper are caught year-round but are best in the colder months.

A good operator up in Little River is **Longway Fishing Charters** (843/249-7813, www.longwaycharters.com), which specializes in offshore fishing. Another in the same area is **Capt. Smiley's Inshore Fishing** (843/361-7445, www.captainsmiley-fishingcharters.com). **Fish Hook Charters** (2200 Little River Neck Rd., 843/283-7692, www.fishhookcharters.com) takes a 34-foot boat out from North Myrtle Beach.

For surf fishing on the beach, you do not need a license of any type. All other types of fishing require a valid South Carolina fishing license, available for a nominal fee online (http://dnr.sc.gov) or at any tackle shop and most grocery stores.

Cruises

Except in the winter months, there are plenty of places to cruise in the Strand, from Little River down to Murrells Inlet, and from the Waccamaw River to the Intracoastal Waterway. The **Great American Riverboat Company** (8496 Enterprise Rd., 843/650-6600, www.mbriverboat.com) offers sightseeing and dinner cruises along the Intracoastal Waterway. **Island Song Charters** (4374 Landing Rd., 843/467-7088, www.sailingmyr-tlebeach.com) out of Little River takes you on sunset and dolphin cruises on the 32-foot sailboat *Island Song*.

Up in North Myrtle, **Getaway Adventures** (843/663-1100, www.myrtle-beachboatcruises.com) specializes in dolphin tours. Also in North Myrtle, **Thomas**

Outdoors Watersports (2200 Little River Neck Rd., 843/280-2448, www.mbjetski.com) runs dolphin cruises.

ON LAND
Golf

The Grand Strand in general, and Myrtle Beach in particular, is world golf central. There are over 120 courses in this comparatively small area, and if golfers can't find something they like here, they need to sell their clubs. While the number of truly great courses is few—the best courses are farther down the Strand near Pawleys Island—the quality overall is still quite high.

A great bonus is affordability. Partially because of dramatically increased competition due to the glut of courses, and partially because of savvy regional marketing, greens fees here are significantly lower than you might expect, in many cases under $100. For even more savings, finding a golf-lodging package deal in Myrtle Beach is like finding sand on the beach—almost too easy. Check with your hotel to see if they offer any golf packages. At any time of year, some good one-stop shops on the Internet are at www.mbn.com and www.myrtlebeachgolf.com.

Some highlights of area golf include the Davis Love III-designed course at **Barefoot Resort** (4980 Barefoot Resort Ridge Rd., 843/390-3200, www.barefootgolf.com, $105-185) in North Myrtle, maybe the best in the Strand outside Pawleys Island. Or would that be the Greg Norman course, or the Tom Fazio course, or the Pete Dye course, all also at Barefoot? You get the picture.

Also up near North Myrtle is a favorite with visitors and locals alike, the challenging **Glen Dornoch Golf Club** (4840 Glen Dornoch Way, 800/717-8784, www.glensgolfgroup.com, from $100), on 260 beautiful acres. Affiliated with Glen Dornoch are the 27 holes at Little River's **Heather Glen** (4650 Heather Glen Way, 800/868-4536, www.glensgolfgroup.com, $130), which are divided into Red, White, and Blue courses. They combine for what's consistently rated one of the best public courses in the United States.

And no list of area golf is complete without a nod to **Myrtle Beach National** (4900 National Dr., 843/347-4298, www.mbn.com, from $80). With three distinct courses—King's North, West, and South Creek, with its South Carolina-shaped sand trap at hole 3—the National is one of the state's legendary courses, not to mention a heck of a deal.

Miniature Golf

Don't scoff—miniature golf, or "putt-putt" to an older generation, is a big deal in Myrtle Beach. If you thought there were a lot of regular golf courses here, the 50 miniature golf courses will also blow your mind. Sadly, almost all of the classic old-school miniature golf courses are no more, victims of the demand for increased production values and modernized gimmick holes. But here are some of the standouts, including the best of the North Myrtle courses as well.

Down near the older section of Myrtle, the completely over-the-top **Mount Atlanticus Minotaur Goff** (707 N. Kings Hwy., 843/444-1008, $10 for 18 holes) is garish yet wonderful. And yes, that's how it's spelled—get it? Legend has it that this one course cost $3 million to build. Literally the stuff of dreams—or maybe hallucinations—this sprawling course mixes the mythological with the nautical to wonderful effect. You don't actually encounter the Minotaur until the bonus 19th hole, a fiendish water trap. If you get a hole in one, you get free golf here for life.

My favorite course is a bit farther north on the main drag. **Captain Hook's Miniature Golf** (2205 N. Kings Hwy., www.captainhooksminigolf.com, $10 for 18 holes) has two courses depicting the world of Peter Pan and Neverland, including a hole entirely on board the eponymous captain's pirate ship! I wouldn't call it particularly difficult, but it's a lot of fun.

Hawaiian Rumble (3210 U.S. 17, 843/458-2585, www.prominigolf.com) in North Myrtle is not only a heck of a fun, attractive course,

Mount Atlanticus Minotaur Goff

it's also the official training center for the U.S. Professional Miniature Golf Association (the folks who generally get a hole in one on every hole). The Rumble's sister course is **Hawaiian Village** (4205 U.S. 17, 843/361-9629, www.prominigolf.com) in North Myrtle, which is also the home of serious professional miniature golf competitions.

For a bit of retro action, try **Rainbow Falls** (9550 Kings Hwy., 843/497-2557). It's not as garish as some of the newer courses, but fans of old-school putt-putt will love it.

While at Broadway at the Beach, you might want to try the popular medieval-themed **Dragon's Lair** (1197 Celebrity Circle, 843/913-9301). Yep, it has a 30-foot fire-breathing dragon, Sir Alfred, that you have to make your way around. While the dinosaur craze has cooled somewhat, the golf at **Jurassic Golf** (445 29th Ave., 843/448-2116), festooned with dozens of velociraptors and the like, certainly has stayed hot. There is a similarly themed site in North Myrtle, the **Dinosaur Adventure** (700 7th Ave., 843/272-8041).

Tennis

There are over 200 tennis courts in the Myrtle Beach area. The main municipal site is the **Myrtle Beach Tennis Center** (3302 Robert Grissom Pkwy., 843/918-2440, www.myrtlebeachtennis.com, $2 pp per hour), which has 10 courts, 8 of them lighted. The city also runs six lighted courts at **Midway Park** (U.S. 17 and 19th Ave. S.).

The privately owned **Kingston Plantation** (843/497-2444, www.kingstonplantation.com) specializes in tennis vacations, and you don't even have to be a guest. They have a pro on staff and offer lessons. Down in Pawleys Island, the **Litchfield Beach and Golf Resort** (14276 Ocean Hwy., 866/538-0187, www.litchfieldbeach.com) has two dozen nice courts.

Cycling

In Myrtle Beach, when they say "biker," they mean a Harley dude. Bicycling—or safe bicycling, anyway—is largely limited to fat-tire riding along the beach and easy pedaling through the quiet residential neighborhoods near Little River. There is a bike lane on North Ocean Boulevard from about 29th Avenue North to about 82nd Avenue North. Riding on the sidewalk is strictly prohibited.

As for bike rentals, a good operator is **Beach Bike Shop** (711 Broadway St., 843/448-5335, www.beachbikeshop.com). In North Myrtle, try **Wheel Fun Rentals** (91 S. Ocean Blvd., 843/280-7900, www.wheelfunrentals.com).

Horseback Riding

A horse ride along the surf is a nearly iconic image of South Carolina, combining two of the state's chief pursuits: equestrian sports and hanging out on the beach. A great way to enjoy a horseback ride along the Grand Strand without having to bring your own equine is to check out **Horseback Riding of Myrtle Beach** (843/294-1712, www.myrtlebeachhorserides.com). They offer a variety of group rides, each with a guide, going to nature-preserve or beach locales. While they'll take you out any day of the week, advance reservations are required. Ninety minutes on a nature preserve costs about $50 per person, while a 90-minute ride on the beach is about $75 per person.

You can go horseback riding on Myrtle Beach from the third Saturday in November until the end of February, with these conditions: You must access the beach from Myrtle Beach State Park, you cannot ride over sand dunes in any way, and you must clean up after your horse.

SPECTATOR SPORTS

Playing April-early September in a large stadium near Broadway at the Beach are the **Myrtle Beach Pelicans** (1251 21st Ave. N., 843/918-6000, www.myrtlebeachpelicans.com, $8-11), a single-A affiliate of the Chicago Cubs.

NASCAR fans already know of the **Myrtle Beach Speedway** (455 Hospitality Ln., www.myrtlebeachspeedway.com, $12, free under age 10) off U.S. 501, one of the more vintage tracks in the country, dating back to 1958 (it was actually a dirt track well into the 1970s). Currently the main draws are the NASCAR Whelen All-American Series races (Apr.-Nov. Sat. 7:30pm).

Other spectator sports in the area tend to revolve around the Chanticleer teams of **Coastal Carolina University** (132 Chanticleer Dr. W., 843/347-8499, www.goccusports.com), just inland from Myrtle Beach in Conway. The baseball team won the school's first national title in 2016. By the way, *chanticleer* is an old name for a rooster, and in this case is a self-conscious derivative of the mascot of the University of South Carolina, the gamecock.

Food

There are about 2,000 restaurants in the Myrtle Beach area, not counting hotel room service and buffets. You can find any dining option that floats your boat at almost any price level. Seafood, of course, is heartily recommended, but there are steak houses, rib joints, pizza places, and vegetarian restaurants galore as well. We can only explore a small fraction here, but following are some of the unique and tasty experiences on the bustling Grand Strand.

Food is never far away, with the biggest concentration of restaurants—including the gigantic seafood buffet places—on "Restaurant Row," a stretch of Kings Highway/U.S. 17 between Myrtle Beach and North Myrtle Beach, from about the merge of U.S. 17 Bypass and U.S. 17 Business in the south and the Tanger Outlets to the north.

BREAKFAST

Pancakes are big on the Strand, with many flapjack places open daily 24 hours to accommodate partiers and night owls. A prime purveyor of pancakes is **Harry's Breakfast Pancakes** (2306 N. Kings Hwy., 843/448-8013, www.harryspancake.com, daily 5:30am-2pm, $4-10). They're not open all day, but there's enough time to enjoy their fluffy stacks and rich omelets.

BARBECUE, BURGERS, AND STEAKS

The best barbecue in town—and a delightfully low-key experience in this often too-flashy area—is at ★ **Little Pigs Barbecue** (6102 Frontage Rd., 843/692-9774, Mon.-Sat. 11am-8pm, $8-12). This is a local-heavy place dealing in no-frills pulled pork, piled high at the counter and reasonably priced with a selection of sauces. The lack of atmosphere *is* the atmosphere, and they prefer to let the barbecue (and the hush puppies and onion rings) do the talking.

Since opening 30 years ago, ★ **Thoroughbreds** (9706 N. Kings Hwy., 843/497-2636, www.thoroughbredsrestaurant.com, Sun.-Thurs. 5pm-10pm, Fri.-Sat. 5pm-11pm, $20), on the old Restaurant Row, has been considered the premier fine-dining place in Myrtle Beach, dealing in the kind of wood-heavy, clubby, Old World-meets-New World ambience you'd expect to see in Palm Beach, Florida. That said, the prices are definitely more Myrtle Beach; you can easily have a romantic dinner for two for under $100. The menu is a carnivore's delight: Beef includes the signature prime rib, a great steak au poivre, and a nod to cowboy machismo, the 22-ounce bone-in rib eye.

The darling of the steak-loving set is **Rioz Brazilian Steakhouse** (2920 Hollywood Dr., 843/839-0777, www.rioz.com, daily 4pm-10pm, $20-40). It's not cheap—the recommended 15-item meat sampler is about $35 per person—but then again, an experience this awesome shouldn't be cheap (a big plus is that kids under age 7 eat for free). The meats are fresh and vibrant, slow-cooked over a wood fire in the simple but succulent style typical of the gaucho *churrascaria* tradition. The service is widely considered to be the best in the area. But the biggest surprise may turn out to be the salad and seafood bar, which even has sushi.

There is no dearth of places to nosh at Barefoot Landing, but meat lovers (not to mention golfers) will probably enjoy **Greg Norman's Australian Grille** (4930 Kings Hwy. S., 843/361-0000, www.gregnorman-saustraliangrille.com, lunch daily 11am-3pm, dinner daily 5pm-10pm, $20-30), which, despite the chain-sounding name, is the only restaurant of its kind. It's the place to enjoy a cocktail by the lake and a premium entrée like the lobster-crusted swordfish.

I normally shy away from mentioning national chain-type places, but I'll make an exception for Myrtle Beach, where you expect things to be a little cheesy. **Jimmy Buffett's Margaritaville** (1114 Celebrity Circle, 843/448-5455, www.margaritavillemyrtlebeach.com, Sun.-Thurs. 11am-10pm, Fri.-Sat. 11am-midnight, $13-22) at Broadway at the Beach is widely regarded as the best single location of the national chain. The signature Cheeseburger in Paradise is the obvious big hit. You get a lot of entertainment for your money as well, with balloon-twisting performers coming to your table and a bizarre whirling "hurricane" that acts up in the main dining area every now and then. As you'd expect, the margaritas are good, if expensive.

Many locals insist the better burger is at another Buffett-owned chain, the succinctly titled **Cheeseburger in Paradise** (7211 N. Kings Hwy., 843/497-3891, www.cheeseburgerinparadise.com, Sun.-Thurs. 11:30am-11pm, Fri.-Sat. 11:30am-midnight, $10-15), which offers a range of burgers on the menu with sweet potato chips on the side, all served up in a less flashy but still very boisterous atmosphere than the flagship restaurant.

CLASSIC SOUTHERN

If you've got a hankering for some spicy Cajun-Creole food, go no farther than the **House of Blues** (4640 U.S. 17 S., 843/272-3000, www.hob.com, Mon.-Fri. 4pm-9pm, Sat. 8am-9pm, Sun. 9am-2pm and 3pm-9pm, $10-25) at Barefoot Landing in North Myrtle Beach. With 11 similarly themed locations around North America, this particular venue deals in the same kind of retro delta vibe, with specially commissioned folk art festooning the walls and live music cranking up at about 10pm. At your table, a gregarious server will walk you through the limited but intense menu, which includes such tasty bits as buffalo tenders (boneless chicken wings in a perfectly spicy sauce) and a couple of excellent jambalaya-type dishes. All portions are enormous and richly spiced. It's a loud, clanging room, so keep in mind that this is less a romantic experience than an exuberant, earthy one.

A special experience at House of Blues is the weekly **Gospel Brunch** (Sun. 9am-2pm, $20 adults, $10 ages 6-12, free under age 6), an opportunity not only to enjoy some tasty Southern-style brunch treats like cheese grits, jambalaya, and catfish tenders but to enjoy some outstanding gospel entertainment at the same time. The Gospel Brunch is served in seatings, and reservations are recommended.

CONTINENTAL

In Myrtle Beach it can be difficult to find a good meal that's not fried or smothered or both. For a highbrow change of pace, try **The Library** (1212 N. Kings Hwy., 843/448-4527, www.thelibraryrestaurantsc.com, Mon.-Sat. 5pm-10pm, $20-50), which is hands-down the most romantic dining experience in Myrtle proper. It's not cheap, but then again, nothing about this place is pedestrian, from the very attentive European-style service to the savvy wine list and the signature dishes (many of them prepared tableside), like she-crab soup, Caesar salads, steak Diane, and the ultimate splurge, steak and lobster.

Like art? Like food? Try the **Collector's Café** (7726 N. Kings Hwy., 843/449-9370, www.collectorscafeandgallery.com, $10-20), which, as the name implies, is a combined gallery and dining space. Don't be daunted by the strip mall setting—inside is a totally different ball game with a trendy open kitchen and plush, eclectic furniture awaiting you amid the original artwork. As for the menu, you may as well go for what's widely regarded as the best single dish, the scallop cakes. Make sure you save room for dessert.

ITALIAN

The best-regarded Italian place in Myrtle Beach—though it could just as easily go in the *Steaks* category, since that's its specialty—is **Angelo's** (2011 S. Kings Hwy., 843/626-2800, www.angelosteakandpasta.com, Sun.-Thurs. 4pm-8:30pm, Fri.-Sat. 4pm-9pm, $12-25). The signature dishes are intriguingly spiced cuts of steak (request beforehand if you don't want them seasoned), cooked medium and under for an exquisite tenderness. You can get spaghetti as a side with the steaks, or just go with the classic baked potato. Don't forget to check out the Italian buffet, including lasagna, Italian sausage, chicken cacciatore, ravioli, and, of course, pizza.

MEXICAN

If you need a fix of absolutely authentic Mexican food, head straight to ★ **La Poblanita** (311 Hwy. 15, 843/448-3150, daily 11am-10pm, $7-10). Don't be put off by the humble exterior in a small strip mall; the food is simply amazing—and amazingly inexpensive. Eighty percent of the diners are Mexican American families, which attests to the authenticity of the cuisine. Everything on the menu is handmade, including the tortillas. The empanadas and burritos are quite simply the best I've eaten anywhere. Even the rice melts in your mouth. Don't forget the Mexican Coke!

SEAFOOD

The grandest old Calabash seafood joint in town, **Original Benjamin's** (9593 N. Kings Hwy., 843/449-0821, daily 3:30pm-10pm, buffet $25 adults, $12 children), on the old Restaurant Row, is one of the more unique dining experiences in Myrtle Beach. With themed rooms overlooking the Intracoastal Waterway, including the concisely named Bus Room—yes, it has an old school bus in it—you'll find yourself in the mood to devour copious amounts of fresh seafood at its humongous 170-item buffet line.

Closer to Broadway at the Beach, try **George's** (1401 29th Ave. N., 843/916-2278, www.captaingeorges.com, Mon.-Sat. 3pm-10pm, Sun. noon-9pm, buffet $31, $16 ages 5-12, free under age 5). Despite the usual kitschy nautical decor, this is the kind of place even locals will admit going to for the enormous seafood buffet, widely considered a cut above the norm.

With old reliables like crab cakes and sea scallops as well as signature house dishes like pecan-encrusted grouper and stuffed flounder, you can't go wrong at **The Sea Captain's House** (3002 N. Ocean Blvd., 843/448-8082, daily 6am-10:30am, 11:30am-2:30pm, and 5pm-10pm, $10-20), one of Myrtle Beach's better seafood restaurants. This opinion is widely held, however, so prepare to wait—often up to

two hours. Luckily, you can sip a cocktail and gaze out over the Atlantic Ocean as you do so. Old hands will tell you it's not as good as back in the day, but it's still a cut above.

When you're at Ocean Drive Beach up in North Myrtle, check out another venerable old name, the **Duffy Street Seafood Shack** (202 Main St., 843/281-9840, www.duffyst.com, daily noon-10pm, $10). This is a humble, unkempt roadside affair dealing in the kind of down-home treats Myrtle Beach seems to love ("pigskin" shrimp, fried pickles, and the like). Overall, it's a good place to get a tasty bite and soak in the flavor of this Cherry Grove neighborhood at the heart of the old shag culture.

Accommodations

There is no dearth of lodging in the Myrtle Beach area, from the typical high-rise "resorts" (think condos on steroids) to chain hotels, vacation villas, house rentals, and camping. Because of the plethora of options, prices are generally reasonable, and competition to provide more and more on-site amenities—free breakfasts, "lazy river" pools, washers and dryers, hot tubs, poolside grills, and so on—has only increased. You are the beneficiary, so you might as well take advantage of it.

Note that the stated price range may be very broad because so many Myrtle Beach lodgings offer several room options, from one-bed guest rooms to full three-bedroom suites. Here are a few general tips to consider when booking a room:

- The larger suites are generally "condo apartments," meaning they're privately owned. While they're usually immaculately clean for your arrival, it means that housekeeping is minimal and you won't get lots of complimentary goodies whenever you call the front desk.

- The entire Myrtle Beach area is undergoing

growth, and that includes the accommodations. This means that many properties have older sections and newer ones. Ask beforehand which section you're being booked in.

- Check www.myrtlebeachhotels.com for last-minute deals and specials at 11 well-run local resorts.

- By the end of September, prices drop dramatically.

- Almost all area lodgings, especially the high-rises, feature on-site pools galore; lounge chairs and tables are at a premium and go very quickly during high season when the sun's out.

- Always keep in mind that summer is the high season here, unlike the rest of South Carolina, and guest rooms, especially at beachfront places, get snapped up very early.

UNDER $150

For 75 years, ★ **Driftwood on the Oceanfront** (1600 N. Ocean Blvd., 843/448-1544, www.driftwoodlodge.com, $100-120) has been a favorite place to stay. Upgraded over the years, but not *too* upgraded, this five-story, 90-room complex is family-owned and takes pride in delivering personalized service that is simply impossible to attain in the larger high-rises nearby. As you'd expect, the guest rooms and suites are a bit on the small side by modern Myrtle Beach standards—with none of the increasingly popular three-bedroom suites available—but most everyone is impressed by the value.

Probably the best-regarded bed-and-breakfast in Myrtle Beach (yes, there are a precious few) is the ★ **Serendipity Inn** (407 71st Ave. N., 843/449-5268, www.serendipityinn.com, $90-150). A short walk from the beach but sometimes seemingly light-years away from the typical Myrtle sprawl, this 15-room gem features a simple but elegant pool, an attractive courtyard, and sumptuous guest rooms. The full breakfast is simple but hearty. There's free Wi-Fi throughout the property.

If you're looking for a basic, inexpensive, one-bed hotel experience on the beach, ask for a room at the new oceanfront section of the **Best Western Grand Strand Inn and Suites** (1804 S. Ocean Blvd., 843/448-1461, $80-140), a smallish but clean and attentively run chain hotel. The property's other buildings are significantly older and are located across busy Ocean Boulevard, and the walk across the street to the beach can be difficult, especially if you have small kids. That said, this is a great value and a quality property.

If water park-style entertainment is your thing, try **Dunes Village Resort** (5200 N. Ocean Blvd., 877/828-2237, www.dunesvillage.com, $140-300), also one of the better values in Myrtle. Its huge indoor water park has copious waterslides, including several for adults, and various other aquatic diversions. The buildings themselves—the property comprises two high-rise towers—are modern and well equipped, although since this is a time-share-style property, housekeeping is minimal.

$150-300

My favorite place to stay at Myrtle Beach is the ★ **Island Vista Oceanfront Resort** (6000 N. Ocean Blvd., 855/732-6250, www.islandvista.com). While not the flashiest or heaviest in amenities by any means, Island Vista's location in a quiet residential area overlooking a mile of the Strand's best and least-traveled beach makes it a standout alternative to the often crowded and logistically challenging environment you'll find in the more built-up high-rise blocks farther south on the beach. In the high season you'll pay about $300 for a one-bedroom suite, but the prices on the spacious and very well equipped two- and three-bedroom suites are competitive. They have the usual multiple-pool option, including an indoor heated pool area. A big plus is the fact that the in-house fine-dining restaurant, the **Cypress Room,** is a definite cut above most area hotel kitchens.

Consistently one of the best-regarded properties in Myrtle proper, the **Hampton Inn & Suites Oceanfront** (1803 S. Ocean Blvd., 843/946-6400, www.hamptoninnoceanfront.com, $169-259) has been made even better by a thorough upgrade. This is a classic beachfront high-rise (not to be confused with the Hampton Inn at Broadway at the Beach), clean inside and out, with elegant, tasteful guest rooms in various sizes. Guest rooms range from typical one-bed, one-bath hotel-style rooms to larger condo-style suites with a fridge.

Situated more toward North Myrtle, the **Sea Watch Resort** (161 Sea Watch Blvd., $171-395) is a good choice for those who want the full-on condo high-rise Myrtle Beach experience but not necessarily the crowds that usually go with it. Guest rooms are clean and well equipped.

One of the better-quality stays for the price in Myrtle is the **Roxanne Towers** (1604 N. Ocean Blvd., 843/839-1016, www.theroxanne.com, $150-250). Known for attentive service, this is a busy property in a busy area. Parking is historically something of a problem. Keep in mind that room size is capped at two bedrooms, so there are none of the sprawling three-bedroom suites that many other local places have.

For a quality stay in the heart of Myrtle's beach bustle, go for the **Sandy Beach Resort** (201 S. Ocean Blvd., 800/844-6534, www. sandybeachoceanfrontresort. com, $200-300). The guest rooms are top-notch, and the service is professional. As is the case with many local properties, there is a newer section, the Palmetto Tower, and an "old" section, the venerable Magnolia Tower. There are one-, two-, and three-bedroom units available, the latter a particularly good value.

Considered one of the major remaining centers of the shag subculture on the Strand, the **Ocean Drive Beach and Golf Resort** (98 N. Ocean Blvd., $200-350) up in North Myrtle Beach hosts many events surrounding the notable regional dance, including the Shaggers Hall of Fame. Its on-site lounge, **The Spanish Galleon,** specializes in beach music. It's also just a great place to stay, with amenities such as a "lazy river," a whirlpool, full galley-style kitchens, and, of course, proximity to the beach.

Also up in North Myrtle is the ★ **Tilghman Beach and Golf Resort** (1819 Ocean Blvd., 843/280-0913, www.til-ghmanresort.com, $200-350), owned by the same company as the Ocean Drive Beach Resort. It's not directly on the beach, but since the buildings in front of it are pretty low, you can still get awesome ocean views. Even the views from the back of the building aren't bad, since they overlook a golf course. But you don't have to be a duffer to enjoy the Tilghman—the pool scene is great, the balconies are roomy, and the suites are huge and well enough equipped (a flat-screen TV in every room) to make you feel right at home.

VACATION RENTALS

There are hundreds, probably thousands, of privately rented condo-style lodgings at Myrtle Beach, in all shapes and forms. Most, however, do a great job of catering to what vacationers here really seem to want: space, convenience, and a working kitchen. All rental agencies basically work with the same listings, so looking for and finding a rental is easier than you might think.

Some of the key brokers are **Myrtle Beach Vacation Rentals** (800/845-0833, www. mb-vacationrentals.com), **Beach Vacations** (866/453-4818, www.beachvacationsmb.com), **Barefoot Vacations** (800/845-0837, www. barefootvacations.info), **Elliott Realty and Beach Rentals** (www.elliottrealty.com), and **Atlantic Dunes Vacation Rentals** (866/544-2568, www.atlanticdunesvacations. com).

BEACH CAMPING

Myrtle Beach is not where you go for a pristine, quiet camping experience. For that, I suggest Huntington State Park down near Murrells Inlet. However, there is plenty of camping, almost all of it heavily RV-oriented, if you want it. For more info, visit www.camp-myrtlebeach.com.

The closest thing to a real live campground is good old **Myrtle Beach State Park** (4401 S. Kings Hwy., 843/238-5325, www.southcarolinaparks.com, daily 6am-10pm, $4 adults, $1.50 ages 6-15, free under age 6), which despite being only a short drive from the rest of the beachfront sprawl is still a fairly relaxing place to stay, complete with its own scenic fishing pier (daily fishing fee $4.50). There's even a nature center with a little aquarium and exhibits.

The park's charming and educational atmosphere is largely due to the fact that this is one of the 17 Civilian Conservation Corps parks built during the Great Depression. There are four cabins ($54-125) available, all fully furnished and about 200 yards from the beach. The main campground is about 300 yards from the beach and comprises 300 sites with electricity and water ($23-25) and a 45-site tent and overflow campground ($17-19) that is only open during the summer high season.

The **Myrtle Beach KOA** (613 6th Ave. S., 800/562-7790, www.myrtlebeachkoa. com), though not at all cheap ($40-50 even for tenters), offers the usual safe, dependable amenities of that well-known chain, including rental "kabins" and activities for kids.

Willow Tree RV Resort and Campground (520 Southern Sights Dr., 843/756-4334, www.willowtreervr.com) is set inland on a well-wooded 300-acre tract with large sites well away from the sprawl, and it offers lakeside fishing and bike trails. In the summer high season, basic sites are $50-82, and the one- and two-bedroom cabins range $120-190.

Information and Services

The main visitors center for Myrtle Beach is the **Myrtle Beach Area Chamber of Commerce and Visitor Center** (1200 N. Oak St., 843/626-7444, www.visitmybeach. com, Mon.-Fri. 8:30am-5pm, Sat. 10am-2pm). There's an **Airport Welcome Center** (1180 Jetport Rd., 843/626-7444) as well, and a visitors center in North Myrtle Beach, the **North Myrtle Beach Chamber of Commerce and Convention & Visitors Bureau** (270 U.S. 17 N., 843/281-2662, www.northmyrtle-beachchamber.com).

The main health care facility in the Myrtle Beach area is **Grand Strand Regional Medical Center** (809 82nd Pkwy., 843/692-1000, www.grandstrandmed.com). Myrtle Beach is served by the **Myrtle Beach Police Department** (1101 N. Oak St., 843/918-1382, www.cityofmyrtlebeach.com). The separate municipality of North Myrtle Beach is served by the **North Myrtle Beach Police Department** (843/280-5555, www.nmb.us).

Transportation

GETTING THERE
The Myrtle Beach area is served by the fast-growing **Myrtle Beach International Airport** (MYR, 1100 Jetport Rd., 843/448-1589, www.flymyrtlebeach.com), which hosts Allegiant (www.allegiantair.com), American (www.aa.com), Delta (www.delta.com), Porter Airlines (www.flyporter.com), Spirit (www.spiritair.com), United (www.ual.com), and WestJet (www.westjet.com).

Unusual for South Carolina, a state that is exceptionally well served by the interstate highway system, the main route into the area is the smaller U.S. 17, which runs north-south, with a parallel business spur, from Georgetown up to the North Carolina border. The approach from the west is by U.S. 501, called Black Skimmer Trail as it approaches Myrtle Beach.

The local **Greyhound Bus Terminal** (511 7th Ave. N., 843/231-2222, www.greyhound. com) is in "downtown" Myrtle Beach.

GETTING AROUND
In practice, the Myrtle Beach municipalities blend and blur into each other in one long sprawl parallel to the main north-south route, U.S. 17. However, always keep this in mind: Just north of Murrells Inlet, U.S. 17 divides into two distinct portions. There's the U.S. 17 Bypass, which continues to the west of much of the coastal growth, and there's Business U.S. 17, also known as Kings Highway, the main drag along which most key attractions and places of interest are located.

The other key north-south route, Ocean Boulevard, runs along the beach. This is a two-lane road that can get pretty congested in the summer.

Thankfully, area planners have provided a

THE GRAND STRAND
TRANSPORTATION

great safety valve for some of this often horrendous traffic. Highway 31, the Carolina Bays Parkway, begins inland from Myrtle Beach at about 16th Avenue. This wide and modern highway roughly parallels the Intracoastal Waterway and takes you on a straight shot, with a 65 mph speed limit, all the way to Highway 22 (the Conway Bypass) or all the way to Highway 9 at Cherry Grove Beach, the farthest extent of North Myrtle Beach. If time is of the essence, you should use Highway 31 whenever possible.

Rental Car, Taxi, and Bus

You will need a vehicle to make the most of this area. Rental cars are available at the airport. Rental options outside the airport include **Enterprise** (1377 U.S. 501, 843/626-4277; 3401 U.S. 17 S., 843/361-4410, www.enterprise.com), **Hertz** (851 Jason Blvd., 843/839-9530, www.hertz.com), and the unique **Rent-a-Wreck** (901 3rd Ave. S., 843/626-9393).

Taxi service on the Strand is plentiful but fairly expensive. Look in the local Yellow Pages for full listings; a couple of good services are **Yellow Cab** (917 Oak St., 843/448-5555) and **Beach Checker Cab** (843/272-6212) in North Myrtle.

The area is served by the **Coastal Rapid Public Transit Authority** (1418 3rd Ave., 843/248-7277), which runs several bus routes up and down the Strand. Ask for information at a visitors center or call for a schedule.

Bicycle

Bicyclists in Myrtle Beach can take advantage of some completed segments of the South Carolina portion of the **East Coast Greenway** (www.greenway.org), which, generally speaking, is Ocean Boulevard. You can actually ride Ocean Boulevard all the way from 82nd Avenue North down to the southern city limit.

In North Myrtle Beach, from Sea Mountain Highway in Cherry Grove, you can bike Ocean Boulevard clear down to 46th Avenue South, with a detour from 28th to 33rd Avenues. A right on 46th Avenue South takes you to Barefoot Landing. And, of course, for a scenic ride, you can pedal on the beach itself for miles. But remember: Bicycling on the sidewalk is strictly prohibited.

For bike rentals, try **Beach Bike Shop** (711 Broadway St., 843/448-5335, www.beachbikeshop.com). In North Myrtle, try **Wheel Fun Rentals** (91 S. Ocean Blvd., 843/280-7900, www.wheelfunrentals.com).

Points Inland

CONWAY

A nice day trip west of Myrtle Beach—and a nice change from that area's intense development—is to the charming town of Conway, just northwest of Myrtle Beach on U.S. 501 and the Waccamaw River. Founded in 1733 with the name Kingston, it originally marked the frontier of the colony. It was later renamed Conwayborough, soon shortened to Conway, in honor of local leader Robert Conway, and now serves as the seat of Horry County.

Conway's heyday was during Reconstruction, when it became a major trade center for timber products and naval stores from the

interior. The railroad came through town in 1887 (later being extended to Myrtle Beach), and most remaining buildings date from this period or later. The most notable Conway native is perhaps an unexpected name: William Gibson, originator of the cyberpunk genre of science fiction, was born here in 1948.

Conway is small and easily explored. Make your first stop the **Conway Visitors Center** (903 3rd Ave., 843/248-1700, www.cityofconway.com, Mon.-Fri. 9am-5pm), where you can pick up maps. It also offers guided tours ($2 pp) that depart from City Hall (3rd Ave. and Main St.); call for a schedule. You can also visit the **Conway Chamber of Commerce** (203 Main St.) for maps and information.

Sights

Conway's chief attraction is the 850-foot **Riverwalk** (843/248-2273, www.conwayscchamber.com, daily dawn-dusk) along the blackwater Waccamaw River, a calming location with shops and restaurants nearby. Waterborne tours on the *Kingston Lady* leave from the Conway Marina at the end of the Riverwalk.

Another key stop is the **Horry County Museum** (428 Main St., 843/248-1542, www.horrycountymuseum.org, Tues.-Sat. 9am-4pm, free), which tells the story of this rather large South Carolina county from prehistory to the present. It holds an annual Quilt Gala in February, which features some great regional examples of the art.

Across from the campus of Coastal Carolina University is the circa-1972 Traveler's Chapel, aka **The Littlest Church in South Carolina** (U.S. 501 and Cox Ferry Rd.). At 12 by 24 feet, it seats no more than a dozen people. Weddings are held here throughout the year. Admission is free, but donations are accepted.

Accommodations

The best stay in town is at the four-star **Cypress Inn** (16 Elm St., 843/248-8199, www.acypressinn.com, $145-235), a beautiful and well-appointed 12-room B&B right on the Waccamaw River.

LEWIS OCEAN BAY HERITAGE PRESERVE

The humongous (over 9,000 acres) **Lewis Ocean Bay Heritage Preserve** (803/734-3886, www.dnr.sc.gov, daily dawn-dusk, free) is one of the more impressive phenomena in the Palmetto State, from a naturalist's viewpoint, made all the more special by its location a short drive from heavily developed Myrtle Beach. Managed by the state, it contains an amazing 23 Carolina bays, by far the largest concentration in South Carolina. These elliptical depressions, scattered throughout the Carolinas and all oriented in a northwest-southeast direction, are typified by a cypress-tupelo bog environment.

To get here from Myrtle Beach, take U.S. 501 north to Highway 90 and head east. After about seven miles, turn east onto the unpaved International Drive across from the Wild Horse subdivision. After about 1.5 miles on International Drive, veer left onto Old Kingston Road. The preserve is shortly ahead on both sides of the road; park along the shoulder.

The Lower Grand Strand

Tiny **Pawleys Island** (year-round population about 200) likes to call itself "America's first resort" because of its early role, in the late 1700s, as a place for planters to go with their families to escape the mosquito-infested rice and cotton fields. It's still a vacation getaway and still has a certain elite understatement, an attitude the locals call "arrogantly shabby." While you can visit casually, most people who enjoy the famous Pawleys Island beaches do so from one of the many vacation rental properties.

Shabby arrogance does have its upside, however—there is a ban on further commercial development in the community, allowing Pawleys to remain slow and peaceful. For generations, Pawleys was famous for its cypress cottages, many on stilts. Sadly, 1989's Hurricane Hugo destroyed a great many of these iconic structures—27 out of 29 on the south end alone, most of which have been replaced by far less aesthetically pleasing homes. Hurricane Matthew in 2016, while nowhere near as catastrophic, caused extensive damage to the beach itself and surrounding dunes.

Directly adjacent to Pawleys, **Litchfield**

Beach offers similar low-key enjoyment along with a world-class golf resort. **Murrells Inlet** is chiefly known for a single block of seafood restaurants on its eponymous waterway.

SIGHTS
★ Brookgreen Gardens

One of the unique—and most unlikely—sights in the developed Grand Strand area is bucolic **Brookgreen Gardens** (1931 Brookgreen Dr., 843/235-6000, www.brookgreen.org, May-Mar. daily 9:30am-5pm, Apr. daily 9:30am-8pm, $15 adults, $7 ages 6-12, free under age 6), directly across U.S. 17 from Huntington Beach State Park. Once one of several massive contiguous plantations in the Pawleys Island area, the modern Brookgreen is a result of the charity and passion of Archer Milton Huntington and his wife, Anna. Quite the sculptor in her own right, Anna Huntington saw to it that Brookgreen's 9,000 acres would host by far the largest single collection of outdoor sculpture in the United States. To learn more, visit the on-site **Carroll A. Campbell Jr. Center for American Sculpture,** which offers seminars and workshops throughout the year. A highlight of the year is the **Night of a Thousand Candles** in early December. It's actually closer to 6,000 candles, lit all across the grounds to gorgeous seasonal effect.

On the other end of the grounds opposite the gardens is the **E. Craig Wall Jr. Lowcountry Nature Center,** which includes a small enclosed cypress swamp with a boardwalk, herons and egrets, and a delightful river otter exhibit.

To add an extra layer of enjoyment to your visit, you can explore this massive preserve much more deeply by taking one of several tours offered on Brookgreen's pontoon boat ($7 adults, $4 children, on top of regular admission); check the website for a schedule.

★ Huntington Beach State Park

Right across the street from Brookgreen is **Huntington Beach State Park** (16148 Ocean Hwy., 843/237-4440, www.southcarolinaparks.com, daily 6am-10pm, $5 adults, $3 ages 6-15, free under age 6), probably the best of South Carolina's state parks not built by the Civilian Conservation Corps. Once a part of the same vast parcel of land owned by Archer Huntington and his wife, Anna, the state has leased it from the trustees of their estate since the 1960s.

You can tour the "castle" on the beach,

salt marsh at Huntington Beach State Park

Atalaya, former home of the Huntingtons and now the yearly site of the Atalaya Arts and Crafts Festival. This evocative Moorish-style National Historic Landmark is open to the public for free guided tours (Memorial Day-Sept. daily noon-1pm, Oct. Sun.-Mon. noon-1pm, Tues.-Sat. noon-2pm). You can stroll three miles of beach, view birds and wildlife from boardwalks into the marsh, hike several nature trails, and visit the well-done **Environmental Education Center** (843/235-8755, Tues.-Sun. 10am-5pm), which features a saltwater touch tank and a baby alligator.

While Hurricane Matthew in 2016 felled many trees at the park, thankfully it avoided major long-term damage.

Pawleys Island Historic District

Although many of the island's homes were leveled by Hurricane Hugo, the **Pawleys Island Historic District** (843/237-1698, www.townofpawleysisland.com), in the central portion of the island, still has a dozen contributing structures, almost all on Myrtle Avenue. Among them are the **Weston House** (506 Myrtle Ave.), or Pelican Inn, and the **Ward House** (520 Myrtle Ave.), or Liberty Lodge. As you view the structures, many with their own historical markers, note the architecture. Because these were intended to be lived in May-November, they resemble open and airy Caribbean homes, with extensive porches and plenty of windows.

EVENTS

The highlight of the lower Grand Strand calendar is the annual **Atalaya Arts and Crafts Festival** (www.atalayafestival.com, $6 adults, free under age 16), which takes place on the grounds of Huntington Beach State Park each September. There's music, food, and about 100 vendors who show their art and wares within the exotic Atalaya home. Admission to the park is free during the festival.

Also in September is the **Pawleys Island Festival of Music and Art** (www.

pawleysmusic.com, prices vary), which happens outdoors, across U.S. 17 under the stars in Brookgreen Gardens, with a few performances at nearby Litchfield Plantation.

A main event in Murrells Inlet is the annual **Fourth of July Boat Parade** (843/651-0900, free), which celebrates American independence with a patriotically themed procession of all kinds of streamer- and flag-bedecked watercraft down the inlet. It begins at about 6pm and ends, of course, with a big fireworks display.

Another big deal in Murrells Inlet is the annual **Blessing of the Inlet** (843/651-5099, www.belinumc.org), always held the first Saturday in May and sponsored by a local Methodist church. Enjoy food vendors, goods baked by local women, and a great family atmosphere.

SHOPPING

The shopping scene revolves around the famous Pawleys Island hammock, a beautiful and practical bit of local handiwork sold primarily at the **Hammock Shops Village** (10880 Ocean Hwy., 843/237-8448, Mon.-Sat. 10am-6pm, Sun. 1pm-5pm). To purchase a Pawleys Island hammock, go to **The Original Hammock Shop** (843/237-9122, www.the-hammockshop.com), housed in a century-old cottage. Next door is the affiliated **Hammock Shop General Store,** which, as the name implies, sells a variety of other goods such as beachwear, books, and a notable style of local fudge. The actual hammocks are handcrafted in the shed next door, the way they have been since 1889.

SPORTS AND RECREATION

Beaches

Public access to the beach that remains after 2016's Hurricane Matthew is very limited. The best way to enjoy the beach is to rent one of the many private beach homes for a week or so. Beach access with parking at Pawleys Island includes a fairly large lot at the south end of the island and parking areas off Atlantic

Avenue at Hazard, 1st, Pearce, 2nd, and 3rd Streets, and Shell Road.

Kayaking and Canoeing

The Waccamaw River and associated inlets and creeks are peaceful and scenic places to kayak, with plenty of bird-watching opportunities to boot. For a two-hour guided tour of the area salt marsh, reserve a spot on the kayak trips sponsored by the **Environmental Education Center** (Huntington Beach State Park, 843/235-8755, office Tues.-Sun. 10am-5pm, $30 pp). Call for tour days and times. Or you can put in yourself at Oyster Landing, about one mile from the entrance to the state park.

Golf

Home to some of the best links in the Carolinas, the lower part of the Grand Strand recently organized its courses under the umbrella moniker **Waccamaw Golf Trail** (www.waccamawgolftrail.com), chiefly for marketing purposes. No matter, the courses are still as superb as ever, if generally pricier than their counterparts up the coast.

The best course in the area, and one of the best in the country, is the **Caledonia Golf and Fish Club** (369 Caledonia Dr., 843/237-3675, www.fishclub.com, $195). While the course itself is almost ridiculously young—it opened in 1995—this masterpiece is built, as so many area courses are, on the grounds of a former rice plantation. The clubhouse, in fact, dates from before the Civil War. Packages (800/449-4005, www.myrtlebeachcondo-rentals.com) are available. Affiliated with Caledonia is the fine **True Blue Golf Club** (900 Blue Stem Dr., 843/235-0900, www.fishclub.com, $100), considered perhaps the most challenging single course on the Strand.

Another excellent Pawleys course is the **Litchfield Country Club** (U.S. 17 and Magnolia Dr., 843/237-3411, www.litchcc.com, $60), one of the Grand Strand's oldest. The facilities are self-consciously dated—this is a country club, after all—setting it apart from the flashier, newer courses sprouting

like mushrooms farther up the Strand. It's a deceptive course that's short on yards but heavy on doglegs.

The Jack Nicklaus-designed **Pawleys Plantation Golf and Country Club** (70 Tanglewood Dr., 843/237-6100, www.pawleysplantation.com, $150) has set a tough example for the last 20 years. The front nine is a traditional layout, while the back nine melts into the marsh.

FOOD
Breakfast and Brunch

The high-end strip mall setting isn't the most romantic, but by broad consensus the best breakfast on the entire Strand is at **Applewood House of Pancakes** (14361 Ocean Hwy., 843/979-1022, daily 6am-2pm, $5-10) in Pawleys. Eggs Benedict, specialty omelets, crepes, waffles, and pancakes abound in this roomy, unpretentious dining room. Do it; you won't regret it.

Seafood

Murrells Inlet has several good places clustered together along the marsh on U.S. 17. The best is ★ **Lee's Inlet Kitchen** (4460 Business U.S. 17, 843/651-2881, www.leesinletkitchen.com, Mar.-Nov. Mon.-Sat. 4:30pm-10pm, $20-40), the only joint still in the original family—in this case the Lee family, who started the place in the mid-1940s. The seafood is simply but delectably prepared (your choice of fried or broiled). They close down December-February.

Everything from the fried green tomatoes to the crab cakes is fresh, hot, and tasty at **Flo's Place Restaurant** (3797 Business U.S. 17, 843/651-7222, www.flosplace.com, daily 11am-10pm, $15-25). Flo is sadly no longer with us, but her place still eschews schlock for a humble, down-home feel. In recent years the menu has added more New Orleans-style Creole seafood dishes.

On the other end of the spectrum stylewise is **Divine Fish House** (3993 Business U.S. 17, 843/651-5800, www.divinefishhouse.com, daily 5pm-10pm, $20-33), which offers more adventurous high-end cuisine like the fine San Antonio salmon (smothered with pepper-jack cheese and bacon) and the Asian-flavored banana leaf mangrove grouper.

ACCOMMODATIONS
Under $150

Similarly named but not to be confused with Litchfield Plantation is the nearby **Litchfield Beach and Golf Resort** (14276 Ocean Hwy., 866/538-0187, www.litchfieldbeach.com, $100-170). In typical Grand Strand fashion, this property delivers a lot of service for a surprisingly low price and offers a wide range of lodging choices, from a basic room at the Seaside Inn on the low end to four-bedroom villas ($230) on the other. A regular free shuttle takes you to the beach. There are also lots of water activities right on the premises, including a "lazy river" tube course.

$150-300

The premier B&B-style lodging on the entire Grand Strand is ★ **Litchfield Plantation** (Kings River Rd., 843/237-9121, www.litchfieldplantation.com, $230-275) on Pawleys Island, built, as you've probably come to expect by now, on an old plantation. There is a host of lodging choices, all of them absolutely splendid. The Plantation House has four sumptuous suites, all impeccably decorated. The humbly named Guest House—actually an old mansion—has six bedrooms, and the entire 2nd floor is an executive suite. Lastly, the newer outparcel villas contain an assortment of two- and three-bedroom suites.

Vacation Rentals

Many who enjoy the Pawleys area do so using a vacation rental as a home base rather than a traditional hotel or B&B. **Pawleys Island Realty** (88 N. Causeway Rd., 800/937-7352, www.pawleysislandrealty.com) can hook you up.

Camping

At **Huntington Beach State Park** (16148 Ocean Hwy., 843/237-4440, www.southcarolinaparks.com, daily 6am-10pm, $5 adults, $3 ages 6-15, free under age 6), the beach is beautiful, there are trails and an education center, and the bird-watching is known as some of the best on the East Coast. While there are 131 RV-suitable sites ($23-28), tenters should go to one of the six walk-in tent sites ($17-19).

INFORMATION AND SERVICES

On Pawleys Island is the **Georgetown County Visitors Bureau** (95-A Centermarsh Ln., 843/235-6595, www.visitgeorgetowncountysc.com). The **Myrtle Beach Area Chamber of Commerce** (1200 N. Oak St., 843/626-7444, www.visitmybeach.com) and the **Waccamaw Community Hospital** (4070 U.S. 17 Bypass, 843/652-1000, www.georgetownhospitalsystem.org) are in Murrells Inlet. Pawleys Island is served by the **Pawleys Island Police Department** (321 Myrtle Ave., 843/237-3008, www.townofpawleysisland.com).

Georgetown and Vicinity

Think of Georgetown as Beaufort's lesser-known cousin. Like Beaufort, it's an hour away from Charleston, it boasts a tidy historic downtown, and it was once a major center of Lowcountry plantation culture. However, Georgetown gets significantly less attention and less traffic. The fact that the entrance to town is dominated by the sprawling, ominous-looking Georgetown Steel mill on one side of the road and the massive International Paper plant on the other has something to do with it. Making matters worse was a disastrous fire in September 2013, which destroyed seven historic waterfront buildings.

Georgetown

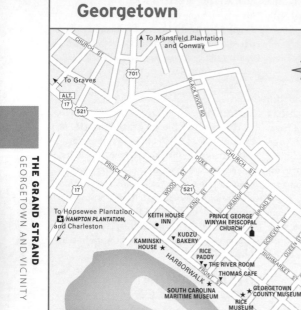

© AVALON TRAVEL

HISTORY

The third-oldest city in South Carolina, after Charleston and Beaufort, Georgetown was founded in 1729 on a four- by eight-block grid, most of which still exists today, complete with original street names. The Revolutionary War hero Francis Marion, the "Swamp Fox," was born in nearby Berkeley County and conducted operations in and around the area throughout the war.

While Charleston-area plantations get most of the attention, the truth is that by 1840 about 150 rice plantations on the Sampit and Little Pee Dee Rivers were producing half of the entire national output of the staple crop. After the Civil War, the collapse of the slave-based economy (at its height, 90 percent of Georgetown's population were enslaved) meant the collapse of the rice economy as well.

In 1905, Bernard Baruch—native South Carolinian, Wall Street mover and shaker, and adviser to presidents—came to town, purchasing Hobcaw Barony, a former plantation. It became his winter residence and hunting ground, and his legacy of conservation lives on there today in an education center on the site.

On the national level Georgetown is perhaps best known for being the hometown of comedian Chris Rock. Although he moved away long ago, many members of his family continue to live here.

SIGHTS
Kaminski House

The city of Georgetown owns and operates the historic **Kaminski House** (1003 Front St., 843/546-7706, www.kaminskimuseum.org, Mon.-Sat. 9am-5pm, $7 adults, $3 ages 6-12, free under age 6). Not to be confused with the

the Old Market building, part of the Rice Museum

1842 timepiece, hosts the bulk of the archival information on the impact of rice growing on the region's history and economy. The adjacent **Kaminski Hardware Building** includes a 17-minute video on the rice industry, a good Gullah-Geechee cultural exhibit, and a gift shop.

Most visitors to the Rice Museum take a one-hour **guided tour,** included in the price of admission. The highlight is the "Browns Ferry Vessel," the remains of a wrecked local colonial-era boat, circa 1730, which has its own listing in the National Register of Historic Places.

South Carolina Maritime Museum

As the Palmetto State's second-largest port, Georgetown has more than its share of nautical history. Check it out at the burgeoning **South Carolina Maritime Museum** (729 Front St., 843/520-0111, www.scmaritimemuseum.org, Mon.-Sat. 11am-5pm, free). The 2013 downtown fire caused a bit of damage to the building, but the museum is still humming. It sponsors the fun Wooden Boat Show each October on the waterfront.

Georgetown County Museum

For a more complete look at various aspects of local history, check out the **Georgetown County Museum** (632 Prince St., 843/545-7020, Tues.-Fri. 10am-5pm, Sat. 10am-3pm, $4 adults, $2 ages 6-18, free under age 6). The highlight is a recently discovered letter written by Revolutionary War hero Francis Marion.

Prince George Winyah Episcopal Church

It has seen better days—the British partially burned it during the Revolutionary War—but **Prince George Winyah Episcopal Church** (301 Broad St., 843/546-4358, www.pgwinyah.org, Mon.-Fri. 11:30am-4:30pm, services Sun. 8am, 9am, and 11am) is still a fine example of the Anglican tradition of the Lowcountry rice culture. Built in 1750 out

Kaminski Hardware Building down the block, this grand home was built in 1769 and was the executive residence of several city mayors. It is furnished with a particularly exquisite selection of 18th- and 19th-century antiques.

The grounds are beautiful as well, overlooking the Sampit River and lined with Spanish moss-covered oaks. Take the free 45-minute **guided tour** departing Monday-Saturday at 11am, 1pm, and 3pm; call ahead to confirm tour times.

Rice Museum

The succinctly named **Rice Museum** (633 Front St., 843/546-7423, www.ricemuseum.org, Mon.-Sat. 10am-4:30pm, $7 adults, $3 ages 6-21, free under age 6) is a look back at the all-important staple crop and its massive effects on Georgetown, which at one point accounted for half of the country's rice production.

There are actually two parts of the museum. The **Old Market building,** often simply called "the Town Clock" because of its

The Swamp Fox and the Coming of Guerrilla Warfare

Short, bowlegged, and moody, Francis Marion was as far away from the template of the war hero as his tactics were from the storybook exploits of military literature. The father of modern guerrilla warfare was born an unimpressively small and sickly baby, the youngest of seven, somewhere in Berkeley County, South Carolina, in 1732 to hardworking French Huguenot parents. Soon his family would move near Georgetown on the coast, and the teenage Marion became enamored with the sea. While his infatuation with maritime life lasted exactly one voyage—a whale rammed and sank his ship—a taste for adventure remained.

During the French and Indian War, Marion fought local Cherokee people, using irregular tactics that would resurface during the Revolutionary War. His first experience in the Revolutionary War was in more textbook engagements, such as the defenses of Fort Moultrie and Fort Sullivan and the siege of Savannah. But with the fall of Charleston in 1780, a vengeful Marion and his ragged band of volunteer fighters—who, unusual for the time, included African Americans—vanished into the bogs of the Pee Dee and took up a different way of warfare: ambush and retreat, harass and vanish. In a foreshadowing of the revolutionary movements of the 20th century, "Marion's Men" provisioned themselves with food and supplies from a sympathetic local populace, offering receipts for reimbursement after the war.

Astride small agile mounts called Marsh Tackies, descendants of horses originally left by the

of ballast stones (the parish itself dates from substantially earlier, 1721), the sanctuary features classic box pews, expert stained glass, and ornate woodwork on the inside. The bell tower dates from 1824.

Hopsewee Plantation

Beautiful in an understated way, **Hopsewee Plantation** (494 Hopsewee Rd., 843/546-7891, www.hopsewee.com, Feb.-Nov. Tues.-Fri. 10am-4pm, Sat. 11am-4pm, Dec.-Jan. by appointment only, $17.50 adults, $10.50 ages 12-17, $7.50 ages 5-11, free under age 5), on the Santee River 12 miles south of Georgetown, was the birthplace of Thomas Lynch Jr., one of South Carolina's signers of the Declaration of Independence. Some key archaeological work is going on at the former slave village on this old indigo plantation; you can visit two of the original slave cabins on the tour. The 1740 main house is a masterpiece of colonial architecture, and all the more impressive because it's very nearly original, with the black cypress exterior largely intact. There's a fairly active calendar of events throughout the year, including sweetgrass basket-weaving classes.

★ Hampton Plantation

Tucked away three miles off U.S. 17 on the South Santee River is **Hampton Plantation State Historic Site** (1950 Rutledge Rd., 843/546-9361, www.southcarolinaparks.com, grounds daily 9am-5pm, free, house tours Sat.-Tues. 1pm, 2pm, and 3pm, $7.50 adults, $3.50 ages 6-15, free under age 6). This Georgian gem, one of the grandest of the antebellum Lowcountry homes, hosted George Washington in 1791. Supposedly the grand "Washington Oak" nearby provided shade for a picnic at which our first president dined. It was also the home of South Carolina poet laureate Archibald Rutledge, who sold it to the state in 1971. Because it's now a state-run project, admission fees are significantly lower than at most of the private plantation homes in the area. The imposing antebellum main house, built in 1735 and expanded in 1757, is magnificent both inside and out. If you want to skip the house tour, visiting the scenic grounds is free.

St. James-Santee Episcopal Church

This redbrick church doesn't look that old,

Spanish, the Patriots rode where bigger British cavalry horses balked. Marion's nocturnal cunning and his superior intelligence network frustrated the British army and their Loyalist supporters to no end, leading to his nickname, "the Swamp Fox."

British colonel Banastre Tarleton, himself known as "the Butcher" for atrocities committed against civilians, was dispatched to neutralize Marion. The savage cat-and-mouse game between the two formed the basis for the storyline of Mel Gibson's *The Patriot* (Gibson's character was reportedly a composite of Marion and several other South Carolina irregulars). Filmed entirely in South Carolina—including at Middleton Plantation, Cypress Gardens, and Historic Brattonsville—*The Patriot* is far from an exact chronicle, but it does accurately portray the nature of the war in the Southern theater, in which quarter was rarely asked or given, and little distinction was made between combatant and civilian.

While certainly the most famous, the Swamp Fox was merely first among equals in a veritable menagerie of hit-and-run fighters. Thomas Sumter, a Virginian by birth, became known as "the Carolina Gamecock" for his ferocity on the battlefield; Andrew Pickens, "the Wizard Owl," and his militiamen played a key role in the Battle of Cowpens in the Upstate.

After the war, Marion served in elected office, married, and settled down at his Pine Bluff Plantation, now submerged under the lake that bears his name. He died in 1795 at the age of 63.

but the sanctuary of **St. James-Santee Episcopal Church** (Old Georgetown Rd., 843/887-4386), south of Georgetown near Hampton Plantation State Historic Site, dates from before the Revolutionary War. Known locally as "the Old Brick Church," this building dates from 1768, but the St. James-Santee parish it serves was actually the second in the colony after St. Michael's in Charleston. The parish was notable for incorporating large numbers of French Huguenots. The interior is nearly as Spartan as the exterior, featuring the rare sight of old-fashioned family box pews. While the brick was imported from Britain, the columns are made of cypress. Today, only one official service is held each year in the Old

Hampton Plantation

Brick Church, during Easter. You can have a look at the exterior and walk through the cemetery during daylight hours anytime, though. You get here by following the signs via a very long dirt road, not recommended in rainy weather unless you have a good four-wheel-drive vehicle.

McClellanville

The almost unbearably cute little fishing village of McClellanville is nestled among the woods of Francis Marion National Forest and is known mostly for the annual **Lowcountry Shrimp Festival and Blessing of the Fleet** (http://lowcountryshrimpfestival.com), held on the waterfront in early May. This is the place to go for any kind of delectable fresh shrimp dish you might want, from fried shrimp to shrimp kebabs and shrimp tacos. The event culminates with the colorful and touching Blessing of the Fleet ceremony.

Hobcaw Barony

Once a plantation, then a winter home for a Wall Street investor, **Hobcaw Barony** (22 Hobcaw Rd., 843/546-4623, www.hobcawbarony.org, hours and prices vary) is now an environmental education center. Hobcaw entered its modern period when 11 former plantations were purchased en masse in 1905 by Wall Street investor Bernard Baruch, a South Carolina native who wanted a winter residence to escape the brutal Manhattan winters. Presidents and prime ministers came to hunt and relax on its nearly 18,000 acres. Fifty years later, Baruch died, and his progressive-minded daughter Belle took over, immediately wanting to open the grounds to universities for scientific research.

Still privately owned by the Belle W. Baruch Foundation, much of Hobcaw Barony is open only to researchers, but the **Hobcaw Barony Discovery Center** (843/546-4623, www.hobcawbarony.org, Mon.-Fri. 9am-5pm, free) has various exhibits on local history and culture, including Native American artifacts and a modest but fun aquarium with a touch tank. To experience the rest of Hobcaw Barony, you

must take one of the various themed guided tours (call for days and times). The basic Hobcaw tour ($20) takes you on a three-hour van ride all around the grounds, including the main Hobcaw House, the historic stables, and the old slave quarters, with an emphasis on the natural as well as human history of the area. Other special tours include Birding on the Barony ($30), Christmas in the Quarters ($20), and a catch-and-release fly-fishing tour ($250) of local waters.

Georgetown Lighthouse

While you can't access the state-owned **Georgetown Lighthouse,** you can indeed take a trip to the beach on North Island, where the lighthouse stands. The 1811 structure, repaired after heavy damage in the Civil War, is still an active beacon, now entirely automated.

North Island was part of lands bequeathed to the state by former Boston Red Sox owner Tom Yawkey; North Island is now part of a wildlife preserve bearing Yawkey's name. In 2001, the Georgetown Lighthouse, listed in the National Register of Historic Places, was added to the preserve.

Tours and Cruises

One of the most sought-after tour tickets in the Georgetown area is for the annual **Plantation Home Tour** (843/545-8291). Sponsored by the Episcopal Church Women of Prince George Winyah Parish, this event, generally happening the first week in April, brings visitors onto many local private antebellum estates that are not open to the public at any other time. Each ticket is for either the Friday or Saturday tour, both of which feature a different set of homes. Tickets include tea at the Winyah Indigo Society Hall each afternoon.

For a standard downtown tour, get on one of the blue-and-white trams of **Swamp Fox Historic District Tours** (1001 Front St., 843/527-6469, $10 pp), which leave daily on the hour starting at 10am near the Harborwalk.

The best walking tour of Georgetown is

Miss Nell's Tours (843/546-3975, Tues. and Thurs. 10:30am and 2:30pm, other times by appointment, $7-24 depending on length of tour). Leaving from the Harborwalk Bookstore (723 Front St.), Miss Nell, who's been doing this for over 20 years, takes you on a delightful trek through Georgetown's charming downtown waterfront.

One of the more interesting local waterborne tours is on board the *Jolly Rover* and *Carolina Rover* (735 Front St., 843/546-8822, www.rovertours.com, Mon.-Sat., times and prices vary). The *Jolly Rover* is an honest-to-goodness tall ship that takes you on a two-hour tour of beautiful Winyah Bay and the Intracoastal Waterway, all with a crew in period dress. The *Carolina Rover* takes you on a three-hour ecotour to nearby North Island, site of the historic Georgetown Lighthouse. You can't tour the lighthouse itself, but you can get pretty darn close to it on this tour.

ENTERTAINMENT AND EVENTS

The **Winyah Bay Heritage Festival** (632 Prince St., 843/833-9919, www.winyahbay.org, free) happens each January at various venues and benefits the local historical society. The focus is on wooden decoys and waterfowl paintings, similar to Charleston's well-known Southeast Wildlife Exposition.

Each October brings the delightful **Wooden Boat Show** (843/545-0015, www.woodenboatshow.com, free) to the waterfront, a celebration of, you guessed it, wooden boats. These aren't toys but the real thing—sleek, classic, and beautiful in the water. There are kids' activities, canoe-making demonstrations, a boat contest, and the highlight, a boatbuilding challenge involving two teams working to build a skiff in four hours.

SPORTS AND RECREATION

Kayaking and Canoeing

Kayakers and canoeists will find a lot to do in the Georgetown area, which includes the confluence of five rivers and the Atlantic Ocean.

A good trip for more advanced paddlers is to go out on **Winyah Bay** to undeveloped North Island. With advance permission from the state's Department of Natural Resources (803/734-3888), you can camp here. Any paddling in Winyah Bay is pleasant, whether you camp or not.

Another long trip is on the nine-mile blackwater **Wambaw Creek Wilderness Canoe Trail** in the Francis Marion National Forest, which takes you through some beautiful cypress and tupelo habitats. Launch sites are at the Wambaw Creek Boat Ramp and a bridge landing. Other good trips in the national forest are on the Santee River and Echaw Creek.

For rentals and guided tours, contact **Nature Adventures Outfitters** (800/673-0679), which runs daylong paddles (about $85 pp); and **Black River Outdoors Center and Expeditions** (21 Garden Ave., 843/546-4840, www.blackriveroutdoors.com), which runs a good half-day tour ($55 adults, $35 under age 13). For those who want to explore the intricate matrix of creeks and tidal canals that made up the Georgetown rice plantation empire, a guided tour is essential.

Occasional kayak ecotours leave from the **Hobcaw Barony Discovery Center** (22 Hobcaw Rd., 843/546-4623, www.hobcawbarony.org, Mon.-Fri. 9am-5pm, $50) under the auspices of the **North Inlet Winyah Bay National Estuarine Research Reserve** (843/546-6219, www.northinlet.sc.edu).

Hiking

The **Francis Marion National Forest** (www.fs.fed.us) hosts a number of great hiking opportunities, chief among them the Swamp Fox passage of the **Palmetto Trail** (www.palmettoconservation.org). This 47-mile route winds through longleaf pine forests, cypress swamps, bottomland hardwood swamps, and various bogs, much of the way along an old logging railbed. The main entrance to the trail is near Steed Creek Road off U.S. 17; the entrance is clearly marked on the west side of the highway.

Another way to access the Swamp

Fox passage is at **Buck Hall Recreation Area** (843/887-3257) on the Intracoastal Waterway. This actually marks the trailhead of the Awendaw Connector of that part of the Palmetto Trail, a more maritime environment. Another trailhead from which to explore Francis Marion hiking trails is farther down U.S. 17 at the **Sewee Visitor Center** (5821 U.S. 17, 843/928-3368, www.fws.gov/seweecenter, Tues.-Sat. 9am-5pm).

Golf

The closest really good links to Georgetown are the courses of the **Waccamaw Golf Trail** (www.waccamawgolftrail.com), a short drive north on U.S. 17. The best public course close to Georgetown is the **Wedgefield Plantation Golf Club** (129 Clubhouse Ln., 843/546-8587, www.wedgefield.com, $69), on the grounds of an old rice plantation on the Black River about four miles west of town.

FOOD

Don't be fooled by Georgetown's small size—there's often a wait for tables at the better restaurants.

Breakfast and Brunch

The *Southern Living*-recommended **Thomas Cafe** (703 Front St., 843/546-7776, www.thomascafe.net, Mon.-Fri. 7am-2pm, Sat. 7am-1pm, $5-9) offers awesome omelets and pancakes in addition to more Lowcountry-flavored lunch dishes like crab cake sandwiches and fried green tomatoes.

Classic Southern

Georgetown's best-known fine-dining establishment is **The Rice Paddy** (732 Front St., 843/546-2021, www.ricepaddyrestaurant.com, lunch Mon.-Sat. 11:30am-2pm, dinner Mon.-Sat. 6pm-10pm, $20-30), with the name implying not an Asian menu but rather a nod to the town's Lowcountry culture. The seafood is strong, but they do a mean veal scaloppine and rack of lamb as well. Reservations are strongly recommended.

Coffee, Tea, and Sweets

A perennial favorite is ★ **Kudzu Bakery** (120 King St., 843/546-1847, Mon.-Fri. 9am-5:30pm, Sat. 9am-2pm), renowned for its fresh-baked goodies such as delectable breakfast muffins, velvety chocolate cakes, and seasonal pies with fresh ingredients like strawberries, peaches, and pecans.

Seafood

Find the best shrimp and grits in town at **The River Room** (801 Front St., 843/527-4110, www.riverroomgeorgetown.com, Mon.-Sat. 11:30am-2:30pm and 5pm-10pm, $15-25), which combines a gourmet attitude in the kitchen with a casual attitude on the floor. However, dishes like the herb-encrusted grouper or the signature crab cakes taste like fine dining all the way. Reservations are not accepted, and dress is casual. Literally right on the waterfront, the dining room in this former hardware store extends 50 feet over the Sampit River, adjacent to a public dock where many diners arrive by boat. There's even a large aquarium inside to complete the atmosphere.

ACCOMMODATIONS
Under $150

Close to the historic district is **Quality Inn & Suites** (210 Church St., 843/546-5656, www.qualityinn.com, $90-140), which has an outdoor pool and an included breakfast. On the north side of town on U.S. 17 you'll find the **Hampton Inn Georgetown-Marina** (420 Marina Dr., 843/545-5000, www.hamptoninn.com, $140-170), which also offers a pool and complimentary breakfast.

$150-300

By far the most impressive lodging near Georgetown—and indeed among the most impressive in the Southeast—is ★ **Mansfield Plantation** (1776 Mansfield Rd., 843/546-6961, www.mansfieldplantation.com, $150-200), a bona fide antebellum estate dating from a 1718 king's grant. It is so evocative and so authentic that Mel Gibson shot part of his film *The Patriot* here, and renovation was recently completed on a historic slave chapel and cabin. You can stay in one of nine guest rooms situated in three guesthouses on the grounds, each within easy walking distance of the public areas in the main house, which include a 16-seat dining room.

With the closing of two longtime favorite B&Bs, the Dupre House and the Harbour House Inn, it's left to another B&B, the **Keith House Inn** (1012 Front St., 843/485-4324, www.thekeithhouseinn.com, $149-169), to carry on the tradition. Its four 2nd-floor suites, with balconies, each have a different theme. The public areas are wonderfully and whimsically furnished.

INFORMATION AND SERVICES

In the historic waterfront area, you'll find the **Georgetown County Chamber of Commerce and Visitor Center** (531 Front St., 843/546-8436, www.georgetownchamber.

com). **Georgetown Memorial Hospital** (606 Black River Rd., 843/527-7000, www.georgetownhospitalsystem.org) is the main medical center in the area. If you need nonemergency law-enforcement help, call the **Georgetown Police** (2222 Highmarket St., 843/545-4300, www.cityofgeorgetownsc.com).

GETTING THERE AND AROUND

Georgetown is at the extreme southern tip of the Grand Strand, accessible by U.S. 17 from the east and south and U.S. 521 (called Highmarket St. in town) from the west. Very centrally located for a tour of the coast, it's about an hour north of Charleston and slightly less than an hour from Myrtle Beach.

Although there's no public transportation in Georgetown, its small size makes touring fairly simple. Metered parking is available downtown.

Charleston

Everyone who spends time in Charleston comes away with a story about the locals' courtesy and hospitality.

Mine came while walking through the French Quarter and admiring a handsome old single house on Church Street, one of the few that survived the fire of 1775. To my surprise, the woman chatting with a friend nearby turned out to be the homeowner. Noticing my interest, she invited me, a total stranger, inside to check out the progress of her renovation. This is a city that takes civic harmony seriously—it even boasts the country's only "Livability Court," a legally binding board that meets regularly to enforce local quality-of-life ordinances.

In 2015, however, Charleston gained national prominence when a white gunman murdered nine worshippers in the historically black Emanuel AME Church on Calhoun Street downtown. The nation was transfixed not only by the horror of the incident, but also by Charleston's community response, which was wholly in keeping with its character: hopeful, forgiving, resilient, and compassionate. Charleston's nickname, the "Holy City," derives from the skyline's abundance of church steeples rather than any excess of piety among its citizens, but its response to the Mother Emanuel tragedy seemed to lend a new meaning.

While many visitors come to see the historical south of Charleston—finding it and then some, of course—they leave impressed by the diversity of Charlestonian life. It's a surprisingly cosmopolitan mix of students, professionals, and longtime inhabitants—who discuss the finer points of Civil War history as if it were last year, party on Saturday night like there's no tomorrow, and go to church on Sunday morning dressed in their finest.

This city, so known for its history, is also quietly booming as one of the nation's key centers of tech and digital development. Highly educated and motivated millennials from all over the country are flocking to Charleston for its blend of start-up friendliness, great nightlife, eco-friendly sensibilities, and vibrant arts and cultural scene.

HISTORY

Unlike the many English colonies in America that were based on freedom from religious persecution, Carolina was strictly a commercial venture from the beginning. The tenure

---

Previous: the view down Broad Street from the Old Exchange; Charles Towne Landing. **Above:** the veranda at Husk.

Look for ★ to find recommended sights, activities, dining, and lodging.

Highlights

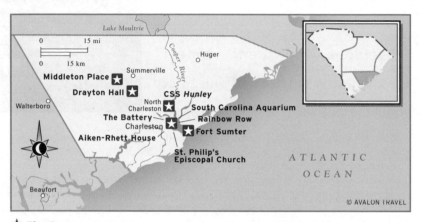

© AVALON TRAVEL

★ **The Battery:** Tranquil surroundings combine with beautiful views of Charleston Harbor, historical points key to the Civil War, and amazing mansions (page 145).

★ **Rainbow Row:** Painted in warm pastels, these old merchant homes near the cobblestoned waterfront take you on a journey to Charleston's antebellum heyday (page 147).

★ **South Carolina Aquarium:** Experience the state's surprising breadth of habitat (page 151).

★ **Fort Sumter:** Take the ferry to this historic place where the Civil War began, with gorgeous views along the way (page 151).

★ **St. Philip's Episcopal Church:** A sublimely beautiful sanctuary and two historic graveyards await you in the heart of the evocative French Quarter (page 153).

★ **Aiken-Rhett House:** There are certainly more ostentatious house museums in Charleston, but none that provide such a virtually intact glimpse into real antebellum life (page 160).

★ **Drayton Hall:** Don't miss Charleston's oldest surviving plantation home and one of the country's best examples of professional historic preservation (page 162).

★ **Middleton Place:** Wander around one of the world's most beautifully landscaped gardens—and the first in North America (page 163).

★ **CSS *Hunley:*** The first submarine to sink a ship in battle is a moving example of bravery and sacrifice (page 165).

Charleston and Vicinity

MAGNOLIA PLANTATION
AND GARDENS

CHARLESTON
INTERNATIONAL
AIRPORT

Hanahan

REMOUNT RD

Goose Creek

NURSERY RD

642

26
52
78

526

To MIDDLETON PLACE
and The Inn at
Middleton Place

DORCHESTER ACCESS RD

AVIATION ACCESS RD

RIVERS AVE

MONTAGUE AVE

RHETT AVE

North
Charleston

DRAYTON
HALL

61

ASHLEY RIVER RD

DORCHESTER RD

MONTAGUE AVE

NORTH CHARLESTON AND
AMERICAN LAFRANCE
FIRE MUSEUM AND
EDUCATIONAL CENTER

CHARLESTON
NAVY YARD

NAVY YARD
AT NOISETTE

526

Ashley River

DORCHESTER AVE

642

NOISETTE BLVD

SPRUILL AVE

CSS
HUNLEY

Clouter Creek

Cooper River

Daniel
Island

7

52
78

526

61

SAM RITTENBERG BLVD

171

Duck
Island

26

West
Ashley

7

OLD TOWN RD

CHARLES TOWNE
LANDING

Ashley River

MAGNOLIA
CEMETERY

Wando River

17

SAVANNAH HWY

ST ANDREWS BLVD

61
171

THE CITADEL

Hampton
Park

JOSEPH P. RILEY
JR. BALLPARK

KING ST

MEETING ST

MORRISON DR

Town Creek

Drum
Island

Mount
Pleasant

THE
COBURG
COW

61

CALHOUN

ST

EAST BAY ST

FERRY TO
FORT SUMTER

To Wild Dunes
Resort and KOA
at Mt Pleasant

17

700

MAY BANK HWY

CITY MARINA

BROAD

ST

PATRIOTS POINT RD

COLEMAN BLVD

James
Island

RIVERLAND DR

Wappoo Creek

171

30

HARBOR VIEW RD

SEE CHARLESTON MAPS

703

PATRIOTS
POINT

Sullivan's
Island

JAMES ISLAND
COUNTY PARK

CENTRAL PARK RD

James Creek

FOLLY BEACH RD

To Holiday Inn
Folly Beach Oceanfront

Charleston Harbor

To FORT SUMTER

© AVALON TRAVEL

Stono River

Wappoo Creek

526

0   1 mi

0   1 km

of the Lords Proprietors—the eight English aristocrats who literally owned the colony—began in 1670 when the *Carolina* finished its journey from Barbados at Albemarle Creek on the west bank of the Ashley River.

Those first colonists set up a small fortification called Charles Towne, named for Charles II, the first monarch of the Restoration. A year later they were joined by settlers from the prosperous but overcrowded British colony of Barbados, who brought a Caribbean sensibility that exists in Charleston to this day.

Finding the first Charles Towne not very fertile and vulnerable to attack from Native Americans and the Spanish, they moved to the peninsula and down to "Oyster Point," what Charlestonians now call White Point Gardens. Just above Oyster Point they set up a walled town, bounded by modern-day Water Street to the south (then a marshy creek, as the name indicates), Meeting Street to the west, Cumberland Street to the north, and the Cooper River on the east.

Charles Towne came into its own after two nearly concurrent events in the early 1700s: the decisive victory of a combined force of Carolinians and Native American allies against the fierce Yamasee people, and the final eradication of the pirate threat with the deaths of Blackbeard and Stede Bonnet.

Flush with a new spirit of independence, Charles Towne threw off the control of the anemic, disengaged Lords Proprietors, tore down the old defensive walls, and was reborn as an outward-looking, expansive, and increasingly cosmopolitan city that came to be called Charleston. With safety from hostile incursions came the time of the great rice and indigo plantations. Springing up all along the Ashley River soon after the introduction of the crops, they turned the labor and expertise of imported Africans into enormous profit for their owners. However, the planters preferred the pleasures and sea breezes of Charleston, and gradually summer homes became year-round residences.

As the storm clouds of civil war gathered in the early 1800s, the majority of Charleston's population was of African descent, and the city had long been America's main importation point for the transatlantic slave trade. The worst fears of white Charlestonians seemed confirmed during the alleged plot by slave leader Denmark Vesey in the early 1820s to start a rebellion. The Lowcountry's reliance on slave labor put it front and center in the coming national confrontation over abolition, which came to a head with the bombardment of Fort Sumter in Charleston Harbor in April 1861.

By war's end, not only did the city lay in ruins—mostly from a disastrous fire in 1861, as well as from a 545-day Union siege—so did its way of life.

World War II brought the same economic boom that came to much of the South, most notably through an expansion of the Navy Yard and the addition of a military air base. By the 1950s, the automobile suburb and a thirst for "progress" had claimed so many historic buildings that the inevitable backlash inspired the formation of the Historic Charleston Foundation, which continues to lead the fight to keep intact the Holy City's architectural legacy.

Civil rights came to Charleston in earnest with a landmark suit to integrate the Charleston Municipal Golf Course in 1960. The biggest battle, however, would be the 100-day strike in 1969 against the Medical University of South Carolina—then, as now, a large employer of African Americans.

Charleston's next great renaissance—still ongoing today—came with the redevelopment of its downtown and the fostering of the tourism industry under the nearly 40-year tenure of Mayor Joe Riley, during which so much of the current visitor-friendly infrastructure became part of daily life here. Today, Charleston is completing the transition away from a military and manufacturing base, and by some measures is the nation's leader in tech start-ups, even ahead of Silicon Valley.

PLANNING YOUR TIME

Even if you're just going to confine yourself to the peninsula, plan on spending at least **two nights** in Charleston. You'll want half a day for shopping on King Street and a full day for seeing various attractions and museums. Keep in mind that one of Charleston's key sights, Fort Sumter, takes almost half a day to see once you factor in ticketing and boarding time for the ferry out to the fort and back; plan accordingly.

If you have a car, there are several great places to visit off the peninsula, especially the three plantations along the Ashley—Drayton Hall, Magnolia Plantation, and Middleton Place—and Charles Towne Landing. They are all no more than 30 minutes from downtown, and because they're roughly adjacent, you can visit all of them in a single day if you get an early start. The sites and excellent down-home restaurants on Johns Island are about 45 minutes out of downtown.

ORIENTATION

Charleston occupies a peninsula bordered by the Ashley River to the west and the Cooper River to the east, which "come together to form the Atlantic Ocean," according to the haughty phrase once taught to generations of Charleston schoolchildren. Although the lower tip of the peninsula actually points closer to southeast, that direction is regarded locally as due south, and anything toward the top of the peninsula is considered due north.

The peninsula is ringed by islands, many of which have become heavily populated suburbs. Clockwise from the top of the peninsula, they are: Daniel Island, Mount Pleasant, Isle of Palms, Sullivan's Island, Morris Island, Folly Island, and James Island. The resort island of Kiawah and the less-developed Edisto Island are farther south down the coast.

Charleston is made up of many small neighborhoods, many of them quite old. The boundaries are confusing, so your best bet is to simply look at the street signs (signage in general is excellent in Charleston). If you're in a historic neighborhood, such as the French Quarter or Ansonborough, a smaller sign above the street name will indicate that.

Other key terms you'll hear are "the Crosstown," the portion of U.S. 17 that goes across the peninsula; "Savannah Highway," the portion of U.S. 17 that traverses "West Ashley," which is the suburb across the Ashley River; "East Cooper," the area across the Cooper River that includes Mount Pleasant, Isle of Palms, and Daniel and Sullivan's Islands; and "the Neck," up where the peninsula narrows. These are the terms that locals use, and hence what you'll see in this guide.

Sights

TOP EXPERIENCE

TOURS

Because of the city's small, fairly centralized layout, the best way to experience Charleston is on foot—either yours or via hooves of an equine nature. For more tour information in Charleston, visit the **Charleston Visitor Reception and Transportation Center** (375 Meeting St., 800/774-0006, www.charlestoncvb.com, Mon.-Fri. 8:30am-5pm), where they have entire walls of brochures for all the latest tours and an on-site staff of local tourism experts.

Walking Tours

Since 1996, **Ed Grimball's Walking Tours** (Waterfront Park, Concord St., 843/813-4447, www.edgrimballtours.com, $22 adults, $8 children) has run twice-weekly historical tours that take you through the heart of Charleston, courtesy of the knowledgeable and sprightly Ed himself, a native Charlestonian. All of Ed's walks start from the big Pineapple Fountain in Waterfront Park, and reservations are a must.

Original Charleston Walks (Market St. and State St., 843/408-0010, www.charlestonwalks.com, times and prices vary) has received much national TV exposure. Its two-hour tours leave from the corner of Market and State Streets and cover a full slate, including a popular adults-only pub crawl.

Charleston Strolls (Mills House Hotel, 115 Meeting St., 843/722-8687, www.charlestonstrolls.com, daily 10am and 2pm, $25 adults, $10 children) is another popular tour good for a historical overview and tidbits. The two-hour tours leave twice daily from the Mills House Hotel.

Art lovers should check out the offerings from **Charleston Art Tours** (53 Broad St., 843/860-3327, www.charlestonarttours.com, $48-55). Sandra and Teri provide a selection of visual art-themed packages, including a French Quarter Tour and a Charleston Renaissance Tour.

Ghost tours are very popular in Charleston. **Bulldog Tours** (18 Anson St., 843/722-8687, www.bulldogtours.com, $22 adults, $10 children) has exclusive access to the Old City Jail, which features prominently in most of its tours. The most popular tour, the Haunted Jail Tour, leaves daily at 7pm, 8pm, 9pm, and 10pm; meet at the jail at 21 Magazine Street. The Ghosts and Dungeons Tour runs March-November Tuesday-Saturday at 7pm and 9pm and leaves from 18 Anson Street.

Carriage Tours

There's not a lot of difference in service or price among the carriage companies, and that's chiefly by design. The city divides the tours into three routes, or "zones." Which zone your driver explores is determined by lottery at the embarkation point—you don't get to decide the zone and neither does your driver. Typically, rides take 1-1.5 hours and hover around $25 per adult, about half that per child.

Tours sometimes book up early, so call ahead. The oldest and in my opinion best

service in town is **Palmetto Carriage Works** (40 N. Market St., 843/723-8145, www.palmettocarriage.com), which offers free parking at its "red barn" base near City Market. Another popular tour is **Old South Carriage Company** (14 Anson St., 843/723-9712, www.oldsouthcarriage.com) with its Confederate-clad drivers. **Carolina Polo & Carriage Company** (16 Hayne St., 843/577-6767, www.cpcc.com) leaves from several spots, including the Doubletree Hotel and the company's Hayne Street stables.

Motorized Tours

Adventure Sightseeing (Charleston Visitor Reception and Transportation Center, 375 Meeting St., 843/762-0088, www.adventuresightseeing.com, daily various times, $20 adults, $11 children) offers several comfortable 1.5- to 2-hour rides, including the only motorized tour to the Citadel area, leaving the visitors center at various times throughout the day.

You can make a day of it with **Charleston's Finest Historic Tours** (Charleston Visitor Reception and Transportation Center, 375 Meeting St., 843/577-3311, www.historictoursofcharleston.com, daily 10:30am, $21 adults, $10.50 children), which has a basic two-hour city tour each day at 10:30am and offers some much longer tours to outlying plantations. The company offers free downtown pickup from most lodgings.

The old faithful **Gray Line of Charleston** (Charleston Visitor Reception and Transportation Center, 375 Meeting St., 843/722-4444, www.graylineofcharleston.com, Mar.-Nov. daily 9:30am-3pm, Dec.-Feb daily 9:30am-2pm, $21-34 adults, $12-19 children) offers a 90-minute Historic Charleston Tour. Tours depart from the visitors center every 30 minutes. Hotel pickup is available by reservation. The last tour leaves at 2pm during the off-season.

African American History Tours

Al Miller's **Sites & Insights Tours**

(Charleston Visitor Reception and Transportation Center, 375 Meeting St., 843/552-9995, www.sitesandinsightstours.com, tour times vary, $13-18) has several packages, including a Black History and Porgy & Bess Tour as well as a good combo city and island tour, all departing from the visitors center.

Alphonso Brown's **Gullah Tours** (African American Art Gallery, 43 John St., 843/763-7551, www.gullahtours.com, Mon.-Fri. 11am and 1pm, Sat. 11am, 1pm, and 3pm, $18) features stories told in the Gullah dialect. Tours run Monday-Saturday and leave from the African American Art Gallery, near the visitors center.

SOUTH OF BROAD

Wander among these narrow streets and marvel at the lovingly restored old homes, but keep in mind that almost everything down here is in private hands. Don't wander into a garden or take photos inside a window unless you're invited to do so.

The Battery

★ The Battery

For many, **The Battery** (S. Battery St. and Murray Blvd., 843/724-7321, daily 24 hours, free) is the single most iconic Charleston spot, drenched in history and boasting dramatic views. South is the Cooper River, with views of Fort Sumter, Castle Pinckney, and Sullivan's Island; north is the old carrier *Yorktown* moored at Mount Pleasant; and landward is the adjoining, peaceful **White Point Gardens,** the sumptuous mansions of the Battery.

Once the bustling (and sometimes seedy) heart of Charleston's maritime activity, the Battery was where "the gentleman pirate" Stede Bonnet and 21 of his men were hanged in 1718. The area got its name for hosting cannons during the War of 1812, with the current distinctive seawall structure built in the 1850s.

Contrary to popular belief, no guns fired from here on Fort Sumter, as they would have been out of range. However, many inoperable cannons, mortars, and piles of shot still reside here, much to the delight of kids. This is where Charlestonians gathered in a giddy, party-like atmosphere to watch the shelling of Fort Sumter in 1861, blissfully ignorant of the horrors to come.

Edmondston-Alston House

The most noteworthy attraction on the Battery is the 1825 **Edmondston-Alston House** (21 E. Battery St., 843/722-7171, www.middletonplace.org, Sun.-Mon. 1pm-4:30pm, Tues.-Sat. 10am-4:30pm, $12 adults, $8 students), the only Battery home open to the public for tours. This is one of the most unique and well-preserved historic homes in the United States, thanks to the ongoing efforts of the Alston family, who acquired the house from shipping merchant Charles Edmondston after the Panic of 1837 and still lives on the 3rd floor (tours only visit the first two stories).

Over 90 percent of the home's furnishings are original items from the Alston era. Originally built in the Federal style, second owner Charles Alston added several Greek

Charleston Sights

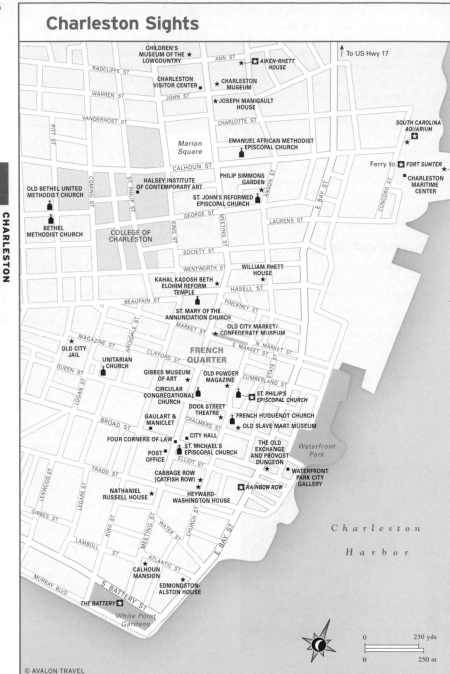

CHILDREN'S MUSEUM OF THE ★ LOWCOUNTRY

ANN ST

★ AIKEN-RHETT HOUSE

To US Hwy 17

RADCLIFFE ST

CHARLESTON VISITOR CENTER

★ CHARLESTON MUSEUM

WARREN ST

JOHN ST

★ JOSEPH MANIGAULT HOUSE

VANDERHOST ST

CHARLOTTE ST

SOUTH CAROLINA AQUARIUM

PITT ST

Marion Square

EMANUEL AFRICAN METHODIST EPISCOPAL CHURCH

Ferry to ★ FORT SUMTER

CALHOUN ST

CONCORD ST

E BAY ST

■ CHARLESTON MARITIME CENTER

OLD BETHEL UNITED METHODIST CHURCH

COMING ST

ST PHILIP ST

HALSEY INSTITUTE OF CONTEMPORARY ART

PHILIP SIMMONS GARDEN

ANSON ST

ST. JOHN'S REFORMED EPISCOPAL CHURCH

BETHEL METHODIST CHURCH

GEORGE ST

MEETING ST

LAURENS ST

COLLEGE OF CHARLESTON

KING ST

SOCIETY ST

WENTWORTH ST

WILLIAM RHETT HOUSE

KAHAL KADOSH BETH ELOHIM REFORM TEMPLE

HASELL ST

BEAUFAIN ST

PINCKNEY ST

ST. MARY OF THE ANNUNCIATION CHURCH

MAGAZINE ST

MARKET ST

OLD CITY MARKET/ CONFEDERATE MUSEUM

OLD CITY JAIL

ARCHDALE ST

CLIFFORD ST

FRENCH QUARTER

S MARKET ST

N. MARKET ST

STATE ST

UNITARIAN CHURCH

QUEEN ST

LOGAN ST

GIBBES MUSEUM OF ART ★

OLD POWDER MAGAZINE

CUMBERLAND ST

CIRCULAR CONGREGATIONAL CHURCH

ST. PHILIP'S EPISCOPAL CHURCH

DOCK STREET THEATRE

GAULART & MANICLET

CHALMERS ST

FRENCH HUGUENOT CHURCH

OLD SLAVE MART MUSEUM

BROAD ST

FOUR CORNERS OF LAW

CITY HALL

ST. MICHAEL'S EPISCOPAL CHURCH

THE OLD EXCHANGE AND PROVOST DUNGEON

Waterfront Park

POST OFFICE

ELLIOT ST

TRADD ST

LENWOOD ST

LEGARE ST

CABBAGE ROW (CATFISH ROW)

WATERFRONT PARK CITY GALLERY

NATHANIEL RUSSELL HOUSE

HEYWARD-WASHINGTON HOUSE

★ RAINBOW ROW

GIBBES ST

KING ST

MEETING ST

WATER ST

CHURCH ST

E BAY ST

Charleston

LAMBOLL

ST

Harbor

ATLANTIC ST

MURRAY BLVD

CALHOUN MANSION

S BATTERY ST

EDMONDSTON-ALSTON HOUSE

THE BATTERY ★

White Point Gardens

0   250 yds

0   250 m

© AVALON TRAVEL

Revival elements, notably the parapet, balcony, and piazza, from which General P. G. T. Beauregard watched the attack on Fort Sumter. Today, the house is owned and administered by the Middleton Place Foundation, best known for its stewardship of Middleton Place along the Ashley River.

★ Rainbow Row

At 79-107 East Bay Street, between Tradd and Elliot Streets, is one of the most photographed sights in the United States: colorful **Rainbow Row,** nine pastel-colored mansions facing the Cooper River. The bright, historically accurate colors are one of the vestiges of Charleston's Caribbean heritage, a legacy of the English settlers from the colony of Barbados who were among the city's first citizens.

The homes are unusually old for this fire-, hurricane-, and earthquake-ravaged city, with most dating from 1730 to 1750. These houses were originally right on the Cooper River, their lower stories serving as storefronts on the wharf. The street was created later on top of landfill, or "made land" as it's called locally.

Besides its grace and beauty, Rainbow Row is of vital importance to American historic preservation. These were the first Charleston homes to be renovated and brought back from early 20th-century seediness. The restoration projects on Rainbow Row directly inspired the creation of the Preservation Society of Charleston, the first such group in the United States.

Nathaniel Russell House

Considered one of Charleston's grandest homes despite being built by an outsider from Rhode Island, the **Nathaniel Russell House** (51 Meeting St., 843/724-8481, www. historiccharleston.org, Mon.-Sat. 10am-5pm, Sun. 2pm-5pm, last tour begins 4:30pm, $12 adults, $5 children) is now a National Historic Landmark and one of the country's best examples of neoclassicism. Built in 1808 by Nathaniel Russell, aka "King of the Yankees," the home is furnished as accurately as possible to represent not only the lifestyle of the Russell family, but also the 18 African American servants who shared the premises.

When you visit, keep in mind that you're in the epicenter of not only Charleston's historic preservation movement but perhaps the nation's as well. In 1955 the Nathaniel Russell House was the first major project of the Historic Charleston Foundation, which raised $65,000 to purchase it. For an extra $6, you can gain admission to the Aiken-Rhett

Rainbow Row

Know Your Charleston Houses

Charleston's homes boast not only a long pedigree, but an interesting and unique one as well. Here are the basics of local architecture.

- **Single House:** Thus named for its single-room width. With full-length piazzas, or long verandas, on the south side to take advantage of breezes, the single house is perhaps the nation's first sustainable house design. The house is lengthwise on the lot, with the entrance on the side. This means the "backyard" is actually the side yard. Church Street has great examples, including 90, 92, and 94 Church Street, and the oldest single house in town, the 1730 Robert Brewton House (71 Church St.).

- **Double House:** This layout is two rooms wide with a central hallway and a porched facade facing the street. Double houses often had separate carriage houses. The Aiken-Rhett and Heyward-Washington Houses are good examples.

- **Charleston Green:** This uniquely Charlestonian color—extremely dark green that looks pitch black in low light—has its roots in the aftermath of the Civil War. The government distributed surplus black paint to contribute to the reconstruction of the ravaged peninsula, but Charlestonians were too proud to use it as-is. So they added a tiny bit of yellow, producing Charleston green.

- **Earthquake Bolt:** Due to structural damage after the 1886 earthquake, many buildings were retrofitted with one or more wall-to-wall iron rods to keep them stable. The rod was capped at both ends by a "gib plate," often disguised with a decorative element such as a lion's head, an S or X shape, or some other design. Notable examples are at 235 Meeting Street, 198 East Bay Street, 407 King Street, and 51 East Battery (a rare star design); 190 East Bay Street is unusual for having both an X and an S plate on the same building.

- **Joggling Board:** This long (10-15 ft.) flexible plank of cypress, palm, or pine with a handle at each end served various recreational purposes. Babies were bounced to sleep, small children used it as a trampoline, and it was also a method of courtship. A couple would start out at opposite ends and bounce until they met in the middle.

- **Carolopolis Award:** The Preservation Society of Charleston hands out these badges, to be mounted near the doorway, to local homeowners who have renovated historic properties downtown. On the award is "Carolopolis," the Latinized name of the city; "Condita AD 1670," the Latin word for "founding" with the date of Charleston's inception; and the date the award was given.

- **Ironwork:** Wrought iron was a widely used ornament before the mid-1800s. Charleston's best-known blacksmith, Philip Simmons, worked in wrought iron. His masterpieces are visible most notably at the Philip Simmons Garden (91 Anson St.), a gate for the visitors center (375 Meeting St.), and the Philip Simmons Children's Garden at Josiah Smith Tennent House (Blake St. and E. Bay St.). Chevaux-de-frise are iron bars on top of a wall that project menacing spikes. They became popular after the Denmark Vesey slave revolt conspiracy of 1822. The best example is at the Miles Brewton House (27 King St.).

House farther uptown, also administered by the Historic Charleston Foundation.

Calhoun Mansion

The single largest of Charleston's surviving grand homes, the 1876 **Calhoun Mansion** (16 Meeting St., 843/722-8205, www.calhounmansion.net, tours daily 11am-5pm, $16) boasts 35 opulent rooms (with 23 fireplaces!) in a striking Italianate design taking up a whopping 24,000 square feet. The grounds feature some charming garden spaces. A 90-minute "grand tour" is available for $75 per person; call for an appointment. Though the interiors at this privately run house are packed with antiques and furnishings, not all of them are accurate for the period.

Heyward-Washington House

The **Heyward-Washington House** (87 Church St., 843/722-0354, www.charleston-museum.org, Mon.-Sat. 10am-5pm, Sun. noon-5pm, $12 adults, $5 children, combo tickets to Charleston Museum and Manigault House available) takes the regional practice of naming a historic home for the two most significant names in its pedigree to its logical extreme. Built in 1772 by the father of Declaration of Independence signer Thomas Heyward Jr., the house also hosted George Washington during the president's visit to Charleston in 1791. It's now owned and operated by the Charleston Museum. The main attraction at the Heyward-Washington House is its masterful woodwork, exemplified by the cabinetry of legendary Charleston carpenter Thomas Elfe.

Cabbage Row

You'll recognize the addresses that make up **Cabbage Row** (89-91 Church St.) as "Catfish Row" from Gershwin's opera *Porgy and Bess* (based on the book *Porgy* by the Charleston author DuBose Heyward, who lived at 76 Church St.). Today this complex—which once housed 10 families—is certainly upgraded from years past, but the row still has the humble appeal of the tenement housing it once was, primarily for freed African American slaves after the Civil War. The house nearby at 94 Church Street was where John C. Calhoun and others drew up the infamous Nullification Acts that eventually led to the South's secession.

St. Michael's Episcopal Church

The oldest church in South Carolina, **St. Michael's Episcopal Church** (71 Broad St., 843/723-0603, services Sun. 8am and 10:30am) is actually the second sanctuary built on this spot, the first being St. Philip's, which was rebuilt on Church Street. As a response to the overflowing congregation at the new St. Philip's, St. Michael's was built from 1752 to 1761, in the style of Christopher Wren. Other than a small addition on the southeast corner in 1883, the St. Michael's you see today is unchanged, including the massive pulpit, outsized in the style of the time.

Services here over the years hosted such luminaries as the Marquis de Lafayette, George Washington, and Robert E. Lee, the latter two of whom are known to have sat in the "governor's pew." Two signers of the U.S. Constitution, John Rutledge and Charles Cotesworth Pinckney, are buried in the sanctuary.

St. Michael's offers informal, free guided **tours** after Sunday services; contact the greeter for more information.

Four Corners of Law

The famous intersection of Broad and Meeting Streets, named the **Four Corners of Law** for its confluence of federal law (the post office building), state law (the state courthouse), municipal law (city hall), and God's law (St. Michael's Episcopal Church), has been key to Charleston from the beginning. Meeting Street was laid out around 1672 and takes its name from the White Meeting House of early Dissenters, meaning non-Anglicans. Broad Street was also referred to as Cooper Street in the early days. Right in the middle of the street once stood the very first statue in the United States, a figure of William Pitt erected in 1766.

WATERFRONT
The Old Exchange and Provost Dungeon

The **Old Exchange and Provost Dungeon** (122 E. Bay St., 843/727-2165, www.oldexchange.com, daily 9am-5pm, $10 adults, $5 children and students) is brimming with history. The last building erected by the British before the American Revolution, it's also one of the three most historically significant colonial buildings in the United States, along with Philadelphia's Independence Hall and Boston's Faneuil Hall.

The Great Charleston Earthquake

The Charleston peninsula is bordered by three faults: the Woodstock Fault above North Charleston, the Charleston Fault running along the east bank of the Cooper River, and the Ashley Fault to the west of the Ashley River. On August 31, 1886, one of them buckled, causing one of the most damaging earthquakes ever to hit the United States.

The earthquake of 1886 was signaled by foreshocks earlier that week, but Charlestonians remained unconcerned. Then, that Tuesday at 9:50pm, came the big one. With an epicenter somewhere near the Middleton Place Plantation, the Charleston earthquake is estimated to have measured about 7 on the Richter scale. Tremors were felt across the country, with the ground shaking in Chicago and a church damaged in Indianapolis. A dam 120 miles away in Aiken gave way, washing a train off the tracks. Cracks opened up parallel to the Ashley River, with part of the riverbank falling into the water. Thousands of chimneys all over the state fell or were rendered useless. The quake brought a series of "sand blows," a phenomenon where craters open and spew sand and water into the air. In Charleston's case, some of the craters were 20 feet wide, shooting debris another 20 feet into the air. The whole event lasted less than a minute.

In crowded Charleston, the damage was horrific: over 2,000 buildings destroyed, a quarter of the city's value gone, 27 killed immediately and almost 100 more to die from injuries and disease. Because of the large numbers of newly homeless, tent cities sprang up in every available park and green space. The American Red Cross's first field mission soon brought some relief, but the scarcity of food and especially fresh water made life difficult.

Almost every surviving building had experienced structural damage, in some cases severe. This led to the widespread use of the "earthquake bolt" now seen throughout older Charleston homes. Essentially acting as a very long screw with a washer on each end, the idea of the earthquake bolt is simple: Poke a long iron rod through two walls that need stabilizing, and cap the ends. Charleston being Charleston, the caps were often decorated with a pattern or symbol.

The seismic activity of Charleston's earthquake was so intense that more than 300 aftershocks occurred in the 35 years after the event. Geologists think that most seismic events measured in the region today are probably also aftershocks.

This is actually the former Royal Exchange and Custom House, the cellar of which served as a British prison. The complex was built in 1771 over a portion of the original 1698 seawall, some of which you can see today during the short but fascinating tour of the "dungeon" (actually built as a warehouse). Three of Charleston's four signers of the Declaration of Independence did time downstairs for sedition against the crown. Later, happier times were experienced in the ballroom upstairs, as it was here that the state selected its delegates to the Continental Congress and ratified the U.S. Constitution; it's also where George Washington took a spin on the dance floor during his raucous "Farewell Tour" in 1791.

While the highlight for most is the basement dungeon, or provost, where the infamous "gentleman pirate" Stede Bonnet was imprisoned in 1718 before being hanged, visitors shouldn't miss the sunny upstairs ballroom and its selection of Washington-oriented history.

Waterfront Park

Dubbing it "this generation's gift to the future," Mayor Joe Riley made this eight-acre project another part of his downtown renovation. Situated on Concord Street roughly between Exchange Street and Vendue Range, **Waterfront Park** (Concord St., 843/724-7327, daily dawn-dusk, free) was, like many waterfront locales in Charleston, built on what used to be marsh and water. This particularly massive chunk of "made land" juts about a football field's length farther out than the old waterline. Children will enjoy the large "Vendue" wading fountain at the park's entrance off Vendue Range, while a bit farther south is the large and quite artful Pineapple Fountain with its surrounding wading pool. Contemporary art lovers of all ages will appreciate the nearby **Waterfront Park City Gallery** (34 Prioleau St., www.citygalleryatwaterfrontpark.com, Tues.-Fri. 10am-6pm, Sat.-Sun. noon-5pm, free).

★ South Carolina Aquarium

The **South Carolina Aquarium** (100 Aquarium Wharf, 843/720-1990, www.scaquarium.org, Mar.-Aug. daily 9am-5pm, Sept.-Feb. daily 9am-4pm, $29.95 adults, $22.95 children, 4-D film extra, combo tickets with Fort Sumter tour available) is a great place for the whole family to have some fun while getting educated about the rich aquatic life off the coast and throughout this small but ecologically diverse state.

When you enter you're greeted with the 15,000-gallon Carolina Seas tank, with placid nurse sharks and vicious-looking moray eels. Other exhibits highlight the five key South Carolina ecosystems: beach, salt marsh, coastal plain, piedmont, and mountain forest. Another neat display is the Touch Tank, a hands-on collection of invertebrates found along the coast, such as sea urchins and horseshoe crabs. The pièce de résistance, however, is the three-story Great Ocean Tank with its hundreds of deeper-water marine creatures, including sharks, puffer fish, and sea turtles.

A key part of the aquarium's research and outreach efforts is the Turtle Hospital, which, in partnership with the state of South Carolina, attempts to rehabilitate and save sick and injured specimens. The hospital has saved many sea turtles, the first one being a 270-pound female affectionately known as "Edisto Mama." Tour the hospital or visit the interactive Sea Turtle Recovery exhibit to learn more about these efforts.

★ Fort Sumter National Monument

This is the place that brought about the beginning of the Civil War, a Troy for modern times. Though many historians insist the war would have happened regardless of President Lincoln's decision to keep **Fort Sumter** (843/883-3123, www.nps.gov/fosu, hours seasonal, free) in federal hands, the stated casus belli was Major Robert Anderson's refusal to surrender the fort when requested to do so in the early-morning hours of April 12, 1861. A few hours later came the first shot of the

Fort Sumter National Monument

Mayor Joe's Legacy

the entrance to Joseph P. Riley Jr. Park

Few cities anywhere have been as greatly influenced by one mayor as Charleston has by Joseph P. "Joe" Riley, who finally declined to run for reelection in 2015 after his 10th four-year term. "Mayor Joe," or just "Joe," as he's usually called, is not only responsible for the majority of redevelopment in the city; he also set the bar for its award-winning tourism industry.

Riley won his first mayoral race at the age of 32, the second Irish American mayor of the city. The lawyer, Citadel grad, and former member of the state legislature had a clear vision for his administration: to bring unprecedented numbers of women and minorities into city government, rejuvenate then-seedy King Street, and enlarge the city's tax base by annexing surrounding areas (during Riley's tenure the city grew from 16.7 square miles to over 100).

Here's only a partial list of the major projects and events Mayor Joe has made happen in Charleston:

- Charleston Maritime Center
- Charleston Place
- Children's Museum of the Lowcountry
- Hampton Park rehabilitation
- King Street-Market Street retail district
- Joseph P. Riley Jr. Park (named after the mayor at the insistence of city council)

- MOJA Arts Festival
- Piccolo Spoleto
- South Carolina Aquarium
- Spoleto USA
- Waterfront Park
- West Ashley Bikeway & Greenway

war, fired from Fort Johnson by Confederate captain George James. That 10-inch mortar shell, a signal for the general bombardment to begin, exploded above Fort Sumter. The first return shot from Fort Sumter was fired by none other than Captain Abner Doubleday, the man once credited as the father of baseball. Today the battered but still-standing Fort Sumter remains astride the entrance to Charleston Harbor on an artificial 70,000-ton sandbar, being part of the Third System of fortifications ordered after the War of 1812.

You can only visit by boats run by the approved concessionaire **Fort Sumter Tours** (843/881-7337, www.fortsumtertours.com, $18 adults, $11 ages 6-11, $16 seniors). Once at the fort, there's no charge for admission. Ferries leave from Liberty Square at Aquarium Wharf on the peninsula three times a day during the high season (Apr.-Oct.); call or check the website for times. Make sure to arrive about 30 minutes before the ferry departs. You can also get to Fort Sumter by ferry from Patriots Point at Mount Pleasant through the same concessionaire.

Budget at least 2.5 hours for the whole trip, including an hour at Fort Sumter. At Liberty Square on the peninsula is the **Fort Sumter Visitor Education Center** (340 Concord St., www.nps.gov/fosu, daily 8:30am-5pm, free), so you can learn more about where you're about to go. Once at the fort, you can be enlightened by the regular ranger talks on the fort's history and construction (generally at 11am and 2:30pm), take in the interpretive exhibits throughout the site, and enjoy the view of the spires of the Holy City from afar.

Some visitors are disappointed to find many of the fort's gun embrasures bricked over. This was done during the Spanish-American War, when the old fort was turned into an earthwork and the newer Battery Huger (huge-EE) was built on top of it.

FRENCH QUARTER

★ St. Philip's Episcopal Church

With a pedigree dating back to the colony's fledgling years, **St. Philip's Episcopal Church** (142 Church St., 843/722-7734, www.stphilipschurchsc.org, sanctuary Mon.-Fri. 10am-noon and 2pm-4pm, services Sun. 8:15am) is the oldest Anglican congregation south of Virginia. The first St. Philip's was built in 1680 at the corner of Meeting Street and Broad Street, the present site of St. Michael's Episcopal Church. It was badly damaged by a hurricane in 1710, so the city fathers approved the building of a new sanctuary dedicated to the saint on Church Street. Alas, the second St. Philip's burned to the ground in 1835. Construction immediately began on a replacement, and it's that building you see today. Heavily damaged by Hurricane Hugo in 1989, a $4.5 million renovation kept the church usable.

South Carolina's great statesman John C. Calhoun—who ironically despised Charlestonians for what he saw as their loose morals—was originally buried across Church Street in the former "stranger's churchyard," or West Cemetery, after his death in 1850. (Charles Pinckney and Edward Rutledge are two other notable South Carolinians buried here.) But near the end of the Civil War, Calhoun's body was moved to an unmarked grave closer to the sanctuary in an attempt to hide its location from Union troops.

Circular Congregational Church

The historic **Circular Congregational Church** (150 Meeting St., 843/577-6400, www.circularchurch.org, services fall-spring Sun. 11am, summer Sun. 10:15am, tours Mon.-Fri. 10:30am) has one of the most interesting pedigrees of any house of worship in Charleston. Services were originally held on the site of the "White Meeting House," for which Meeting Street is named; they were moved here beginning in 1681 and catered to a polyglot mix of Congregationalists, Presbyterians, and Huguenots. For that reason it was often called the Church of Dissenters ("dissenter" being the common term at the time for anyone not an Anglican). As with many structures in town, the 1886 earthquake necessitated a rebuild, and the current edifice dates from 1891.

French Huguenot Church

One of the oldest congregations in town, the **French Huguenot Church** (44 Queen St., 843/722-4385, www.frenchhuguenotchurch. org, liturgy Sun. 10:30am) also has the distinction of being the only remaining independent Huguenot church in the country. Founded around 1681 by French Calvinists, the church had about 450 congregants by 1700. The original sanctuary was built in 1687, but was deliberately destroyed as a firebreak during the great conflagration of 1796. The church was replaced in 1800, but that building was in turn demolished in favor of the picturesque, stucco-coated Gothic Revival sanctuary you see today, which was completed in 1845. Sunday services are conducted in English now, but a single annual service in French is still celebrated in April.

Dock Street Theatre

Any thespian or lover of the stage must pay homage to the first theater built in North America, the **Dock Street Theatre** (135 Church St., 843/720-3968, www.charleston-stage.com, box office Mon.-Fri. 1pm-5pm, tickets $63-67). The original 1736 Dock Street Theatre burned down, but a second theater opened on the same site in 1754. That building was in turn demolished for a grander edifice in 1773, which, you guessed it, also burned down. The current building dates from 1809, when the Planter's Hotel was built near the site of the original Dock Street Theatre. To mark the theater's centennial, the hotel added a stage facility in 1835, and it's that building you see now. In addition to a very active and well-regarded annual season from the resident Charleston Stage Company, the 464-seat venue has hosted umpteen events of the Spoleto Festival over the past three decades and continues to do so.

Old Powder Magazine

The **Old Powder Magazine** (79 Cumberland St., 843/722-9350, www.powdermag.org, Mon.-Sat. 10am-4pm, Sun. 1pm-4pm, $5 adults, $2 children) may be small, but the building is quite historically significant. The 1713 edifice is the oldest public building in South Carolina and the only one remaining from the days of the Lords Proprietors. As the name indicates, this was where the city's gunpowder was stored during the Revolution. The magazine is designed to implode rather than

the restored Dock Street Theatre

French Huguenots

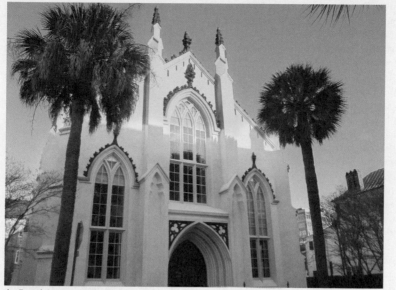

the French Huguenot Church

A visitor can't spend a few hours in Charleston without coming across many French-sounding names. Some are common surnames, such as Ravenel, Manigault (MAN-i-go), Gaillard, Laurens, or Huger (huge-EE). Some are street or place names, such as Mazyck or Legare (Le-GREE). The Gallic influence in Charleston was of the Calvinist Protestant variety. Known as Huguenots, these French immigrants—refugees from an increasingly intolerant Catholic regime in France—were numerous enough in the settlement by the 1690s that they were granted full citizenship and property rights if they swore allegiance to the British crown.

Unlike other colonies, Carolina never put much of a premium on religious conformity, a trait that exists to this day despite the area's overall conservatism. And unlike many who fled European monarchies to come to the New World, the French Huguenots were far from poverty-stricken. Most arrived already well educated and skilled in one or more useful trades. In Charleston's early days, they were mostly farmers or tar burners (makers of tar and pitch for maritime use). Their pragmatism and work ethic would lead them to higher positions in local society, such as lawyers, judges, and politicians. One of the wealthiest Charlestonians, the merchant Gabriel Manigault, was by some accounts the richest person in the American colonies during the early 1700s. South Carolina's most famous French Huguenot was Francis Marion, the "Swamp Fox" of Revolutionary War fame. Born on the Santee River, Marion grew up in Georgetown and is now interred near Moncks Corner.

The library of the **Huguenot Society of Carolina** (138 Logan St., 843/723-3235, www.huguenotsociety.org, Mon.-Fri. 9am-2pm) is a great research tool for anyone interested in French Protestant history and genealogy.

To this day, the spiritual home of Charleston's Huguenots is the same as always: the French Huguenot Church on Church Street, one of the earliest congregations in the city. The church still holds a liturgy in French every April.

explode in the event of a direct hit. This is another labor of love of the Historic Charleston Foundation, which has leased the building from The Colonial Dames since 1993. It was opened to the public as an attraction in 1997. Next door is the privately owned, circa-1709 **Trott's Cottage,** the first brick dwelling in Charleston.

Old Slave Mart Museum

Slave auctions became big business in the South after 1808, when the United States banned the importation of slaves, thus increasing both price and demand. The auctions generally took place in public buildings where everyone could watch the wrenching spectacle. In the 1850s, public auctions in Charleston were put to a stop when city leaders discovered that visitors from European nations—all of which had banned slavery years before—were horrified at the practice. The slave trade was moved indoors to "marts" near the waterfront, where sales could be conducted out of the public eye. The last remaining such structure is the **Old Slave Mart Museum** (6 Chalmers St., 843/958-6467, www.charleston-sc.gov, Mon.-Sat. 9am-5pm, $7 adults, $5 children, free under age 6). Built in 1859, its last auction was held in November 1863. There are two main areas: the orientation area, where visitors learn about the transatlantic slave trade and the architectural history of the building itself, and the main exhibit area, where visitors can see documents, tools, and displays re-creating what happened inside during this sordid chapter in local history and celebrating the resilience of the area's African American population.

NORTH OF BROAD
Confederate Museum

Located on the 2nd floor of City Market's iconic main building, Market Hall on Meeting Street, the small **Confederate Museum** (188 Meeting St., 843/723-1541, Tues.-Sat. 11am-3:30pm, $5 adults, $3 children, cash only) hosts an interesting collection of Civil War memorabilia, with an emphasis on the military side, and is the local headquarters of the United Daughters of the Confederacy. Perhaps its best contribution, however, is its research library.

Gibbes Museum of Art

The **Gibbes Museum of Art** (135 Meeting St., 843/722-2706, www.gibbesmuseum.org, Tues.-Sat. 10am-5pm, Sun. 1pm-5pm, $9 adults, $7 students, $5 ages 6-12) is one of those rare Southern museums that manages a good blend of the modern and the traditional, the local and the international. Their permanent collection spans a wide range of Southern art from the colonial era on, and they arguably have the most distinctive collection of portrait miniatures in the nation. Begun in 1905 as the Gibbes Art Gallery—the final wish of James Shoolbred Gibbes, who willed $100,000 for its construction—the complex has grown through the years in size and influence. The Gibbes Art School in the early 20th century formed a close association with the Woodstock School in New York, bringing important ties and prestige to the fledgling institution. Georgia O'Keeffe brought an exhibit here in 1955.

Kahal Kadosh Beth Elohim Reform Temple

The birthplace of Reform Judaism in the United States and the oldest continuously active synagogue in the nation is **Kahal Kadosh Beth Elohim Reform Temple** (90 Hasell St., 843/723-1090, www.kkbe.org, services Sat. 11am, tours Mon.-Fri. 10am-noon, Sun. 10am-4pm). The congregation—*Kahal Kadosh* means "holy community" in Hebrew—was founded in 1749, with the current temple dating from 1840 and built in the Greek Revival style. The temple's Reform roots came about indirectly because of the great fire of 1838. In rebuilding, some congregants wanted to bring an organ into the temple, and the Orthodox contingent lost the debate. So the new building became the first home of Reform Judaism in the country, a fitting testament to Charleston's long-standing

The New Charleston Green

Most people know "Charleston green" as a unique local color, the result of adding a few drops of yellow to post-Civil War surplus black paint. But these days the phrase also refers to environmentally friendly development in Charleston.

The most obvious example is the ambitious Navy Yard redevelopment, which seeks to repurpose the closed-down facility. From its inception in 1902 at the command of President Theodore Roosevelt through the end of the Cold War, the Charleston Navy Yard was one of the city's biggest employers. Though the yard was closed in 1995, a 340-acre section now hosts an intriguing mix of green-friendly design firms, small nonprofits, and commercial maritime companies. Clemson University—with the help of a massive federal grant, the largest in the school's history—will oversee one of the world's largest wind turbine research facilities, centered on Building 69.

Also in North Charleston, local retail chain Half Moon Outfitters has a green-friendly warehouse facility in an old grocery store. The first LEED (Leadership in Energy and Environmental Design) Platinum-certified building in South Carolina, the warehouse features solar panels, rainwater reservoirs, and locally harvested or salvaged interiors. There's also the LEED-certified North Charleston Elementary School as well as North Charleston's adoption of a "dark skies" ordinance to cut down on light pollution. On the peninsula, the historic meetinghouse of the Circular Congregational Church has a green addition with geothermal heating and cooling, rainwater cisterns, and Charleston's first vegetative roof.

For many Charlestonians, the green movement manifests in simpler things: the pedestrian and bike lanes on the Ravenel Bridge, the thriving city recycling program, and the Sustainable Seafood Initiative, a partnership of local restaurants, universities, and conservation groups that brings the freshest, most environmentally responsible dishes to your table when you dine out in Charleston.

This forward-thinking mode doesn't just mean enhanced quality of life for Charleston residents. It also pays off in attracting tech businesses and other cutting-edge employers, and the well-educated millennial knowledge workers who founded and staff them.

Charleston's tech economy is among the fastest growing in the nation, 26 percent faster than the national average, faster even than Austin, Texas, and Raleigh/Durham, North Carolina. Nearly 100 firms are part of the public/private Charleston Digital Corridor (www.charlestondigitalcorridor.com). The growth has garnered so much attention that some are using the nickname "Silicon Harbor" for the Charleston region.

ecumenical spirit of religious tolerance and inclusiveness.

Old City Jail

If you were to make a movie called *Dracula Meets the Lord of the Rings*, the imposing **Old City Jail** (21 Magazine St., 843/577-5245) might make a great set. Its history is also the stuff from which movies are made. Built in 1802 on a lot set aside for public use since 1680, the edifice was the Charleston County lockup until 1939. Some of the last pirates were jailed here in 1822 while awaiting hanging, as was slave rebellion leader Denmark Vesey. During the Civil War, prisoners of both armies were held here at various times.

The Old City Jail currently houses the American College of the Building Arts. Unless you're a student there, the only way to tour the Old Jail is through **Bulldog Tours** (18 Anson St., 843/722-8687, www.bulldogtours. com). Their Haunted Jail Tour ($20 adults, $10 children) starts daily at 7pm, 8pm, 9pm, and 10pm; all tours are paid for at 40 North Market Street, within a short walk, with jail tours starting at the jail itself.

Old City Market

Part kitschy tourist trap, part glimpse into the Old South, part community gathering place, **Old City Market** (Meeting St. and Market St., 843/973-7236, daily 6am-11:30pm) remains Charleston's most reliable attraction. It is certainly the practical center of the city's tourist trade, not least because so many tours originate nearby. No matter what anyone tries to tell you, Charleston's City Market never hosted a single slave auction. When the Pinckney family donated this land to the city for a "Publick Market," one stipulation was that no slaves were ever to be sold here—or else the property would immediately revert to the family's descendants. A recent multi-million-dollar renovation has prettified the bulk of City Market into more of a big-city air-conditioned pedestrian shopping mall. It's not as shabbily charming as it once was, but it certainly offers a more comfortable stroll during the warmer months.

Philip Simmons Garden

Charleston's most beloved artisan is the late Philip Simmons. Born on nearby Daniel Island in 1912, Simmons became one of the most sought-after decorative ironworkers in the United States. In 1982 the National Endowment for the Arts awarded him its National Heritage Fellowship. His work is on display at the Smithsonian Institution and the Museum of International Folk Art in Santa Fe, New Mexico, among many other places. In 1989, the congregation at Simmons's **St. John's Reformed Episcopal Church** (91 Anson St., 843/722-4241, http://philipsimmons.us) voted to make the church garden a commemoration of the life and work of this legendary African American artisan, who died in 2009 at age 97. Completed in two phases, the Bell Garden and the Heart Garden, the project is a delightful blend of Simmons's signature graceful, sinuous style and fragrant flowers.

Unitarian Church

In a town filled with cool old church cemeteries, the coolest belongs to the **Unitarian Church** (4 Archdale St., 843/723-4617, www.charlestonuu.org, services Sun. 11am, free tours Sat. 10am-1pm). As a nod to the beauty and power of nature, vegetation and shrubbery in the cemetery have been allowed to take their natural course (walkways excepted).

The church itself—the second-oldest such

the cemetery at Unitarian Church

edifice in Charleston and the oldest Unitarian sanctuary in the South—was built in 1776 because of overcrowding at the Circular Congregational Church, but the building saw rough usage by British troops during the Revolution. Repairs were made in 1787 and an extensive modernization took place in 1852. Sadly, the 1886 earthquake toppled the original tower, and the version you see today is a subsequent and less grand design.

To see the sanctuary at times other than weekend mornings, go by the office next door Monday-Friday 9am-2pm and they'll let you take a walk through the interior.

William Rhett House

The oldest standing residence in Charleston is the circa-1713 **William Rhett House** (54 Hasell St.), which once belonged to the colonel who captured the pirate Stede Bonnet. It's now a private residence, but you can admire this excellent prototypical example of a Charleston single house easily from the street and read the nearby historical marker.

UPPER KING

Marion Square

While the Citadel moved lock, stock, and barrel almost a century ago, the college's old home, the South Carolina State Arsenal, still overlooks 6.5-acre **Marion Square** (between King St. and Meeting St. at Calhoun St., 843/965-4104, daily dawn-dusk), a reminder of the days when this was the institute's parade ground, the "Citadel Green" (the old Citadel is now a hotel). Marion Square is named for the "Swamp Fox" himself, Revolutionary War hero and father of modern guerrilla warfare Francis Marion. Marion Square hosts many events, including a farmers market every Saturday early April-late November.

College of Charleston

The oldest college in South Carolina and the first municipal college in the country, the **College of Charleston** (66 George St., 843/805-5507, www.cofc.edu) represents a chunk of the city's history, but its 12,000-plus students bring a modern, youthful touch to many of the city's public activities. Though the college has its share of modernistic buildings, a stroll around the gorgeous campus will uncover some historic gems. The oldest building on campus, the Bishop Robert Smith House, dates from the year of the college's founding, 1770, and is now the president's house; find it on Glebe Street between Wentworth and George. Movies that have had scenes shot on campus include *Cold Mountain*, *The Patriot*, and *The Notebook*. If you have an iPhone or iPod Touch, you can download a neat self-guided tour, complete with video, from the iTunes App Store (www.apple.com, search "College of Charleston Tour," free).

Emanuel African Methodist Episcopal Church

Known simply as "Mother Emanuel," **Emanuel African Methodist Episcopal Church** (110 Calhoun St., www.emanuelamechurch.org, services Sun. 9:30am) has a distinguished history as one of the South's oldest African American congregations. Prior to the Civil War, one of the church's founders, Denmark Vesey, was implicated in planning a slave uprising. The edifice was burned as retaliation for Vesey's involvement (and the founding of the Citadel as a military academy nearby was directly related to white unrest over the plot). In the wake of the Nat Turner revolt in 1834, open worship by African Americans was outlawed in Charleston and went underground until after the Civil War. The congregation adopted the "Emanuel" name with the building of a new church in 1872, a wooden structure that unfortunately didn't survive the great earthquake of 1886. The simple, elegant, and deceptively large church you see today dates from 1891, and has hosted luminaries such as Booker T. Washington, Dr. Martin Luther King Jr., and Coretta Scott King. In 2015, the historically black church was the site of the horrific murders of nine worshippers—including its pastor, Clementa Pinckney—by a white racist.

Emanuel African Methodist Episcopal Church

At Pinckney's memorial service, President Barack Obama spoke and led the congregation in singing *Amazing Grace*.

Charleston Museum

During its long history, the **Charleston Museum** (360 Meeting St., 843/722-2996, www.charlestonmuseum.org, Mon.-Sat. 9am-5pm, Sun. noon-5pm, $12 adults, $5 children, combo tickets to Heyward-Washington and Manigault Houses available) has moved literally all over town. It's currently housed in a noticeably modern building, but make no mistake: This is the nation's oldest museum, founded in 1773. It strives to stay as fresh and relevant as any new museum, with a rotating schedule of special exhibits in addition to its very eclectic permanent collection. For a long time this was the only place to get a glimpse of the CSS *Hunley*, albeit just a fanciful replica in front of the main entrance. (Now you can see the real thing at its conservation site in North Charleston, and it's even smaller than the replica would indicate.) Much of the museum's collection focuses on aspects of everyday life of Charlestonians, from the aristocracy to slaves, including items such as utensils, clothing, and furniture. There are quirks as well, such as the Egyptian mummy and the fine lady's fan made out of turkey feathers. A particular and possibly surprising specialty includes work and research by noted regional naturalists like John James Audubon, André Michaux, and Mark Catesby.

Joseph Manigault House

Owned and operated by the nearby Charleston Museum, the **Joseph Manigault House** (350 Meeting St., 843/723-2926, www.charlestonmuseum.org, Mon.-Sat. 10am-5pm, Sun. noon-5pm, last tour 4:30pm, $12 adults, $5 children, combo tickets to Charleston Museum and Heyward-Washington House available) is sometimes called the "Huguenot House." This grand circa-1803 National Historic Landmark was designed by wealthy merchant Gabriel Manigault for his brother, Joseph, a rice planter of local repute. The three-story brick town house is a great example of Adams, or Federal, architecture.

★ Aiken-Rhett House

An acquisition of the Historic Charleston Foundation, the **Aiken-Rhett House** (48 Elizabeth St., 843/723-1159, www.historic-charleston.org, Mon.-Sat. 10am-5pm, Sun. 2pm-5pm, last tour 4:15pm, $12 adults, $5 children) shows another side of the

the Aiken-Rhett House

Family Fun in Charleston

Let's face it: A steady diet of house museums and long-ago history will bore anyone to tears, not just the young folks in your traveling party. Fortunately, Charleston has a range of options to please children of all ages. You just have to know where to look.

- **Children's Museum of the Lowcountry:** Conveniently located in the city's "Museum Row," this indoor playground offers a variety of hands-on activities for kids ages 3 months-12 years.

- **Old Exchange and Provost Dungeon:** For a real-life Pirates of the Caribbean experience, take a guided tour of this spooky spot from colonial times, complete with animatronic-style figures of pirates and scoundrels.

- **Sewee Visitor and Environmental Education Center:** Visit a pack of red wolves (indigenous to the coastal area) at this center devoted to preserving the species and educating people about these magnificent little animals.

- **South Carolina Aquarium:** The closest thing to a zoo, this easily managed and very informative installation features aspects of every habitat in the ecologically diverse Palmetto State—from Lowcountry marshland to Upstate mountain rivers—anchored by an enormous three-floor central observation tank filled with marine life.

- **Waterfront Park:** The park's outdoor fountain sculptures are sure to please any carefree spirit in your group.

organization's mission. Whereas the Historic Charleston-run Nathaniel Russell House seeks to re-create a specific point in time, work at the Aiken-Rhett House emphasizes conservation and research. Built in 1818 and expanded by South Carolina governor William Aiken Jr., after whom we know the house today, parts of this rambling, almost Dickensian house remained sealed from 1918 until 1975, when the family relinquished the property to the Charleston Museum. While the docents are friendly and helpful, the main way to enjoy the Aiken-Rhett House is by way of a self-guided MP3 player audio tour, which is unique in Charleston.

Children's Museum of the Lowcountry

Another example of Charleston's savvy regarding the tourist industry is the **Children's Museum of the Lowcountry** (25 Ann St., 843/853-8962, www.explorecml.org, Tues.-Sat. 9am-5pm, Sun. noon-5pm, $12 non-SC residents). Recognizing that historic homes and Civil War memorabilia aren't enough to keep a family with young children in town for long, the city established this museum in 2005 specifically to give families with kids ages 3 months-12 years a reason to spend more time (and money) downtown.

HAMPTON PARK
The Citadel

The Citadel (171 Moultrie St., 843/953-3294, www.citadel.edu, grounds daily 8am-6pm) was originally sited at the Old State Arsenal at Marion Square, born out of panic over the threat of a slave rebellion organized in 1822 by Denmark Vesey. The school moved to its current 300-acre site farther up the peninsula along the Ashley River in 1922. The Citadel (technically named The Citadel, The Military College of South Carolina) has entered popular consciousness through the works of graduate Pat Conroy, especially his novel *Lords of Discipline*, starring a thinly disguised "Carolina Military Institute."

There's a lot for visitors to see, including **The Citadel Museum** (843/953-6779, daily noon-5pm, free), on your right just as you enter campus; the "Citadel Murals" in the Daniel Library; "Indian Hill," the highest point in Charleston and former site of an Indian trader's home; and the grave of U.S. general Mark Clark of World War II fame, who was Citadel president from 1954 to 1966. Ringing vast Summerall Field—the huge open space where you enter campus—are the many castle-like cadet barracks.

The most interesting single experience for visitors to the Citadel is the Friday afternoon dress parade on Summerall Field, in which cadets pass for review in full dress uniform (the fabled "long gray line") accompanied by a marching band and pipers. Often called "the best free show in Charleston," the parade happens almost every Friday at 3:45pm during the school year; you might want to consult the website before your visit to confirm. Arrive well in advance to avoid parking problems.

WEST ASHLEY
Charles Towne Landing

Any look at West Ashley must start where everything began, with the 600-acre state historic site **Charles Towne Landing** (1500 Old Town Plantation Rd., 843/852-4200, www. southcarolinaparks.com/ctl, daily 9am-5pm, $10 adults, $6 students, free under age 6). This is where Charleston's original settlers first arrived and camped in 1670, remaining only a few years before eventually moving to the more defensible peninsula where the Holy City now resides. A beautiful and fully seaworthy replica of a settlers' ship is the main highlight, docked in the creek on the far side of the long and well-done exploration trail through the site.

★ Drayton Hall

A mecca for historic preservationists from all over the country, **Drayton Hall** (3380 Ashley River Rd., 843/769-2600, www.draytonhall. org, Mon.-Sat. 9am-5pm, Sun. 11am-5pm, tours on the half hour, $22 adults, $10 ages 12-18, $6 ages 6-11, grounds only $10) is remarkable not only for its pedigree, but also for the way in which it has been preserved. This stately redbrick Georgian-Palladian building, the oldest plantation home in the country open to the public, is literally historically preserved—as in no electricity, heat, or running water.

Since its construction in 1738 by John Drayton, son of Magnolia Plantation founder Thomas, Drayton Hall has survived almost completely intact through the ups and downs of Lowcountry history. In its heyday before

Drayton Hall

the American Revolution, Drayton Hall was widely considered the finest home in all the colonies, the very symbol of the extraordinary wealth of the South Carolina aristocracy. John Drayton died while fleeing the British in 1779; subsequently his house served as the headquarters of British generals Henry Clinton and Charles Cornwallis. During the Civil War, Drayton Hall escaped the depredations of the conquering Union army, one of only three area plantation homes to survive.

The guides hold degrees in the field, and a tour of the house, which starts on the half hour, takes every bit of 50 minutes. A separate 45-minute program called "Connections: From Africa to America" chronicles the diaspora of the slaves who originally worked this plantation, from their capture to their eventual freedom. "Connections" is presented at 11:15am, 1:15pm, and 3:15pm.

The site comprises not only the main house, but two self-guided walking trails as well, one along the peaceful Ashley River and another along the marsh. Also on-site is an African American cemetery with at least 33 known graves. It's kept deliberately untended and unlandscaped to honor the final wish of Richmond Bowens (1908-1998), the seventh-generation descendant of some of Drayton Hall's original slaves.

Magnolia Plantation and Gardens

A different legacy of the Drayton family is **Magnolia Plantation and Gardens** (3550 Ashley River Rd., 843/571-1266, www.magnoliaplantation.com, daily 8:30am-4:30pm, $15 adults, $10 children, free under age 6). It claims not only the first garden in the United States, dating back to the 1680s, but also the first public garden, dating to 1872. Thomas Drayton Jr.—scion of Norman aristocracy, son of a wealthy Barbadian planter—came from the Caribbean to build his own fortune; he immediately married the daughter of Stephen Fox, who began this plantation in 1676. Magnolia has stayed in the possession

of an unbroken line of Drayton descendants to this day.

As a privately run attraction, Magnolia has little of the academic veneer of other plantation sites in the area, and there's a slightly kitschy feel here, the opposite of the quiet dignity of Drayton Hall. And unlike Middleton Place a few miles down the road, the gardens here are anything but manicured, with a wild, almost playful feel. That said, Magnolia can claim fame to being one of the earliest bona fide tourist attractions in the United States and the beginning of Charleston's now-booming tourist industry.

While spring remains the best—and the most crowded—time to come, a huge variety of camellias bloom in early winter, a time marked by a yearly Winter Camellia Festival. Children will enjoy finding their way through "the Maze" of manicured camellia and holly bushes, complete with a viewing stand to look within the giant puzzle. Plant lovers will enjoy the themed gardens such as the Biblical Garden, the Barbados Tropical Garden, and the Audubon Swamp Garden, complete with alligators and named after John James Audubon, who visited here in 1851. House tours, the 45-minute Nature Train tour, the 45-minute Nature Boat tour, and a visit to the Audubon Swamp Garden run about $8 per person extra for each offering.

★ Middleton Place

With the first landscaped garden in North America and still one of the most magnificent in the world, **Middleton Place** (4300 Ashley River Rd., 843/556-6020, www.middletonplace.org, daily 9am-5pm, $28 adults, $15 students, $10 children, guided house tour $15 extra) is a sublime, unforgettable combination of history and sheer natural beauty. Nestled along a quiet bend in the Ashley River, the grounds contain a historic restored home, working stables, 60 acres of breathtaking gardens, and the Inn at Middleton Place, a stunning piece of modern architecture.

First granted in 1675, Middleton Place is the culmination of the Lowcountry rice plantation aesthetic. In 1741 the plantation became the family seat of the Middletons, one of the most notable surnames in U.S. history. As the Civil War wound down, on February 22, 1865, the 56th New York Volunteers burned the main house and destroyed the gardens, leaving only the circa-1755 guest wing, which today is the excellently restored **Middleton Place House Museum** (4300 Ashley River Rd., 843/556-6020, www.middletonplace.org, guided tours Mon. 1:30pm-4:30pm, Tues.-Sun. 10am-4:30pm, $15). The 1886 earthquake added its mark, and it wasn't until 1916 that renovation of the property began. In 1971 Middleton Place was named a National Historic Landmark.

A short walk takes you to the **Plantation Stableyards,** where costumed craftspeople work using historically authentic tools and methods, all while surrounded by a happy family of domestic animals. The Stableyards is also home to a pair of magnificent male water buffalo. Henry Middleton originally imported a pair to work the rice fields—the first in North America—but these guys are just there to relax and add atmosphere. Meet them daily 9am-5pm.

The 53-room **Inn at Middleton Place** (www.theinnatmiddletonplace.com) has a bold Frank Lloyd Wright-influenced design, comprising four units joined by walkways. But both inside and outside it manages to blend quite well with the surrounding fields, trees, and riverbanks. The inn also offers kayak tours and instruction—a particularly nice way to enjoy the grounds from the waters of the Ashley—and features its own organic garden and labyrinth, intriguing modern counterpoints to the formal gardens of the plantation itself.

They still grow the exquisite Carolina Gold rice in a field at Middleton Place, harvested in the old style each September. You can sample some of it in many dishes at the **Middleton Place Restaurant** (843/556-6020, www.middletonplace.org, lunch daily 11am-3pm, dinner Tues.-Thurs. 6pm-8pm, Fri.-Sat. 6pm-9pm, Sun. 6pm-8pm, $15-25). You can tour the gardens for free if you arrive for a dinner reservation at 5:30pm or later.

The Coburg Cow

The entire stretch of U.S. 17 (Savannah Hwy.) heading into Charleston from the west is redolent of a particularly Southern brand of retro Americana. The chief example is the famous **Coburg Cow,** a large, rotating dairy cow accompanied by a bottle of chocolate milk. The

Middleton Place

current installation dates from 1959, though a version of it was on this site as far back as the early 1930s, when this area was open countryside. During Hurricane Hugo the Coburg Cow was moved to a safe location. In 2001 the attached dairy closed down, and the city threatened to have the cow moved or demolished. But community outcry preserved the delightful landmark, which is visible today on the south side of U.S. 17 in the 900 block. You can't miss it—it's a big cow on the side of the road!

Caw Caw Interpretive Center

About 10 minutes west of Charleston on U.S. 17 you'll find the unique **Caw Caw Interpretive Center** (5200 Savannah Hwy., Ravenel, 843/889-8898, www.ccprc.com, Tues.-Sun. 9am-5pm, $2), a treasure trove for history buffs and naturalists wanting to learn more about the old rice culture of the South. Most Wednesday and Saturday mornings, guided bird walks are held at 8:30am ($5 pp). You can put in your own canoe for $10 October-April on Saturdays and Sundays. Bikes and dogs aren't allowed on the grounds.

NORTH CHARLESTON

Magnolia Cemetery

Although not technically in North Charleston, historic **Magnolia Cemetery** (Cunnington Ave. at Huguenin Ave., 843/722-8638, Sept.-May daily 8am-5pm, June-Aug. daily 8am-6pm) is well north of the downtown tourist district in the area called "the Neck." This historic burial ground, while not quite the aesthetic equal of Savannah's famed Bonaventure Cemetery, is still a stirring site for its natural beauty and ornate memorials as well as for its historical aspects. Here are buried the crewmen who died aboard the CSS *Hunley,* reinterred after their retrieval from Charleston Harbor. In all, over 2,000 Civil War dead are buried here, including 5 Confederate generals and 84 rebels who fell at Gettysburg and were moved here.

★ CSS *Hunley*

In 1864, the Confederate submarine CSS *Hunley* mysteriously sank right after successfully destroying the USS *Housatonic* with the torpedo attached to its bow, marking the first time a sub ever sank a ship in battle. For the longest time, the only glimpse of the ill-fated Confederate submarine afforded to visitors was a not-quite-accurate replica outside the Charleston Museum. But in 1995, after a 15-year search, maritime novelist and adventurer Clive Cussler and his team finally found the submarine off Sullivan's Island. In 2000, a team comprising the nonprofit **Friends of the Hunley**, the federal government, and private partners successfully implemented a plan to safely raise the vessel.

Today you can view the sub, see the life-size model from the TNT movie *The Hunley,* and look at artifacts such as the "lucky" gold piece of the commander at the **Warren Lasch Conservation Center** (1250 Supply St., Bldg. 255, 866/866-9938, www.hunley.org, Sat. 10am-5pm, Sun. noon-5pm, $16 adults, $8 students, free under age 5). You can even see facial reconstructions of some of the eight sailors who died on board. The remains of the crew lie in Magnolia Cemetery, where they were buried in 2004 with full military honors.

The Lasch Center is only open to the public on weekends so that research and conservation can be performed during the week. Because of this limited window of opportunity and the popularity of the site, reserve tickets ahead of time.

To get to the Warren Lasch Conservation Center from Charleston, take I-26 north to exit 216B. Take a left onto Spruill Avenue and a right onto McMillan Avenue. Once in the Navy Yard, take a right on Hobson Avenue, and after about one mile take a left onto Supply Street. The Lasch Center is the low white building on the left.

Fire Museum

The **North Charleston and American**

LaFrance Fire Museum and Education Center (4975 Centre Pointe Dr., North Charleston, 843/740-5550, www.legacyofheroes.org, Mon.-Sat. 10am-5pm, Sun. 1pm-5pm, last ticket 4pm, $6 adults, free under age 14), which shares a huge 25,000-square-foot space with the North Charleston Convention and Visitors Bureau, is primarily dedicated to maintaining and increasing its collection of antique American LaFrance firefighting vehicles and equipment. The 18 fire engines here date from 1857 to 1969. The museum's exhibits have taken on greater poignancy in the wake of the tragic loss of nine Charleston firefighters killed trying to extinguish a warehouse blaze on U.S. 17 in summer 2007—second only to the 9/11 attacks as the largest single loss of life for a U.S. firefighting department.

SUMMERVILLE

Founded as Pineland Village in 1785, Summerville made its reputation as a place for plantation owners and their families to escape the insects and heat of the swampier areas of the Lowcountry. Summerville boasts a whopping 700 buildings in the National Register of Historic Places. For a walking tour of the historic district, download the map at www.visitsummerville.com or pick up a hard copy at the **Summerville Visitors Center** (402 N. Main St., 843/873-8535, Mon.-Fri. 9am-5pm, Sat. 10am-3pm, Sun. 1pm-4pm).

Azalea Park

Much visitor activity in Summerville centers on **Azalea Park** (S. Main St. and W. 5th St. S., daily dawn-dusk, free), rather obviously named for its most scenic inhabitants. Several fun yearly events take place here, most notably the **Flowertown Festival** (www.flowertownfestival.com, free) each April, a three-day affair heralding the coming of spring and the blooming of the flowers. One of the biggest festivals in South Carolina, 250,000 people usually attend. Another event, **Sculpture in the South** (www.sculptureinthesouth.com) in May, takes advantage of the extensive public sculpture in the park.

Colonial Dorchester State Historic Site

Just south of Summerville on the way back to Charleston is the interesting **Colonial Dorchester State Historic Site** (300 County Rd. S-18-373, 843/873-1740, www.southcarolinaparks.com, daily 9am-6pm, $2 adults, free under age 16), chronicling a virtually unknown segment of Carolina history. A contingent of Massachusetts Puritans ("Congregationalists" in the parlance of the time) were given special dispensation in 1697 to form a settlement of their own specifically to enhance commercial activity on the Ashley River. Today little is left of old Dorchester but the tabby walls of the 1757 fort overlooking the Ashley. Don't miss the unspectacular but still historically vital remains of the wooden wharf on the walking trail along the river, once the epicenter of a thriving port. The most-photographed thing on-site is the bell tower of the Anglican church of St. George—which actually wasn't where the original settlers worshipped and was in fact quite resented by them since they were forced to pay for its construction.

Summerville-Dorchester Museum

To learn more about Summerville's interesting history, go just off Main Street to the **Summerville-Dorchester Museum** (100 E. Doty Ave., 843/875-9666, www.summervilledorchestermuseum.org, Mon.-Sat. 9am-2pm, donations accepted). Located in the former town police station, the museum has a wealth of good exhibits. The museum opened in 1992 thanks to a group of Summerville citizens who wanted to preserve the region's history.

MOUNT PLEASANT AND EAST COOPER

The main destination in this area on the east bank of the Cooper River is the island of Mount Pleasant, primarily known as a peaceful, fairly affluent suburb of Charleston—a role it has played for about 300 years now.

Greater Charleston

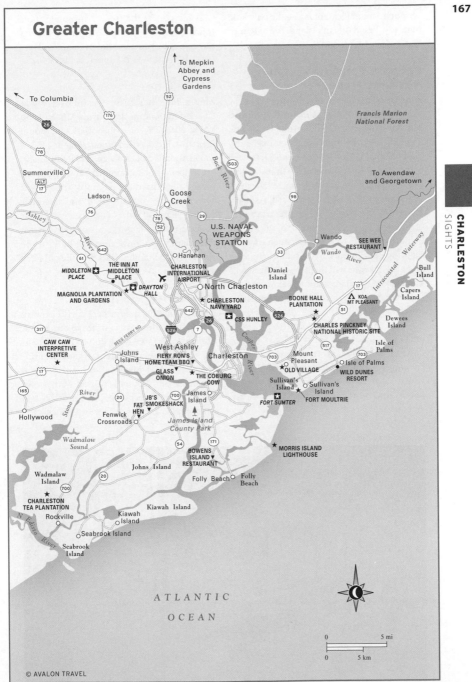

To Mepkin
Abbey and
Cypress
Gardens

To Columbia

Francis Marion
National Forest

To Awendaw
and Georgetown

Summerville

Ladson

Goose
Creek

U.S. NAVAL
WEAPONS
STATION

Wando

SEE WEE
RESTAURANT

Bull
Island

Hanahan

Daniel
Island

Wando River

Capers
Island

THE INN AT
MIDDLETON
PLACE

MIDDLETON
PLACE

CHARLESTON
INTERNATIONAL
AIRPORT

KOA
MT PLEASANT

Dewees
Island

MAGNOLIA PLANTATION
AND GARDENS

DRAYTON
HALL

North Charleston

BOONE HALL
PLANTATION

CHARLESTON
NAVY YARD

CHARLES PINCKNEY
NATIONAL HISTORIC SITE

Isle of
Palms

CAW CAW
INTERPRETIVE
CENTER

Johns
Island

CSS HUNLEY

West Ashley

Charleston

Mount
Pleasant

FIERY RON'S
HOME TEAM BBQ

Isle of Palms

GLASS
ONION

THE COBURG
COW

Old Village

WILD DUNES
RESORT

Sullivan's
Island

Sullivan's
Island

Hollywood

Fenwick
Crossroads

JB'S
SMOKESHACK

FAT
HEN

James
Island

FORT SUMTER

FORT MOULTRIE

James Island
County Park

Wadmalaw
Sound

BOWENS
ISLAND
RESTAURANT

MORRIS ISLAND
LIGHTHOUSE

Wadmalaw
Island

Johns Island

Folly Beach

Folly
Beach

CHARLESTON
TEA PLANTATION

Rockville

Kiawah Island

Kiawah
Island

Seabrook Island

Seabrook
Island

N Edisto River

ATLANTIC

OCEAN

0   5 mi

0   5 km

© AVALON TRAVEL

Through Mount Pleasant is also the only land route to access Sullivan's Island, Isle of Palms, and historic Fort Moultrie.

Patriots Point Naval and Maritime Museum

Directly across Charleston Harbor from the old city lies the **Patriots Point Naval and Maritime Museum** (40 Patriots Point Rd., 843/884-2727, www.patriotspoint.org, daily 9am-6:30pm, $20 adults, $12 ages 6-11, free for active-duty military), one of the first chapters in Charleston's tourism renaissance. The project began in 1975 with what is still its main attraction, the World War II aircraft carrier USS *Yorktown*, named in honor of the carrier lost at the Battle of Midway. Much of "The Fighting Lady" is open to the public, and kids and nautical buffs will thrill to walk the decks and explore the many stations below deck on this massive 900-foot vessel, a veritable floating city.

Other ships moored beside the *Yorktown* and open for tours are the Coast Guard cutter USCG *Ingham,* the submarine USS *Clamagore,* and the destroyer USS *Laffey,* which survived being hit by three Japanese bombs and five kamikaze attacks—all within an hour.

A big plus is the free 90-minute guided tour. If you want to make a family history day out of it, you can hop on the ferry from Patriots Point to Fort Sumter and back.

Old Village

Mount Pleasant's history is almost as old as Charleston's, encapsulated by the **Old Village** (West of Royall Ave. to the waterfront, Mount Pleasant). First settled for farming in 1680, it soon acquired cachet as a great place for planters to spend the hot summers away from the mosquitoes inland. The main drag is Pitt Street, where you can shop and meander among plenty of stores and restaurants (try an ice cream soda at the historic Pitt Street Pharmacy). The huge meeting hall on the waterfront, Alhambra Hall, was the old ferry terminal.

Boone Hall Plantation

Unusual for this area, where fortunes were originally made mostly on rice, **Boone Hall Plantation**'s (1235 Long Point Rd., 843/884-4371, www.boonehallplantation.com, mid-Mar.-Labor Day Mon.-Sat. 8:30am-6:30pm, Sun. noon-5pm, Labor Day.-mid-Mar. Mon.-Sat. 9am-5pm, Sun. noon-5pm, $20 adults, $10 children) main claim to fame was as a cotton

restored slave cabin at Boone Hall Plantation

plantation as well as a noted brickmaking plant. Boone Hall takes the phrase "living history" to its extreme: It's not only an active agricultural facility, it also lets visitors go on "u-pick" walks through its fields, which boast succulent strawberries, peaches, tomatoes, and even pumpkins in October—as well as free hayrides. Keep in mind that the plantation's "big house" is not original; it's a 1935 reconstruction. The most poignant and educational structures by far are the nine humble brick slave cabins from the 1790s, expertly restored and most fitted with interpretive displays. Summers see some serious Civil War reenacting going on. In all, three different tours are available: a 30-minute house tour, a tour of Slave Street, and a garden tour.

Charles Pinckney National Historic Site

The **Charles Pinckney National Historic Site** (1240 Long Point Rd., 843/881-5516, www.nps.gov/chpi, daily 9am-5pm, free) is one of my favorite sights in Charleston, for its uplifting, well-explored subject matter as well as its tastefully maintained house and grounds. Sometimes called "the forgotten founder," Charles Pinckney was not only a hero of the American Revolution and a notable early abolitionist, but also one of the main authors of the U.S. Constitution. His great-aunt Eliza Lucas Pinckney was the first woman agriculturalist in the United States, responsible for opening up the indigo trade. The current main house, doubling as the visitors center, dates from 1828, 11 years after Pinckney sold Snee Farm to pay off debts. That said, it's still a great example of Lowcountry architecture. It replaces Pinckney's original home, where President George Washington slept and had breakfast under a nearby oak tree in 1791 while touring the South.

Isle of Palms

This primarily residential area of about 5,000 people received the state's first "Blue Wave" designation from the Clean Beaches Council for its well-managed and preserved beaches.

Like adjacent Sullivan's Island, there are pockets of great wealth here, but also a laid-back, windswept beach-town vibe. Aside from the whole scene, the main attraction here is the **Isle of Palms County Park** (14th Ave., 843/886-3863, www.ccprc.com, May-Labor Day daily 9am-7pm, Mar.-Apr. and Sept.-Oct. daily 10am-6pm, Nov.-Feb. daily 10am-5pm, $7 per vehicle, free for pedestrians and cyclists), with its oceanfront beach, complete with an umbrella rental front, volleyball court, playground, and lifeguards. The island's other claim to fame is the excellent (and surprisingly affordable) **Wild Dunes Resort** (5757 Palm Blvd., 888/778-1876, www.wilddunes.com), with its two Fazio golf courses and 17 clay tennis courts. Breach Inlet, between Isle of Palms and Sullivan's Island, is where the Confederate sub *Hunley* sortied to do battle with the USS *Housatonic.*

To get here from Mount Pleasant, take the Isle of Palms Connector (Hwy. 517) off U.S. 17 (Johnnie Dodds/Chuck Dawley Blvd.). To get to the county park, go through the light at Palm Boulevard and take the next left at the gate.

Sullivan's Island

Part funky beach town, part ritzy getaway, Sullivan's Island has a certain timeless quality. While much of it was rebuilt after Hurricane Hugo's devastation, plenty of local character remains, as evidenced by some cool little bars in its tiny "business district" on the main drag of Middle Street. There's a ton of history on Sullivan's, but you can also just while the day away on the quiet, windswept beach on the Atlantic or ride a bike all over the island and back. Unless you have a boat, you can only get here from Mount Pleasant. From U.S. 17, follow the signs for Highway 703 and Sullivan's Island. Cross the Ben Sawyer Bridge, and then turn right onto Middle Street; continue for about 1.5 miles.

FORT MOULTRIE

While Fort Sumter gets the bulk of the attention, the older **Fort Moultrie** (1214

Middle St., 843/883-3123, www.nps.gov/fosu, daily 9am-5pm, $3, free under age 16) on Sullivan's Island has a much more sweeping history. Furthering the irony, Major Robert Anderson's detachment at Fort Sumter at the opening of the Civil War was actually the Fort Moultrie garrison, reassigned to Sumter because Moultrie was thought too vulnerable from the landward side. Moultrie's first incarnation, a perimeter of felled palm trees, didn't even have a name when it was unsuccessfully attacked by the British in the summer of 1776, the first victory by the colonists in the Revolution. The redcoat cannonballs bounced off those flexible trunks, and thus was born South Carolina's nickname, "the Palmetto State."

In 1809 a brick fort was built here; it soon gained notoriety as the place where the great chief Osceola was detained after his capture. The chief died at the fort in 1838, and his modest grave site is still here, in front of the fort on the landward side. Other famous people to have trod on Sullivan's Island include Edgar Allan Poe, who was inspired by Sullivan's lonely, evocative environment to write *The Gold Bug* and other works. There's a Gold Bug Avenue and a Poe Avenue here today, and the local library is named after him as well. A young Lieutenant William Tecumseh Sherman was also stationed here during his Charleston stint in the 1830s, well before his encounter with history in the Civil War.

Moultrie's main Civil War role was as a target for Union shot during the long siege of Charleston. It was pounded so hard and for so long that its walls fell below a nearby sand hill and were finally unable to be hit anymore. A full military upgrade happened in the late 1800s, extending over most of Sullivan's Island (some private owners have even bought some of the old batteries and converted them into homes). It's the series of later forts that you'll visit on your trip to the Moultrie site, which is technically part of the Fort Sumter

National Monument and administered by the National Park Service.

Most of the outdoor tours are self-guided, but ranger programs typically happen Memorial Day-Labor Day daily at 11am and 2:30pm. There's a bookstore and visitors center across the street offering a 20-minute video on the hour and half hour 9am-4:30pm. Keep in mind there's no regular ferry to Fort Sumter from Fort Moultrie; the closest ferry to Sumter leaves from Patriots Point on Mount Pleasant.

BENCH BY THE ROAD

Scholars say that about half of all African Americans alive today had an ancestor who once set foot on Sullivan's Island. As the first point of entry for at least half of all slaves imported to the United States, the island's "pest houses" acted as quarantine areas so slaves could be checked for communicable diseases before going to auction in Charleston proper. But few people seem to know this. In a 1989 magazine interview, African American author and Nobel laureate Toni Morrison said about historic sites concerning slavery, "There is no suitable memorial, or plaque, or wreath or wall, or park or skyscraper lobby. There's no 300-foot tower, there's no small bench by the road." In 2008, that last item became a reality, as the first of several planned "benches by the road" was installed on Sullivan's Island to mark the sacrifice of enslaved African Americans. It's a simple black steel bench with an attached marker and a nearby plaque. The Bench by the Road is at the Fort Moultrie visitors center (1214 Middle St.).

Awendaw and Points North

This area just north of Charleston along U.S. 17—named for the Sewee Indian village originally located here and known to the world chiefly as the place where Hurricane Hugo made landfall in 1989—is seeing some new growth but still hews to its primarily rural, nature-loving roots.

CAPE ROMAIN NATIONAL WILDLIFE REFUGE

One of the best natural experiences in the area is about a 30-minute drive north of Charleston at **Cape Romain National Wildlife Refuge** (5801 U.S. 17 N., 843/928-3264, www.fws.gov/caperomain, daily dawn-dusk, free). Essentially comprising four barrier islands, the 66,000-acre refuge—almost all of which is marsh—provides a lot of great paddling opportunities, chief among them **Bulls Island** (no overnight camping). A fairly lengthy trek from where you put in is famous Boneyard Beach, where hundreds of downed trees lie on the sand, bleached by sun and salt. Slightly to the south within the refuge, **Capers Island Heritage Preserve** (843/953-9300, www.dnr.sc.gov, daily dawn-dusk, free) is still a popular camping locale despite heavy damage from 1989's Hurricane Hugo. Get permits in advance by calling the South Carolina Department of Natural Resources. You can kayak to the refuge yourself or take the only approved ferry service from **Coastal Expeditions** (514-B Mill St., Mount Pleasant, 843/881-4582, www.coastalexpeditions.com, $40 adults, $20 children, 30 minutes). **Barrier Island Eco Tours** (50 41st Ave., Isle of Palms, 843/886-5000, www.nature-tours.com, 3.5-hour boat excursions $38 adults, $28 children) on Isle of Palms also runs trips to the area.

SEWEE VISITOR AND ENVIRONMENTAL EDUCATION CENTER

Twenty miles north of Charleston is the **Sewee Visitor and Environmental Education Center** (5821 U.S. 17, 843/928-3368, www.fws.gov/seweecenter, Wed.-Sat. 9am-5pm, free). Besides being a gateway of sorts for the almost entirely aquatic Cape Romain National Wildlife Refuge, Sewee is primarily known for housing several rare red wolves, which were part of a unique release program on nearby Bull Island begun in the late 1970s. They're kept at the center to maintain the genetic integrity of the species.

FOLLY BEACH AND THE SOUTHWEST ISLANDS

Folly Beach

A large percentage of the town of **Folly Beach** (south of Charleston via Hwy. 30 and Hwy. 171) was destroyed by Hurricane Hugo in 1989, and erosion since then has increased and hit the beach itself pretty hard. All that said, enough of Folly's funky charm is left to make it worth visiting. Called "the Edge of America" during its heyday as a swinging resort getaway from the 1930s through the 1950s, Folly Beach is now a slightly beaten but enjoyable little getaway on this barrier island. Folly's main claim to larger historical fame is playing host to George Gershwin, who stayed at a cottage on West Arctic Avenue to write the score for *Porgy and Bess,* set across the harbor in downtown Charleston. (Ironically, Gershwin's opera couldn't be performed in its original setting until 1970 because of segregationist Jim Crow laws.) Original *Porgy* author DuBose Heyward stayed around the corner at a summer cottage on West Ashley Avenue that he dubbed "Follywood."

Called Folly Road until it gets to the beach, Center Street is the main drag here, dividing the beach into east and west. In this area you'll find the **Folly Beach Fishing Pier** (101 E. Arctic Ave., 843/588-3474, Apr.-Oct. daily 6am-11pm, Nov. and Mar. daily 7am-7pm, Dec.-Feb. daily 8am-5pm, $5-7 parking, $8 fishing fee), which replaced the grand old wooden pier-and-pavilion structure that burned down in 1960.

To get to Folly Beach from Charleston, go west on Calhoun Street and take the James Island Connector. Take a left on Folly Road (Hwy. 171), which becomes Center Street once in Folly Beach.

At the far east end of Folly Island, about 300 yards offshore, you'll see the **Morris Island Lighthouse,** an 1876 beacon that was once surrounded by lush green landscape, but is now completely surrounded by water after the land eroded around it. Now privately owned, there's an extensive effort to save and preserve the lighthouse (www.savethelight.

org). There's also an effort to keep high-dollar condo development off beautiful bird-friendly Morris Island itself (www.morrisisland.org). To get there while there's still something left to enjoy, take East Ashley Street until it deadends. Park in the lot and take a 0.25-mile walk to the beach.

Kiawah Island

The beautiful island of Kiawah—about 45 minutes from downtown Charleston—has as its main attraction the sumptuous **Kiawah Island Golf Resort** (12 Kiawah Beach Dr., 800/654-2924, www.kiawahgolf.com, $600-800), a key location for PGA tournaments. But even if you don't play golf, the resort is an amazing stay. The main component is **The Sanctuary,** an upscale hotel featuring an opulent lobby complete with grand staircases, a large pool area overlooking the beach, tasteful Spanish Colonial-style architecture, and 255 smallish but excellently appointed guest rooms. Several smaller private, family-friendly resorts also exist on Kiawah, with fully furnished homes and villas and every amenity you could ask for. Go to www.explorekiawah.com for a full range of options or call 800/877-0837.

Through the efforts of the **Kiawah Island Conservancy** (23 Beachwalker Dr., 843/768-2029, www.kiawahconservancy.org), over 300 acres of the island have been kept as an undeveloped nature preserve. The island's famous bobcat population has made quite a comeback; the bobcats are vital to the island ecosystem, since as top predator they help cull what would otherwise become untenably large populations of deer and rabbit.

The beach at Kiawah is a particular delight, set as it is on such a comparatively undeveloped island. No matter where you stay on Kiawah, a great thing about the island is the notable lack of light pollution—don't forget to look up at night and enjoy the stars!

Seabrook Island

Like its neighbor Kiawah, **Seabrook Island** is a private resort-dominated island. In addition to offering miles of beautiful beaches, on its 2,200 acres are a wide variety of golfing, tennis, equestrian, and swimming facilities as well as extensive dining and shopping options. There are a lot of kids' activities as well. For information on lodging options and packages, go to www.seabrook.com or call 866/249-9934. Seabrook Island is about 45 minutes from Charleston. From downtown, take Highway 30 West to Maybank Highway, then take a left onto Cherry Point Road.

Johns Island

ANGEL OAK PARK

The outlying community of Johns Island is where you'll find the inspiring **Angel Oak Park** (3688 Angel Oak Rd., Mon.-Sat. 9am-5pm, Sun. 1pm-5pm, free), home of a massive live oak, 65 feet in circumference, that's over 1,000 years old and commonly considered the oldest tree east of the Mississippi River. As is the case with all live oaks, don't expect impressive height—when oaks age they spread *out*, not up. The sprawling, picturesque tree and the park containing it are owned by the city of Charleston, and the scenic grounds are often used for weddings and special events. Angel Oak Park is about 30 minutes from Charleston. Take U.S. 17 over the Ashley River, then Highway 171 to Maybank Highway. Take a left onto Bohicket Road, and then look for signs on the right.

LEGARE FARMS

Legare Farms (2620 Hanscombe Point Rd., 843/559-0763, www.legarefarms.com, hours vary) is open to the public for various activities, including its annual pumpkin patch in October, its "sweet corn" festival in June, and bird walks (Sat. 8:30am, $6 adults, $3 children) in fall. To make the 20-minute drive from downtown Charleston, take Highway 30 West to Maybank Highway, then make a left onto River Road and a right onto Jenkins Farm Road.

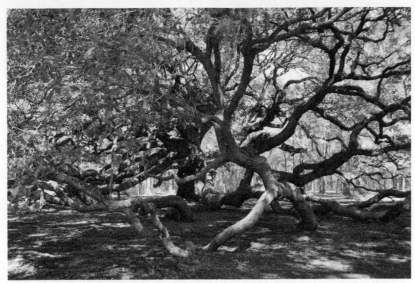

the ancient Angel Oak

Wadmalaw Island

CHARLESTON TEA PLANTATION

Currently owned by the R. C. Bigelow Tea corporation, the **Charleston Tea Plantation** (6617 Maybank Hwy., 843/559-0383, www. charlestonteaplantation.com, Mon.-Sat. 10am-4pm, Sun. noon-4pm, free) is no cute living-history exhibit: It's a big working tea plantation—the only one in the United States—with acre after acre of *Camellia sinensis* being worked by modern farm machinery. Visitors get to see how the tea is brought "from the field to the cup." Factory tours are free, and a trolley tour of the "Back 40" is $10. And, of course, there's a gift shop where you can sample and buy all types of teas and tea-related products. Growing season is April-October. The tea bushes, direct descendants of plants brought over in the 1800s from India and China, "flush up" 2-3 inches every few weeks during growing season. Charleston Tea Plantation is about 30 minutes from Charleston. Take the Ashley River Bridge, stay left to Folly Road (Hwy. 171), turn right onto Maybank Highway and follow it 18 miles, and look for the sign on the left.

DEEP WATER VINEYARDS

South Carolina has several good wineries, among them Wadmalaw's own **Deep Water Vineyards** (6775 Bears Bluff Rd., 843/559-6867, www.deepwatervineyard. com, Tues.-Sat. 10am-5pm), formerly Irvin House Vineyards, the Charleston area's only vineyard. They make several varieties of muscadine wine here, with $5 tastings and a gift shop. Every Saturday they host a "Wine-Down" party (noon-4pm). Also on the grounds you'll find **Firefly Distillery** (6775 Bears Bluff Rd., 843/559-6867, www.firefly-vodka.com, Tues.-Sat. 10am-5pm), home of their signature Firefly Sweet Tea Vodka. To get here from Charleston, go west on Maybank Highway about 10 miles to Bears Bluff Road, veering right on the latter. The vineyard entrance is on the left after about eight miles.

Entertainment and Events

NIGHTLIFE

Unlike the locals-versus-tourists divide you find so often in other destination cities, in Charleston it's nothing for a couple of visitors to find themselves at a table next to four or five college students enjoying themselves in true Charlestonian fashion: loudly and with lots of good food and strong drink nearby.

Bars close in Charleston at 2am, though there is a movement afoot to make the closing time earlier in some areas of town, mostly the Upper King neighborhood, the youngest and most vibrant nightlife area in Charleston. All hard-liquor sales stop at 7pm, with none at all on Sundays. You can buy beer and wine in grocery stores 24-7.

Pubs and Bars

One of Charleston's favorite neighborhood spots is **Moe's Crosstown Tavern** (714 Rutledge Ave., 843/722-3287, daily 11am-2am) in the Hampton Square area.

In the French Quarter, the Guinness flows freely at touristy **Tommy Condon's Irish Pub** (160 Church St., 843/577-3818, www.tommycondons.com, Sun.-Thurs. 11am-2am, dinner until 10pm, Fri.-Sat. 11am-2am, dinner until 11pm), as do the patriotic Irish songs performed live most nights.

If it's a nice day, a good place to relax and enjoy happy hour outside is **Vickery's Bar and Grill** (15 Beaufain St., 843/577-5300, www.vickerysbarandgrill.com, Mon.-Sat. 11:30am-2am, Sun. 11am-1am, kitchen closes 1am), part of a small regional chain based in Atlanta. Start with the oyster bisque and maybe try the turkey and brie sandwich or crab cakes for your entrée.

The hottest hipster dive bar is the **Recovery Room** (685 King St., 843/727-0999, Mon.-Fri. 4pm-2am, Sat. 3pm-2am, Sun. noon-2am) in Upper King. The drinks are cheap and stiff, and the bar food is addictively tasty (two words: Tater Tots!).

Located not too far over the Ashley River on U.S. 17, Charleston institution **Gene's Haufbrau** (17 Savannah Hwy., 843/225-4363, www.geneshaufbrau.com, daily 11:30am-2am) is worth making a special trip into West Ashley. Boasting the largest beer selection in Charleston—from the Butte Creek Organic Ale from California to a can of PBR—Gene's also claims to be the oldest bar in town, established in 1952.

Though Sullivan's Island has a lot of high-dollar homes, it still has friendly watering holes like **Dunleavy's Pub** (2213-B Middle St., 843/883-9646, Sun.-Thurs. 11:30am-1am, Fri.-Sat. 11:30am-2am). Inside is a great bar festooned with memorabilia, or you can enjoy a patio table.

The other Sullivan's watering hole of note is **Poe's Tavern** (2210 Middle St., 843/883-0083, www.poestavern.com, daily 11am-2am, kitchen closes 10pm) across the street, a nod to Edgar Allan Poe and his service on the island as a clerk in the U.S. Army. It's a lively, mostly local scene, set within a fun but suitably dark interior (though you might opt for one of the outdoor tables on the raised patio). Simply put, no trip to Sullivan's is complete without a stop at one (or possibly both) of these two local landmarks, which are within a stone's throw of each other.

If you're in Folly Beach, enjoy the great views and cocktails at **Blu Restaurant and Bar** (1 Center St., 843/588-6658, www.blu-follybeach.com, daily 7am-10pm) inside the Tides Folly Beach hotel. There's nothing like a Spiked Lemonade on a hot Charleston day at the beach.

Another notable Folly Beach watering hole is the **Sand Dollar Social Club** (7 Center St., 843/588-9498, Sun.-Fri. noon-1am, Sat. noon-2am), the kind of cash-only, mostly local dive you often find in little beach towns. You have to pony up for a "membership" to this private club, but it's only a buck. There's a catch,

Craft Breweries

The craft beer revolution has hit Charleston hard. Here are a few notable places to try:

- **Palmetto Brewing** (289 Huger St., 843/937-0903, www.palmettobrewery.com, tasting room Tues.-Wed. 3pm-7pm, Thurs. 3pm-9pm, Fri. 1pm-10pm, Sat. 1pm-7pm) has roots in Charleston going back before the Civil War and was the city's first post-Prohibition brewery. Known for their nitro beers and their Espresso Porter, among many others, they have an extensive outdoor seating area and often feature live music on weekends.

- **COAST Brewing** (1250 2nd St. N., 843/343-4727, www.coastbrewing.com, Thurs.-Fri. 4pm-7pm, Sat. 11am-4pm) in North Charleston focuses on sustainable and organic ingredients. Try the Blackbeerd Stout if it's available, and any Kölsch. This is more of a casual, all-outdoor tasting experience, so keep weather in mind.

- **Holy City Brewing** (4155C Dorchester Rd., www.holycitybrewing.com, Mon.-Thurs. 11am-8pm, Fri.-Sat. 11am-9pm, Sun. 11am-5pm), also in North Charleston, is known for its porters and stouts. This is also a great choice if you're hungry, as they have a full menu. Try the namesake Holy City Burger.

though: You can't get in until your 24-hour "waiting period" is over.

If you find yourself up in North Charleston, stop by **Madra Rua Irish Pub** (1034 E. Montague Ave., 843/554-2522, daily 11am-1am), an authentic watering hole with a better-than-average pub-food menu that's also a great place to watch a soccer game.

Lounges

On the waterfront, the aptly named **Rooftop Bar and Restaurant** (23 Vendue Range, 843/723-0485, Tues.-Sat. 6pm-2am) at the Vendue is a very popular happy hour spot from which to enjoy the sunset over the Charleston skyline.

If artisan cocktails are your thing, head straight to another waterfront spot, **The Gin Joint** (182 E. Bay St., 843/577-6111, www.theginjoint.com, Thurs.-Fri. 5pm-2am, Sat. 3pm-2am, Sun.-Wed. 5pm-midnight), where you can get drinks with names like Thieve's Tonic (rum, turmeric, lime, coconut, ginger honey) and Studmuffin (Madeira, chicory liqueur, coffee liqueur, and bay leaf ice cubes). With most cocktails running about $11 each, they're actually bargains when you consider the curated ingredients going into each one. Got a big party? Order one of four signature punches to share, prepared tableside (about

$40). Fair warning: These aren't your typical office party punches and pack a commensurately large, well, punch. Thankfully, there is a good little menu of tapas to soak up all the alcohol.

Across the street from Gene's Haufbrau in West Ashley, the retro-chic **Voodoo Lounge** (15 Magnolia Rd., 843/769-0228, Mon.-Fri. 4pm-2am, Sat.-Sun. 5:30pm-2am, kitchen until 1am) is another very popular hangout. It has a wide selection of trendy cocktails and killer gourmet tacos.

Live Music

Charleston's live music scene is hit or miss. With the long-ago passing of the heyday of Hootie & the Blowfish, there's no distinct "Charleston sound" to speak of (though Hootie frontman-turned-country-star Darius Rucker still plays frequently in the area), but the venues do a good job of bringing in well-regarded national and regional touring acts. The best place to find up-to-date music listings is the local free weekly *Charleston City Paper* (www.charlestoncitypaper.com).

The venerable **Music Farm** (32 Ann St., 843/722-8904, www.musicfarm.com) in Upper King isn't much to look at from the outside, but the cavernous space has played host to all sorts of bands over the past two

Doin' the Charleston

It has been called the biggest song-and-dance craze of the 20th century. It first entered the American public consciousness via New York City in a 1923 Harlem musical called *Runnin' Wild,* but the roots of the dance soon to be known as the Charleston were indeed in the Holy City. No one is quite sure of the day and date, but local lore assures us that members of Charleston's legendary Jenkins Orphanage Band were the first to start dancing that crazy "Geechie step," a development that soon became part of the band's act.

The Jenkins Orphanage was started in 1891 by the African American Baptist minister Reverend D. J. Jenkins and was originally housed in the Old Marine Hospital at 20 Franklin Street (which you can see today, although it's not open to the public). To raise money, Reverend Jenkins acquired donated instruments and started a band comprising talented orphans from the house. The orphans traveled as far away as London, where they were a hit with the locals but not with the constabulary, who unceremoniously fined them for stopping traffic. A Charleston attorney who happened to be in London at the time, Augustine Smyth, paid their way back home, becoming a lifelong supporter of the orphanage in the process.

From then on, playing in donated old Citadel uniforms, the Jenkins Orphanage Band frequently took their act on the road. They played at the St. Louis and Buffalo expositions and even at President Taft's inauguration. They also frequently played in New York, and it was there that African American pianist and composer James P. Johnson heard the Charlestonians play and dance to their Gullah rhythms, considered exotic at the time. Johnson would incorporate what he heard into the tune "Charleston," one of many songs in the revue *Runnin' Wild.* The catchy song and its accompanying loose-limbed dance seemed tailor-made for the Roaring '20s and its liberated, hedonistic spirit. Before long the Charleston had swept the nation, becoming a staple of jazz clubs and speakeasies across the country and, indeed, the world.

decades. Recent concerts have included Fitz and the Tantrums, the Dropkick Murphys, and the Drive-By Truckers.

The hippest music spot in town is out on James Island at **The Pour House** (1977 Maybank Hwy., 843/571-4343, www.charlestonpourhouse.com, 9pm-2am on nights with music scheduled), where the local characters are sometimes just as entertaining as the acts onstage.

Dance Clubs

The **Trio Club** (139 Calhoun St., 843/965-5333, Thurs.-Sat. 9pm-2am), right off Marion Square, is a favorite place to make the scene. There's a relaxing outdoor area with piped-in music, an intimate sofa-filled upstairs bar for dancing and chilling, and the dark candlelit downstairs with frequent live music leaning toward hip-hop sounds.

Gay-Friendly

Most gay-oriented nightlife centers on the Upper King area. Charleston's hottest dance spot of any type, gay or straight, is **Cure** (28 Ann St., 843/577-2582, Fri.-Sun. 10pm-2am), on the lower level of the parking garage across from the visitors center (375 Meeting St.). This space was for years known as Club Pantheon but has changed ownership. Cover charges are typically not cheap, but it's worth it for the great DJs, the dancing, and the people watching, not to mention the frequent drag cabaret shows.

Just down the street from Cure—and owned by the same people—is a totally different kind of gay bar, **Dudley's** (42 Ann St., 843/577-6779, daily 4pm-2am). Mellower and more appropriate for conversation or a friendly game of pool, Dudley's is a nice contrast to the thumping club a few doors down.

North of Broad, **Vickery's Bar and Grill** (15 Beaufain St., 843/577-5300, www.vickerysbarandgrill.com, Mon.-Sat. 11:30am-2am, Sun. 11am-1am, kitchen closes 1am) does not market itself as a gay establishment, but it has nonetheless become quite popular with the gay community—not least because of the good reputation its parent tavern in Atlanta has with that city's large and influential gay community.

PERFORMING ARTS
Theater

Unlike the more (literally) puritanical colonies farther up the North American coast, Charleston was an arts-friendly settlement from the beginning. The first theatrical production on the continent happened in Charleston in January 1735, when a nomadic troupe rented a space at Church and Broad Streets to perform Thomas Otway's *The Orphan*. The play's success led to the building of the Dock Street Theatre on what is now Queen Street. Notable thespians performing in town included Edwin Booth, Junius Booth Jr. (brothers of Lincoln's assassin, John Wilkes), and Edgar Allan Poe's mother, Eliza.

Several high-quality troupes continue to keep Charleston's proud theater tradition alive, chief among them **Charleston Stage** (Dock Street Theatre, 135 Church St., 843/577-7183, www.charlestonstage.com), the resident company of the Dock Street Theatre. In addition to its well-received regular season of classics and modern staples, Charleston Stage has debuted more than 30 original scripts over the years, a recent example being *Gershwin at Folly*, recounting the composer's time at Folly Beach working on *Porgy and Bess*.

The Footlight Players (Footlight Players Theatre, 20 Queen St., 843/722-4487, www.footlightplayers.net) make up the oldest continuously active company in town, founded in 1931. This community-based amateur company performs a mix of crowd-pleasers (*Who's Afraid of Virginia Woolf?*) and creative adaptations (*Miracle in Bedford Falls,* a musical based on *It's a Wonderful Life*) at its space at 20 Queen Street.

The players of **PURE Theatre** (477 King St., 843/723-4444, www.puretheatre.org) perform in a black-box space in the heart of the Upper King entertainment/nightlife district.

Their shows emphasize compelling, mature drama, beautifully performed. This is where to catch less glitzy, grittier productions like *Rabbit Hole, American Buffalo,* and *Cold Tectonics,* a hit at Piccolo Spoleto.

The city's most unusual players are **The Have Nots!** (Theatre 99, 280 Meeting St., 843/853-6687, www.theatre99.com, Wed. 8pm, Fri.-Sat. 8pm and 10pm, $5-12.50), with a rotating ensemble of dozens of comedians who perform their brand of edgy, adults-only improv at Theatre 99. Friday is the most reliable improve night, while Wednesday and Saturday may feature more sketch comedy.

Music

The **Charleston Symphony Orchestra** (Gaillard Center, 95 Calhoun St., 843/554-6060, www.charlestonsymphony.com) performed for the first time on December 28, 1936, at the Hibernian Hall on Meeting Street. During that first season the CSO accompanied *The Recruiting Officer,* the inaugural show at the renovated Dock Street Theatre. For seven decades, the CSO continued to provide world-class orchestral music, gaining "Metropolitan" status in the 1970s, when it accompanied the first-ever local performance of *Porgy and Bess,* which despite its Charleston setting couldn't be performed locally before then due to segregation laws. Now under the direction of conductor Ken Lam, the CSO performs at the renovated and reimagined Gaillard Center, modeled on European concert halls. Check the website for upcoming concerts.

The excellent music department at the College of Charleston sponsors the annual **Charleston Music Fest** (Simons Center for the Arts, 54 St. Philip St., $25), a series of chamber music concerts at various venues around the beautiful campus, featuring many faculty members of the college as well as visiting guest artists. Other college musical offerings include the **College of Charleston Concert Choir** (www.cofc.edu/music), which performs at various venues, usually churches, around town during the fall; the **College of**

Charleston Opera, which performs at least one full-length production during the school year and often takes the stage at Piccolo Spoleto; and the popular Yuletide Madrigal Singers, who sing in early December at a series of concerts in historic Randolph Hall.

Chamber Music Charleston (various locations, 843/763-4941, www.chambermusiccharleston.org), which relies on many core Charleston Symphony Orchestra musicians, continues to perform around town, including at Piccolo Spoleto. They play a wide variety of picturesque venues, including the Sottile Theatre (44 George St.) and Kiawah Island. They can also be found at private house concerts, which sell out quickly.

CINEMA

The most interesting art-house and indie venue in town is The Terrace (1956D Maybank Hwy., 843/762-4247, www.terracetheater.com), and not only because it offers beer and wine that you can enjoy at your seat. Shows before 5pm are $7. It's west of Charleston on James Island; get there by taking U.S. 17 west from Charleston and going south on Highway 171, after which you take a right on Maybank Highway (Hwy. 700).

FESTIVALS AND EVENTS

Charleston is a festival-mad city, especially in the spring and early fall. And new festivals are being added every year, further enhancing the hedonistic flavor of this city that has also mastered the art of hospitality.

January

Held on a Sunday in late January at historic Boone Hall Plantation in Mount Pleasant, the Lowcountry Oyster Festival (www.charlestonlowcountry.com, Sun. 11am-5pm, $8, food additional) features literal truckloads of the sweet shellfish for your enjoyment. Gates open at 10:30am, and there's plenty of parking. Oysters are sold by the bucket and served with crackers and cocktail sauce. Bring your own shucking knife or glove, or buy them on-site.

February

One of the unique events in town is the Southeastern Wildlife Exposition (various venues, 843/723-1748, www.sewe.com, $12.50 per day, $30 for three days, free under age 13). For the last quarter century, the Wildlife Expo has brought together hundreds of artists and exhibitors to showcase just about any kind of naturally themed art you can think of in over a dozen galleries and venues all over downtown. Kids will enjoy the live animals on hand as well.

North Charleston is home to Brewvival (adjacent to COAST Brewing, 1250 2nd St. N., www.brewvival.com, $75). This daylong craft brew-tasting festival features brewers from the rapidly growing South Carolina craft beer industry. There is live music, and food vendors are available as well.

March

Generally straddling late February and the first days of March, the four-day Charleston Food & Wine Festival (www.charlestonfoodandwine.com, various venues and admission) is a glorious celebration of one of the Holy City's premier draws: its amazing culinary community. While the emphasis is on Lowcountry chefs, guest chefs from New York, New Orleans, and Los Angeles routinely come to show off their skills. Oenophiles, especially of domestic wines, will be in heaven as well. This event has boomed in recent years and downtown gets quite crowded. Tickets aren't cheap—an all-event pass is over $500 per person—but then again, this is one of the nation's great food cities.

Immediately before the Festival of Houses and Gardens is the Charleston International Antiques Show (40 E. Bay St., 843/722-3405, www.historiccharleston.org, admission varies), held at Historic Charleston's headquarters at the Missroon House on the High Battery. It features over 30 of the nation's best-regarded dealers and offers lectures and tours.

Mid-March-April, the perennial favorite Festival of Houses and Gardens

(843/722-3405, www.historiccharleston.org, admission varies) is sponsored by the Historic Charleston Foundation and held at the very peak of the spring blooming season for maximum effect. In all, the festival goes into a dozen historic neighborhoods to view about 150 homes. Each day sees a different three-hour tour of a different area, at about $50 per person. This is a fantastic opportunity to peek inside some amazing old privately owned properties that are inaccessible to visitors at all other times. A highlight is a big oyster roast and picnic at Drayton Hall.

Not to be confused with the above festival, the **Garden Club of Charleston House and Garden Tours** (843/530-5164, www.thegardenclubofcharleston.com, $35) are held over a weekend in late March. Highlights include the Heyward-Washington House and the private garden of the late great Charleston horticulturalist Emily Whaley.

One of Charleston's newest and most fun events, the five-night **Charleston Fashion Week** (www.charlestonfashionweek.com, admission varies) benefits local women's and children's charities. Mimicking New York's Fashion Week events under tenting in Bryant Park, Charleston's version features runway action under big tents in Marion Square—and, yes, past guests have included former contestants on *Project Runway*.

April

The annual **Cooper River Bridge Run** (www.bridgerun.com) happens the first Saturday in April (unless that's Easter weekend, in which case it runs the week before) and features a six-mile jaunt across the massive Arthur Ravenel Bridge over the Cooper River, the longest cable span in the Western Hemisphere. It's not for those with a fear of heights, but it's still one of Charleston's best-attended events—there are well over 30,000 participants.

Previously known as the Family Circle Cup, the **Volvo Car Open** (161 Seven Farms Dr., Daniel Island, 843/856-7900, www.volvocaropen.com, admission varies) is held at

Daniel Island's Family Circle Tennis Center, specifically built for the event. Almost 100,000 people attend the multiple-week event. Individual session tickets go on sale the preceding January.

Mount Pleasant is the home of Charleston's shrimping fleet, and each April sees all the boats parade by the Alhambra Hall and Park for the **Blessing of the Fleet** (843/884-8517, www.townofmountpleasant.com). Family events and lots and lots of seafood are also on tap.

May

Free admission and free parking are not the only draws at the outdoor **North Charleston Arts Festival** (5000 Coliseum Dr., www.northcharleston.org), but let's face it, that's important. Held beside North Charleston's Performing Arts Center and Convention Center, the festival features music, dance, theater, multicultural performers, and storytellers. There are a lot of kids' events as well.

Held over three days at the Holy Trinity Greek Orthodox Church up toward the Neck, the **Charleston Greek Festival** (30 Race St., 843/577-2063, www.charlestongreekfestival.com, $5 admission, food extra) offers a plethora of live entertainment, dancing, Greek wares, and, of course, fantastic Greek cuisine cooked by the congregation. Parking is not a problem, and there's even a shuttle to the church from the lot.

Indisputably Charleston's single biggest and most important event, **Spoleto Festival USA** (843/579-3100, www.spoletousa.org, admission varies) has come a long way since it was a sparkle in the eye of the late Gian Carlo Menotti three decades ago. Though Spoleto long ago broke ties with its founder, his vision remains indelibly stamped on the event from start to finish. There's plenty of music, to be sure, in genres that include orchestral, opera, jazz, and avant-garde, but you'll find something in every other performing art, such as dance, drama, and spoken word, in traditions from Western to African to Southeast Asian. For 17 days from Memorial Day weekend through early June, Charleston hops and hums nearly 24 hours a day to the energy of this vibrant, cutting-edge (yet accessible) artistic celebration.

As if all the hubbub around Spoleto didn't give you enough to do, there's also **Piccolo Spoleto** (843/724-7305, www.piccolospoleto. com, various venues and admission), literally "little Spoleto," running concurrently. The intent of Piccolo Spoleto—begun just a couple of years after the larger festival came to town and run by the city's Office of Cultural Affairs—is to give local and regional performers a time to shine, sharing some of that larger spotlight on the national and international performers at the main event. Of particular interest to visiting families will be Piccolo's children's events, a good counter to some of the decidedly more adult fare at Spoleto USA.

June

Technically part of Piccolo Spoleto but gathering its own following, the **Sweetgrass Cultural Arts Festival** (www.sweetgrassfestival.org) is held the first week in June in Mount Pleasant at the Laing Middle School (2213 U.S. 17 N.). The event celebrates the traditional sweetgrass basket-making skills of African Americans in the historic Christ Church Parish area of Mount Pleasant. If you want to buy some sweetgrass baskets made by the world's foremost experts in the field, this would be the time.

July

Each year over 30,000 people come to see the **Patriots Point Fourth of July Blast** (866/831-1720), featuring a hefty barrage of fireworks shot off the deck of the USS *Yorktown* moored on the Cooper River in the Patriots Point complex. Food, live entertainment, and kids' activities are also featured.

September

From late September into the first week of October, the city-sponsored **MOJA Arts Festival** (843/724-7305, www.mojafestival.com, various venues and admission)

highlights the cultural contributions of African Americans and people from the Caribbean with dance, visual art, poetry, cuisine, crafts, and music in genres that include gospel, jazz, reggae, and classical. In existence since 1984, MOJA's name comes from the Swahili word for "one," and its diverse range of offerings in so many media have made it one of the Southeast's premier events. Some events are ticketed, while others, such as the kids' activities and many of the dance and film events, are free.

For five weeks from the last week of September into October, the Preservation Society of Charleston hosts the much-anticipated **Fall Tours of Homes & Gardens** (843/722-4630, www.preservationsociety. org, $45). The tour takes you into more than a dozen local residences and is the nearly 90-year-old organization's biggest fund-raiser. Tickets typically go on sale the previous June, and they tend to sell out very quickly.

Another great food event in this great food city, the **Taste of Charleston** (1235 Long Point Rd., 843/577-4030, www.charlestonrestaurantassociation.com, 11am-5pm, $12) is held on a weekend in October at Boone Hall Plantation in Mount Pleasant and sponsored by the Greater Charleston Restaurant Association. Over 50 area chefs and restaurants come together so you can sample their wares, including a wine and food pairing, with proceeds going to charity.

October

Local company **Half Moon Outfitters** (280 King St., 843/853-0990, 425 Coleman Blvd., 843/881-9472, www.halfmoonoutfitters.com, Mon.-Sat. 10am-7pm, Sun. noon-6pm) sponsors an annual six-mile Giant Kayak Race at Isle of Palms Marina in late October benefiting the Coastal Conservation League.

November

Plantation Days at Middleton Place (4300 Ashley River Rd., 843/556-6020, www.middletonplace.org, daily 9am-5pm, last tour 4:30pm, guided tour $10) happen each Saturday in

A Man, a Plan: Spoleto!

People gather in Marion Square to enjoy Piccolo Spoleto.

Sadly, Gian Carlo Menotti is no longer with us, having died in 2007 at the age of 95. But the overwhelming success of the composer's brainchild and labor of love, **Spoleto Festival USA**, lives on, enriching the cultural and social life of Charleston and serving as the city's chief calling card to the world at large.

Menotti began writing music at age seven in his native Italy. As a young man he moved to Philadelphia to study music, where he shared classes—and lifelong connections—with Leonard Bernstein and Samuel Barber. His first full-length opera, *The Consul,* would garner him the Pulitzer Prize, as would 1955's *The Saint of Bleecker Street.* But by far Menotti's best-known work is the beloved Christmas opera *Amahl and the Night Visitors,* composed especially for NBC television in 1951. At the height of his fame in 1958, the charismatic and mercurial genius—fluent and witty in five languages—founded the "Festival of Two Worlds" in Spoleto, Italy, specifically as a forum for young American artists in Europe. But it wasn't until nearly two decades later, in 1977, that Menotti was able to make his long-imagined dream of an American counterpart a reality.

Attracted to Charleston because of its long-standing support of the arts, its undeniable good taste, and its small size—ensuring that his festival would always be the number one activity in town while it was going on—Menotti worked closely with the man who was to become the other key part of the equation: Charleston mayor Joe Riley, then in his first term in office. Since then, the city has built on Spoleto's success by founding its own local version, **Piccolo Spoleto**—literally, "little Spoleto"—which focuses exclusively on local and regional talent.

Things haven't always gone smoothly. Menotti and the stateside festival parted ways in 1993, when he took over the Rome Opera. Making matters more uneasy, the Italian festival—run by Menotti's longtime partner (and later adopted son), Chip—also became estranged from what was intended to be its soul mate in South Carolina. (Chip was later replaced by the Italian Culture Ministry.) But perhaps this kind of creative tension is what Menotti intended all along. Indeed, each spring brings a Spoleto USA that seems to thrive on the inherent conflict between the festival's often cutting-edge offerings and the very traditional city that hosts it. Spoleto still challenges its audiences, just as Menotti intended it to. Depending on the critic and the audience member, that modern opera debut you see may be groundbreaking or gratuitous. The drama you check out may be exhilarating or tiresome.

Each year, a total of about 500,000 people attend both Spoleto and Piccolo Spoleto. Nearly one-third of the attendees are Charleston residents—the final proof that when it comes to supporting the arts, Charleston puts its money where its mouth is.

November, giving visitors a chance to wander the grounds and see artisans at work practicing authentic crafts, as they would have done in antebellum days, with a special emphasis on the contributions of African Americans. A special treat comes on Thanksgiving, when a full meal is offered on the grounds at the Middleton Place Restaurant (843/556-6020, www.middletonplace.org, reservations strongly recommended).

One of Charleston's newest annual events is the **Charleston International Film Festival** (843/817-1617, www.charlestoniff.com, various venues and prices). Despite being a relative latecomer to the film-festival circuit, the event is pulled off with Charleston's usual aplomb.

Though the **Battle of Secessionville** actually took place in June 1862 much farther south, November is the time the battle is reenacted at Boone Hall Plantation (1235 Long Point Rd., 843/884-4371, www.boonehallplantation.com, $17.50 adults, $7.50 children) in Mount Pleasant. Call for specific dates and times.

December

A yuletide in the Holy City is an experience you'll never forget, as the **Christmas in Charleston** (843/724-3705) events clustered around the first week of the month prove. For some reason—whether it's the old architecture, the friendly people, the churches, the carriages, or all of the above—Charleston feels right at home during Christmas. The festivities begin with the mayor lighting the city's 60-foot Tree of Lights in Marion Square, followed by a parade of brightly lit boats from Mount Pleasant all the way around Charleston up the Ashley River. The key event is the Sunday Christmas Parade through downtown, featuring bands, floats, and performers in the holiday spirit. The Saturday farmers market in the square continues through the middle of the month with a focus on holiday items.

Shopping

Shopping in Charleston centers on King Street, unique not only for the fact that so many national-name stores are lined up so close to each other, but also because there are so many great restaurants of so many different types scattered in and among the retail outlets, ideally positioned for when you need to take a break to rest and refuel. **Lower King** is primarily top-of-the-line antiques stores (most are closed Sundays, so plan your trip accordingly); **Middle King** is where you'll find upscale name-brand outlets such as Banana Republic and American Apparel as well as some excellent shoe stores; and **Upper King,** north of Calhoun Street, is where you'll find funky housewares shops, generally locally owned.

FRENCH QUARTER
Antiques and Vintage

A cute little shop tucked away in an alley,

Curiosity (56½ Queen St., 843/647-7763, www.curiositycharleston.com) is a find even by the standards of antiques/vintage-crazy Charleston. A nice plus is the prices here are a bit lower than in the premier antiques shops on Lower King Street, which would never be accused of being bargain priced.

Art Galleries

While not considered a visual arts mecca, the Holy City has been fertile ground for visual artists since native son Joseph Allen Smith began one of the country's first art collections in Charleston in the late 1700s. For most visitors, the center of gallery activity is in the French Quarter between South Market and Tradd Streets.

Incorporating works from the estate of Charleston legend Elizabeth O'Neill Verner is **Ann Long Fine Art** (54 Broad St., 843/577-0447, www.annlongfineart.com, Mon.-Sat.

Art Walks

The best way to experience visual art galleries in Charleston is to go on one of the popular and free **Charleston Gallery Association ArtWalks** (843/724-3424, www.charlestongalleryassociation.com, first Friday of March, May, October, and December 5pm-8pm), which feature lots of wine, food, and, of course, art. Over 40 galleries throughout downtown, with a special focus on the French Quarter, are featured. You can download a map at the website and visit them all yourself, whether or not you're here for the ArtWalk.

11am-5pm), which seeks to combine the painterly aesthetic of the Old World with the edgy vision of the New.

One of the French Quarter's most beloved galleries, the **Corrigan Gallery** (62 Queen St., 843/722-9868, www.corrigangallery.com, daily 10am-5pm) deals in some of the best current local artists, along with a focus on the Charleston Renaissance and the Charleston printmaking tradition.

The **Pink House Gallery** (17 Chalmers St., 843/723-3608, http://pinkhousegallery.tripod.com, Mon.-Sat. 10am-5pm) is housed in the oldest tavern building in the South, built circa 1694. The exhibits here offer a glimpse into old Charleston, including exclusive antique prints.

Robert Lange Studios (2 Queen St., 843/805-8052, www.robertlangestudios.com, daily 11am-5pm) is oriented toward modern art. It hosts not only the work of its owners, Robert and Megan Lange, but also a slate of up-and-coming regional artists. This is a great place to be on the regular first Friday art walks and events.

Books and Music
The great **Shops of Historic Charleston Foundation** (108 Meeting St., 843/724-8484, www.historiccharleston.org) is housed in a beautiful building and has plenty of tasteful Charleston-themed gift ideas, from books to kitchenware.

NORTH OF BROAD
Antiques
Alexandra AD (156 King St., 843/722-4897, Mon.-Sat. 10am-5pm) features great chandeliers, lamps, and fabrics.

Since 1929, **George C. Birlant & Co.** (191 King St., 843/722-3842, Mon.-Sat. 9am-5:30pm) has been importing 18th- and 19th-century furniture, silver, china, and crystal, and it deals in the famous "Charleston Battery Bench."

Art Galleries
For a more modern take from local artists, check out the **Sylvan Gallery** (171 King St., 843/722-2172, www.thesylvangallery.com, Mon.-Fri. 9am-5pm, Sat. 10am-5pm, Sun. 11am-4pm), which specializes in 20th- and 21st-century art and sculpture.

Specializing in original Audubon prints and antique botanical prints is **The Audubon Gallery** (190 King St., 843/853-1100, www.audubonart.com, Mon.-Sat. 10am-5pm), the sister store of the Joel Oppenheimer Gallery in Chicago.

Within City Market is **Gallery Chuma** (188 Meeting St., 843/722-1702, www.gallerychuma.com, daily 9:30am-6pm), which specializes in the art of the Gullah people of the South Carolina coast. They put on lots of cultural and educational events about Gullah culture as well as display art on the subject.

Art Mecca (427 King St., 843/577-0603, www.artmeccaofcharleston.com, Mon.-Fri. 10am-6pm, Sat. 10am-7pm, Sun. 11am-5pm) is an inviting modernist space that specializes in local and regional contemporary artists. It's a great place to get a flavor of what Charleston's younger up-and-coming artists are doing.

Books and Music
The charming **Pauline Books and Media** (243 King St., 843/577-0175, Mon.-Sat. 10am-6pm) is run by the Daughters of Saint Paul and

carries Christian books, Bibles, rosaries, and images from a Roman Catholic perspective.

It's easy to overlook at the far southern end of the retail development on King, but the excellent **Preservation Society of Charleston Book and Gift Shop** (147 King St., 843/722-4630, Mon.-Sat. 10am-5pm) is perhaps the best place in town to pick up books on Charleston lore and history as well as locally themed gift items.

Clothes

A charmingly old-school and notable locally owned clothing store on King Street is the classy **Berlins Men's and Women's** (114-120 King St., 843/722-1665, Mon.-Sat. 9:30am-6pm), dating from 1883. Despite the name, Berlins focuses on men's clothing, offering designs from Canali, Coppley, Jack Victor, and more.

Big companies' losses are your gain at **Oops!** (326 King St., 843/722-7768, Mon.-Fri. 10am-6pm, Sat. 10am-7pm, Sun. noon-6pm), which buys factory mistakes and discontinued lines from major brands at a discount, passing along the savings to you. The range here tends toward colorful and preppy.

The incredible consignment store **The Trunk Show** (281 Meeting St., 843/722-0442, Mon.-Sat. 10am-6pm) offers one-of-a-kind vintage and designer wear and accessories. Some finds are bargains, some not so much, but there's no denying the quality and breadth of the offerings.

For a locally owned clothing shop, try the innovative **Worthwhile** (268 King St., 843/723-4418, www.shopworthwhile.com, Mon.-Sat. 10am-6pm, Sun. noon-5pm), which has lots of organic fashions.

Jewelry

Art Jewelry by Mikhail Smolkin (312 King St., 843/722-3634, www.fineartjewelry.com, Mon.-Sat. 10am-5pm) features one-of-a-kind pieces by this St. Petersburg, Russia, native.

Since 1919, **Croghan's Jewel Box** (308 King St., 843/723-3594, www. croghansjewelbox.com, Mon.-Fri. 9:30am-5:30pm, Sat. 10am-5pm) has offered amazing locally crafted diamonds, silver, and designer pieces to generations of Charlestonians. An expansion in the late 1990s tripled the size of the historic location.

Joint Venture Estate Jewelers (185 King St., 843/722-6730, www.jventure.com, Mon.-Sat. 10am-5:30pm) specializes in antique, vintage, and modern estate jewelry as well as pre-owned watches, including Rolex, Patek Philippe, and Cartier, with a fairly unique consignment emphasis.

Shoes

A famous locally owned place for footwear is **Bob Ellis Shoe Store** (332 King St., 843/722-2515, www.bobellisshoes.com, Mon.-Sat. 10am-6pm), which has served Charleston's elite with high-end shoes since 1950.

Copper Penny Shooz (317 King St., 843/723-3838, Mon.-Sat. 10am-7pm, Sun. noon-6pm) combines hip and upscale footwear for women, "curated with a Southern eye," as this Charleston-based regional chain's motto goes.

Funky and fun **Phillips Shoes** (320 King St., 843/965-5270, Mon.-Sat. 10am-6pm) deals in Dansko for men, women, and kids (don't miss the awesome painting above the register of Elvis fitting a customer).

Rangoni of Florence (270 King St., 843/577-9554, Mon.-Sat. 9:30am-6pm, Sun. 12:30pm-5:30pm) imports the best women's shoes from Italy, with a few men's designs as well.

Shopping Centers and Malls

Belmond Charleston Place (205 Meeting St., 843/722-4900, www.charlestonplace-shops.com, Mon.-Wed. 10am-6pm, Thurs.-Sat. 10am-8pm, Sun. noon-5pm), usually just called "Charleston Place," is a combined retail-hotel development with highlights such as Gucci, Talbots, Louis Vuitton, Yves Delorme, Everything But Water, and Godiva.

For years dominated by a flea market vibe,

City Market (Meeting St. and Market St., 843/973-7236, daily 9:30am-10:30pm) was recently upgraded and is now chockablock with boutique retail all along its lengthy interior. The humbler crafts tables are toward the back. If you must have one of the handcrafted sweetgrass baskets, try out your haggling skills—the prices have wiggle room built in. In addition to the myriad tourist-oriented shops in the City Market itself, there are a few gems in the surrounding area that also appeal to locals.

Sporting Goods

With retail locations in Charleston and throughout South Carolina and Georgia and a new cutting-edge, eco-friendly warehouse in North Charleston, **Half Moon Outfitters** (280 King St., 843/853-0990, www.halfmoonoutfitters.com, Mon.-Sat. 10am-7pm, Sun. noon-6pm) is something of a local legend. Here you can find not only top-of-the-line camping and outdoor gear and tips on local recreation, but also some really stylish outdoorsy apparel as well.

UPPER KING
Art Galleries

One of the most important single venues for art, the nonprofit **Redux Contemporary Art Center** (136 St. Philip St., 843/722-0697, www.reduxstudios.org, Tues.-Fri. 10am-6pm, Sat. noon-5pm) features modernistic work in a variety of media, including illustration, video installation, blueprints, performance art, and graffiti. Outreach is hugely important to this venture and includes lecture series, classes, workshops, and internships.

Books and Music

Housed in an extremely long and narrow storefront, Jonathan Sanchez's funky and friendly **Blue Bicycle Books** (420 King St., 843/722-2666, www.bluebicyclebooks.com, Mon.-Sat. 10am-7:30pm, Sun. 1pm-6pm) deals primarily in used books and has a particularly nice stock of local and regional titles, art books, and fiction.

Home Goods

Head to **Haute Design Studio** (489 King St., 843/577-9886, www.hautedesign.com, Mon.-Fri. 9am-5:30pm) for upper-end furnishings with an edgy feel.

WATERFRONT
Art Galleries

The **City Gallery at Waterfront** (34 Prioleau St., 843/958-6484, www.citygalleryatwaterfrontpark.com, Tues.-Fri. 10am-6pm, Sat.-Sun. noon-5pm) is funded by the city, with exhibits focusing on local and regional culture and folkways. It's mostly an exhibit space, though art is also sold here.

Home Goods

Affiliated with the hip local restaurant chain Maverick Kitchens, **Charleston Cooks!** (194 E. Bay St., 843/722-1212, www.charlestoncooks.com, Mon.-Sat. 10am-9pm, Sun. 11am-6pm) has an almost overwhelming array of gourmet items and kitchenware, and even offers cooking classes.

Indigo (4 Vendue Range, 800/549-2513, Sun.-Thurs. 10am-6pm, Fri.-Sat. 10am-7pm), a favorite home accessories store, has plenty of one-of-a-kind pieces, many of them by regional artists and rustic in flavor, almost like outsider art.

SOUTH OF BROAD
Art Galleries

Charleston Renaissance Gallery (103 Church St., 843/723-0025, www.fineartsouth.com, Mon.-Sat. 10am-5pm) specializes in 19th- and 20th-century oils and sculpture and features artists from the American South, including some splendid pieces from the Charleston Renaissance.

Helena Fox Fine Art (106-A Church St., 843/723-0073, www.helenafoxfineart.com, Mon.-Sat. 10am-5pm) deals in 20th-century representational art.

WEST ASHLEY
Home Goods

Probably Charleston's best-regarded home

goods store is the nationally recognized **ESD, Elizabeth Stuart Design** (422 Savannah Hwy./U.S. 17, 843/225-6282, www.esdcharleston.com, Mon.-Sat. 10am-6pm), with a wide range of antique and new furnishings, art, lighting, jewelry, and more.

Music

In an age when it's harder and harder to find brick-and-mortar music/movie stores, **Monster Music and Movies** (946 Orleans Rd., 843/571-4657, Mon.-Sat. 10am-9pm, Sun. noon-7pm) is a great discovery. They have new and used vinyl and CDs, and they feature great sales and in-store performances for the annual Record Store Day in April.

NORTH CHARLESTON
Music

Fox Music House (3005 W. Montague Ave., 843/740-7200, Mon.-Fri. 10am-6pm, Sat. 10am-5pm) is a neighborhood favorite, and has been locally owned since 1928. They specialize in pianos and keyboards.

Shopping Centers

The **Tanger Outlet** (4840 Tanger Outlet Blvd., 843/529-3095, www.tangeroutlet.com, Mon.-Sat. 10am-9pm, Sun. 11am-6pm) has factory-priced bargains from stores such as Adidas, Banana Republic, Brooks Brothers,

CorningWare, Old Navy, Timberland, and more.

MOUNT PLEASANT AND EAST COOPER
Antiques

Mount Pleasant boasts a fun antiques and auction spot, **Page's Thieves Market** (1460 Ben Sawyer Blvd., 843/884-9672, www.pagesthievesmarket.com, Mon.-Fri. 9am-5:30pm, Sat. 9am-5pm). Its rambling interior has hosted bargain and vintage shoppers for 50 years, and it's routinely voted Charleston's best antiques store.

Shopping Centers

The most pleasant mall in the area is the retro-themed, pedestrian-friendly **Mount Pleasant Towne Center** (1600 Palmetto Grande Dr., 843/216-9900, www.mtpleasanttownecentre.com, Mon.-Sat. 10am-9pm, Sun. noon-6pm). In addition to national chains you'll find a few cool local stores in here, like Stella Nova spa and day salon and Copper Penny Shooz.

In a Harris Teeter grocery shopping center, **Gwynn's of Mount Pleasant** (916 Houston Northcutt Blvd., 843/884-9518, Mon.-Sat 10am-7pm) is an old-fashioned department store specializing in women's clothing and shoes, with a distinct local and Southern sensibility.

Sports and Recreation

ON THE WATER
Beaches

In addition to the charming town of Folly Beach itself, there's the modest county-run **Folly Beach County Park** (1100 W. Ashley Ave., Folly Beach, 843/588-2426, www.ccprc.com, May-Labor Day 9am-8pm, Mar.-Apr. and Sept.-Oct. 10am-7pm, Nov.-Feb. 10am-6pm, $7 per vehicle, free for pedestrians and cyclists) at the far west end of Folly Island. It has a picnic area, restrooms, outdoor showers, and beach chair and umbrella rentals. Get

there by taking Highway 171 (Folly Rd.) until it turns into Center Street, and then take a right on West Ashley Avenue.

On Isle of Palms you'll find **Isle of Palms County Park** (14th Ave., Isle of Palms, 843/886-3863, www.ccprc.com, fall-spring daily 10am-dark, summer daily 9am-dark, $5 per vehicle, free for pedestrians and cyclists), which has restrooms, showers, a picnic area, a beach volleyball area, and beach chair and umbrella rentals. Get there by taking the Isle of Palms Connector (Hwy. 517) to the island, go through the light at Palm Boulevard, and take the next left at the park gate. There's good public beach access near the Pavilion Shoppes on Ocean Boulevard, accessed via J. C. Long Boulevard.

On the west end of Kiawah Island to the south of Charleston is **Kiawah Island Beachwalker Park** (Kiawah Island, 843/768-2395, www.ccprc.com, Mar.-Apr. and Oct. Sat.-Sun. 10am-6pm, May-Aug. daily 9am-7pm, Sept. daily 10am-6pm, $7 per vehicle, free for pedestrians and cyclists), the only public facility on this mostly private resort island. It has restrooms, showers, a picnic area with grills, and beach chair and umbrella rentals. Get there from downtown Charleston by taking Lockwood Avenue onto the Highway 30 Connector bridge over the Ashley River. Turn right onto Folly Road, then take a left onto Maybank Highway. After about 20 minutes you'll take another left onto Bohicket Road, which leads you to Kiawah in 14 miles. Turn left from Bohicket Road onto the Kiawah Island Parkway. Just before the security gate, turn right on Beachwalker Drive and follow the signs to the park.

For a totally go-it-alone type of beach day, go to the three-mile-long beach on the Atlantic Ocean at **Sullivan's Island.** There are no facilities, no lifeguards, strong offshore currents, and no parking lots on this residential island (park on the side of the street). There's also a lot of dog walking on this beach, since no leash is required November-February. Get there from downtown by crossing the Ravenel Bridge over the Cooper River and bearing right onto Coleman Boulevard, which turns into Ben Sawyer Boulevard. Take the Ben Sawyer Bridge onto Sullivan's Island. Beach access is plentiful and marked.

Diving

Offshore diving centers on a network of **artificial reefs** (see www.dnr.sc.gov for a list and locations), particularly the "Charleston 60" sunken barge and the popular "Train Wreck," comprising 50 deliberately sunk New York City subway cars. Probably Charleston's best-regarded outfitter and charter operator is **Charleston Scuba** (335 Savannah Hwy., 843/763-3483, www.charlestonscuba.com) in West Ashley. They offer training classes, charters, and offshore diving trips. In addition to Charleston Scuba, you also might want to check out **Cooper River Scuba** (843/572-0459, www.cooperriverdiving.com) and **Atlantic Coast Dive Center** (209 Scott St., 843/884-1500).

Kayaking

Many kayakers put in at the Shem Creek Marina or the public Shem Creek Landing in Mount Pleasant. From here it's a safe, easy paddle—sometimes with appearances by dolphins or manatees—to the Intracoastal Waterway. Another good place to put in is at **Isle of Palms Marina** (50 41st Ave., 843/886-0209) behind the Wild Dunes Resort on Morgan Creek, which empties into the Intracoastal Waterway.

An excellent outfit for guided kayak tours is **Coastal Expeditions** (654 Serotina Ct., 843/881-4582, www.coastalexpeditions.com), which also runs the only approved ferry service to the Cape Romain National Wildlife Refuge. They'll rent you a kayak for roughly $50 per day. Coastal Expeditions also sells an outstanding kayaking, boating, and fishing map of the area (about $12).

The best tour operator close to downtown is **Nature Adventures Outfitters** (Shrimp Boat Ln., 843/568-3222, www.kayakcharlestonsc.com), which puts in on Shem Creek in Mount Pleasant for most of its 2-, 2.5-, 3-, and 3.5-hour and full-day guided trips, with prices from $40 to $85. They also offer blackwater tours out of landings at other locations; see the website for specific directions for those tours.

Fishing and Boating

For casual fishing off a pier, try the well-equipped **Folly Beach Fishing Pier** (101 E. Arctic Ave., Folly Beach, 843/588-3474, daily dawn-dusk, $5-7 parking, $8 fishing fee, rod rentals available) on Folly Beach or the **North Charleston Riverfront Park** (843/745-1087, www.northcharleston.org, daily dawn-dusk) along the Cooper River on the grounds of the old Navy Yard. Get onto the Navy Yard grounds by taking I-26 north to exit 216B. Take a left onto Spruill Avenue and a right onto McMillan Avenue.

Key local marinas include **Shem Creek Marina** (526 Mill St., 843/884-3211, www.shemcreekmarina.com), **Charleston Harbor Marina** (24 Patriots Point Rd., 843/284-7062, www.charlestonharbormarina.com), **Charleston City Marina** (17 Lockwood Dr., 843/722-4968), **Charleston Maritime Center** (10 Wharfside St., 843/853-3625, www.cmcevents.com), and the **Cooper River Marina** (1010 Juneau Ave., 843/554-0790, www.ccprc.com).

Good fishing charter outfits include **Barrier Island Eco Tours** (50 41st Ave., 843/886-5000, www.nature-tours.com, about $80) out of Isle of Palms, **Bohicket Boat Adventure & Tour Co.** (2789 Cherry Point Rd., 843/559-3525, www.bohicketboat.com, $375 per half day for 1-2 passengers) out of the Edisto River, and **Reel Fish Finder Charters** (315 Yellow Jasmine Ct., Moncks Corner, 843/697-2081, www.reelfishfinder.com, $400 per half day for 1-3 passengers), which picks up clients at many different marinas in the area. For a list of all public landings in Charleston County, go to www.ccprc.com.

Surfing and Kiteboarding

The surfing at the famous Washout area on the east side of Folly Beach isn't what it used to be due to storm activity and beach erosion. But diehards still gather at this area when the swell hits. Check out the conditions yourself from the three views of the **Folly Surfcam** (www.follysurfcam.com).

The best local surf shop is undoubtedly the historic **McKevlin's Surf Shop** (8 Center St., Folly Beach, 843/588-2247, www.mckevlins.com, spring-summer daily 10am-6pm, fall-winter daily 10am-5:30pm) on Folly Beach, one of the first surf shops on the East Coast, dating to 1965.

Folly Beach Shaka Surf School (107 E. Indian Ave., Folly Beach, 843/607-9911, www.shakasurfschool.com) offers private and group surf lessons, including youth surf camps throughout summer, women-only weekend outings, and yoga classes geared toward surfers. Surf camps are located on the east end of Folly Beach.

Mount Pleasant is home to **Sol Surfers Surf Camp** (1170 Lazy Ln., Mount Pleasant, 843/881-6700, www.solsurfers.net), which offers surf camps during the summer and private and group lessons throughout the year. The surf camp shuttle picks up students at the Parrot Surf Shop (811 Coleman Blvd.). Surf camps take place on the eastern end of Folly Beach.

Water Parks

During the summer months, Charleston County operates three water parks: **Splash Island Waterpark** (444 Needlerush Pkwy., Mount Pleasant, 843/884-0832); **Whirlin' Waters Adventure Waterpark** (University Blvd., North Charleston, 843/572-7275); and **Splash Zone Waterpark at James Island County Park** (871 Riverland Dr., 843/795-7275), on James Island west of town. Admission runs about $10 per person. Go to www.ccprc.com for more information.

Water Tours

The best all-around tour of Charleston Harbor is the 90-minute ride offered by **Spiritline Cruises** (Charleston Harbor, 800/789-3678, www.spiritlinecruises.com, $22 adults, $12 ages 4-11), which leaves from either Aquarium Wharf or Patriots Point. Allow about 30 minutes for ticketing and boarding. Spiritline also has a three-hour dinner cruise in the evening leaving from Patriots Point (about $50 pp) and a cruise to Fort Sumter.

Sandlapper Water Tours (Charleston Maritime Center, 10 Wharfside St., 843/849-8687, www.sandlappertours.com, Mar.-Aug., $20-27) offers many types of evening and dolphin cruises on a 45-foot catamaran. The company also offers Charleston's only waterborne ghost tour. Most of the tours leave from the Maritime Center near East Bay and Calhoun Streets.

Barrier Island Eco Tours (50 41st Ave., 843/886-5000, www.nature-tours.com, from $40) can take you on a passenger boat ride up to Cape Romain NWR out of Isle of Palms, with a focus on undeveloped Capers Island. Plan on seeing plenty of dolphins!

Coastal Expeditions (514-B Mill St., 843/884-7684, www.coastalexpeditions.com, prices vary) is based on Shem Creek in Mount Pleasant and offers several sea kayak adventures of varying lengths.

ON LAND
Golf

The country's first golf course was constructed in Charleston in 1786, so as you'd expect there's great golfing in the area, generally on the outlying islands. The folks at the nonprofit **Charleston Golf, Inc.** (423 King St., 843/958-3629, www.charlestongolfguide.com) are your best one-stop resource for tee times and packages.

The main public course is the 18-hole, renovated and upgraded **Charleston Municipal Golf Course** (2110 Maybank Hwy., 843/795-6517, www.charleston-sc.gov/golf, $22-24 for 18 holes), affectionately referred to as the Muni. To get there from the peninsula, take U.S. 17 south over the Ashley River, take Highway 171 (Folly Rd.) south, and then take a right onto Maybank Highway.

Probably the most renowned area facilities are at the acclaimed **Kiawah Island Golf Resort** (12 Kiawah Beach Dr., Kiawah Island, 800/654-2924, www.kiawahresort.com/golf, $150-350 for 18 holes, 25 percent discount for resort guests), about 20 miles from Charleston. The resort has five courses in all, the best known of which is the **Kiawah Island Ocean Course,** site of the famous "War by the Shore" 1991 Ryder Cup. This 2.5-mile course, which is walking-only until noon each day, hosted the Senior PGA Championship in 2007 and the PGA Championship in 2012. The resort offers a golf academy and private lessons galore. These are public courses, but be aware

that tee times are limited for golfers who aren't guests at the resort.

Two excellent resort-style public courses are at **Wild Dunes Resort** (5757 Palm Blvd., Isle of Palms, 888/845-8932, www.wilddunes.com, $165 for 18 holes) on Isle of Palms. The resort has been named one of the state's best by *Golf Digest.*

The 18-hole **Patriots Point Links** (1 Patriots Point Rd., Mount Pleasant, 843/881-0042, www.patriotspointlinks.com, $100 for 18 holes) on Charleston Harbor, right over the Ravenel Bridge, is one of the most convenient courses in the area, and it boasts some phenomenal views.

In Mount Pleasant you will find perhaps the best course in the area for the money, the award-winning **Rivertowne Golf Course** at the **Rivertowne Country Club** (1700 Rivertowne Country Club Dr., Mount Pleasant, 843/856-9808, www.rivertowne-countryclub.com, $150 for 18 holes). Opened in 2002, the course was designed by Arnold Palmer.

Hiking and Biking

The **West Ashley Greenway** (South Windermere Shopping Center [80 Folly Rd.] to Johns Island, paralleling U.S. 17, dawn-dusk) is an urban walking and biking trail built on a former railbed. The 10-mile trail runs parallel to U.S. 17 and passes parks, schools, and the Clemson Experimental Farm, ending near Johns Island. To get to the trailhead from downtown, drive west on U.S. 17. About 0.5 mile after you cross the bridge, turn left onto Folly Road (Hwy. 171). At the second light, turn right into South Windermere Shopping Center; the trail is behind the center on the right.

The most ambitious trail in South Carolina is the **Palmetto Trail,** begun in 1997 and eventually covering 425 miles from the Atlantic to the Appalachians. The coastal terminus of the Palmetto Trail, the 7-mile **Awendaw Passage,** winds through the Francis Marion National Forest. It begins at the trailhead at the Buck Hall Recreational

Area (McClellanville, 843/887-3257, www.palmettoconservation.org, $5 vehicle fee), which has parking and restroom facilities. Get there by taking U.S. 17 north from Charleston about 20 miles and through the Francis Marion National Forest and then Awendaw. Take a right onto Buck Hall Landing Road.

Charleston-area beaches are perfect for a leisurely bike ride on the sand. Sullivan's Island is a particular favorite, and you might be surprised at how long you can ride in one direction on these beaches. Those desiring a more demanding use of their legs can walk or ride their bike in the dedicated pedestrian and bike lane on the massive **Arthur Ravenel Jr. Bridge** over the Cooper River, the longest cable-stayed bridge in the Western Hemisphere.

Tennis

Tennis fans are in for a treat at the **Family Circle Tennis Center** (161 Seven Farms Dr., 800/677-2293, www.volvocaropen.com, Mon.-Thurs. 8am-8pm, Fri. 8am-7pm, Sat. 8am-5pm, Sun. 9am-5pm, $15/hour) on Daniel Island. This multimillion-dollar facility is owned by the city of Charleston and was built in 2001 specifically to host the annual Family Circle Cup women's competition, which is now known as the Volvo Car Open. But it's also open to the public year-round (except when the Volvo Car Open is on) with 17 courts.

The best resort tennis activity is at the **Kiawah Island Golf Resort** (12 Kiawah Beach Dr., Kiawah Island, 800/654-2924, www.kiawahresort.com, $44 per hour for nonguests). The resort's Roy Barth Tennis Center has nine clay and three hard courts, while the West Beach Tennis Club has 10 Har-Tru courts and 2 lighted hard courts.

There are four free, public, city-funded facilities on the peninsula: **Moultrie Playground** (Broad St. and Ashley Ave., 843/769-8258, www.charlestoncity.info, six lighted hard courts), **Jack Adams Tennis Center** (290 Congress St., six lighted hard courts), **Hazel Parker Playground** (70 E. Bay St., on the Cooper River, one hard court),

and **Corrine Jones Playground** (Marlowe St. and Peachtree St., two hard courts).

Bird-Watching

Right in Charleston Harbor is the little **Crab Bank Seabird Sanctuary** (803/734-3886, www.dnr.sc.gov, Oct. 16-Mar. 14 daily dawn-dusk), where thousands of migratory birds can be seen, depending on the season. The sanctuary has been designated an Important Bird Area by Audubon. Mid-October-mid-March you can either kayak there yourself or take a charter with **Nature Adventures Outfitters** (1900 Iron Swamp Rd., Awendaw Island, 800/673-0679). During nesting season, mid-March-mid-October, the sanctuary is closed to the public.

On Johns Island southwest of Charleston is **Legare Farms** (2620 Hanscombe Point Rd., Johns Island, 843/559-0788, www.legare-farms.com, farm hours vary), which holds migratory bird walks ($6 adults, $3 children) in the fall each Saturday at 8:30am.

Once part of a rice plantation, the **I'on Swamp Trail** (15 miles northeast of Charleston via U.S. 17, 843/928-3368, www.fs.fed.us, daily dawn-dusk, free) is one of the premier bird-watching sites in South Carolina, particularly during spring and fall migrations. The rare Bachman's warbler, commonly considered one of the most elusive birds in North America, has been seen here. To get here, make the 10-minute drive to Mount Pleasant, then head north on U.S. 17 and take a left onto I'on Swamp Road (Forest Service Rd. 228). The parking area is 2.5 miles ahead on the left.

Ice-Skating

Ice-skating in South Carolina? Yep, 100,000 square feet of it, year-round at the two NHL-size rinks of the **Carolina Ice Palace** (7665 Northwoods Blvd., North Charleston, 843/572-2717, www.carolinaicepalace.com, daily public sessions, $7 adults, $6 children). This is also the practice facility for the local hockey team, the Stingrays, as well as where the Citadel's hockey team plays.

SPECTATOR SPORTS

A New York Yankees Class A affiliate in the South Atlantic League, the **Charleston River Dogs** play April-August at **Joseph P. Riley Jr. Park** (360 Fishburne St., 843/577-3647, www.riverdogs.com, $8-11 general admission), aka "the Joe." There are a lot of fun promotions to keep things interesting should the play on the field be less than stimulating. Expect to pay $5 for parking.

The professional USL Pro soccer team **Charleston Battery** plays April-July at **MUSC Health Stadium** (MUSC Health Stadium, 1990 Daniel Island Dr., 843/971-4625, www.charlestonbattery.com, about $10) on Daniel Island, north of Charleston.

An ECHL professional hockey team, the **South Carolina Stingrays** get a good crowd out to their rink at the **North Charleston Coliseum** (5001 Coliseum Dr., 843/744-2248, www.stingrayshockey.com, $15), playing October-April.

The Citadel (171 Moultrie St., 843/953-3294, www.citadelsports.com, ticket prices vary) plays Southern Conference football home games at **Johnson Hagood Stadium,** next to the campus on the Ashley River near Hampton Park. The basketball team plays home games at **McAlister Field House** on campus. The school's ice hockey team has its home games at the **Carolina Ice Palace** (7665 Northwoods Blvd., North Charleston).

Food

Charleston's long history of good taste and livability combines with an affluent and sophisticated population to attract some of the brightest chefs and restaurateurs in the country. A long list of James Beard Award nominees each year confirms the city's role as perhaps the preeminent hub of culinary excellence in the American South.

Kitchens here eschew fickle trends, instead emphasizing quality, professionalism, and, most of all, freshness of ingredients. The farm-to-table movement is as strong here as anywhere in the country and drives the menus of most of the premier establishments.

If you come here in the first week or two of the New Year, keep in mind that is usually the time when Charleston's more popular restaurants might close briefly for renovations.

WATERFRONT
New Southern

Few restaurants in Charleston have inspired such impassioned advocates as legendary chef Sean Brock's flagship restaurant, ★ **McCrady's** (2 Unity Alley and 155 Bay St., www.mccradysrestaurant.com, Wed.-Thurs. and Sun. 7pm seating, Fri.-Sat. seatings at 6:30pm and 8:45pm, $125 pp, $85 pp wine pairing). In the restaurant's early days, Brock's then-groundbreaking sous vide (or vacuum cooking technique) was spoken of in reverent tones by his clientele. In an expansion and reimagining, Brock moved the original McCrady's to a spot right next door, where it continues to offer the sophisticated, almost frighteningly delicious tasting-menu experience for which it is renowned. Brock repurposed the former McCrady's space as **McCrady's Tavern,** a return to the original use of the building as a watering hole and community gathering spot back in the 1770s. In a nod to a more egalitarian dining experience, the tavern has a more casual New Southern menu. Either spot is a core stop of any Charleston foodie pilgrimage.

Magnolias (185 E. Bay St., 843/577-7771, www.magnoliascharleston.com, Mon.-Sat. 11:30am-10pm, Sun. 3:45pm-10pm, $25-35) began life as one of Charleston's first serious eating spots. While the interior has since been given a warm renovation, the menu remains as attractive as ever, with a delightful take on Southern classics like the lump crab cakes, the shellfish over grits, and the rainbow trout. The appetizers are particularly strong—start with the famous fried green tomatoes or maybe the boiled peanut hummus.

Slightly North of Broad (192 E. Bay St., 843/723-3424, www.snobcharleston.com, daily 11:30am-2:30pm and 5pm-10pm, $25-35), or "SNOB," is an ironic play on the often pejorative reference to the insular South of Broad neighborhood. This hot spot, routinely voted best restaurant in town in such contests, is anything but snobby. Hopping with happy foodies for lunch and dinner, the fun is enhanced by the long, open kitchen with its own counter area. The dynamic but comforting menu here is practically a bible of the new wave of Lowcountry cuisine, with dishes like beef tenderloin, jumbo lump crab cakes, grilled barbecue tuna—and, of course, the pan-seared flounder. An interesting twist at SNOB is the selection of "medium plates," dishes that are a little more generous than an appetizer but with the same adventurous spirit.

For many visitors to Charleston, there comes a point when they just get tired of stuffing themselves with seafood. If you find yourself in that situation, the perfect antidote is **High Cotton** (199 E. Bay St., 843/724-3815, www.mavericksouthernkitchens.com, Mon.-Thurs. 5:30pm-10pm, Fri. 5:30pm-11pm, Sat. 11:30am-2:30pm and 5:30pm-11pm, Sun. 10am-2pm and 5:30pm-10pm, $35-45), a meat lover's paradise offering some of the best steaks in town as well as a creative menu of assorted lamb and pork dishes. Chef Anthony Gray places heavy emphasis on using fresh local ingredients, both veggies and game, and the rotating menu always reflects that. None of this comes particularly cheap, but splurges rarely do. In the woody (and popular) bar area there's usually a solo live pianist or sax player after 6pm.

NORTH OF BROAD
Classic Southern

Executive chef Sean Brock of McCrady's fame already had a reputation as one of the country's leading purveyors of the farm-to-table fine-dining movement, but he cemented that reputation with **Husk** (76 Queen St., 843/577-2500, www.huskrestaurant.com, Mon.-Thurs. 11:30am-2pm and 5:30pm-10pm, Fri.-Sat. 11:30am-2pm and 5:30pm-11pm, Sun. 10am-2:30pm and 5:30pm-10pm, $25-35), voted "Best New Restaurant in the U.S." by *Bon Appétit* magazine soon after its 2011 opening. Brock says of his ingredients, "If it doesn't come from the South, it's not coming through the door." The spare, focused menu is constantly changing with the seasons. On a recent lunch visit my party enjoyed two types of catfish (a fried catfish BLT on Texas toast and a lightly cornmeal-dusted broiled catfish with local vegetables), Husk's signature cheeseburger, and—wait for it—lamb barbecue. Reservations are strongly recommended.

In business for over 40 years now, **Poogan's Porch** (72 Queen St., 843/577-2337, www.poogansporch.com, Mon.-Fri. 11:30am-2:30pm and 5pm-9:30pm, Sat.-Sun. 9am-3pm and 5pm-9:30pm, $25-30) is the prototype of a classic Charleston restaurant: lovingly restored old home, professional but unpretentious service, great fried green tomatoes, and rich, calorie-laden Lowcountry classics like crab cakes and shrimp and grits. Brunch is the big thing here, a bustling affair with ample portions, Bloody Marys, mimosas, and soft sunlight.

Walk through the gaslit courtyard of the Planter's Inn at Market and Meeting Streets into the intimate dining room of the ★ **Peninsula Grill** (112 N. Market St., 843/723-0700, www.peninsulagrill.com, daily from 5:30pm, $35-50) and begin an epicurean journey you'll not soon forget. Peninsula Grill might be Charleston's quintessential purveyor of high-style Lowcountry cuisine. You'll want to start with the sampler trio of soups and finish with the legendary coconut cake. Reservations are strongly recommended.

Follow Rachael Ray's lead and wait in the long lines outside **Jestine's Kitchen** (251 Meeting St., 843/722-7224, Tues.-Thurs. 11am-9:30pm, Fri.-Sat. 11am-10pm, $15-20) to enjoy a simple Southern take on such meat-and-three comfort food classics as meat loaf, pecan-fried fish, and fried green tomatoes. Most of the recipes are handed down from the restaurant's namesake, Jestine Matthews, the African American woman who raised owner Dana Berlin.

New Southern

Cru Café (18 Pinckney St., 843/534-2434, www.crucafe.com, Tues.-Thurs. 11am-3pm and 5pm-10pm, Fri.-Sat. 11am-3pm and 5pm-11pm, $20-30) boasts an adventurous menu within a traditional-looking Charleston single house just around the corner from the main stable for the city's carriage tours, with a choice of interior or exterior seating. Sample entrées include poblano and mozzarella fried chicken and seared maple leaf duck breast.

The intimate bistro and stylish bar ★ **FIG** (232 Meeting St., 843/805-5900, www.eatatfig.com, Mon.-Thurs. 6pm-11pm, Fri.-Sat. 6pm-midnight, $30-35) has a passion for fresh, simple ingredients. FIG—short for "Food Is Good"—attracts young professional scenesters as well as die-hard foodies. Chef Mike Lata won James Beard's Best Chef of the Southeast award in 2009. FIG is one of Charleston's great champions of the Sustainable Seafood Initiative, and the kitchen staff strives to work as closely as possible with local farmers and anglers in determining its seasonal menu.

Inside the plush Charleston Place Hotel you'll find **Charleston Grill** (224 King St., 843/577-4522, www.charlestongrill.com, dinner daily from 6pm, $30-60), one of the city's favorite (and priciest) fine-dining spots for locals and visitors alike. The menu specializes in French-influenced Lowcountry cuisine, with dishes like the niçoise vegetable tart. There are a lot of great fusion dishes as well, such as the tuna and *hamachi* sashimi topped with pomegranate molasses and lemongrass oil. Reservations are a must.

Focusing on purely seasonal offerings that never stay on the menu longer than three months, ★ **Circa 1886** (149 Wentworth St., 843/853-7828, www.circa1886.com,

Mon.-Sat. 5:30pm-9:30pm, $30-35) combines the best old-world tradition of Charleston with the vibrancy of its more adventurous kitchens. The restaurant—surprisingly little known despite its four-star Mobil rating—is located in the former carriage house of the grand Wentworth Mansion B&B just west of the main College of Charleston campus. The menu has featured such entrées as robust beef au poivre and shrimp-and-crab-stuffed flounder. Be sure to check the daily prix fixe offerings; they can be a great deal.

Coffee, Tea, and Sweets

Considered the best coffeehouse in town, **Black Tap Coffee** (70½ Beaufain St., 843/793-4402, Mon.-Fri. 7am-7pm, Sat.-Sun. 8am-6pm) features an array of Counter Culture beans roasted and served to perfection by skilled baristas. Cold brew and pour-over cups are specialties of the house, as is their signature Lavender Latte. It's smallish and a bit off the beaten King Street path but still well within walking distance of that shopping thoroughfare.

If you find yourself needing a quick pick-me-up while shopping on King Street, avoid the lines at the two Starbucks locations on the avenue and instead turn east on Market Street and duck inside **City Lights Coffeehouse** (141 Market St., 843/853-7067, Mon.-Thurs. 7am-9pm, Fri.-Sat. 7am-10pm, Sun. 8am-6pm). The sweet goodies are delectable in this cozy little Euro-style place, and the Counter Culture organic coffee is to die for. If you're lucky, they'll have some of their Ethiopian Sidamo brewed.

Routinely voted as having the best desserts in the city, the cakes alone at **Kaminsky's** (78 N. Market St., 843/853-8270, daily noon-2am) are worth the trip to the City Market area. The fresh fruit torte, the red velvet, and the "Mountain of Chocolate" are the three best sellers.

French

On the north side of Broad Street you'll find **Gaulart & Maliclet** (98 Broad St.,

843/577-9797, www.fastandfrenchcharleston.com, Mon. 8am-4pm, Tues.-Thurs. 8am-10pm, Fri.-Sat. 8am-10:30pm, $20-25), subtitled "Fast and French." This is a gourmet bistro with a strong takeout component. Prices are especially reasonable for this area of town, with great lunch specials under $10, Thursday night Fondue for Two specials at about $20, and breakfast all day.

Queen Street Grocery (133 Queen St., 843/723-4121, www.queenstreetgrocerycafe.com, kitchen Mon.-Sat. 10am-5pm, Sun. 11am-3pm, $10, store Mon.-Sat. 8am-8:30pm) is the kind of place frequented almost exclusively by locals. At this corner store you can load up on some of the tastiest made-to-order crepes this side of France—as well as light groceries, beer, wine, and cigarettes.

Mediterranean

The cuisine of northern Italy comes alive in the bustling, dimly lit room of **Fulton Five** (5 Fulton St., 843/853-5555, www.fulton-five.com, Mon.-Sat. 5:30pm-close, $30-40), from the *insalata de funghi* to the sublime risotto. It's not cheap, and the portions aren't necessarily the largest, but with these tasty, non-tomato-based dishes and this romantic, gusto-filled atmosphere, you'll be satiated with life itself.

Seafood

Hyman's Seafood (215 Meeting St., 843/723-6000, www.hymanseafood.com, Mon.-Thurs. 11am-9pm, Fri.-Sun. 11am-11pm, $20-40) is thought by many locals to border on a tourist trap, and it's mostly tourists who line up for hours to get in. To keep things manageable, Hyman's offers the same menu and prices for both lunch and dinner. After asking for some complimentary fresh boiled peanuts in lieu of bread, start with the Carolina Delight, a delicious appetizer (also available as an entrée) involving a lightly fried cake of grits topped with your choice of delectable seafood, or maybe a half-dozen oysters from the Half Shell oyster bar. Definitely try the she-crab soup, one of the best you'll find anywhere. As for entrées, the ubiquitous Lowcountry crispy scored flounder is always a good bet.

UPPER KING
Classic Southern

One of a comparatively few great Charleston restaurants with an equally expert focus on breakfast as on the other meals, **Virginia's on King** (412 King St., 912/735-5800, www.holycityhospitality.com, Mon.-Fri. 7am-10pm, Sat. 8am-10pm, Sun. 10am-3pm, $15-25) is a great place to enjoy Southern classics like fried green tomatoes, tomato pie, and their signature she-crab soup. The salmon BLT lunch dish (or in their old Southern parlance, "dinner," with "supper" being the name of the last meal of the day) is one of the best seafood dishes I've had anywhere. As for breakfast, the omelets are solid and most of the lunch menu is also available.

Rapidly gaining a reputation as one of the best brunch scenes in town, **The Macintosh** (479 King St., 843/789-4299, www.themacintoshcharleston.com, Mon.-Sat. 6:30am-7pm, Sun. 9am-6pm, $25-40) combines the best of Charleston's Classic/New South style with a gastropub sensibility, complete with an extensive craft beer menu. The chef is three-time James Beard semifinalist Jeremiah Bacon, which means you can't really go wrong. But for brunch I'd suggest the baked chorizo, and from the small but artfully curated dinner menu, any seafood dish is good. Happy hour (Mon.-Fri. 5pm-7pm) is also a big draw here, with its own special $5 small-plate bar food menu.

American

Charleston's fave rave is ★ **Edmund's Oast** (1081 Morrison Dr., 843/727-1145, www.edmundsoast.com, Mon.-Thurs. 5:30pm-10pm, Fri.-Sat. 5:30pm-11pm, Sun. 10am-2:30pm and 5:30pm-10pm, $25-40), a boisterous beer garden/brewpub on the Upper Peninsula, boasting a 40-tap array, several brews made

Lowcountry Locavores

Charleston has merged its own indigenous and abiding culinary tradition with the "new" idea that you should grow your food as naturally as possible and purchase it as close to home as you can. From bacon and snapper to sweet potatoes, the typical Charleston dish of today harkens back to its soulful Southern roots, before the days of factory food.

Spurred in part by an influx of trained chefs after the establishment of the Spoleto Festival in the 1970s, the locavore movement in Charleston came from the efforts of epicureans committed to sustainability and the principles of community-supported agriculture (CSA). Spearheaded by visionaries like the James Beard Award-winning Mike Lata of the bistro FIG and Sean Brock of Mc-Crady's, sustainable food initiatives have sprung up in Charleston and the Lowcountry, such as the South Carolina Aquarium's Sustainable Seafood Initiative (http://scaquarium.org), partnering with local restaurants to ensure a sustainable wild-caught harvest; Certified South Carolina (www.certifiedsc.com), guaranteeing that the food you eat was grown in the Palmetto State; and a local chapter of the Slow Food Movement (http://slowfoodcharleston.org).

The list of Holy City restaurants relying almost exclusively on local and sustainable sources is long, but here are a few notable examples:

- **Husk** (76 Queen St., 843/577-2500, www.huskrestaurant.com)
- **Charleston Grill** (224 King St., 843/577-4522, www.charlestongrill.com)
- **FIG** (232 Meeting St., 843/805-5900, www.eatatfig.com)
- **Al Di La** (25 Magnolia Rd., 843/571-2321, www.aldilarestaurant.com)
- **Queen Street Grocery** (133 Queen St., 843/723-4121, www.queenstreetgrocerycafe.com)
- **Middleton Place Restaurant** (4300 Ashley River Rd., 843/556-6020, www.middleton-place.org)
- **Circa 1886** (149 Wentworth St., 843/853-7828, www.circa1886.com)
- **COAST Bar and Grill** (39D John St., 843/722-8838, www.coastbarandgrill.com)
- **Cru Café** (18 Pinckney St., 843/534-2434, www.crucafe.com)
- **Hominy Grill** (207 Rutledge Ave., 912/937-0930, www.hominygrill.com)
- **Peninsula Grill** (112 N. Market St., 843/723-0700, www.peninsulagrill.com)

on-site, and, perhaps surprisingly, an excellent cocktail menu. The small plates, though, might be what stay with you. Expressive, excellent charcuterie and pitch-perfect sliders are the highlights. If you sit at the bar, the $4 per plate happy hour items (4:30pm-6:30pm) are a must-try; I suggest the smoked wings.

Asian

There's usually a long wait to get a table at the great Thai place **Basil** (460 King St., 843/724-3490, www.basilthairestaurant.com, Mon.-Thurs. 11:30am-2:30pm and 5pm-10:30pm, Fri.-Sat. 5pm-11pm, Sun. 5pm-10pm, $15-20) on Upper King, since they don't take reservations. But Basil also has one of the hippest, most happening bar scenes in the area, so you won't necessarily mind. Revelers enjoy fresh, succulent takes on Thai classics like cashew chicken and pad thai. The signature dish is the basil duck.

Barbecue

The Downtown/Upper Peninsula outpost of Charleston's favorite barbecue chain, **Fiery Ron's Home Team BBQ** (126 Williman St.,

843/225-7427, www.hometeambbq.com, daily 11am-10pm, $10-20), boasts a bit of an upscale feel from the original West Ashley location and the Sullivan's Island version. But don't be deceived by the excellent artisanal cocktail menu; the barbecue here is just as good.

Coffee, Tea, and Sweets

One of the best java joints in Charleston is **Kudu Coffee** (4 Vanderhorst St., 843/853-7186, Mon.-Sat. 6:30am-7pm, Sun. 9am-6pm). A kudu is an African antelope, and the Africa theme extends to the beans, which all have an African pedigree. Poetry readings and occasional live music add to the mix. A lot of green-friendly, left-of-center community activism goes on here as well.

French

The best mussels I've ever had were at ★ **39 Rue de Jean** (39 John St., 843/722-8881, www.holycityhospitality.com, Mon.-Thurs. 11:30am-11pm, Fri.-Sat. 11:30am-1am, Sun. 10am 11pm, $20-30). But anything off the bistro-style menu is unbelievably tasty, from the foie gras to the confit to the coq au vin to the steak frites. There are incredible Prohibition-style cocktails to go along with the extensive wine list.

Italian

One of Upper King's "it" restaurants, **Indaco** (525 King St., 843/727-1218, www.indaco-charleston.com, Sun.-Thurs. 5pm-10pm, Fri.-Sat. 5pm-midnight, $15-25) features a small but well-curated menu of antipasti, custom wood-fired gourmet pizzas, and delicious Italian specialties like black pepper tagliatelle. Yes, there's brussels sprout pizza, and it's quite delicious! Indaco is set in a stylish, bustling restored warehouse.

Mexican

The quesadillas at **Juanita Greenberg's Nacho Royale** (439 King St., 843/723-6224, www.juanitagreenbergs.com, daily 11am-11pm, $10-15) are perfectly packed with jack cheese, spicy sausage, and a delightful *pico de gallo*. This modest Mexican joint caters primarily to a college crowd, as you can tell from the reasonable prices, the large patio out back, the extensive tequila list, and the bar that stays open until 2am on weekends.

Seafood

Near 39 Rue de Jean you'll find the affiliated **COAST Bar and Grill** (39D John St., 843/722-8838, www.coastbarandgrill.com, daily 5:30pm-close, $20-25), which makes the most of its loud, hip setting in a former warehouse. The raw bar is satisfying, with a particularly nice selection of ceviche. COAST is a strong local advocate of the Sustainable Seafood Initiative, whereby restaurants work directly with the local fishing industry.

HAMPTON PARK

Classic Southern

With a motto like "Grits are good for you," you know what you're in store for at **Hominy Grill** (207 Rutledge Ave., 912/937-0930, www.hominygrill.com, Mon.-Fri. 7:30am-8:30pm, Sat.-Sun. 9am-8:30pm, $15-20), set in a renovated barbershop at Rutledge Avenue and Cannon Street near the Medical University of South Carolina. Primarily revered for his Sunday brunch, chef Robert Stehling has fun—almost mischievously so—breathing new life into American and Southern classics. Because this is largely a locals' place, you can impress your friends back home by saying you had the rare pleasure of the Hominy's sautéed shad roe with bacon and mushrooms—when the shad are running, that is.

Moe's Crosstown Tavern (714 Rutledge Ave., 843/722-3287, Mon.-Sat. 11am-midnight, bar until 2am, $10-15) is not only one of the classic Southern dives, but also has one of the best kitchens on this side of town, known for hand-cut fries, great wings, and, most of all, excellent burgers. On Tuesdays, the burgers are half price at happy hour—one of Charleston's best deals.

Italian

A rave of Charleston foodies is the

Tuscan-inspired fare of chef Ken Vedrinski at **Trattoria Lucca** (41 Bogard St., 843/973-3323, www.luccacharleston.com, Mon.-Sat. 6pm-10pm, $25-30). The menu is simple but perfectly focused, featuring handmade pasta and signature items like the pork chop or the fresh cheese plate. You'll be surprised at how much food your money gets you here. Monday evenings see a family-style prix fixe communal dinner.

WEST ASHLEY
Classic Southern
Tucked away on the grounds of the Middleton Place Plantation is the romantic **Middleton Place Restaurant** (4300 Ashley River Rd., 843/556-6020, www.middletonplace.org, Tues.-Thurs. and Sun. 11am-3pm and 6pm-8pm, Fri.-Sat. 11am-3pm and 6pm-9pm, $25-30). Theirs is a respectful take on traditional plantation fare like hoppin' John, gumbo, she-crab soup, and collards. The special annual Thanksgiving buffet is a real treat. Reservations are required for dinner. A nice plus is being able to wander the gorgeous landscaped gardens before dusk if you arrive at 5:30pm or later with a dinner reservation.

New Southern
One of the more unassuming advocates of farm-to-table dining, ★ **The Glass Onion** (1219 Savannah Hwy., 843/225-1717, www.ilovetheglassonion.com, Mon.-Thurs. 11am-9pm, Fri. 11am-10pm, Sat. 10am-3pm and 4pm-10pm, $20-30) is in an equally unassuming location on U.S. 17 (Savannah Hwy.) on the western approach to town. That said, their food is right in the thick of the sustainable food movement and is incredibly tasty to boot (not to mention that there is more parking there than there is downtown). The interior says "diner," and indeed the emphasis here is on Southern soul and comfort-food classics. The Glass Onion also boasts a good variety of specialty craft brews to wash it all down. Another plus: In this town full of Sunday brunches, Glass Onion's specialty is a Saturday brunch!

American
Gene's Haufbrau (17 Savannah Hwy., 843/225-4363, www.genes-haufbrau.com, daily 11:30am-2am, $10) is worth making a special trip into West Ashley. Claiming to be the oldest bar in continuous operation in town (1952), Gene's complements its fairly typical bar-food menu with some good wraps. Start with the "Drunken Trio" (beer-battered cheese sticks, mushrooms, and onion rings) and follow with a portobello wrap or a good old-fashioned crawfish po'boy. One of the best meals in town for the money is Gene's $8.50 blue plate special, a rotating comfort food entrée like country-fried steak or pot roast, offered Monday-Friday 11:30am-4pm. The late-night kitchen hours, until 1am, are a big plus.

If you're any kind of fan of fried chicken, whether good old-fashioned Southern fried or the type of sandwich you might get at Chick-fil-A, you will want to check out **Boxcar Betty's** (1922 Savannah Hwy., 843/225-7470, www.boxcarbetty.com, daily 11am-9pm, $10). Be warned, these juicy, incredibly tasty flour-breaded fried chicken sandwiches are addictive.

Barbecue
My favorite barbecue joint, the rowdy and always hopping ★ **Fiery Ron's Home Team BBQ** (1205 Ashley River Rd., 843/225-7427, www.hometeambbq.com, Mon.-Sat. 11am-9pm, Sun. 11:30am-9pm, $10-20) has pulled pork and ribs that rank with the best I've had anywhere in the country. Even the sides are amazing here, including perfect collards and tasty mac and cheese. Pitmaster Madison Ruckel provides an array of tableside sauces, including hot sauce, indigenous South Carolina mustard sauce, and his own "Alabama white," a light and delicious mayonnaise-based sauce. As if that weren't enough, the owners' close ties to the regional jam-band community mean there's great live blues and indie rock after 10pm most nights (Thursday is bluegrass night) to spice up the bar action, which goes until 2am.

Fiery Ron's Home Team BBQ is one of the state's best.

Mediterranean

Anything on this northern Italian-themed menu is good, but the risotto—a legacy of original chef John Marshall—is the specialty dish at **Al Di La** (25 Magnolia Rd., 843/571 2321, www.aldilarestaurant.com, Tues.-Sat. 6pm-10pm, $15-20), a very popular West Ashley fine-dining spot. Reservations are recommended.

NORTH CHARLESTON
Pizza

If you have a hankering for pizza in North Charleston, don't miss **EVO Pizzeria** (1075 E. Montague Ave., 843/225-1796, www.evo-pizza.com, Tues.-Fri. 11am-2:30pm and 5pm-10pm, Sat. 6pm-10pm, $15) in the Olde North Charleston area at Park Circle. They specialize in a small but rich menu of unusual gourmet pizza toppings, like pistachio pesto.

SUMMERVILLE
American

For a down-home-style pancakes-and-sandwich place that's popular with the locals at all hours of the day, try **Alex's Restaurant** (120 E. 5th N. St., 843/871-3202, daily 24 hours, $10).

A popular local landmark is **Guerin's Pharmacy** (140 S. Main St., 843/873-2531, Mon.-Fri. 9am-6pm, Sat. 9am-5pm, $5), which claims to be the state's oldest pharmacy. Complete with an old-fashioned soda fountain, they offer malted milk shakes and lemonade.

MOUNT PLEASANT AND EAST COOPER

In Mount Pleasant, most of the restaurant action centers on the picturesque shrimping village of Shem Creek, which is dotted on both banks with bars and restaurants, most dealing in fresh local seafood. As with Murrells Inlet up the coast, some spots on Shem Creek border on tourist traps. Don't be afraid to go where the lines aren't.

American

For a burger and an adult beverage or two, go straight to friendly **Poe's Tavern** (2210 Middle St., Sullivan's Island, 843/883-0083, www.poestavern.com, daily 11am-2am, kitchen until 10pm, $10-15), a nod to Edgar Allan Poe's stint at nearby Fort Moultrie.

Seafood

At the **Red Drum Gastropub** (803 Coleman Blvd., 843/849-0313, www.reddrumrestaurant.com, daily 5:30pm-10pm, lunch/brunch

To Market, to Market

A fun and favorite local fixture April-mid-December, the **Charleston Farmers Market** (843/724-7309, www.charlestoncity.info, Sat. 8am-2pm) rings beautiful Marion Square with stalls of local produce, street eats, local arts and crafts, and kids' activities.

Running April-October, East Cooper has its own version in the **Mount Pleasant Farmers Market** (843/884-8517, http://townofmountpleasant.com, Tues. 3pm-dark) at the Moultrie Middle School on Coleman Boulevard.

Sat.-Sun. 10:30am-2pm, $20-40), the food is just as important as the drink. While you're likely to need reservations for the dining room, where you can enjoy Lowcountry-Tex-Mex fusion-style cuisine with a typically Mount Pleasant-like emphasis on seafood, the bar scene is very hopping and fun, with live music every Wednesday-Thursday night.

A must-stop roadside diner in the Awendaw area is ★ **See Wee Restaurant** (4808 U.S. 17 N., 843/928-3609, Mon.-Thurs. 11am-8:30pm, Fri.-Sat. 11am-9:30pm, Sun. 11am-8pm, $15-25), about 20 minutes north of Charleston by car. Housed in a humble former general store on the west side of U.S. 17 (the restrooms are still outside), this diner draws folks from far and wide to enjoy signature menu items like the grouper and the unreal she-crab soup, considered by some epicures to be the best in the world. You can't miss with any of their seafood entrées. Occasionally the crowds can get thick, but rest assured it's worth any wait.

A popular spot, especially for the younger crowd, **Vickery's Shem Creek Bar and Grill** (1313 Shrimp Boat Ln., 843/884-4440, daily 11:30am-1am, $15-20) has a similar menu to its partner location on the peninsula, but this Vickery's has the pleasant added bonus of a beautiful view overlooking the creek. You'll get more of the Vickery's Cuban flair here, with a great black bean soup and an awesome Cuban sandwich.

A well-regarded spot on Shem Creek is **Water's Edge** (1407 Shrimp Boat Ln., 843/884-4074, daily 11am-11pm, $20-35), which consistently takes home a *Wine*

Spectator Award of Excellence for its great selection of vintages. Native Charlestonian Jimmy Purcell concentrates on fresh seafood with a slightly more upscale flair than many Shem Creek places.

Vegetarian

For a real change of pace, try **The Sprout Cafe** (629 Johnnie Dodds Blvd., 843/849-8554, www.thehealthysprout.com, Mon.-Fri. 6am-8pm, Sat. 9am-3pm, Sun. 11am-3pm, $10) on U.S. 17. Dealing totally in raw foods, the restaurant emphasizes healthy and fresh ingredients. You might be surprised at the inventiveness of their breakfast-through-dinner seasonal menu, which might include a tasty crepe topped with a pear-and-nut puree and maple syrup, or a raw squash and zucchini "pasta" dish topped with walnut "meatballs."

FOLLY BEACH AND THE SOUTHWEST ISLANDS

American

Three words: duck fat fries. The **Tattooed Moose** (3328 Maybank Hwy., 843/277-2990, www.tattooedmoose.com, daily 11:30am-1am, $10-15) is a dive bar sensation on Johns Island, combining classic bar food with a typically Charlestonian touch of Old South culinary bravado. While the fries—served straight up with roasted garlic and blue cheese or with gravy—are the signature menu item, the sandwiches are simply fantastic. Try the duck confit sandwich or the pork belly sandwich. Brunch is becoming huge here, too, and live music is featured most nights.

Barbecue

If barbecue is your thing, head straight to **JB's Smokeshack** (3406 Maybank Hwy., 843/557-0426, www.jbssmokeshack.com, Wed.-Sat. 11am-8:30pm, $8-18), considered one of the better 'cue joints in the Lowcountry. True connoisseurs will tell you it's the chicken that's really awesome, however. JB's offers a buffet for $8.88 per person ($5 under age 11), or you can opt for a barbecue plate, including hash, rice, and two sides. In a nice twist, the plates include a three-meat option: pork, chicken, ribs, or brisket.

Breakfast and Brunch

The closest thing to a taste of old Folly is the **Lost Dog Café** (106 W. Huron Ave., 843/588-9669, daily 6:30am-3pm, $10-15), so named for its bulletin board stacked with alerts about lost pets, pets for adoption, and new pups and kittens for sale or giveaway. It opens early to offer a tasty, healthy breakfast to the surfing crowd. It's a great place to pick up a quick, inexpensive, and tasty meal while you're near the beach.

For a hearty and delicious breakfast, go to **Sunrise Bistro** (1797 Main Rd., 843/718-1858, www.sunrise-bistro.com, Tues.-Thurs. 7am-2:30pm, Fri.-Sat. 7am-2:30pm and 5pm-9pm, Sun. 9am-1pm, $10-15), one of those unassuming diners that always seems to have an eager crowd. Everything, from the omelets to the pancakes down to the simplest bagel with coffee, is spot-on, and a great value to boot. The best offerings here are during the day.

French

★ **Fat Hen** (3140 Maybank Hwy., 843/559-9090, Tues.-Sat. 11:30am-3pm and 5:30pm-10pm, Sun. 10am-3pm, $20-40) is a self-styled "country French bistro" begun by a couple of old Charleston restaurant hands. The fried oysters are a particular specialty. There's also a bar menu (4pm-10pm).

Mexican

Taco Boy (15 Center St., 843/588-9761, Sun.-Thurs. 11am-10pm, Fri.-Sat. 11am-11pm, $10) is a fun place to get a fish taco, have a margarita, and take a walk on the nearby beach afterward. Though no one is under any illusions that this is an authentic Mexican restaurant, the fresh guacamole is particularly rave-worthy, and there's a good selection of tequilas and beers *hecho en México,* with the bar staying open until 2am on weekends.

Seafood

Set within the trendy Tides Folly Beach boutique hotel, **Blu** (1 Center St., 843/588-6658, www.blufollybeach.com, breakfast daily 7am-11am, lunch daily 11am-5pm, dinner Sun.-Thurs. 5pm-9pm, Fri.-Sat. 5pm-10pm, $15-30) offers an equally high standard of food and decor, along with some amazing views of the ocean. The menu isn't particularly pretentious, but it does offer high-quality Sustainable Seafood Initiative options, all of which are recommended.

Fans of the legendary **Bowens Island Restaurant** (1870 Bowens Island Rd., 843/795-2757, Tues.-Sat. 5pm-10pm, $15-20, cash only) on James Island went into mourning when it burned to the ground in 2006. But you can't keep a good oysterman down, and owner Robert Barber rebuilt. A universe removed from the Lexus-and-khaki scene downtown, Bowens Island isn't the place for the uptight. This is the spot to go when you want shovels of oysters literally thrown onto your table, freshly steamed and delicious and all-you-can-eat.

To get to Bowens Island from the peninsula, take Calhoun Street west onto the James Island Connector (Hwy. 30). Take exit 3 onto Highway 171 south and look for Bowens Island Road on the right. The restaurant will be on the left in a short while, after passing by several ritzy McMansions that in no way resemble the restaurant you're about to experience.

Accommodations

Due to the city's long-standing tradition of hospitality and the high standards it has set for itself, hotels and bed-and-breakfasts are generally well maintained and have a high level of service.

The price differential is not that much between the peninsula and the outskirts. You'll pay more to stay in the tourist areas, but not *that* much more, with the bonus of being able to walk to most places you want to see. The farther south you go on the peninsula, the quieter and more affluent it tends to be. Folks looking for a more wild and woolly good time will be drawn to the Upper King area farther north.

SOUTH OF BROAD
$150-300

On the south side of Broad Street is a great old Charleston lodging, **Governor's House Inn** (117 Broad St., 843/720-2070, www.governorshouse.com, $200-350). This circa-1760 building, a National Historic Landmark, is associated with Edward Rutledge, signer of the Declaration of Independence. Though most of its 11 guest rooms—all with four-poster beds, period furnishings, and high ceilings—go for around $300, some of the smaller guest rooms can be had for closer to $200 in the off-season.

The nine guest rooms of ★ **Two Meeting Street Inn** (2 Meeting St., 843/723-7322, www.twomeetingstreet.com, $200-450) down by the Battery are individually appointed, with themes like "the Music Room" and the "the Spell Room." The decor in this 1892 Queen Anne bed-and-breakfast is very traditional, with lots of floral patterns and hunt club-style pieces and artwork. It's considered by many to be the most romantic lodging in town, and you won't soon forget the experience of sitting on the veranda enjoying the sights, sounds, and breezes. Three of the guest rooms—the Canton, Granite, and Roberts—can be had for not much over $200.

WATERFRONT
$150-300

The guest rooms and the thoroughly hospitable service are the focus at nearby ★ **The Vendue** (19 Vendue Range, 800/845-7900, www.thevendue.com, $250-450). All guest rooms are sumptuously appointed in boutique style, with lots of warm, rich fabrics, unique pieces, and high-end bath amenities. That said, the public spaces are cool as well, with a focus on featuring quality art that essentially turns the property into one huge exhibition space. The inn gets a lot of traffic in the evenings because of the popular and hopping Rooftop Bar, which has amazing views.

Over $300

About as close to the Cooper River as a hotel gets, the **Harbourview Inn** (2 Vendue Range, 843/853-8439, www.harbourviewcharleston.com, $300-500) comprises a "historic wing" and a larger, newer, but still tastefully done main building. For the best of those eponymous harbor views, try to get a room on the 3rd floor or you might have some obstructions. It's the little touches that keep guests happy here, with wine, cheese, coffee, tea, and cookies galore and an emphasis on smiling, personalized service. The guest rooms are quite spacious, with big baths and 14-foot ceilings. You can take your complimentary breakfast—good but not great—in your room or eat it on the nice rooftop terrace.

FRENCH QUARTER
Over $300

A great place in this part of town is the **French Quarter Inn** (166 Church St., 843/722-1900, www.fqicharleston.com, $350-500). The decor in the 50 surprisingly spacious guest rooms is suitably high-period French, with low-style noncanopied beds and crisp fresh linens. Many guest rooms feature fireplaces, whirlpool baths, and private balconies.

NORTH OF BROAD
$150-300

It calls itself a boutique hotel, perhaps because each room is unique and sumptuously appointed. But the charming ★ **Andrew Pinckney Inn** (199 Church St., 843/937-8800, www.andrewpinckneyinn.com, $250-350) is very nearly in a class by itself in Charleston not only for its great rates but for its casual West Indies-style decor, charming courtyard, gorgeous three-story atrium, and rooftop terrace on which you can enjoy your complimentary (and delicious) breakfast. For the money and the amenities, it's possibly the single best lodging package in town.

If you plan on some serious shopping, you might want to stay right on the city's main shopping thoroughfare at the **Kings Courtyard Inn** (198 King St., 866/720-2949, www.kingscourtyardinn.com, $200-300). This 1853 Greek Revival building houses a lot more guest rooms—more than 40—than meets the eye, and it can get a little crowded at times. Still, its charming courtyard and awesome location on King Street are big bonuses, as is the convenient but cramped parking lot right next door (about $12 per day, a bargain for this part of town), with free in-and-out privileges.

Affiliated with the Kings Courtyard—and right next door, in fact—is the smaller, cozier **Fulton Lane Inn** (202 King St., 866/720-2940, www.fultonlaneinn.com, $240-350), with its lobby entrance on tiny Fulton Lane between the two inns. Small, simple guest rooms—some with fireplaces—have comfortable beds and spacious baths. This is the kind of place for active people who plan to spend most of their days out and about but want a cozy place to come back to at night. You mark down your continental breakfast order at night, leave it on your doorknob, and it shows up at the *exact* time you requested the next morning. Then when you're ready to shop and walk, just go down the stairs and take the exit right out onto busy King Street. Also nice is the $12-per-day parking with free in-and-out privileges.

Although it is a newer building by Charleston standards, the **Mills House Hotel** (115 Meeting St., 843/577-2400, www.millshouse.com, $250-400) boasts an important pedigree. Dating to 1853, the first incarnation was a grand edifice that hosted luminaries such as Robert E. Lee. Through the years, fire and restoration wrought their changes, and the modern version basically dates from an extensive renovation in the 1970s. The hotel

Andrew Pinckney Inn

has a very good restaurant and lounge inside, the Barbadoes Room (breakfast, lunch, dinner, and Sunday brunch), as well as a healthy banquet and event schedule. So this isn't the place to go for peace and quiet. Rather, this Wyndham-affiliated property is where you go to feel the bustle of downtown Charleston and to be conveniently close to its main sightseeing and shopping attractions. Some of the upper floors of this seven-story building offer spectacular views.

Over $300

Considered Charleston's premier hotel, Charleston Place maintains a surprisingly high level of service and decor for its massive 440-room size. Currently owned by the London-based Orient-Express Hotels, ★ **Belmond Charleston Place** (205 Meeting St., 843/722-4900, www.charlestonplace.com, $300-500) is routinely rated as one of the best hotels in North America by *Condé Nast Traveler* and other publications. The guest rooms aren't especially large, but they are well appointed, featuring Italian marble baths, high-speed Internet, and voice messaging—and, of course, there's a pool available. A series of suite offerings—Junior, Junior Executive, Parlor, and the 800-square-foot Senior—feature enlarged living areas and multiple TVs and phones. The on-site **spa** (843/937-8522) offers all kinds of massages, including couples and "mommy to be" sessions. Diners and tipplers have three fine options to choose from: the famous **Charleston Grill** (843/577-4522, daily 6pm-close, $27-65) for fine dining; the breakfast, lunch, and brunch hot spot **Palmetto Cafe** (843/722-4900, daily 6:30am-3pm, $24-31); and the **Thoroughbred Club** (daily 11am-midnight) for cocktails and, for groups of 10 or more, afternoon tea.

On the north side of Broad Street, the magnificent ★ **John Rutledge House Inn** (116 Broad St., 843/723-7999, www.johnrutledgehouseinn.com, $300-400) is very close to the old South of Broad neighborhood not only in geography but in feel. Known as "America's most historic inn," the Rutledge House boasts a fine old pedigree indeed: Built for Constitution signer John Rutledge in 1763, it's one of only 15 homes belonging to the original signers to survive. George Washington breakfasted here with Mrs. Rutledge in 1791. The interior is stunning: Italian marble fireplaces, original plaster moldings, and masterful ironwork abound in the public spaces. The inn's 19 guest rooms are divided among the original mansion and two carriage houses.

UPPER KING
$150-300

Stretching the bounds of the "Upper King" definition, the **Ashley Inn** (201 Ashley Ave., 843/723-1848, www.charleston-sc-inns.com, $200-300) is located well northwest of Marion Square, almost in the Citadel area. Although it's too far to walk from here to most any historical attraction in Charleston, the Ashley Inn does provide free bikes to its guests as well as free off-street parking, a particularly nice touch. It also deserves a special mention not only because of the romantic, well-appointed nature of its six guest rooms, suite, and carriage house but for its outstanding breakfasts. You get to pick a main dish, such as Carolina sausage pie, stuffed waffles, or cheese blintzes.

In a renovated 1924 building overlooking beautiful Marion Square, the **Francis Marion Hotel** (387 King St., 843/722-0600, www.francismarionhotel.com, $200-300) offers quality accommodations in the hippest, most bustling area of the peninsula—but be aware that it's quite a walk down to the Battery from here. The guest rooms are plush and big, though the baths can be cramped. The hotel's parking garage costs a reasonable $12 per day, with valet parking available until about 8pm. A Starbucks in the lobby pleases many guests on their way out or in. Most rooms hover around $300, but some are a real steal.

HAMPTON PARK
Under $150

Downtown Charleston's least-expensive lodging is also its most unique: the **Not So Hostel** (156 Spring St., 843/722-8383, www.

notsohostel.com, $30-70). The already-reasonable prices also include a make-your-own bagel breakfast, off-street parking, bikes, high-speed Internet access in the common room, and even an airport, train, and bus shuttle. The inn actually comprises three 1840s Charleston single houses, all with the obligatory piazzas. (However, unlike some hostels, there's air-conditioning in all the rooms.) Because the free bike usage makes up for its off-the-beaten-path location, a stay at the Not So Hostel is a fantastic way to enjoy the Holy City on a budget. They now have an annex at 33 Cannon Street with all-private rooms ($75-85).

WEST ASHLEY
$150-300

Looking like Frank Lloyd Wright parachuted into a 300-year-old plantation and got to work, ★ The Inn at Middleton Place (4290 Ashley River Rd., 843/556-0500, www.theinnatmiddletonplace.com, $200-300) is one of Charleston's unique lodgings and not only because it's on the grounds of the historic and beautiful Middleton Place Plantation. The four connected buildings, comprising over 50 guest rooms, are modern yet deliberately blend in with the forested, neutral-colored surroundings. The spacious guest rooms have that same woodsy minimalism, with excellent fireplaces, spacious Euro-style baths, and huge floor-to-ceiling windows overlooking the grounds and the river. Guests also have full access to the rest of the gorgeous Middleton grounds. The only downside is that you're a lengthy drive from the peninsula and all its attractions, restaurants, and nightlife. But don't worry about food—the excellent Middleton Place Restaurant is open for lunch and dinner. There are nightly happy hours at the lodge, a great way to meet some of your fellow lodging mates and relax.

SUMMERVILLE
Over $300

The renowned Woodlands Resort & Inn (125 Parsons Rd., 843/875-2600, www.

woodlandsmansion.com, $500 and up) is one of a handful of inns in the United States with a five-star rating both for lodging and dining. Its 18 guest rooms within the 1906 great house are decorated in a mix of old-fashioned plantation high style and contemporary designer aesthetics, with modern, luxurious baths. There's also a freestanding guest cottage ($950) that seeks to replicate a hunting lodge vibe. There's a full day spa on the premises; the most basic offering, a one-hour massage, will run you about $120. Within Woodlands is its award-winning world-class restaurant, simply called The Dining Room (Mon.-Sat. 11am-2pm and 6pm-9pm, brunch Sun. 11:30am-2pm, $40-50). The 900-entry wine list and sommelier are collectively fantastic, as are the desserts. Jackets are required, and reservations are strongly advised.

MOUNT PLEASANT AND EAST COOPER
$150-300

One of the more accessible and enjoyable resort-type stays in the Charleston area is on the Isle of Palms at Wild Dunes Resort (5757 Palm Blvd., 888/778-1876, www.wilddunes.com, $275-350). This is the place to go for relaxing, beach-oriented vacation fun in your choice of a traditional hotel room, a house, or a villa. Bustling Mount Pleasant is only a couple of minutes away, and Charleston proper not much farther.

FOLLY BEACH AND THE SOUTHWEST ISLANDS
$150-300

The upbeat but still cozy Tides Folly Beach (1 Center St., 843/588-6464, www.tidesfollybeach.com, $200-300) boutique hotel has a combination of attentive staff, great oceanfront views, and an excellent on-site restaurant, Blu.

Over $300

The beautiful island of Kiawah—about 45 minutes from downtown Charleston—has as its main attraction the sumptuous

★ **Kiawah Island Golf Resort** (1 Sanctuary Beach Dr., 800/654-2924, www.kiawahgolf.com, $500-1000), a frequent venue for PGA tournaments. But even if you don't play golf, the resort is an amazing stay. The main component is The Sanctuary, an upscale hotel featuring an opulent lobby complete with grand staircases, a large pool area overlooking the beach, tasteful Spanish Colonial-style architecture, and 255 smallish but excellently appointed guest rooms.

CAMPING

Charleston County runs a family-friendly, fairly boisterous campground at **James Island County Park** (871 Riverland Dr., 843/795-7275, www.ccprc.com, $31 tent site, $37 pull-through site). A neat feature here is the $5-per-person round-trip shuttle to the visitors center downtown, Folly Beach Pier, and Folly Beach County Park. The park also has 10 furnished cottages (843/795-4386, $138) for rent, sleeping up to eight people. Reservations are recommended. For more commercial camping in Mount Pleasant, try the **KOA of Mount Pleasant** (3157 U.S. 17 N., 843/849-5177, www.koa.com, from $30 tent sites, from $50 pull-through sites).

Transportation and Services

AIR

Way up in North Charleston is **Charleston International Airport** (CHS, 5500 International Blvd., 843/767-1100, www.chs-airport.com), served by American (www.aa.com), Delta (www.delta.com), JetBlue (www.jetblue.com), and Southwest (www.southwest.com).

It'll take about 20 minutes to make the 12-mile drive from the airport to downtown, and vice versa. The airport is conveniently located just off the I-526/Mark Clark Expressway perimeter highway off I-26. As in most cities, taxi service from the airport is regulated. This translates to about $30 for two people from the airport to Charleston Place downtown.

CAR

There are two main routes into Charleston: I-26 from the west-northwest (which dead-ends downtown) and U.S. 17 from the west (called Savannah Highway when it gets close to Charleston proper), which continues east over the Ravenel Bridge into Mount Pleasant and beyond. There's a fairly new perimeter highway, I-526 (Mark Clark Expressway), which loops around the city from West Ashley to North Charleston to Daniel Island and into Mount Pleasant. It's accessible both from I-26 and U.S. 17.

Keep in mind that I-95, while certainly a gateway to the region, is actually a good ways out of Charleston, about 30 miles west of the city. Charleston is almost exactly two hours from Savannah by car, and about an hour's drive from Beaufort and Hilton Head.

Car Rentals

Charleston International Airport has rental kiosks for **Avis** (843/767-7031), **Budget** (843/767-7051), **Dollar** (843/767-1130), **Enterprise** (843/767-1109), **Hertz** (843/767-4550), **National** (843/767-3078), and **Thrifty** (843/647-4389). There are a couple of rental locations downtown: **Budget** (390 Meeting St., 843/577-5195) and **Enterprise** (398 Meeting St., 843/723-6215). **Hertz** has a location in West Ashley (3025 Ashley Town Center Dr., 843/573-2147), as does **Enterprise** (2004 Ashley Hwy., 843/556-7889).

BUS

Public transportation by **Charleston Area Regional Transit Authority** (CARTA, 843/724-7420, www.ridecarta.com) is a convenient and inexpensive way to enjoy Charleston without the more structured nature of an organized tour. There's a wide variety of routes, but most visitors will limit their acquaintance to the tidy, trolley-like **DASH** (Downtown Area Shuttle, free) buses run by CARTA primarily for visitors. Keep in mind that DASH only stops at designated places.

TAXI

The South is generally not big on taxis, and Charleston is no exception. The best bet is simply to call rather than try to flag one down. Charleston's most fun service is **Charleston Black Cabs** (843/216-2627, www.charlestonblackcabcompany.com), using Americanized versions of the classic British taxi. A one-way ride anywhere on the peninsula below the bridges is about $10 per person, and rates go up from there. They're very popular, so call as far ahead as you can or try to get one at their stand at Charleston Place. Two other good services are **Safety Cab** (843/722-4066) and **Yellow Cab** (843/577-6565).

You can also try a human-powered taxi service from **Charleston Rickshaw** (843/723-5685). A cheerful (and energetic) young cyclist will pull you and a friend to most points on the Lower Peninsula for about $10-15. Call 'em or find one by City Market. They work late on Friday and Saturday nights too.

PARKING

As you'll quickly see, parking is at a premium in downtown Charleston. An exception seems to be the large number of free spaces all along the Battery, but unless you're an exceptionally strong walker, that's too far south to use as a reliable base from which to explore the whole peninsula.

Metered spaces are enforced 8am-6pm Monday-Saturday. Most metered parking downtown is on and around Calhoun Street, Meeting Street, King Street, Market Street, and East Bay Street.

The city has several conveniently located and comparatively inexpensive parking garages. I strongly suggest that you make use of them. They're located at the aquarium,

Camden and Exchange Streets, Charleston Place, Concord and Cumberland Streets, East Bay and Prioleau Streets, Marion Square, Gaillard Auditorium, Liberty and St. Philip Streets, Majestic Square, the Charleston Visitor Reception and Transportation Center, and Wentworth Street.

The city's website (www.charlestoncity. info) has a good interactive map of parking.

TOURIST INFORMATION
Visitors Centers

I highly recommend a stop at the **Charleston Visitor Reception and Transportation Center** (375 Meeting St., 800/774-0006, www.charlestoncvb.com, Mon.-Fri. 8:30am-5pm). I also recommend using the attached parking garage not only for your stop at the center but also anytime you want to see the many sights this part of town has to offer, such as the Charleston Museum, the Manigault and Aiken-Rhett Houses, and the Children's Museum. Go to the center to take advantage of the great deal offered by the **Charleston Heritage Passport** (www. heritagefederation.org), which gives you 40 percent off admission to all of Charleston's key historic homes, the Charleston Museum, and the two awesome plantation sites on the Ashley River: Drayton Hall and Middleton Place. You can get the Heritage Passport *only* at the Charleston Visitor Reception and Transportation Center on Meeting Street.

Other area visitors centers include the **Mount Pleasant-Isle of Palms Visitors Center** (99 Harry M. Hallman Jr. Blvd., 800/774-0006, daily 9am-5pm) and the **North Charleston Visitors Center** (4975B Centre Pointe Dr., 843/853-8000, Mon.-Sat. 10am-5pm).

Hospitals

If there's a silver lining in getting sick or injured in Charleston, it's that there are plenty of high-quality medical facilities available. The premier institution is the **Medical University of South Carolina** (171 Ashley Ave., 843/792-2300, www.muschealth.com)

in the northwest part of the peninsula. Two notable facilities are near each other downtown: **Roper Hospital** (316 Calhoun St., 843/402-2273, www.roperhospital.com) and **Charleston Memorial Hospital** (326 Calhoun St., 843/792-2300). In Mount Pleasant there's **East Cooper Regional Medical Center** (1200 Johnnie Dodds Blvd., www.eastcoopermedctr.com). In West Ashley there's **Bon Secours St. Francis Hospital** (2095 Henry Tecklenburg Ave., 843/402-2273, www.ropersaintfrancis.com).

Police

For nonemergencies in Charleston, West Ashley, and James Island, contact the **Charleston Police Department** (843/577-7434, www.charlestoncity.info). You can also contact the police department in Mount Pleasant (843/884-4176). North Charleston is a separate municipality with its own police department (843/308-4718, www.northcharleston.org). Of course, for emergencies always call **911.**

Media

The daily newspaper of record is the *Post and Courier* (www.charleston.net). Its entertainment insert, *Preview,* comes out on Thursdays. The free alternative weekly is the *Charleston City Paper* (www.charlestoncitypaper.com), which comes out on Wednesdays and is the best place to find local music and arts listings. A particularly well-done and lively metro glossy is *Charleston* magazine (www.charlestonmag.com), which comes out once a month.

The National Public Radio affiliate is the South Carolina ETV radio station WSCI at 89.3 FM. South Carolina ETV is on television at WITV. The local NBC affiliate is WCBD, the CBS affiliate is WCSC, the ABC affiliate is WCIV, and the Fox affiliate is WTAT.

Libraries

The main branch of the **Charleston County Public Library** (68 Calhoun St.,

843/805-6801, www.ccpl.org, Mon.-Thurs. 9am-9pm, Fri.-Sat. 9am-6pm, Sun. 2pm-5pm) has been at its current site since 1998. Named for Sullivan's Island's most famous visitor, the **Edgar Allan Poe Library** (1921 I'on Ave., 843/883-3914, www.ccpl.org, Mon. and Fri. 2pm-6pm, Tues., Thurs., and Sat. 10am-2pm) has been housed in Battery Gadsden, a former Spanish-American War gun emplacement, since 1977.

The College of Charleston's main library is the **Marlene and Nathan Addlestone Library** (205 Calhoun St., 843/953-5530, www.cofc.edu), home to special collections, the Center for Student Learning, the main computer lab, the media collection, and even a café. The college's **Avery Research Center for African American History and Culture** (125 Bull St., 843/953-7609, www.cofc.edu/avery, Mon.-Fri. 10am-5pm, Sat. noon-5pm) houses documents relating to the history and culture of African Americans in the Lowcountry.

For other historical research on the area, check out the collections of the **South Carolina Historical Society** (100 Meeting St., 843/723-3225, www.southcarolinahistoricalsociety.org, Mon.-Fri. 9am-4pm, Sat. 9am-2pm). There's a $5 research fee for nonmembers.

LGBTQ Resources

Contrary to many media portrayals of the region, Charleston is quite open to the LGBTQ community, which plays a major role in arts, culture, and business. As with any other place in the South, however, it's generally expected that people—straights as well—will keep personal matters and politics to themselves in public settings. A key local advocacy group is the **Alliance for Full Acceptance** (29 Leinbach Dr., Ste. D-3, 843/883-0343, www.affa-sc.org). The **Lowcountry Gay and Lesbian Alliance** (843/720-8088) holds a potluck the last Sunday of each month. For the most up-to-date happenings, try the *Charleston City Paper.*

Hilton Head and the Lowcountry

For many people around the world, the Lowcountry is the first image that comes to mind when they think of the American South.

History hangs in the humid air where first the Spanish and French came to interrupt the native tribes' ancient reverie, followed by the English. Although time, erosion, and development have erased most traces of these various occupants, you can almost hear their ghosts in the rustle of the branches in a sudden sea breeze or in the piercing call of a heron over the marsh.

The defining characteristic of the Lowcountry is its liquid nature—not only literally, in the creeks and waterways that dominate every vista and the seafood cooked in all manner of ways, but figuratively too, in the slow but deep quality of life here. Not so very long ago, before the influx of resort development, retirement subdivisions, and tourism, much of the Lowcountry was like a flatter, more humid Appalachia—poverty-stricken and desperately underserved. While the archetypal South has been marketed in any number of ways to the rest of the world, here you get a sense that this is the real

thing—timeless, endlessly alluring, but somehow very familiar.

South of Beaufort is the historically significant Port Royal area and the East Coast Marine Corps Recruit Depot of Parris Island. East of Beaufort is the center of Gullah culture, St. Helena Island, and the scenic gem of Hunting Island. To the south is the scenic but entirely developed golf and tennis mecca, Hilton Head Island, and Hilton Head's close neighbor but diametrical opposite in every other way, Daufuskie Island, another important Gullah center. Nestled between is the close-knit and gossipy little village of Bluffton on the gossamer May River.

PLANNING YOUR TIME

A commonsense game plan is to use centrally located Beaufort as a home base and spend **three days** exploring the region. Take at least half a day of leisure to walk all over Beaufort, a delightfully walkable place. If you're in the mood for a road trip, dedicate a full day to tour the area to the north and northeast, with

Previous: yoga on the beach; the Harbour Town Lighthouse. **Above:** Old Town Bluffton.

Look for ★ to find recommended sights, activities, dining, and lodging.

Highlights

★ **Henry C. Chambers Waterfront Park:** While away the time on a porch swing at this clean and inviting gathering place on the serene Beaufort River (page 213).

★ **St. Helena's Episcopal Church:** To walk through this Beaufort sanctuary and its walled graveyard is to walk through history (page 215).

★ **Penn Center:** Visit the center of modern Gullah culture and education—and a key site in the history of the civil rights movement (page 224).

★ **Hunting Island State Park:** One of the most peaceful natural getaways on the East Coast is only minutes away from the civilized temptations of Beaufort (page 227).

★ **ACE Basin:** You can take a lifetime to learn your way around this massive, marshy estuary— or just a few hours to soak in its lush beauty (page 227).

★ **Edisto Beach State Park:** Relax at this quiet, friendly, and relatively undeveloped park on Sea Island, a mecca for shell collectors (page 231).

★ **Pinckney Island National Wildlife Refuge:** This well-maintained sanctuary is a major birding location and a great getaway from nearby Hilton Head (page 234).

★ **Coastal Discovery Museum at Honey Horn:** This beautifully repurposed plantation house with spacious grounds is a great place to learn about Hilton Head history, both human and natural (page 235).

© AVALON TRAVEL

★ **Old Town Bluffton:** By turns gossipy and gorgeous, the charming "Old Town" on the May River centers on a thriving artist colony (page 246).

★ **South Carolina Artisans Center:** Visual artists and fine craftspeople from all over the state contribute work to this high-quality collective in Walterboro (page 251).

Hilton Head and the Lowcountry

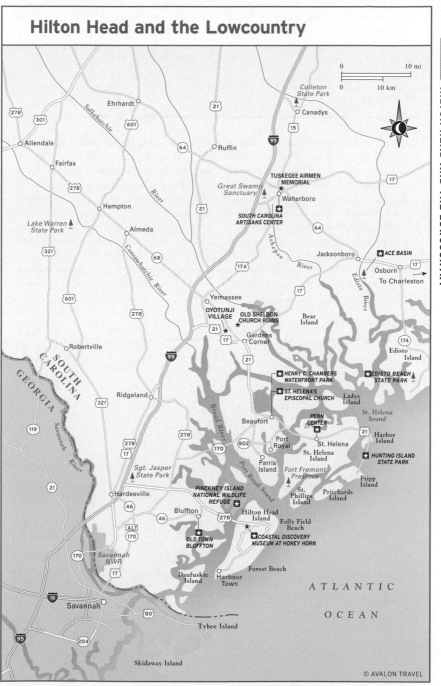

© AVALON TRAVEL

a jaunt to the ACE Basin National Wildlife Refuge. While the New York accents fly fast and furious on Hilton Head Island, that's no reason for you to rush. Plan on at least half a day just to enjoy the fine broad beaches alone. I recommend another half day to tour the island itself, maybe including a stop in Sea Pines for a late lunch or dinner.

Beaufort

Sandwiched halfway between the prouder, louder cities of Charleston and Savannah, Beaufort is in many ways a more authentic slice of life from the past than either of those two. If you want to party, stay in those two cities. If you want to relax in a similar environment, Beaufort's your ticket.

Long a staple of movie crews seeking to portray some archetypal aspect of the Old South (*The Prince of Tides, The Great Santini, Forrest Gump*) or just to film beautiful scenery for its own sake (*Jungle Book, Last Dance*), Beaufort—pronounced "BYOO-fert," by the way, not "BO-fort"—features many well-preserved examples of Southern architecture, most all of them in idyllic, family-friendly neighborhoods.

While you'll run into plenty of charming and gracious locals during your time here, you might be surprised at the number of transplanted Northerners. That's due not only to the high volume of retirees who've moved

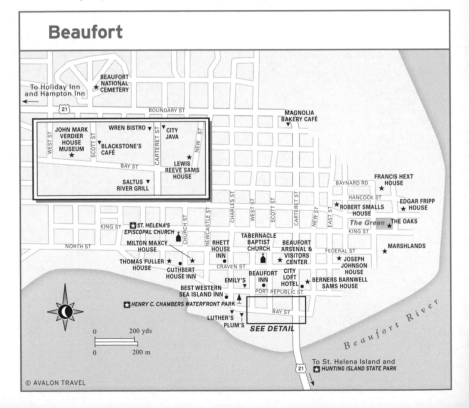

© AVALON TRAVEL

to the area, but also to the active presence of three major U.S. Navy facilities: the Marine Corps Air Station Beaufort, the Marine Corps Recruit Depot on nearby Parris Island, and the Beaufort Naval Hospital.

The two main avenues to remember are Bay Street, along the Beaufort River and the real center of downtown; and Boundary Street, which becomes Carteret Street as you arrive into downtown proper.

HISTORY

This was the site of the second landing by the Spanish on the North American continent, the expedition of Captain Pedro de Salazar in 1514 (Ponce de León's more famous landing at St. Augustine was but a year earlier). A Spanish slaver made a brief stop in 1521, long enough to name the area Santa Elena. Port Royal Sound didn't get its modern name until the first serious attempt at a permanent settlement, Jean Ribault's exploration in 1562. Though ultimately disastrous, Ribault's base of Charlesfort was the first French settlement in America.

In 1776, Beaufort planter Thomas Heyward Jr. was a signer of the Declaration of Independence. After independence, Lowcountry planters turned to cotton as the main cash crop, since England had been their prime customer for indigo. The gambit paid off, and Beaufort soon became one of the wealthiest towns in the new nation. In 1861, only seven months after secessionists fired on Fort Sumter in nearby Charleston, a Union fleet sailed into Port Royal and occupied the Lowcountry for the duration of the war.

Gradually developing their own distinct dialect and culture, much of it linked to their West African roots, isolated Lowcountry African Americans became known as the Gullah. Evolving from an effort by abolitionist missionaries early in the Civil War, in 1864 the Penn School was formed on St. Helena Island specifically to teach the children of the Gullah communities. Now known as the Penn Center, the facility has been a beacon for the study of this aspect of African American culture ever since.

SIGHTS

★ Henry C. Chambers Waterfront Park

A tastefully designed, well-maintained, and user-friendly mix of walkways, bandstands, and patios, **Henry C. Chambers Waterfront Park** (843/525-7054, www.cityofbeaufort.org, daily 24 hours) is a favorite gathering place for locals and visitors

the Henry C. Chambers Waterfront Park

Pat Conroy's Lowcountry

No person was as closely associated with the South Carolina Lowcountry as beloved author Pat Conroy, who passed away in 2016. After moving around as a child in a military family, he began high school in Beaufort. His painful teen years there formed the basis of his first novel, a brutal portrait of his domineering Marine pilot father, Colonel Donald Conroy, aka Colonel Bull Meecham of *The Great Santini* (1976). Many scenes from the 1979 film adaptation were filmed at the famous Tidalholm, the Edgar Fripp House (1 Laurens St.) in Beaufort. (The house was also front and center in *The Big Chill*.)

Conroy's pattern of thinly veiled autobiography actually began with his first book, the self-published *The Boo*, a tribute to a teacher at the Citadel in Charleston while Conroy was still a student there. His second work, *The Water is Wide* (1972), is a chronicle of his experiences teaching in a one-room African American school on Daufuskie Island. Though ostensibly a straightforward first-person journalistic effort, Conroy changed the location to the fictional Yamacraw Island, supposedly to protect Daufuskie's fragile culture from curious outsiders. The 1974 film adaptation starring Jon Voight was titled *Conrack* after the way his students mispronounced his name. You can visit that same one-room school today on Daufuskie. Known as the Mary Field School, the building is now a local community center.

Conroy would go on to publish in 1980 *The Lords of Discipline*, a reading of his real-life experience with the often-savage environment faced by cadets at the Citadel—though Conroy would change the name, calling it the Carolina Military Institute. Still, when it came time to make a film adaptation in 1983, the Citadel refused to allow it to be shot there, so the "Carolina Military Institute" was filmed in England instead. Conroy also wrote the foreword to the cookbook *Gullah Home Cooking the Daufuskie Way: Smokin' Joe Butter Beans, Ol' 'Fuskie Fried Crab Rice, Sticky-Bush Blackberry Dumpling, and Other Sea Island Favorites* by Daufuskie native and current Savannah resident Sallie Ann Robinson.

For many of his fans, Conroy's *The Prince of Tides* is his ultimate homage to the Lowcountry. Surely, the 1991 film version starring Barbra Streisand and Nick Nolte—shot on location and awash in gorgeous shots of the Beaufort River marsh—did much to implant an idyllic image of the area with audiences around the world. According to local legend, Streisand originally didn't intend to make the film in Beaufort, but a behind-the-scenes lobbying effort allegedly coordinated by Conroy himself, and including a stay at the Rhett House Inn, convinced her.

The Bay Street Inn (601 Bay St.) in Beaufort was seen in the film, as was the football field at the old Beaufort High School. The beach scenes were shot on nearby Fripp Island. Interestingly, some scenes set in a Manhattan apartment were actually shot within the old Beaufort Arsenal (713 Craven St.), now a visitors center. Similarly, the Beaufort Naval Hospital doubled as New York's Bellevue.

Despite the many personal tribulations he faced in the area, to the end Conroy never gave up on the Lowcountry. He is interred in the old Gullah Cemetery on St. Helena Island, near the historic Penn Center, beside civil rights heroine Agnes Sherman. As for the "Great Santini" himself, you can visit the final resting place of Colonel Conroy in the Beaufort National Cemetery—Section 62, Grave 182.

alike, beckoning one and all with its open green space and wonderful marsh-front views.

John Mark Verdier House Museum

A smallish but stately Federalist building on the busiest downtown corner, the **John Mark Verdier House Museum** (801 Bay St., 843/379-6335, www.historicbeaufort.org, tours on the half hour Mon.-Sat. 10:30am-3:30pm, $5) is the only historic Beaufort planter's home open to regular tours. Built in 1805 for John Mark Verdier, its main claims to fame are acting as the Union headquarters during the long occupation of Beaufort during the Civil War and hosting Revolutionary War

St. Helena's Episcopal Church

hero the Marquis de Lafayette, who stayed at the Verdier House on his 1825 U.S. tour. In 2011 the Verdier House was extensively and professionally restored, with exterior paint reflecting the home's authentic 1863 look.

Beaufort Arsenal Visitors Center and History Museum

The imposing yellow-gray tabby facade of the 1852 **Beaufort Arsenal** (713 Craven St.) houses the **Beaufort Visitors Center** (843/986-5400, www.beaufortsc.org, Mon.-Sat. 9am-5pm, Sun. noon-5pm) and **Beaufort History Museum** (www.beauforthistorymuseum.com, Mon.-Sat. 10am-4pm, $5). The visitors center is a great place to purchase various tour tickets, and the adjacent museum is a small but informative stop to learn more about the area's long and important history. There are also public restrooms.

★ St. Helena's Episcopal Church

Nestled within a low brick wall surrounding this historic church and cemetery, **St.**

HILTON HEAD AND THE LOWCOUNTRY
BEAUFORT

Helena's Episcopal Church (505 Church St., 843/522-1712, Tues.-Fri. 10am-4pm, Sat. 10am-1pm) has witnessed some of Beaufort's most compelling tales. Built in 1724, this was the parish church of Thomas Heyward, one of South Carolina's signers of the Declaration of Independence. John "Tuscarora Jack" Barnwell, one of Beaufort's founders, is buried on the grounds.

While the cemetery and sanctuary interior are likely to be your focus, take a close look at the church exterior—many of the bricks are actually ships' ballast stones. Also be aware that you're not looking at the church's original footprint; the building has been expanded several times since its construction (a hurricane in 1896 destroyed the entire east end). A nearly $3 million restoration, mostly for structural repairs, was completed in 2000.

Reconstruction Era National Monument

One of Barack Obama's last acts as president was the creation of the **Reconstruction Era National Monument** (www.nps.gov/reer, hours vary, free). Encompassing several sites in the Beaufort area, this isn't a single park you visit but rather a collection of locations that were important in the years immediately following the Civil War.

The easiest site to visit is the Beaufort Firehouse (706 Craven St.) downtown across from the Beaufort Arsenal/Museum. Once home to private businesses and now deeded to the National Park Service, the firehouse marks the site of community gatherings in the post-Civil War occupation era. As the national monument takes shape, it is likely to be a visitors center of some sort.

Two key sites on St. Helena Island are Darrah Hall on the Penn Center campus (for which there's a separate listing in this chapter) and the Brick Baptist Church, just across the street from the Penn Center. Darrah Hall is the epicenter of one of the nation's first schools for emancipated slaves. The Brick Baptist Church was built by slaves in 1855 and is the oldest church on St. Helena Island.

The Camp Saxton/Emancipation Oak site is on the grounds of the Beaufort Naval Hospital. While currently not open to the public, that will likely change at some point in the future.

Tabernacle Baptist Church

Built in 1845, the handsome **Tabernacle Baptist Church** (911 Craven St., 843/524-0376) had a congregation of over 3,000 before the Civil War. Slaves made up most of the congregation, and during the war freed slaves purchased the church. A congregant was the war hero Robert Smalls, who seized the Confederate steamer he was forced to serve on and delivered it to Union forces. He is buried in the church cemetery and has a nice memorial dedicated to him facing the street.

Beaufort National Cemetery

Begun by order of Abraham Lincoln in 1863, **Beaufort National Cemetery** (1601 Boundary St., daily 8am-sunset) is one of the few cemeteries containing the graves of both Union and Confederate troops. This national cemetery is where 19 soldiers of the all-black 54th and 55th Massachusetts Infantries were reinterred after being found on Folly Island near Charleston. Also buried here is "the Great Santini" himself, novelist Pat Conroy's father, Donald.

Santa Elena History Center

The actual historic site is on nearby Parris Island, but in downtown Beaufort you'll find the **Santa Elena History Center** (1501 Bay St., 843/379-1550, www.santa-elena.org, Tues.-Sat. 10am-4pm, Sun. 1pm-4pm, free), detailing the Spanish occupation of the area beginning 450 years ago, long before English-speaking settlers arrived. This is a new and growing venture, and exhibits and resources will be added as funds become available.

A Walking Tour of Beaufort Homes

Here's a walking tour of some of Beaufort's fine historic homes in private hands. You won't be taking any tours of the interiors, but these homes are part of the legacy of the area and are locally valued as such. Be sure to respect the privacy of the inhabitants by keeping the noise level down and not trespassing on private property to take photos.

- **Thomas Fuller House:** Begin at the corner of Harrington and Bay Streets and view the 1796 Thomas Fuller House (1211 Bay St.), one of the oldest in Beaufort and unique in that much of the building material is tabby (hence the home's other name, the Tabby Manse).

- **Milton Maxcy House:** Walk east on Bay Street one block and take a left on Church Street; walk up to the corner of Church and Craven Streets. Otherwise known as the Secession House (113 Craven St.), this 1813 home was built on a tabby foundation dating from 1743. In 1860, when it was the residence of attorney Edmund Rhett, the first Ordinance of Secession was signed here, and the rest, as they say, is history.

- **Lewis Reeve Sams House:** Resume the walking tour on the other side of the historic district at the foot of the bridge in the old neighborhood simply called "the Point." The beautiful Lewis Reeve Sams House (601 Bay St.) at the corner of Bay and New Streets, with its double-decker veranda, dates from 1852 and like many Beaufort mansions served as a Union hospital during the Civil War.

- **Berners Barnwell Sams House:** Continue up New Street, where shortly ahead on the left you'll find the 1818 Berners Barnwell Sams House (310 New St.), which served as the African American hospital during the Union occupation. Harriet Tubman of Underground Railroad fame worked here for a time as a nurse.

- **Joseph Johnson House:** Continue up New Street and take a right on Craven Street. Cross East Street to find the 1850 Joseph Johnson House (411 Craven St.), with the massive live oak in the front yard.

Legend has it that when the Yankees occupied Hilton Head, Mr. Johnson buried his valuables under an outhouse. After the war he returned to find his home for sale due to unpaid back taxes. He dug up his valuables, paid the taxes, and resumed living in the home. You might recognize the home from the film *Forces of Nature*.

- **Marshlands:** Backtrack to East Street, walk north to Federal Street, and go to its end. Built by James R. Verdier, Marshlands (501 Pinckney St.) was used as a hospital during the Civil War, as many Beaufort homes were, and is now a National Historic Landmark. It was the setting of Francis Griswold's 1931 novel *A Sea Island Lady*.

- **The Oaks:** Walk up to King Street and take a right. Soon after you pass a large open park on the left, King Street dead-ends at Short Street. The Oaks (100 Laurens St.) at this corner was owned by the Hamilton family, who lost a son who served with General Wade Hampton's cavalry in the Civil War. After the conflict, the family couldn't afford the back taxes; neighbors paid the debts and returned the deed to the Hamiltons.

- **Edgar Fripp House:** Continue east on Laurens Street toward the water to find this handsome Lowcountry mansion, sometimes called Tidalholm (1 Laurens St.). Built in 1856 by the wealthy planter for whom nearby Fripp Island is named, this house was a key setting in *The Big Chill* and *The Great Santini*.

- **Francis Hext House:** Go back to Short Street, walk north to Hancock Street, and take a left. A short way ahead on the right, the handsome red-roofed estate known as Riverview (207 Hancock St.) is one of the oldest structures in Beaufort; it was built in 1720.

- **Robert Smalls House:** Continue west on Hancock Street, take a short left on East Street, and then a quick right on Prince Street. The 1834 Robert Smalls House (511 Prince St.) was the birthplace of Robert

Smalls, a former slave and Beaufort native who stole the Confederate ship *Planter* from Charleston Harbor while serving as helmsman and delivered it to Union troops in Hilton Head. Smalls and a few compatriots commandeered the ship while the officers were at a party at Fort Sumter. Smalls used the bounty he earned for the act of bravery to buy his boyhood home. After the war, Smalls was a longtime U.S. congressman.

ENTERTAINMENT AND NIGHTLIFE
Performing Arts

Beaufort's fine arts scene is small but professional in outlook. Most performances are based in the nice Performing Arts Center on the oak-lined campus of the **University of South Carolina Beaufort** (USCB, 801 Carteret St., 843/521-4100, www.uscb.edu). A prime mover of the local performing arts scene is **Beaufort Performing Arts Inc.,** formed by a mayoral task force in 2003 specifically to encourage arts and cultural development within the area. Ticket prices typically range $12-40.

Perhaps surprising for such a small place, Beaufort boasts its own full orchestra, the **Beaufort Orchestra** (1106 Carteret St., 843/986-5400, www.beaufortorchestra.org), which plays in the Performing Arts Center.

Cinema

One of only two functional drive-ins in the state, the **Highway 21 Drive In** (55 Parker Dr., 843/846-4500, www.hwy21drivein.com) has two screens, great sound, movies Friday-Sunday, and awesome concessions that include Angus beef hamburgers. All you need to provide is the car and the company.

Festivals and Events

Surprising for a town so prominent in so many films, Beaufort didn't have its own film festival until 2007. The **Beaufort Film Festival** (843/986-5400, www.beaufortfilmfestival.com) is held in February. It's small in scale but growing steadily each year and boasts a diverse range of high-quality, cutting-edge entries, including shorts and animation. Most events are held at the University of South Carolina Beaufort campus.

Now over 20 years old, the **Gullah Festival of South Carolina** (www.theoriginalgullahfestival.org) celebrates Gullah history and culture on Memorial Day weekend at various locations throughout town, mostly focusing on Waterfront Park.

By far the biggest single event on the local festival calendar is the over 50-year-old **Beaufort Water Festival** (www.bftwaterfestival.com), held over two weeks in June or July each year, centering on the Waterfront Park area.

Fall in the Lowcountry means shrimping season, and early October brings the **Beaufort Shrimp Festival** (www.beaufortsc.org). Various cooking competitions are held, obviously centering on the versatile crustaceans that are the raison d'être of the shrimp fleet.

St. Helena Island hosts the three-day **Penn Center Heritage Days** (www.penncenter.com) each November, without a doubt the Beaufort area's second-biggest celebration after the Water Festival. Focusing on Gullah culture, history, and delicious food, Heritage Days does a great job of combining fun with education.

SHOPS

The recently renovated Old Bay Marketplace, with a facade so bright red you can't miss it, hosts a few cute shops, most notably the stylish **Lulu Burgess** (917 Bay St., 843/524-5858, Mon.-Sat. 10am-6pm, Sun. noon-5pm), an eclectic store that brings a rich, quirky sense of humor to its otherwise tasteful assortment of gift items for the whole family.

A great women's clothing store nearby is **Go Fish** (719 Bay St., 843/379-8448, www.shopgofish.com, Mon.-Thurs. 10am-6pm, Fri.-Sat. 10am-8pm), a regional chain with particularly high-quality but affordable garments, jewelry, and shoes.

At the far end of Bay Street is **Bay Street Treasures** (1001 Bay St., 843/379-4488, Mon.-Sat. 10am-5pm), an eclectic home goods/furnishings store, strong with regional and Lowcountry appeal.

My favorite shop in Beaufort is **Nevermore Books** (201 Carteret St., 843/812-9460, www.nevermorebooks.com, Tues.-Fri. 10am-5pm, Sat. 11am-4pm), a very short walk off Bay Street around the corner on Carteret. While Edgar Allan Poe is the ostensible theme of this locally owned shop—check out the awesome window display!—they specialize in fiction of all types and have a range of regional books as well.

Art Galleries

A complete art experience blending the traditional with the cutting edge is at the **I. Pinckney Simons Art Gallery** (711 Bay St., 843/379-4774, www.ipinckneysimonsgallery.com, Tues.-Fri. 11am-5pm, Sat. 11am-3pm), which is pronounced "Simmons" despite the spelling.

For a taste of Gullah-themed art, head to **LyBenson's Gallery & Studio** (211 Charles St., 843/525-9006, www.lybensons.com). Not just a place to enjoy and purchase art, they have some small exhibits on local history and culture, including a room dedicated to local African American hero Robert Smalls.

Right on the water is a fun local favorite, the **Longo Gallery** (103 Charles St., 843/522-8933, Mon.-Sat. 11am-5pm). Owners Suzanne and Eric Longo provide a whimsical assortment of less traditional art than you might find in the more touristy waterfront area. Take Charles Street as it works its way toward the waterfront, and the gallery is right behind a storefront on the corner of Charles and Bay Streets.

You'll find perhaps the area's best-known gallery over the bridge on St. Helena Island. Known regionally as one of the best places to find Gullah folk art, **Red Piano Too** (870 Sea Island Pkwy., 843/838-2241, www.redpianotoo.com, Mon.-Sat. 10am-5pm) is on the corner before you turn onto the road to the historic Penn Center. Over 150 artists from a diverse range of traditions and styles are represented in this charming little 1940 building with a red tin awning.

SPORTS AND ACTIVITIES

Beaufort County comprises over 60 islands, so it's no surprise that nearly all recreation in the area revolves around the water, which dominates so many aspects of life in the Lowcountry. The closer to the ocean you get, the more it's a salt marsh environment. But as you explore more inland, including the sprawling ACE Basin, you'll encounter primarily blackwater.

Kayaking

The Lowcountry is tailor-made for kayaking. Most kayakers put in at the public landings in nearby **Port Royal** (1 Port Royal Landing Dr., 843/525-6664) or **Lady's Island** (73 Sea Island Pkwy., 843/522-0430), across the river from downtown Beaufort. If you don't feel comfortable with your navigation skills, it's a good idea to contact Kim and David at **Beaufort Kayak Tours** (843/525-0810, www.beaufortkayaktours.com), who rent kayaks and can guide you on a number of excellent tours. They charge about $40 for adults and $30 for children for a two-hour trip. A tour with Beaufort Kayak Tours is also the best (and nearly the only) way to access the historically significant ruins of the early British tabby Fort Frederick, now located on the grounds of the Beaufort Naval Hospital and inaccessible by car.

Fishing and Boating

Key marinas in the area are the **Downtown Marina** (1006 Bay St., 843/524-4422) in Beaufort, the **Lady's Island Marina** (73 Sea Island Pkwy., 843/522-0430), and the **Port Royal Landing Marina** (1 Port Royal Landing Dr., 843/525-6664). Hunting Island has a popular 1,000-foot fishing pier at its south end. A good local fishing charter service is Captain Josh Utsey's **Lowcountry Guide Service** (843/812-4919, www.

beaufortscfishing.com). Captain Ed Hardee (843/441-6880) offers good inshore charters.

Biking

Despite the Lowcountry's, well, lowness, biking opportunities abound. It might not get your heart rate up like a ride in the Rockies, but the area lends itself to laid-back two-wheeled enjoyment. Many local B&Bs provide bikes free for guests, and you can rent your own just across the river from Beaufort in Lady's Island at **Lowcountry Bikes** (102 Sea Island Pkwy., 843/524-9585, Mon.-Tues. and Thurs.-Fri. 10am-6pm, Wed. 10am-1pm, Sat. 10am-3pm, about $5 per hour). They can also hook you up with some good routes around the area.

Tours

Colorful character Jon Sharp has retired from his popular walking tours, but filling his shoes is Janet Matlock, who took over the venture and now runs the equally popular **Janet's Walking History Tour** (843/226-4412, www.janetswalkinghistory.com, $25). This highly recommended two-hour jaunt begins and ends at the Downtown Marina (1006 Bay St.) and takes you all through the downtown area. Tours leave at 12:30pm Monday and 11am Tuesday-Saturday; during the hot months of June-September they leave at 10am Monday-Saturday.

The Spirit of Old Beaufort (103 West St. Extension, 843/525-0459, www.thespiritofoldbeaufort.com, Mon.-Sat. 10:30am, 2pm, and 7pm, $18) runs a good year-round series of themed walking tours, roughly two hours long, with guides usually in period dress. If you don't want to walk, you can hire one of their guides to join you in your own vehicle (from $50).

As you might expect, few things could be more Lowcountry than an easygoing carriage ride through the historic neighborhoods. **Southurn Rose Buggy Tours** (843/524-2900, www.southurnrose.com, daily 10am-5pm, $18 adults, $7 children)—yes, that's how they spell it—offers 50-minute narrated

Lowcountry Boil or Frogmore Stew?

Near Beaufort it's called Frogmore stew after the township (now named St. Helena) just over the river. Closer to Savannah it's simply called Lowcountry boil. Supposedly the first pot of this delectable, hearty concoction was made by Richard Gay of the Gay Fish Company. As with any vernacular dish, dozens of local and family variants abound. The key ingredient that makes Lowcountry boil/Frogmore stew what it is—a well-blended mélange with a character all its own rather than just a bunch of stuff thrown together in a pot of boiling water—is some type of crab-boil seasoning. You'll find Zatarain's seasoning suggested on a lot of websites, but Old Bay is far more common in the eponymous Lowcountry where the dish originated.

In any case, here's a simple six-serving recipe to get you started. The only downside is that it's pretty much impossible to make it for just a few people. The dish is intended for large gatherings, whether a football tailgate party on a Saturday or a family afternoon after church on Sunday. Note the typical ratio of one ear of corn and 0.5 pound each of meat and shrimp per person.

- 6 ears fresh corn on the cob, cut into 3-inch sections

- 3 pounds smoked pork sausage, cut into 3-inch sections

- 3 pounds fresh shrimp, shells on

- 5 pounds new potatoes, halved or quartered

- 3 ounces Old Bay Seasoning

Put the sausage and potato pieces, along with the Old Bay, in two gallons of boiling water. When the potatoes are about halfway done, about 15 minutes in, add the corn and boil for about half that time, 7 minutes. Add the shrimp and boil for another 3 minutes, until they just turn pink. Do not overcook the shrimp. Take the pot off the heat and drain; serve immediately. If you cook the shrimp just right, the oil from the sausage will cause those shells to slip right off.

This is but one of dozens of recipes. Some cooks add some lemon juice and beer in the water as it's coming to a boil; others add onion, garlic, or green peppers.

---

carriage rides of the Point, including movie locations, embarking and disembarking near the Downtown Marina about every 40 minutes.

An important specialty bus tour in the area is **Gullah-N-Geechie Man Tours** (843/838-7516, www.gullahngeechietours.net, $20 adults, $18 children), focusing on the rich Gullah history and culture of the St. Helena Island area, including the historic Penn Center. Call for pickup information.

FOOD

Because of Beaufort's small size and insular nature, many of its restaurants double as nightlife hot spots, with hopping bar scenes—or as hopping as it gets here, anyway—at dinner hours and beyond, often with a crowd of regulars. That said, those looking for a rowdy late-night time will be happier seeking it in the notorious party towns of Charleston and Savannah.

New Southern

The stylishly appointed **Wren Bistro, Bar and Market** (210 Carteret St., 843/524-9463, www.wrenbistroandbar.com, Mon.-Sat. 11am-11pm, $15-25) is known for any of its chicken dishes. While the food is great, the interior is particularly well done, simultaneously warm and classy. As seems to be typical of Beaufort, the lunches are as good as the dinners, and the bar scene is quite active.

Breakfast and Brunch

One of the best breakfasts I've had anywhere was a humble two-egg plate for five bucks at Beaufort's most popular morning

Common Ground Coffeehouse and Market Cafe

well-kept little modernist space next to the similarly modernist City Loft Hotel. Their espresso is big-city quality, their periodicals are timely, and their pastries and sandwiches are good for tiding you over when you need some quick energy for more walking around town.

A few blocks across downtown is a great coffee place, **Common Ground Coffeehouse and Market Cafe** (102 West St., 843/524-2326, daily 7:30am-10pm). Located in a historic building facing the river, this is not just a serenely pleasant and convenient place to enjoy your coffee, but the cakes, cookies, light sandwiches, and fresh Italian gelatos are all delightfully delicious. Get here by strolling down Bay Street; it's at the end of an alley between two blocks, and is right on the Waterfront Park. There's an open mike every Friday night.

hangout, ★ **Blackstone's Café** (205 Scott St., 843/524-4330, Mon.-Sat. 7:30am-2:30pm, Sun. 7:30am-2pm, under $10). The dish is complete with tasty hash browns, a comparative rarity in this part of the country, where grits rule as the breakfast starch of choice.

Burgers and Sandwiches

A lunch favorite is **Magnolia Bakery Café** (703 Congress St., 843/524-1961, Mon.-Sat. 9am-5pm, under $10). Lump crab cakes are a specialty item, but you can't go wrong with any of the sandwiches. Vegetarian diners are particularly well taken care of with a large selection of black bean burger plates. As the name indicates, the range of desserts here is tantalizing, with the added bonus of a serious espresso bar.

Coffee, Tea, and Sweets

The closest thing to a hipster coffeehouse in Beaufort is **City Java and News** (301 Carteret St., 843/379-5282, Mon.-Sat. 6am-6:30pm, Sun. 7am-6:30pm), a sunny and

Seafood

The hottest dinner table in town is at the ★ **Saltus River Grill** (802 Bay St., 843/379-3474, Sun.-Thurs. 5pm-9pm, Fri.-Sat. 5pm-10pm, $10-39), famous throughout the state for its raw bar. Other specialties include she-crab bisque, lump crab cakes, and the ubiquitous shrimp and grits. The Saltus River Grill is more upscale in feel and in price than most Lowcountry places, with a very see-and-be-seen attitude and a hopping bar. Reservations are recommended.

The short and focused menu at **Plum's** (904½ Bay St., 843/525-1946, lunch daily 11am-4pm, dinner daily 5pm-10pm, $15-25) keys in on entrées highlighting local ingredients, such as the shrimp penne *all'amatriciana* and fresh black mussel pasta. An outstanding microbrew selection makes Plum's a big nightlife hangout as well.

Steaks

★ **Luther's Rare & Well Done** (910 Bay St., 843/521-1888, daily 10am-midnight, from $8) on the waterfront is the kind of meat-lover's place where even the French onion soup has a morsel of rib eye in it. While the patented succulent rubbed steaks are a no-brainer here, the handcrafted specialty pizzas are also quite popular. Housed in a historic pharmacy building, Luther's is also a great place for late eats after many other places in this quiet town have rolled up the sidewalk. A limited menu of appetizers and bar food to nosh on at the inviting and popular bar is available after 10pm.

Tapas

Emily's (906 Port Republic St., 843/522-1866, www.emilysrestaurantandtapasbar.com, dinner Mon.-Sat. 4pm-10pm, bar until 2am, $10-20) is a very popular fine-dining spot that specializes in a more traditional brand of rich, tasty tapas and is known for its active bar scene.

ACCOMMODATIONS

Beaufort's historic district is blessed with an abundance of high-quality accommodations that blend well with their surroundings.

Under $150

The **Best Western Sea Island Inn** (1015 Bay St., 843/522-2090, www.bestwestern. com, $135-170) is a good value for those for whom the B&B experience is not paramount. Anchoring the southern end of the historic district in a tasteful low brick building, the Best Western offers decent service, basic amenities, and surprisingly attractive rates for the location on Beaufort's busiest street.

$150-300

Any list of upscale Beaufort lodging must highlight the ★ **Beaufort Inn** (809 Port Republic St., 843/379-4667, www.beaufortinn. com, $152-425), consistently voted one of the best B&Bs in the nation. It's sort of a hybrid in that it comprises not only the 1897 historic central home, but also a cluster of freestanding historic cottages, each with a charming little porch and rocking chairs.

The 18-room circa-1820 **Rhett House Inn** (1009 Craven St., 843/524-9030, www. rhetthouseinn.com, $175-320) is the local vacation getaway for the stars. Such arts and entertainment luminaries as Robert Redford, Julia Roberts, Ben Affleck, Barbra Streisand, Dennis Quaid, and Demi Moore have all stayed here at one time or another.

the Beaufort Inn

There's nothing like enjoying the view of the Beaufort River from the expansive porches of the ★ **Cuthbert House Inn** (1203 Bay St., 843/521-1315, www.cuthberthouseinn.com, $205-250). This grand old circa-1790 Federal mansion was once the home of the wealthy Cuthbert family of rice and indigo planters. Some of the king rooms have fireplaces and claw-foot tubs. Of course you get a full Southern breakfast in addition to sunset hors d'oeuvres on the veranda.

While a stay at a B&B is the classic way to enjoy Beaufort, many travelers swear by the **City Loft Hotel** (301 Carteret St., 843/379-5638, www.citylofthotel.com, $200). Housed in a former motel, City Loft represents a total modernist makeover, gleaming from stem to stern with chrome and various art deco touches.

TRANSPORTATION AND SERVICES

The **Beaufort Visitors Information Center** (713 Craven St., 843/986-5400, www.beaufortsc.org, Mon.-Sat. 9am-5pm, Sun. noon-5pm), the headquarters of the Beaufort Chamber of Commerce and Convention and Visitors Bureau, has relocated from its old Carteret Street location and can now be found within the Beaufort Arsenal.

Air

While the Marines can fly their F-18s directly into Beaufort Naval Air Station, you won't have that luxury. The closest major airport to Beaufort is the **Savannah/Hilton Head International Airport** (SAV, 400 Airways Ave., 912/964-0514, www.savannahairport.com) off I-95 outside Savannah. From there it's about an hour to Beaufort. If you're not going into Savannah for any reason, the easiest route to the Beaufort area from the airport is to take I-95's exit 8, and from there take U.S. 278 east to Highway 170.

Alternatively, you could fly into **Charleston International Airport** (CHS, 5500 International Blvd., www.chs-airport.com), but because that facility is on the far north side of Charleston, it will take a bit longer (about an hour and 20 minutes) to get to Beaufort. From the Charleston Airport the best route south to Beaufort is U.S. 17 south, exiting onto U.S. 21 at Gardens Corner and then into Beaufort.

Car

If you're coming into the region by car, I-95 will be your likely primary route, with your main point of entry being exit 8 off I-95 connecting to U.S. 278 east to Highway 170. Beaufort is a little over an hour from Charleston.

Don't be discouraged by the big-box sprawl that assaults you on the approaches to Beaufort on Boundary Street, lined with the usual discount megastores, fast-food outlets, and budget motels. After you make the big 90-degree bend where Boundary turns into Carteret Street—known locally as the "Bellamy Curve"—it's like entering a whole new world of slow-paced, Spanish moss-lined avenues, friendly people, gentle breezes, and inviting storefronts.

Outside Beaufort

The areas outside tourist-traveled Beaufort can take you even further back into sepia-toned Americana, into a time of sharecropper homesteads, sturdy oystermen, and an altogether variable and subjective sense of time.

About 15 minutes east of Beaufort is the center of Gullah culture, St. Helena Island, and the scenic gem of Hunting Island. Just a few minutes south of Beaufort is the East Coast Marine Corps Recruit Depot of Parris Island. About 10 minutes away is the little community of Port Royal.

SIGHTS
★ Penn Center

By going across the Richard V. Woods Memorial Bridge over the Beaufort River on the Sea Island Parkway (which turns into U.S. 21), you'll pass through Lady's Island and reach St. Helena Island. Known to old-timers as Frogmore, the area took back its old Spanish-derived place name in the 1980s. Today St. Helena Island is most famous for the **Penn Center** (16 Martin Luther King Jr. Dr., 843/838-2474, www.penncenter.com, Mon.-Sat. 11am-4pm, $4 adults, $2 seniors and children), the spiritual home of Gullah culture and history. When you visit here among the live oaks and humble but well-preserved buildings, you'll instantly see why Martin Luther King Jr. chose this as one of his major retreat and planning sites during the civil rights era. The Penn Center continues to serve an important civil rights role by providing legal counsel to African American homeowners in St. Helena. Because clear title is difficult to acquire in the area due to the fact that so much of the land has stayed in the families of former slaves, developers are constantly making shady offers so that ancestral land can be opened up to upscale development.

The 50-acre campus is part of the Penn School Historic District, a National Historic Landmark comprising 19 buildings, most of historical significance. The Retreat House was intended for Dr. King to continue his strategy meetings, but he was assassinated before being able to stay there. The museum and bookshop

Penn Center played an important role during the civil rights movement.

are housed in the Cope Building, now called the York W. Bailey Museum, situated right along MLK Jr. Drive.

To get to the Penn Center from Beaufort (about 10 miles), proceed over the bridge until you get to St. Helena Island. Take a right onto MLK Jr. Drive when you see the Red Piano Too Art Gallery. The Penn Center is a few hundred yards down on your right. If you drive past the Penn Center and continue a few hundred yards down MLK Jr. Drive, look for the ancient tabby ruins on the left side of the road. This is the **Chapel of Ease,** the remnant of a 1740 church destroyed by forest fire in the late 1800s.

Fort Fremont Preserve

Military historians and sightseers of a particularly adventurous type will want to drive several miles past the Penn Center on St. Helena Island to visit **Fort Fremont Preserve** (Lands End Rd., www.fortfremont. org, daily 9am-dusk, free). Two artillery batteries remain of this Spanish-American War-era coastal defense fort (an adjacent private residence is actually the old army hospital). The fort was active until 1921, but now the big guns are long gone. Their heavy concrete emplacements, however—along with many dark tunnels and small rooms—are still here and make for a very interesting visit. Guided docent tours happen the fourth Saturday of the month starting at 10:30am at the St. Helena Branch of the Beaufort County Library (6355 Jonathan Francis Senior Rd.). The two-hour tours are free, and reservations aren't required.

Old Sheldon Church

About 20 minutes north of Beaufort are the poignantly desolate ruins of the once-magnificent **Old Sheldon Church** (Old Sheldon Church Rd., off U.S. 17 just past Gardens Corner, daily dawn-dusk, free). One of the first Greek Revival structures in the United States, the house of worship held its first service in 1757. The sanctuary was first burned by the British in 1779. After being rebuilt in 1826, the sanctuary survived until General Sherman's arrival in 1865, whereupon Union troops razed it once more. Nothing remains now but these towering walls and columns made of red brick instead of the tabby often seen in similar ruins on the coast. It's now owned by the nearby St. Helena's Episcopal Church in Beaufort, which holds outdoor services here the second Sunday after Easter.

the ruins of Old Sheldon Church

Port Royal

This sleepy hamlet between Beaufort and Parris Island touts itself as a leader in "small-town New Urbanism," with an emphasis on livability, retro-themed shopping areas, and relaxing walking trails. However, **Port Royal** is still pretty sleepy—but not without very real charms, not the least of which is the fact that everything is within easy walking distance of everything else. The highlight of the year is the annual Softshell Crab Festival, held each April to mark the short-lived harvesting season for that favorite crustacean.

While much of the tiny historic district has a scrubbed, tidy feel, the main historic structure is the charming little **Union Church** (11th St., 843/524-4333, Mon.-Fri. 10am-4pm, donation), one of the oldest buildings in town, with guided docent tours.

Don't miss the boardwalk and observation tower at **The Sands** municipal beach and boat ramp. The 50-foot-tall structure provides a commanding view of Battery Creek. The little beach is artificial (made from dredged material) but still somewhat unusual in this area. To get to The Sands, head east onto 7th Street off the main drag of Parris Avenue. Seventh Street turns into Sands Beach Road for a brief stretch and then merges with 6th Street, taking you directly to The Sands.

A must-stop for families is the **Port Royal Maritime Center** (310 Okatie Hwy., 843/645-7774, www.portroyalsoundfoundation.org, Tues.-Sat. 10am-5pm, free), a new venture that is a great resource for learning about the area's ecological history. Another environmentally oriented point of pride is the **Lowcountry Estuarium** (1402 Parris Ave., 843/524-6600, www.lowcountryestuarium.org, Wed.-Sat. 10am-5pm, feedings at 11:30am and 3pm, $5 adults, $3 children).

If you get hungry in Port Royal, try the waterfront seafood haven **11th Street Dockside** (1699 11th St., 843/524-7433, daily 4:30pm-10pm, $17-27). The Dockside Dinner is a great sampler plate with lobster tail, scallops, crab legs, and shrimp. The views of the waterfront and the adjoining shrimp-boat docks are relaxing and beautiful.

Parris Island

Though more commonly known as the home of the legendary **Marine Corps Recruit Depot Parris Island** (283 Blvd. de France, 843/228-3650, www.mcrdpi.marines.mil, free), the island is also of historical significance as the site of some of the earliest European presence in the New World. Today it's where all female U.S. Marine recruits and most male recruits east of the Mississippi River go through the Corps' grueling 13-week boot camp. Almost every Friday during the year marks the graduation of a company of newly minted Marines. That's why you might notice an influx of visitors to the area each Thursday, aka "Family Day," with the requisite amount of celebration on Fridays after that morning's ceremony.

Unlike many military facilities in the post-9/11 era, Parris Island still hosts plenty of visitors. Just check in with the sentry at the gate and show your valid driver's license, registration, and proof of insurance. Rental car drivers must show a copy of the rental agreement. On your way to the depot proper, there are a couple of beautiful picnic areas. Once inside, stop first at the **Douglas Visitor Center** (Bldg. 283, Blvd. de France, 843/228-3650, Mon. 7:30am-noon, Tues.-Wed. 7:30am-4:30pm, Thurs. 6:30am-7pm, Fri. 7:30am-3pm), a great place to find maps and information. As you go by the big parade ground, or "deck," be sure to check out the beautiful sculpture re-creating the famous photo of Marines raising the flag on Iwo Jima. A short way ahead is the **Parris Island Museum** (Bldg. 111, 111 Panama St., 843/228-2951, www.mcrdpimuseum.com, daily 10am-4:30pm, free), detailing the proud history of the Corps with a particular focus on this Recruit Depot.

The Spanish built Santa Elena nearby the original French settlement, Charlesfort. They then built two other settlements, San Felipe and San Marcos. The Santa Elena site, now on the circa-1950s Parris Island Depot golf course, is a National Historic Landmark. So far, archaeologists have found a residence of a wealthy family in the town and have identified two of Santa Elena's five forts. Many artifacts are viewable at the nearby **clubhouse-interpretive center** (daily 7am-5pm, free). You can take a self-guided tour; to get to the site from the museum, continue on Panama Street and take a right on Cuba Street. Follow the signs to the golf course and continue through the main parking lot of the course.

★ Hunting Island State Park

Rumored to be a hideaway for Blackbeard himself, the aptly named Hunting Island was indeed for many years a notable hunting preserve, and its abundance of wildlife remains to this day. The island is one of the East Coast's best birding spots and also hosts dolphins, loggerheads, alligators, and deer. A true family-friendly outdoor adventure spot, **Hunting Island State Park** (2555 Sea Island Pkwy., 866/345-7275, www.huntingisland.com, winter daily 6am-6pm, during daylight saving time daily 6am-9pm, $5 adults, $3 children) has something for everyone—kids, parents, and newlyweds. Yet it still retains a certain sense of lush wildness—so much so that it doubled as Vietnam in the movie *Forrest Gump*.

At the north end past the campground is the island's main landmark, the historic **Hunting Island Light,** which dates from 1875. Although the lighthouse ceased operations in 1933, a rotating light—not strong enough to serve as an actual navigational aid—is turned on at night. While the 167-step trek to the top (donation $2 pp) is strenuous, the view is stunning.

★ ACE Basin

Occupying pretty much the entire area between Beaufort and Charleston, the **ACE Basin**—the acronym signifies its role as the collective estuary of the Ashepoo, Combahee, and Edisto Rivers—is one of the most enriching natural experiences the country has to offer. The ACE Basin's three core rivers, the Edisto being the largest, are the framework for a matrix of waterways crisscrossing its approximately 350,000 acres of salt marsh. While the ACE Basin can in no way be called "pristine," it's a testament to the power of nature that after 6,000 years of human presence and often intense cultivation, the basin manages to retain much of its untamed feel.

About 12,000 acres of the ACE Basin Project comprise the **Ernest F. Hollings ACE Basin National Wildlife Refuge** (8675

the view from the Hunting Island Light

The Lost Art of Tabby

Tabby is a unique construction technique combining oyster shells, lime, water, and sand found along the South Carolina and Georgia coasts.

Contrary to popular belief, it did not originate with Native Americans. The confusion is due to the fact that the native population left behind many middens, or trash heaps, of oyster shells. While these middens indeed provided the bulk of the shells for tabby buildings to come, Native Americans had little else to do with it. Also contrary to lore, although the Spanish were responsible for the first use of tabby in the Americas, almost all remaining tabby in the area dates from later English settlement. The British first fell in love with tabby after the siege of Spanish-held St. Augustine, Florida, and quickly began building with it in their colonies to the north.

Scholars are divided as to whether tabby was invented by West Africans or its use spread to Africa from Spain and Portugal, circuitously coming to the United States through the knowledge of imported slaves. The origin of the word itself is also unclear, as similar words exist in Spanish, Portuguese, Gullah, and Arabic to describe various types of wall.

We do know for sure how tabby is made: The primary technique was to burn alternating layers of oyster shells and logs in a deep hole in the ground, thus creating lime. The lime was then mixed with oyster shells, sand, and freshwater and poured into wooden molds, or "forms," to dry and then be used as building blocks, much like large bricks. Tabby walls were usually plastered with stucco. Tabby is remarkably strong and resilient, able to survive the hurricanes that often batter the area. It also stays cool in the summer and is insect-resistant, two enormous advantages down here.

Following are some great examples of true tabby you can see today on the South Carolina and Georgia coasts, from north to south:

- **Dorchester State Historic Site** in Summerville, north of Charleston, contains a well-preserved tabby fort.

- Several younger tabby buildings still exist in downtown Beaufort: the **Barnwell-Gough House** (705 Washington St.); the Thomas Fuller House, or **"Tabby Manse"** (1211 Bay St.); and the **Saltus House** (800 block of Bay St.), perhaps the tallest surviving tabby structure.

- The **Chapel of Ease** on St. Helena Island dates from the 1740s. If someone tells you Sherman burned it down, don't believe it; the culprit was a forest fire.

Willtown Rd., 843/889-3084, www.fws.gov/acebasin, grounds year-round daily dawn-dusk, office Mon.-Fri. 7:30am-4pm, free), run by the U.S. Fish and Wildlife Service. The historic 1828 **Grove Plantation House** is in this portion of the basin and houses the refuge's headquarters. Sometimes featured on local tours of homes, it's one of only three antebellum homes left in the ACE Basin. Surrounded by lush, ancient oak trees, it's really a sight in and of itself.

This section of the refuge, the **Edisto Unit,** is about an hour's drive from Beaufort. To get to the Edisto Unit of the Hollings/ACE Basin National Wildlife Refuge, take U.S. 17 to Highway 174 (going all the way down this route takes you to Edisto Island) and turn right onto Willtown Road. The unpaved entrance road is about two miles ahead on the left. There are restrooms and a few picnic tables.

You can also visit the two parts of the **Combahee Unit** of the refuge, which offers a similar scene of trails among impounded wetlands along the Combahee River, with parking; it's farther west near Yemassee. The Combahee Unit is about 30 minutes from Beaufort. Get here by taking a left off U.S. 17 onto Highway 33. The larger portion of the Combahee Unit is soon after the turnoff, and the smaller, more northerly portion is about five miles up the road.

the Chapel of Ease on St. Helena Island

- The **Stoney-Baynard Ruins** in Sea Pines Plantation on Hilton Head are all that's left of the home of the old Braddock's Point Plantation. Foundations of a slave quarters are nearby.

- **Wormsloe Plantation** near Savannah has the remains of Noble Jones's fortification on the Skidaway Narrows.

- **St. Cyprian's Episcopal Church** in Darien is one of the largest tabby structures still in use.

- **Fort Frederica** on St. Simons Island has not only the remains of a tabby fort but many foundations of tabby houses in the surrounding settlement.

- The remarkably intact walls of the **Horton-DuBignon House** on Jekyll Island, Georgia, date from 1738, and the house was occupied into the 1850s.

Recreation
KAYAKING

A good service for rentals and knowledgeable guided tours of the ACE Basin is **Outpost Moe's** (843/844-2514, www.geocities.ws/outpostmoe), where the basic 2.5-hour tour costs $40 per person, and an all-day extravaganza through the basin is $80. Moe's provides lunch for most of its tours. Another premier local outfitter for ACE Basin tours is **Carolina Heritage Outfitters** (U.S. 15 in Canadys, 843/563-5051, www.canoesc.com), which focuses on the Edisto River trail. In addition to guided tours ($30) and rentals, you can camp overnight in their cute tree houses ($125) along the kayak routes. They load you

up with your gear and drive you 22 miles upriver, then you paddle downriver to the tree house for the evening. The next day, you paddle yourself the rest of the way downriver back to home base.

To have a drier experience of the ACE Basin from the deck of a larger vessel, try **ACE Basin Tours** (1 Coosaw River Dr., Beaufort, 843/521-3099, www.acebasintours.com, Mar.-Nov. Wed. and Sat. 10am, $35 adults, $15 children), which will take you on a three-hour tour in the 40-passenger *Dixie Lady*. To get to their dock from Beaufort, take Carteret Street over the bridge to St. Helena Island, and then take a left on Highway 802 east (Sam's Point Rd.). Continue until you cross Lucy Point Creek;

the ACE Basin Tours marina is on your immediate left after you cross the bridge.

The state of South Carolina has conveniently gathered some of the best self-guided kayak trips at www.acebasin.net/canoe.html.

GOLF

Golf is much bigger in Hilton Head than in the Beaufort area, but there are some local highlights. The best-regarded public course in the area, and indeed one of the best military courses in the world, is **Legends at Parris Island** (Bldg. 299, Parris Island, 843/228-2240, www.mccssc.com, $30). Call in advance for a tee time.

Another popular public course is **South Carolina National Golf Club** (8 Waveland Ave., Cat Island, 843/524-0300, www.sc-national.com, $70). Get to secluded Cat Island by taking the Sea Island Parkway onto Lady's Island and continuing south as it turns into Lady's Island Drive. Turn onto

Island Causeway and continue for about three miles.

CAMPING

Hunting Island State Park (2555 Sea Island Pkwy., 866/345-7275, www.huntingisland. com, winter daily 6am-6pm, during daylight saving time daily 6am-9pm, $5 adults, $3 children, $25 RV sites, $19 tent sites, $87-172 cabin) has 200 campsites with individual water and electric hookups on the north end of the island. There used to be plenty of cabins for rent, but beach erosion has sadly made the ones near the water uninhabitable. One cabin near the lighthouse is still available for rent, and it is in such high demand that the park encourages you to camp instead.

Another neat place to camp is **Tuck in the Wood** (22 Tuc In De Wood Ln., St. Helena, 843/838-2267, $25), a very well-maintained 74-site private campground just past the Penn Center on St. Helena Island.

Edisto Island

One of the last truly unspoiled places in the Lowcountry, Edisto Island has been highly regarded as a getaway spot since the Edisto people first started coming here for shellfish. In fact, locals here swear that the island was settled by English-speaking colonists even before Charleston was settled in 1670.

There are rental homes galore on Edisto Island. Because of the lack of hotels, this is the most popular option for most vacationers here—indeed, it's just about the only option. Contact **Edisto Sales and Rentals Realty** (1405 Palmetto Blvd., 800/868-5398, www.edistorealty.com).

SIGHTS

The **Edisto Museum** (8123 Chisolm Plantation Rd., 843/869-1954, www.edistomuseum.org, Tues.-Sat. noon-5pm, $4 adults, $2 children, free under age 10), a project of the Edisto Island Historic Preservation Society,

has recently expanded and incorporated a nearby slave cabin. Its well-done exhibits of local lore and history are complemented by a gift shop. The Edisto Museum is before you get to the main part of the island, off Highway 174.

Opened in 1999 by local snake hunters the Clamp brothers, the **Edisto Island Serpentarium** (1374 Hwy. 174, 843/869-1171, www.edistoserpentarium.com, hours vary, $14.95 adults, $10.95 ages 4-12, free age 3 and younger) is educational and fun, taking you up close and personal with a variety of reptilian creatures native to the area. They usually close Labor Day-April 30.

The **Botany Bay Wildlife Management Area** (www.preserveedisto.org, Wed.-Mon. dawn-dusk, free) is a great way to enjoy the unspoiled nature of Edisto Island. On the grounds of two former rice and indigo plantations comprising 4,000 acres, Botany Bay features several remains of the old plantations and a small, wonderful beach. There are no facilities to speak of, so pack and plan accordingly. Botany Bay is closed on hunt days, which vary depending on the hunting season but are fairly rare.

SPORTS AND ACTIVITIES

As the largest river of the ACE (Ashepoo, Combahee, Edisto) Basin complex, the Edisto River figures large in the lifestyle of residents and visitors. A good public landing is at Steamboat Creek off Highway 174 on the way down to the island. Take Steamboat Landing Road (Hwy. 968) from Highway 174 near the James Edwards School. Live Oak Landing is farther up Big Bay Creek near the interpretive center at the state park. The **Edisto Marina** (3702 Docksite Rd., 843/869-3504) is on the far west side of the island.

Captain Ron Elliott of **Edisto Island Tours** (843/869-1937) offers various ecotours and fishing trips as well as canoe and kayak rentals for about $25 per day. A typical kayak tour runs about $35 per person for a 1.5-2-hour trip, and he offers a "beachcombing" trip for $15 per person. Riding a bike on Edisto

Beach and all around the island is a great and relaxing way to get some exercise and enjoy its scenic, laid-back beauty. The best place to rent a bike—or a kayak or canoe, for that matter—is **Island Bikes and Outfitters** (140 Jungle Rd., 843/869-4444, Mon.-Sat. 9am-4pm). Bike rentals run about $16 per day; single kayaks are about $60 per day.

★ Edisto Beach State Park

Edisto Beach State Park (8377 State Cabin Rd., 843/869-2156, www.southcarolinaparks. com, Nov.-mid-Mar. daily 8am-6pm, mid-Mar.-Oct. daily 6am-10pm, $5 adults, $3 children, free under age 6) is one of the world's foremost destinations for shell collectors. Largely because of fresh loads of silt from the adjacent ACE Basin, there are always new specimens, many of them fossils, washing ashore. The park stretches almost three miles and features the state's longest system of fully accessible hiking and biking trails, including one leading to a 4,000-year-old shell midden, now much eroded from past millennia. The particularly well-done **interpretive center** (Tues.-Sat. 9am-4pm) has plenty of interesting exhibits about the nature and history of the park as well as the surrounding ACE Basin.

Edisto Island

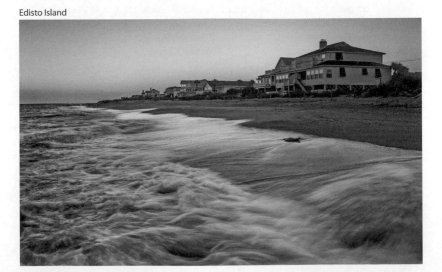

CAMPING

A great thing about Edisto Island is the total absence of ugly chain lodging or beachfront condo development. My recommended option is staying at **Edisto Beach State Park** (843/869-2156, www.southcarolinaparks.com, $25 tent sites, $75-100 cabins) itself, either at a campsite on the Atlantic side or in a marshfront cabin on the northern edge. During high season (Apr.-Nov.), there's a minimum weeklong stay in the cabins; during the off-season, the minimum stay is two days. You can book cabins up to 11 months in advance.

FOOD

One of the all-time great barbecue places in South Carolina is on Edisto: ★ **Po Pigs Bo-B-Q** (2410 Hwy. 174, 843/869-9003, Wed.-Sat. 11:30am-9pm, $4-10), on the way into town. This is the real thing, the full pig cooked in all its many ways: white meat, dark meat, cracklin's, and hash, served in the local style of "all you care to eat." Unlike many barbecue spots, they do serve beer and wine.

Another popular joint on the island is **Whaley's** (2801 Myrtle St., 843/869-2161, Tues.-Sat. 11:30am-2pm and 5pm-9pm, bar daily 5pm-2am, $5-15), a down-home place in an old gas station a few blocks off the beach. This is a good place for casual seafood like boiled shrimp, washed down with a lot of beer. The bar is open seven days a week.

The legendary ★ **Old Post Office** (1442 Hwy. 174, 843/869-2339, www.theoldpostofficerestaurant.com, Tues.-Sun. 5:30pm-10pm, $20), a Lowcountry-style fine-dining spot, served a devoted clientele for 20 years. It recently reopened with a bang and thankfully kept its old-school mystique intact. Specialties include fine crab cakes drizzled with mousseline sauce, the pecan-encrusted Veal Edistonian, and a Carolina rib eye topped with a pimiento cheese sauce.

TRANSPORTATION

Edisto Island is basically halfway between Beaufort and Charleston. There's one main land route here, south on Highway 174 off U.S. 17. It's a long way down from U.S. 17 to Edisto, but the 20- to 30-minute drive is scenic and enjoyable. Most activity on the island centers on the township of Edisto Beach, which voted to align itself with Colleton County for its lower taxes (the rest of Edisto Island is part of Charleston County).

Tours

Edisto has many beautiful plantation homes, relics of the island's longtime role as host to cotton plantations. While all are in private hands and therefore off-limits to the public, an exception is offered through **Edisto Island Tours & T'ings** (843/869-9092, $20 adults, $10 under age 13). You'll take a van tour around Edisto's beautiful churches and old plantations.

Hilton Head Island

Literally the prototype of the modern planned resort community, Hilton Head Island is also a case study in how a landscape can change when money is introduced. From Reconstruction until the post-World War II era, the island consisted almost entirely of African Americans with deep roots in the area. In the mid-1950s Hilton Head began its transformation into an almost all-white, upscale golf, tennis, and shopping mecca populated largely by Northern transplants and retirees. As you can imagine, the flavor here is now quite different from surrounding areas of the Lowcountry, to say the least, with an emphasis on material excellence, top prices, get-it-done-yesterday punctuality, and the attendant aggressive traffic.

These days, Hilton Head gets the most national media attention for the RBC Heritage golf tournament each April, when the entire

Hilton Head Island

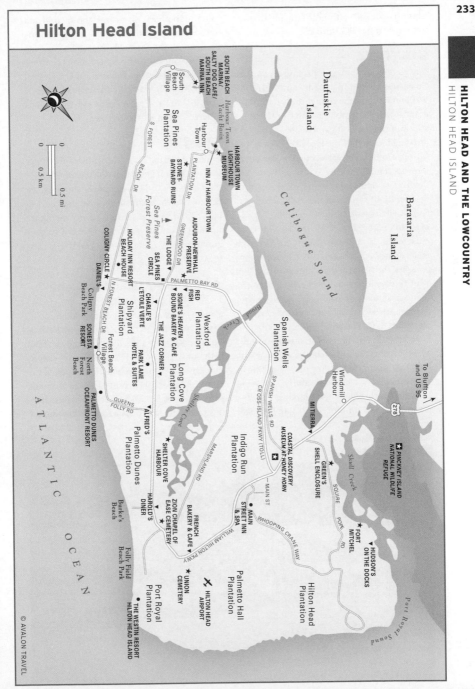

SOUTH BEACH MARINA
SALTY DOG CAFE/
SOUTH BEACH MARINA INN

South Beach Village

Sea Pines Plantation

Harbour Town Yacht Basin

Harbour Town

HARBOUR TOWN LIGHTHOUSE MUSEUM

INN AT HARBOUR TOWN

STONEY-BAYNARD RUINS

AUDUBON-NEWHALL PRESERVE

THE LODGE

SEA PINES CIRCLE

HOLIDAY INN RESORT BEACH HOUSE

COLIGNY CIRCLE

DANIEL'S

Coligny Beach Park

SONESTA RESORT

PALMETTO DUNES OCEANFRONT RESORT

CHARLIE'S L'ETOILE VERTE

THE JAZZ CORNER

PARK LANE HOTEL & SUITES

ALFRED'S

Shipyard Plantation

Forest Beach Village

North Forest Beach

Palmetto Dunes Plantation

RED FISH

SIGNE'S HEAVEN BOUND BAKERY & CAFE

Wexford Plantation

Long Cove Plantation

SHELTER COVE HARBOUR

Sea Pines Forest Preserve

Daufuskie Island

Calibogue Sound

Barataria Island

Spanish Wells Plantation

Windmill Harbour

MI TIERRA

GREEN'S SHELL ENCLOSURE

COASTAL DISCOVERY MUSEUM AT HONEY HORN

Indigo Run Plantation

Skull Creek

To Bluffton and US 95

278

PINCKNEY ISLAND NATIONAL WILDLIFE REFUGE

HUDSON'S ON THE DOCKS

FORT MITCHEL

MAIN STREET INN & SPA

FRENCH BAKERY & CAFE

HAROLD'S DINER

ZION CHAPEL OF EASE CEMETERY

UNION CEMETERY

HILTON HEAD AIRPORT

Palmetto Hall Plantation

Hilton Head Plantation

Port Royal Plantation

THE WESTIN RESORT HILTON HEAD ISLAND

Folly Field Beach Park

Burke's Beach

ATLANTIC OCEAN

PALMETTO BAY RD
N FOREST BEACH DR
QUEENS FOLLY RD
WILLIAM HILTON PKWY
MARSHLAND RD
SPANISH WELLS RD
CROSS-ISLAND PKWY (TOLL)
WHOOPING CRANE WAY
SQUIRE POPE RD
S FOREST DR
BEACH DR
PLANTATION DR
GREENWOOD DR
Broad Creek
Skull Creek
Port Royal Sound
MAIN ST

0   0.5 km
0   0.5 mi

© AVALON TRAVEL

island is packed with golf fans for this extremely popular PGA event.

HISTORY

The second-largest barrier island on the East Coast was named in 1663 by adventurer Sir William Hilton, who thoughtfully named the island—with its notable headland or "Head"—after himself. Later it gained fame as the first growing location of the legendary Sea Island cotton, a long-grain variety that, following its introduction in 1790 by William Elliott II of the Myrtle Bank Plantation, would soon be the dominant version of the cash crop.

Though it seems unlikely given the island's modern demographics, Hilton Head was almost entirely African American through much of the 20th century. When Union troops occupied the island at the outbreak of the Civil War, freed and escaped slaves flocked to the island, and many of the dwindling number of African Americans on the island today are descendants of this original Gullah population.

In the 1950s the Fraser family bought 19,000 of the island's 25,000 acres with the intent to continue forestry on them. But in 1956—not at all coincidentally the same year the first bridge to the island was built—Charles Fraser convinced his father to sell him the southern tip. Fraser's brainchild and decades-long labor of love—some said his obsession—Sea Pines Plantation became the prototype for the golf-oriented resort communities so common today on both U.S. coasts. Fraser himself was killed in a boating accident in 2002 and is buried under the famous Liberty Oak in Harbour Town.

SIGHTS

Contrary to what many think, there are things to do on Hilton Head that don't involve swinging a club at a little white ball or shopping for designer labels, but instead celebrate the area's history and natural setting. The following are some of those attractions, arranged in geographical order from where you first access the island.

★ Pinckney Island National Wildlife Refuge

Consisting of many islands and hammocks, **Pinckney Island National Wildlife Refuge** (912/652-4415, daily dawn-dusk, free) is the only part of this small but very well-managed 4,000-acre refuge that's open to the public. Almost 70 percent of the former rice plantation is salt marsh and tidal creeks, making it a perfect microcosm for the Lowcountry

Pinckney Island National Wildlife Refuge

Green's Shell Enclosure

Less known than the larger Native American shell ring farther south at Sea Pines, **Green's Shell Enclosure** (803/734-3886, daily dawn-dusk) is certainly easier to find, and you don't have to pay $5 to enter the area, as with Sea Pines. This three-acre heritage preserve dates back to at least the 1300s. The heart of the site comprises a low embankment, part of the original fortified village. To get here, take a left at the intersection of U.S. 278 and Squire Pope Road. Turn left into Green's Park, pass the office on the left, and park. The entrance to the shell enclosure is on the left behind a fence.

★ Coastal Discovery Museum at Honey Horn

With the acquisition of Honey Horn's 70-acre spread of historic plantation land, Hilton Head finally has a full-fledged museum worthy of the name, and the magnificent **Coastal Discovery Museum** (70 Honey Horn Dr., 843/689-6767, www.coastaldiscovery.org, Mon.-Sat. 9am-4:30pm, Sun. 11am-3pm, free)

is a must-see, even for those who came to the island mostly to golf and soak up sun.

The facility centers on the expertly restored Discovery House, the only antebellum house still existing on Hilton Head, with exhibits and displays devoted to the history of the island. The museum is also a great one-stop place to sign up for a variety of specialty on-site and off-site guided tours, such as birding and Gullah history tours. The cost for most on-site tours is a reasonable $10 adults and $5 children.

But the real draw is the 0.5-mile trail through the Honey Horn grounds, including several boardwalk viewpoints over the marsh, a neat little butterfly habitat, a few gardens, and a stable and pasture that host Honey Horn May and Tadpole, the museum's two Marsh Tackies—short, tough little ponies descended from Spanish horses and used to great effect by Francis "Swamp Fox" Marion and his freedom fighters in the American Revolution.

While a glance at a map and area signage might convince you that you must pay the $1.25 toll on the Cross Island Parkway to get to Honey Horn, that isn't so. The exit to Honey Horn on the parkway is actually before you get to the toll plaza; therefore access is free.

one of the Coastal Discovery Museum's Marsh Tackies

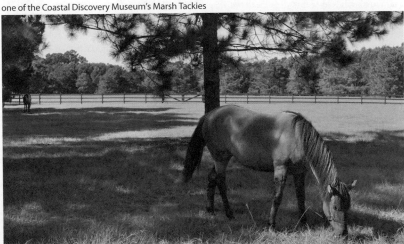

Union Cemetery

A modest but key aspect of African American history on Hilton Head is at **Union Cemetery** (Union Cemetery Rd.), a small burial ground featuring several graves of black Union Army troops (you can tell by the designation "USCI" on the tombstone, for "United States Colored Infantry"). Also of interest are the charming hand-carved cement tombstones of nonveterans. To get here, turn north off William Hilton Parkway onto Union Cemetery Road. The cemetery is a short way ahead on the left. There is no signage or site interpretation.

Zion Chapel of Ease Cemetery

More like one of the gloriously desolate scenes common to the rest of the Lowcountry, this little cemetery in full view of the William Hilton Parkway at Folly Field Road is all that remains of one of the "Chapels of Ease," a string of chapels set up in the 1700s. The **Zion Chapel of Ease Cemetery** (daily dawn-dusk, free) is said to be haunted by the ghost of William Baynard, whose final resting place is in a mausoleum on the site (the remains of his ancestral home are farther south at Sea Pines Plantation).

Audubon-Newhall Preserve

Plant lovers shouldn't miss this small but very well-maintained 50-acre wooded tract in the south-central part of the island on Palmetto Bay Road between the Cross Island Parkway and the Sea Pines Circle. Almost all plant life, even that in the water, is helpfully marked and identified. The **Audubon-Newhall Preserve** (year-round dawn-dusk, free) is open to the public, but you can't camp here. For more information, call the **Hilton Head Audubon Society** (843/842-9246).

Sea Pines Plantation

This private residential resort development at the extreme west end of the island—the first on Hilton Head and the prototype for every other such development in the country—hosts several attractions that collectively are well worth the $5 per vehicle "road use" fee, which you pay at the main entrance gate.

HARBOUR TOWN

It's not particularly historic and not all that natural, but **Harbour Town** is still pretty cool. The dominant element is the squat, colorful **Harbour Town Lighthouse Museum** (149 Lighthouse Rd., 843/671-2810, www.harbourtownlighthouse.com, daily 10am-dusk, $4.25, free age 5 and under), which has never really helped a ship navigate its way near the island. The 90-foot structure was built in 1970 purely to give visitors a little atmosphere, and that it does, as kids especially love climbing the stairs to the top and looking out over the island's expanse.

STONEY-BAYNARD RUINS

The **Stoney-Baynard ruins** (Plantation Dr., dawn-dusk, free), tabby ruins in a residential neighborhood, are what remains of the circa-1790 central building of the old Braddock's Point Plantation, first owned by patriot and raconteur Captain "Saucy Jack" Stoney and later by the Baynard family. Active during the island's heyday as a cotton center, the plantation was destroyed after the Civil War.

SEA PINES FOREST PRESERVE

The **Sea Pines Forest Preserve** (175 Greenwood Dr., 843/363-4530, free) is set amid the Sea Pines Plantation golf resort development, but you don't need a bag of clubs to enjoy this 600-acre preserve, which is built on the site of an old rice plantation (dikes and logging trails are still visible). Here you can ride a horse, fish, or just take a walk on the eight miles of trails (dawn-dusk) and enjoy the natural beauty around you. No bike riding is allowed on the trails, however.

In addition to the Native American shell ring farther north off Squire Pope Road, the Sea Pines Forest Preserve also boasts a shell ring set within a canopy of tall pines.

Tours and Cruises

Most guided tours on Hilton Head focus on

the water. **Harbour Town Cruises** (843/363-9023, www.vagabondcruise.com, $30-60) offers several sightseeing tours as well as excursions to Daufuskie and Savannah. They also offer a tour on a former America's Cup racing yacht.

"Dolphin tours" are extremely popular on Hilton Head, and there is no shortage of operators. **Dolphin Watch Nature Cruises** (843/785-4558, $25 adults, $10 children) departs from Shelter Cove, as does **Lowcountry Nature Tours** (843/683-0187, www.lowcountrynaturetours.com, $40 adults, $35 children, free under age 3). **Outside Hilton Head** (843/686-6996, www.outsidehiltonhead.com) runs a variety of water ecotours and dolphin tours as well as a guided day-trip excursion to Daufuskie, complete with golf cart rental.

There is a notable land-based tour by **Gullah Heritage Trail Tours** (leaves from Coastal Discovery Museum at Honey Horn, 843/681-7066, www.gullahheritage.com, $32 adults, $15 children) delving into the island's rich, if poorly preserved, African American history from slavery through the time of the freedmen.

ENTERTAINMENT AND NIGHTLIFE
Nightlife
The highest-quality live entertainment on the island is at **The Jazz Corner** (1000 William Hilton Pkwy., 843/842-8620, www.thejazzcorner.com, dinner daily 6pm-9pm, late-night menu after 9pm, dinner $15-20, cover varies), which brings in big names in the genre to perform in this space in the unlikely setting of a boutique mall, the Village at Wexford. The dinners are actually quite good, but the attraction is definitely the music. Reservations are recommended. Live music starts around 7pm.

For years islanders jokingly referred to the "Barmuda Triangle," an area named for the preponderance of bars within vague walking distance of Sea Pines Circle. While some of the names have changed over the years, the longtime anchor of the Barmuda Triangle is the **Tiki Hut** (1 S. Forest Beach Dr., 843/785-5126,

Sun.-Thurs. 11am-8pm, Fri.-Sat. 11am-10pm, bar until 2am), actually part of The Beach House hotel at the entrance to Sea Pines. This popular watering hole is the only beachfront bar on the island, which technically makes it the only place you can legally drink alcohol on a Hilton Head beach. Another Triangle fave is **The Lodge** (7 Greenwood Dr., 843/842-8966, www.hiltonheadlodge.com, daily 11:30am-midnight). After the martini-and-cigar craze waned, this popular spot successfully remade itself into a beer-centric place with 36 rotating taps.

Despite its location in the upscale strip mall of the Village at Wexford, the **British Open Pub** (1000 William Hilton Pkwy./Hwy. 278, 843/686-6736, daily 11am-10pm) offers a fairly convincing English vibe with, as the name suggests, a heavy golf theme. The fish-and-chips and shepherd's pie are both magnificent.

Inside Sea Pines is the **Quarterdeck Lounge and Patio** (843/842-1999, www.seapines.com, Sun.-Thurs. 5:30pm-10pm, Fri.-Sat. 5:30pm-midnight) at the base of the Harbour Town Lighthouse. This is where the party's at after a long day on the fairways during the Heritage golf tournament. Within Sea Pines at the South Beach Marina is also where you'll find **The Salty Dog Cafe** (232 S. Sea Pines Dr., 843/671-2233, www.saltydog.com, lunch daily 11am-3pm, dinner daily 5pm-10pm, bar daily until 2am), one of the area's most popular institutions (some might even call it a tourist trap) and something akin to an island empire, with popular T-shirts, a gift shop, books, and an ice cream shop, all overlooking the marina. My suggestion, however, is to make the short walk to the affiliated **Wreck of the Salty Dog** (843/671-7327, daily until 2am), where the marsh views are better and the atmosphere not quite so tacky.

A gay-friendly bar on Hilton Head is **Cool Cats Lounge** (32 Palmetto Bay Rd., Mon.-Fri. 8pm-3am, Sat. 8pm-2am), with a welcoming dive-bar atmosphere and a small but lively dance floor.

Performing Arts

Because so many residents migrated here from art-savvy metropolitan areas in the Northeast, Hilton Head maintains a very high standard of top-quality entertainment. Much of the activity centers on the multimillion-dollar **Arts Center of Coastal Carolina** (14 Shelter Cove Ln., 843/842-2787, www.artshhi.com), which hosts touring shows, resident companies, musical concerts, dance performances, and visual arts exhibits.

Under the direction of maestro John Morris Russell, the **Hilton Head Symphony Orchestra** (843/842-2055, www.hhso.org) performs a year-round season of masterworks and pops programs at various venues, primarily the First Presbyterian Church (540 William Hilton Pkwy./Hwy. 278). They also take their show on the road with several concerts in Bluffton and even perform several "Symphony Under the Stars" programs at Shelter Cove. **Chamber Music Hilton Head** (www.cmhh.org) performs throughout the year with selections ranging from Brahms to Smetana at All Saints Episcopal Church (3001 Meeting St.).

Cinema

There's an art house on Hilton Head, the charming **Coligny Theatre** (843/686-3500, www.colignytheatre.com) in the Coligny Plaza shopping center before you get to Sea Pines. For years this was the only movie theater for miles around, but it has reincarnated as a primarily indie film venue. Look for the entertaining murals by local artist Ralph Sutton. Showtimes are Monday 11:30am and 4pm, Tuesday and Friday 11:30am, 4pm, and 7pm, Wednesday-Thursday and Saturday-Sunday 4pm and 7pm.

Festivals and Events

Late February-early March brings the **Hilton Head Wine and Food Festival** (www.hiltonheadhospitality.org), culminating in what they call "the East Coast's Largest Outdoor Public Tasting and Auction," which is generally held at the Coastal Discovery Museum at Honey Horn. Some events charge admission.

Without question, Hilton Head's premier event is the **RBC Heritage Golf Tournament** (843/671-2248, http://theheritagegolfsc.com), held each April (usually the week after the Masters) at the Harbour Town Golf Links on Sea Pines Plantation. Formerly known as the Verizon Heritage Classic, the event is South Carolina's only PGA Tour event and brings thousands of visitors to town. The entire island gets *quite* crowded during this time, so be aware.

A fun and fondly anticipated yearly event is the **Kiwanis Club Chili Cookoff** (www.hiltonheadkiwanis.org), held each October at Honey Horn on the south end. A low admission price gets you all the chili you can eat plus free antacids. All funds go to charity, and all excess chili goes to a local food bank.

Every November brings Hilton Head's second-largest event, the **Hilton Head Concours d'Elegance & Motoring Festival** (www.hhiconcours.com), a multiday affair bringing together vintage car clubs from throughout the nation and culminating in a prestigious "Best of Show" competition. It started as a fund-raiser for the Hilton Head Symphony, but now people come from all over the country to see these fine vintage cars in a beautiful setting.

SHOPS

As you'd expect, Hilton Head is a shopper's delight, with an emphasis on upscale stores and prices to match. Keep in mind that hours may be shortened in the off-season (Nov.-Mar.). Here's a rundown of the main island shopping areas in the order you'll encounter them as you enter the island.

Shelter Cove

Shelter Cove Towne Centre (40 Shelter Cove Ln., www.sheltercovetownecentre), a repurposed former mall space, centers on a Belk anchor store and a Kroger. New retail locations are steadily opening there. The nearby **Plaza at Shelter Cove** (50 Shelter Cove Ln., www.theplazaatsheltercove.com) features a Whole Foods and the flagship location of **Outside Hilton Head** (843/686-6996, www.outsidehiltonhead.com, Mon.-Sat. 10am-5:30pm, Sun. 11am-5:30pm), a complete outdoor outfitter with a knowledgeable staff.

Village at Wexford

Easily my favorite place to shop on Hilton Head, this well-shaded shopping center on William Hilton Parkway (Hwy. 278) hosts plenty of well-tended shops, including the foodie equipment store **Le Cookery** (843/785-7171, Mon.-Sat. 10am-6pm), the Lily Pulitzer signature women's store **S. M. Bradford Co.** (843/686-6161, Mon.-Sat. 10am-6pm), and the aromatic **Scents of Hilton Head** (843/842-7866, Mon.-Fri. 10am-6pm, Sat. 10am-5pm).

My favorite shop on all Hilton Head is at Wexford, **The Oilerie** (843/681-2722, www.oilerie.com, Mon.-Sat. 10am-7pm, Sun. noon-5pm). This franchise provides free samples of all its high-quality Italian olive oils and vinegars. After you taste around awhile, you pick what you want and the friendly staff bottles it for you in souvenir-quality glassware. They also have a selection of spices, soaps, and other goodies.

Coligny Circle

This is the closest Hilton Head comes to funkier beach towns like Tybee Island or Folly Beach, although it doesn't really come that close. You'll find dozens of delightful and somewhat quirky stores here, many keeping long hours in the summer, like the self-explanatory **Coligny Kite & Flag Co.** (843/785-5483, Mon.-Sat. 10am-9pm, Sun. 11am-6pm), the comprehensive and stylish **Quiet Storm Surf Shop** (843/671-2551, daily 10am-9pm), and **Fresh Produce** (843/842-3410, www.freshproduceclothes.com, Mon.-Sat. 10am-10pm, Sun. 10am-9pm), actually a very cute women's clothing store. Kids will love both **The Shell Shop** (843/785-4900, Mon.-Sat. 10am-9pm, Sun. noon-9pm) and **Black Market Minerals** (843/785-7090, Mon.-Sat. 10am-10pm, Sun. 11am-8pm).

Harbour Town

The **Shoppes at Harbour Town** (www.

seapines.com) are a collection of about 20 mostly boutique stores along Lighthouse Road in Sea Pines Plantation. At **Planet Hilton Head** (843/363-5177, www.planethiltonhead.com, daily 10am-9pm) you'll find some cute, eclectic gifts and home goods. Other clothing highlights include **Knickers Men's Store** (843/671-2291, daily 10am-9pm) and **Radiance** (843/363-5176, Mon.-Tues. 10am-5pm, Wed.-Sat. 10am-9pm, Sun. 11am-9pm), a very cute and fashion-forward women's store.

The **Top of the Lighthouse Shoppe** (843/671-2810, www.harbourtownlighthouse.com, daily 10am-9pm) is where many a climbing visitor has been coaxed to part with some of their disposable income. And, of course, as you'd expect being near the legendary Harbour Town links, there's the **Harbour Town Pro Shop** (843/671-4485, daily 7am-5pm), routinely voted one of the best pro shops in the nation.

South Beach Marina

On South Sea Pines Drive at the marina you'll find several worthwhile shops, including a good marine store and all-around grocery dealer **South Beach General Store** (843/671-6784, daily 8am-10pm). I like to stop in **Blue Water Bait and Tackle** (843/671-3060, daily 7am-8pm) and check out the cool nautical stuff. They can also hook you up with a variety of kayak trips and fishing charters. And, of course, right on the water there's the ever-popular **Salty Dog Cafe** (843/671-2233, www.saltydog.com, lunch daily 11am-3pm, dinner daily 5pm-10pm), whose ubiquitous T-shirts seem to adorn every other person on the island.

Art Galleries

Despite the abundant wealth apparent in some quarters here, there's no freestanding art museum in the area, that role being filled by independent galleries. A good representative example is **Morris & Whiteside Galleries** (220 Cordillo Pkwy., 843/842-4433, www.morris-whiteside.com, Mon.-Fri. 9am-5pm,

Sat. 10am-4pm), located in the historic Red Piano Too Art Gallery building, which features a variety of paintings and sculpture, heavy on landscapes but also showing some fine figurative work. The nonprofit **Art League of Hilton Head** (14 Shelter Cove Ln., 843/681-5060, Mon.-Sat. 10am-6pm) is located in the Walter Greer Art Gallery within the Arts Center of Coastal Carolina and displays work by member artists in all media. The **Nash Gallery** (13 Harbourside Ln., 843/785-6424, Mon.-Fri. 10am-9pm, Sat. 10am-8pm, Sun. 11am-5pm) in Shelter Cove Harbour deals more in North American craft styles. Hilton Head art isn't exactly known for its avant-garde nature, but you can find some whimsical stuff at **Picture This** (78D Arrow Rd., 843/842-5299, Mon.-Fri. 9:30am-5:30pm, Sat. 9:30am-12:30pm), including a selection of Gullah craft items.

SPORTS AND ACTIVITIES
Beaches

First, the good news: Hilton Head Island has 12 miles of some of the most beautiful, safe beaches you'll find anywhere. The bad news is that there are only a few ways to gain access, generally at locations referred to as "beach parks." Don't just drive into a residential neighborhood and think you'll be able to park and find your way to the beach.

Driessen Beach Park has 207 long-term parking spaces, costing $0.25 for 30 minutes. There's free parking but fewer spaces at the Coligny Beach Park entrance and at Fish Haul Creek Park. Also, there are 22 metered spaces at Alder Lane Beach Access, 51 at Folly Field Beach Park, and 13 at Burkes Beach Road. Most other beach parks have permit parking only. Clean, well-maintained public restrooms are available at all the beach parks. You can find **beach information** at 843/342-4580 and www.hiltonheadislandsc. gov. Beach park hours vary: Coligny Beach Park is open daily 24 hours; all other beach parks are open March-September daily 6am-8pm and October-February daily 6am-5pm.

Alcohol is strictly prohibited on Hilton Head's beaches.

Kayaking

Kayakers will enjoy Hilton Head Island, which offers several gorgeous routes, including Calibogue Sound to the south and west and Port Royal Sound to the north. For particularly good views of life on the salt marsh, try Broad Creek, which nearly bisects Hilton Head Island, and Skull Creek, which separates Hilton Head from the natural beauty of Pinckney Island. Broad Creek Marina is a good place to put in.

If you want a guided tour, there are plenty of great kayak tour outfits to choose from in the area. Chief among them is **Outside Hilton Head** (32 Shelter Cove Ln., 800/686-6996, www.outsidehiltonhead.com).

Biking

Although the very flat terrain is not challenging, Hilton Head provides some scenic and relaxing cycling opportunities. Thanks to wise planning and foresight, the island has an extensive and award-winning 50-mile network of biking trails that does a great job of keeping cyclists out of traffic. A big plus is the long bike path paralleling the William Hilton Parkway, enabling cyclists to use that key artery without braving its traffic. There is even an underground bike path beneath the parkway to facilitate crossing that busy road. In addition, there are also routes along Pope Avenue as well as North and South Forest Beach Drive. Go to www.hiltonheadisland. org/biking to download a map of the island's entire bike path network.

Palmetto Dunes Oceanfront Resort (4 Queens Folly Rd., 800/827-3006, www. palmettodunes.com) has a particularly nice 25-mile network of bike paths that all link up to the island's larger framework. Within the resort is **Palmetto Dunes Outfitters** (843/785-2449, www.pdoutfitters.com, daily 9am-5pm), which will rent you any type of bike you might need. Sea Pines Plantation also has an extensive 17-mile network of bike

Golf Galore

With great weather, beautiful land, and an abundance of retirees, the coastal Carolinas offer some of the best golf courses in the world. While a handful of courses are more exclusive, many of the best are public and even have reasonable prices.

MYRTLE BEACH AND VICINITY

- **Barefoot Resort and Golf Club, Fazio Course** (page 115): Strangely not as popular as the affiliated Love course, but many say it's way better.

- **Caledonia Golf and Fish Club and True Blue Golf Club** (page 128): These sister courses compete for the fierce affections of serious golfers; it's sublime.

- **Myrtle Beach National** (page 115): With its South Carolina-shaped sand trap at hole 3, the National is one of the state's legendary courses, not to mention a heck of a deal.

- **Waccamaw Golf Trail** (page 128): Down the road from Myrtle Beach and near Pawleys Island, this area features some of the best courses in the state, including that of the famous Litchfield Resort.

HILTON HEAD ISLAND AND THE LOWCOUNTRY

- **Harbour Town Golf Links** (page 242): The host course of the RBC Heritage features a final three holes that are among the most challenging in the sport.

- **Palmetto Dunes, Arthur Hills Course** (page 242): Put away the drivers at this finesse course artfully situated in a residential area.

- **Legends at Parris Island** (page 230): Always considered one of the best military courses, a recent redesign of the 1957 original has been getting rave reviews.

CHARLESTON AND VICINITY

- **Kiawah Island Golf Resort, Ocean Course** (page 189): This Pete Dye design is considered the most wind-affected course outside the British Isles and possibly the most difficult resort course in the United States.

- **Wild Dunes Links Course** (page 189): This windy, winding beauty is the Holy City's most challenging course.

---

trails; you can pick up a map at most information kiosks within the plantation.

There's a plethora of bike rental facilities on Hilton Head with competitive rates. Be sure to ask if they offer free pickup and delivery. Try **Hilton Head Bicycle Company** (112 Arrow Rd., 843/686-6888, daily 9am-5pm, $16 per day).

Horseback Riding

Within the Sea Pines Forest Preserve is **Lawton Stables** (190 Greenwood Dr., 843/671-2586, www.lawtonstableshhi.com), which features pony rides, a small-animal farm, and guided horseback rides through the preserve. You don't need any riding experience, but you do need reservations.

Bird-Watching

The premier birding locale in the area is the **Pinckney Island National Wildlife Refuge** (U.S. 278 east, just before Hilton Head, 912/652-4415, www.fws.gov, free). You can see bald eagles, ibis, wood storks, painted buntings, and many more species. Birding is best in spring and fall. The refuge has several freshwater ponds that serve as wading bird rookeries. During migration season, so many beautiful birds make such a ruckus that you'll think you've wandered onto an Animal Planet shoot.

Golf

Hilton Head is one of the world's great golf centers, with no fewer than 23 courses. Perhaps contrary to what you might expect, most courses on the island are public, and some are downright affordable. All courses are 18 holes unless otherwise described; greens fees are averages and vary with season and tee time.

The best-regarded course, with prices to match, is **Harbour Town Golf Links** (Sea Pines Plantation, 843/363-4485, www.seapines.com, $239). It's on the island's south end at Sea Pines and is the home of the annual RBC Heritage Classic, far and away the island's number one tourist draw.

There are two Arthur Hills-designed courses on the island, **Arthur Hills at Palmetto Dunes Resort** (843/785-1140, www.palmettodunes.com, $125) and **Arthur Hills at Palmetto Hall** (Palmetto Hall Plantation, 843/689-4100, www.palmettohallgolf.com, $130), both of which now offer the use of Segway vehicles on the fairways. The reasonably priced **Barony Course** at Port Royal Plantation (843/686-8801, www.portroyalgolfclub.com, $98) also boasts some of the toughest greens on the island. Another challenging and affordable course is the **George Fazio at Palmetto Dunes** Resort (843/785-1130, www.palmettodunes.com, $105).

It's wise to book tee times through the **Golf Island Call Center** (888/465-3475, www.golfisland.com), which can also hook you up with good packages.

Tennis

One of the top tennis destinations in the country, Hilton Head has over 20 tennis clubs, some of which offer court time to the public (walk-on rates vary; call for information). They are: **Palmetto Dunes Tennis Center** (Palmetto Dunes Resort, 843/785-1152, www.palmettodunes.com, $30 per hour), **Port** **Royal Racquet Club** (Port Royal Plantation, 843/686-8803, www.portroyalgolfclub.com, $25 per hour), **Sea Pines Racquet Club** (Sea Pines Plantation, 843/363-4495, www.seapines.com, $25 per hour), **South Beach Racquet Club** (Sea Pines Plantation, 843/671-2215, www.seapines.com, $25 per hour), and **Shipyard Racquet Club** (Shipyard Plantation, 843/686-8804, $25 per hour).

Free, first-come, first-served play is available at the following public courts, maintained by the Island Recreation Association (www.islandreccenter.org): **Chaplin Community Park** (Singleton Beach Rd., four courts, lighted), **Cordillo Courts** (Cordillo Pkwy., four courts, lighted), **Fairfield Square** (Adrianna Ln., two courts), **Hilton Head High School** (School Rd., six courts), and **Hilton Head Middle School** (Wilborn Rd., four courts).

Zip Line

Billing itself as the only zip line experience within 250 miles, the **Zip Line Hilton Head** (33 Broad Creek Marina Way, 843/682-6000, www.ziplinehiltonhead.com) offers an extensive canopy tour making great use of the area's natural scenery and features. You generally "fly" in groups of about eight. Reservations are strongly encouraged. The latest offering is "Aerial Adventure," a challenging two-hour trip ($50) with about 50 obstacles.

FOOD

Because of the cosmopolitan nature of the population, with so many transplants from the northeastern United States and Europe, there is uniformly high quality in Hilton Head restaurants. Hilton Head has shed its reputation as a somewhat stodgy food town and does offer some fun, cutting-edge, big-city-style spots to enjoy.

Bistro

Combining rib-sticking comfort food with hearty European-style cuisine is ★ **Lucky Rooster** (841 William Hilton Pkwy., 843/681-3474, www.luckyroosterhhi.com, daily 5pm-10pm, $15). This really is one of the most vibrant and satisfying menus on the island, from the fried green tomatoes to the pan-fried sweetbread starters, to the short rib and shrimp and grits and mushroom lasagna entrées. A lively full bar complements the bistro-style scene.

An upgrade of a longtime island favorite called simply Daniel's, **Crave by Daniel's** (2 N. Forest Beach Dr., 843/341-9379, http://danielshhi.com, daily 4pm-2am, $25) is now an upscale steak house with a twist. In addition to offering gorgeous cuts of meat like a center-cut filet mignon, they specialize in what they call "big small plates." Try a sizzling cinnamon steak kebab or a gyro pizzetta.

Breakfast and Brunch

There are a couple of great diner-style places on the island. Though known more for its hamburgers and Philly cheesesteaks, **Harold's Diner** (641 William Hilton Pkwy., 843/842-9292, Mon.-Sat. 7am-3pm, $4-6) has great pancakes as well as its trademark brand of sarcastic service. The place is small, popular, and does not take reservations.

If you need a bite in the Coligny Plaza area, go to **Skillets** (1 N. Forest Beach Dr., 843/785-3131, www.skilletscafe.com, breakfast daily 7am-5pm, dinner daily 5pm-9pm, $5-23) in Coligny Plaza. Their eponymous stock-in-trade is a layered breakfast dish of sautéed ingredients served in a porcelain skillet, like the "Kitchen Sink" (pancakes ringed with potatoes, sausage, and bacon, topped with two poached eggs).

A great all-day breakfast place with a twist is ★ **Signe's Heaven Bound Bakery & Café** (93 Arrow Rd., 843/785-9118, www.signesbakery.com, Mon.-Fri. 8am-4pm, Sat. 9am-2pm, $5-10). Breakfast is tasty dishes like frittatas and breakfast polenta, while the twist is the extensive artisanal bakery, with delicious specialties like the signature key lime pound cake. Expect a wait during peak periods.

German

I'm pretty sure you didn't come all the way to South Carolina to eat traditional German food, but while you're here, check out ★ **Alfred's** (807 William Hilton Pkwy./ Hwy. 278, 843/341-3117, www.alfredshiltonhead.com, Mon.-Sat. 5pm-11pm, $20-30), one of the more unique spots on Hilton Head and a big favorite with the locals. Expect a wait. Bratwurst, veal cordon bleu, and of course Wiener schnitzel are all standouts. I recommend the German Mix Platter ($25), which features a brat, some sauerbraten, and a schnitzel.

Seafood and Southern

Honest-to-goodness Southern cookin' isn't always that easy to come by on this island full of transplants from outside the South. But a great place to find it is **A Lowcountry Backyard** (32 Palmetto Bay Rd., #4A, www.hhbackyard.com, Mon.-Sat. 11am-3pm and 4:30pm-9pm, Sat. brunch 9am-noon, Sun. brunch 9am-3pm, $15). As the name implies, this is regional cuisine served in a relaxed and casual atmosphere fitting for island life. As with many Hilton Head establishments, it's located within a strip mall setting, the Village Exchange.

Not to be confused with Charley's Crab House next door to Hudson's, seafood lovers will enjoy the experience down near Sea Pines at ★ **Charlie's L'Etoile Verte** (8 New Orleans Rd., 843/785-9277, http://charliesgreenstar.com, lunch Tues.-Sat. 11:30am-2pm, dinner Mon.-Sat. 5:30pm-10pm, $25-40), which is considered by many connoisseurs to be Hilton Head's single best restaurant. The emphasis here is on "French country kitchen" cuisine—think Provence, not Paris. In keeping with that theme, each day's menu is concocted from scratch and handwritten. Reservations are essential.

A longtime Hilton Head favorite is **Red Fish** (8 Archer Rd., 843/686-3388, www.redfishofhiltonhead.com, lunch Mon.-Sat. 11:30am-2pm, dinner daily beginning with early-bird specials at 5pm, $20-37). Strongly Caribbean in decor as well as menu, with romanticism and panache to match, this is a great place for couples. Reservations are essential.

Fresh seafood lovers will enjoy one of Hilton Head's staples, the huge **Hudson's on the Docks** (1 Hudson Rd., 843/681-2772, www.hudsonsonthedocks.com, lunch daily 11am-4pm, dinner daily from 5pm, $14-23) on Skull Creek just off Squire Pope Road on the less-developed north side. Much of the catch—though not all of it, by any means—comes directly off the boats you'll see dockside. Try the stuffed shrimp filled with crabmeat. Leave room for one of the homemade desserts crafted by Ms. Bessie, a 30-year veteran employee of Hudson's.

ACCOMMODATIONS

Generally speaking, accommodations on Hilton Head are often surprisingly affordable given their overall high quality and the breadth of their amenities.

Under $150

You can't beat the price at **Park Lane Hotel and Suites** (12 Park Ln., 843/686-5700, www.hiltonheadparklanehotel.com, $130). This is your basic suite-type hotel (formerly a Residence Inn) with kitchens, laundry, a pool, and a tennis court. The allure here is the price, hard to find anywhere these days at a resort location. For a nonrefundable fee, you can bring your pet. The one drawback is that the beach is a good distance away. The hotel does offer a free shuttle, however, so it would be wise to take advantage of that and avoid the usual beach-parking hassles. As you'd expect given the price, rooms here tend to go quickly; reserve early.

$150-300

A great place for the price is the **South Beach Inn** (232 S. Sea Pines Dr., 843/671-6498, www.sbinn.com, $186) in Sea Pines. Located near the famous Salty Dog Cafe and outfitted in a similar nautical theme, the inn not only has some pretty large guest rooms for the price, it offers a lovely view of the marina and has a very friendly feel. As with all Sea Pines accommodations, staying on the plantation means you don't have to wait in line with other visitors to pay the $5-per-day "road fee." Sea Pines also offers a free trolley to get around the plantation.

One of Hilton Head's favorite hotels for beach lovers is **The Beach House** (1 S. Forest Beach Dr., 855/474-2882, www.beachhousehhi.com, $200), formerly the Holiday Inn Oceanfront and home of the famed Tiki Hut bar on the beach. Staff turnover is less frequent here than at other local accommodations, and while it's no Ritz-Carlton and occasionally shows signs of wear, it's a good value in a bustling area of the island.

One of the better resort-type places for those who prefer the putter and the racquet to the Frisbee and the surfboard is the **Inn and Club at Harbour Town** (7 Lighthouse Ln., 843/363-8100, www.seapines.com, $199) in Sea Pines. The big draw here is the impeccable service, delivered by a staff of "butlers" in kilts, mostly Europeans who take the venerable trade quite seriously. While it's not on the beach, you can take advantage of the free Sea Pines Trolley every 20 minutes.

Recently rated the number one family resort in the United States by *Travel + Leisure,* the well-run ★ **Palmetto Dunes Oceanfront Resort** (4 Queens Folly Rd., 800/827-3006, www.palmettodunes.com, $150-300) offers something for everybody in terms of lodging. There are small, cozy condos by the beach or larger villas overlooking the golf course, and pretty much everything in between. The prices are perhaps disarmingly affordable considering the relative luxury and copious recreational amenities, which include 25 miles of very well-done bike trails, 11 miles of kayak and canoe trails, and, of course, three signature links. As with most developments of this type on Hilton Head, the majority of the condos are privately owned, and therefore each has its own particular set of guidelines and cleaning schedules.

A little farther down the island you'll find the **Sonesta Resort** (130 Shipyard Dr., 843/842-2400, www.sonesta.com/

hiltonheadisland, $160-200), which styles itself as Hilton Head's only green-certified accommodations. The guest rooms are indeed state-of-the-art, and the expansive, shaded grounds near the beach are great for relaxation. No on-site golf here, but immediately adjacent is a well-regarded tennis facility with 20 courts.

Another good resort-style experience heavy on the golf is on the grounds of the Port Royal Plantation on the island's north side, **The Westin Resort Hilton Head Island** (2 Grasslawn Ave., 843/681-4000, www.westin.com/hiltonhead, from $200), which hosts three PGA-caliber links. The beach is also but a short walk away. This AAA four diamond-winning Westin offers a mix of suites and larger villas.

Vacation Rentals

Many visitors to Hilton Head choose to rent a home or villa for an extended stay, and there is no scarcity of availability. Try **Resort Rentals of Hilton Head** (www.hhivacations.com) or **Destination Vacation** (www.destinationvacationhhi.com).

TRANSPORTATION AND SERVICES

The best place to get information on Hilton Head, book a room, or secure a tee time is just as you come onto the island at the **Hilton Head Island Chamber of Commerce Welcome Center** (100 William Hilton Pkwy., 843/785-3673, www.hiltonheadisland.org, daily 9am-6pm).

Air

A few years back, the **Savannah/Hilton Head International Airport** (SAV, 400 Airways Ave., Savannah, 912/964-0514, www.savannahairport.com) added Hilton Head to its name specifically to identify itself with that lucrative market. Keep in mind that when your plane touches down in Savannah, you're still about a 45-minute drive to Hilton Head proper. From the airport, go north on I-95 into South Carolina, and take exit 8 onto U.S. 278 east.

There is a local regional airport as well, the **Hilton Head Island Airport** (HXD, 120 Beach City Rd., 843/689-5400, www.bcgov.net). While attractive and convenient, keep in mind that it only hosts propeller-driven commuter planes because of the runway length and concerns about noise.

Getting Around

Hilton Head Islanders have long referred to their island as the "shoe" and speak of driving to the toe or going to the heel. If you take a look at a map, you'll see why: Hilton Head bears an uncanny resemblance to a running shoe pointed toward the southwest, with the aptly named Broad Creek forming a near facsimile of the Nike "swoosh" symbol.

Running the length and circumference of the shoe is the main drag, U.S. 278 Business (William Hilton Parkway), which crosses onto Hilton Head right at the "tongue" of the shoe, a relatively undeveloped area. The Cross Island Parkway toll route (U.S. 278), beginning up toward the ankle as you first get on the island, is a quicker route straight to the toe near Sea Pines.

While making your way around the island, always keep in mind that the bulk of it consists of private developments, and local law enforcement frowns on people who aimlessly wander among the condos and villas.

Other than taxi services, there is no public transportation to speak of in Hilton Head, unless you want to count the free shuttle around Sea Pines Plantation. Taxi services include **Yellow Cab** (843/686-6666), **Island Taxi** (843/683-6363), and **Ferguson Transportation** (843/842-8088).

Bluffton and Daufuskie Island

Just outside Hilton Head are two of the Lowcountry's true gems, Bluffton and Daufuskie Island. While Bluffton's outskirts have been taken over by the same gated community and upscale strip mall sprawl spreading throughout the coast, at its core it is a delightfully charming little community on the quiet May River, now called Old Bluffton, where you'd swear you just entered a time warp.

Daufuskie Island still maintains much of its age-old isolated, timeless personality, and the island—still accessible only by boat—is one of the spiritual centers of the Gullah culture and lifestyle.

★ OLD TOWN BLUFFTON

Similar to Beaufort, but even quieter and smaller, historic Bluffton is an idyllic village on the banks of the serene May River. Bluffton was the original hotbed of secession, with Charleston diarist Mary Chesnut famously referring to the town as "the center spot of the fire eaters." During their Civil War occupation, Union troops repaid the favor of those original Bluffton secessionists, which is why only nine homes in Bluffton are of antebellum vintage; the rest were torched in a search for Confederate guerrillas.

The center of tourist activity is "Old Town," the **Old Bluffton Historic District,** several blocks of 1800s-vintage buildings clustered between the parallel Boundary and Calhoun Streets (old-timers sometimes call this "the original square mile"). Many of the buildings are private residences, but most have been converted into art studios and antiques stores.

Heyward House Historic Center

The **Heyward House Historic Center** (70 Boundary St., 843/757-6293, www.heyward-house.org, Mon.-Fri. 10am-5pm, Sat. 10am-4pm, tours $5 adults, $2 students) is not only open to tours but also serves as Bluffton's

visitors center. Built in 1840 as a summer home for the owner of Moreland Plantation, John Cole, the house was later owned by George Cuthbert Heyward, grandson of Declaration of Independence signer Thomas Heyward. (Remarkably, it stayed in the family until the 1990s.) The Heyward House also sponsors walking tours of the historic district (843/757-6293, $15, by appointment only). Download your own walking tour map at www.heywardhouse.org.

Church of the Cross

Don't fail to go all the way to the end of Calhoun Street, as it dead-ends on a high bluff on the May River at the Bluffton Public Dock. Overlooking this peaceful marsh-front vista is the photogenic **Church of the Cross** (110 Calhoun St., 843/757-2661, www.the-churchofthecross.net, free tours Mon.-Sat. 10am-2pm). The current sanctuary was built in 1854 and is one of only two local churches not burned in the Civil War. The parish itself began in 1767, with the first services on this spot held in the late 1830s. While the church looks as if it were made of cypress, it's actually constructed of heart pine.

Bluffton Oyster Company

You might want to get a gander at the state's last remaining working oyster house, the **Bluffton Oyster Company** (63 Wharf St., 843/757-4010, www.blufftonoyster.com, Mon.-Sat. 9am-5:30pm), and possibly purchase some of their maritime bounty. Larry and Tina Toomer continue to oversee the oyster-harvesting-and-shucking family enterprise, which has its roots in the early 1900s.

SHOPS

Bluffton's eccentric little art studios, most clustered in a two-block stretch on Calhoun Street, are by far its main shopping draw. Named for the Lowcountry phenomenon you find in the marsh at low tide among the fiddler crabs, Bluffton's **Pluff Mudd Art** (27 Calhoun St., 843/757-5551, Mon.-Sat. 10am-5:30pm) is a cooperative of 16 talented young painters and photographers from throughout the area. The **Guild of Bluffton Artists** (20 Calhoun St., 843/757-5590, Mon.-Sat. 10am-4:30pm) features works from many local artists, as does the outstanding **Society of Bluffton Artists** (48 Boundary St., 843/757-6586, Mon.-Sat. 10am-5pm, Sun. 11:30am-3pm). For cool, custom handcrafted pottery, try **Preston Pottery and Gallery** (10 Church St., 843/757-3084, Tues.-Sat. 10am-5pm). Another great Bluffton place is the hard-to-define **Eggs'n'tricities** (71 Calhoun St., 843/757-3446, Mon.-Sat. 10am-5pm). The name pretty much says it all for this fun and eclectic vintage, junk, jewelry, and folk art store.

If you want to score some fresh local seafood for your own culinary adventure, the no-brainer choice is the **Bluffton Oyster Company** (63 Wharf St., 843/757-4010, Mon.-Sat. 9am-5:30pm), the state's only active oyster facility. They also have shrimp, crab, clams, and fish, nearly all of it from the nearly pristine May River on whose banks the facility sits.

For a much more commercially intense experience, head just outside of town on U.S. 278 on the way to Hilton Head to find the dual **Tanger Outlet Centers** (1414 Fording Island Rd., 843/837-4339, Mon.-Sat. 10am-9pm, Sun. 11am-6pm), an outlet-shopper's paradise with virtually every major brand represented.

FOOD
American

Probably the single most popular place in Bluffton is the friendly **Old Town Dispensary** (15 Captains Cove, 843/837-1893, daily 11am-2am, $15-25), just off the Calhoun Street center of activity. This is an outstanding place to go for some cut-above pub/bar food or casual drinks, with plenty of outdoor seating and usually some live music going on.

Another very popular casual spot in Old Town, and frequented by many locals, is **Captain Woody's Bar & Grill** (17 State of Mind St., 843/757-6222, $10-15). Unpretentious and friendly, this is a good place to enjoy a

Bluffton Oyster Company on the May River

burger and a beer in a relaxed, patio-style environment with plenty going on around you.

Breakfast and Brunch
No discussion of Bluffton cuisine is complete without the famous **Squat 'n' Gobble** (1231 May River Rd., 843/757-4242, daily 24 hours). Long a site of gossiping and politicking as well as, um, squatting and gobbling, this humble diner on May River Road is an indelible part of the local consciousness.

Coffee
If you're looking for a coffeehouse in Old Town, go no farther than ★ **Corner Perk** (1297 May River Rd., Fording Island Rd., 843/816-5674, Tues.-Thurs. 7am-4pm., Fri.-Sat. 7am-11pm, Sun. brunch 7am-4pm, $10-20) in The Promenade, just off the main drag. Their coffee is truly wonderful, and the sandwich-heavy lunch menu compares with anything else in town. Upstairs is The Roasting Room, a more upscale, full-service bourbon bar.

French
Most dining in Bluffton is pretty casual, but you'll get the white-tablecloth treatment at **Claude & Uli's Signature Bistro** (1533 Fording Island Rd., 843/837-3336, lunch Mon.-Fri. 11:30am-2:30pm, dinner Mon.-Sat. from 5pm, $18-25) just outside of town in Moss Village. Chef Claude does a great veal cordon bleu as well as a number of fine seafood entrées, such as an almond-crusted tilapia and an excellent seafood pasta.

Mexican
My favorite restaurant in Bluffton is ★ **Mi Tierra** (101 Mellichamp Center, 843/757-7200, lunch daily 11am-4pm, dinner Mon.-Fri. 4pm-9pm, Sat.-Sun. 4pm-10pm, $3-15). They serve very high-quality but unpretentious Tex-Mex-style food in a fun atmosphere at affordable prices.

ACCOMMODATIONS
Under $150
A quality bargain stay right between Bluffton

and Hilton Head is the **Holiday Inn Express Bluffton** (35 Bluffton Rd., 843/757-2002, www.ichotelsgroup.com, $120), on U.S. 278 as you make the run onto Hilton Head proper. It's not close to the beach or to Old Town Bluffton, so you'll definitely be using your car, but its central location will appeal to those who want to keep their options open.

Over $300
For an ultra-upscale spa and golf resort environment near Bluffton, the clear pick is the **Inn at Palmetto Bluff** (19 Village Park Square, 843/706-6500, www.palmettobluffresort.com, $650-900) just across the May River. This property was picked recently as the number two U.S. resort by *Condé Nast Traveler* magazine. There are three top-flight dining options on the grounds: the fine-dining **River House Restaurant** (843/706-6542, breakfast daily 7am-11am, lunch or "porch" menu daily 11am-10pm, dinner daily 6pm-10pm, $30-40); the **May River Grill** (Tues.-Sat. 11am-4pm, $9-13) at the golf clubhouse; and the casual **Buffalo's** (843/706-6630, Sun.-Tues. 11:30am-5pm, Wed.-Sat. 11:30am-9pm, $10-15).

DAUFUSKIE ISLAND
Sitting between Savannah and Hilton Head Island and accessible only by water, Daufuskie Island—pronounced "da-FUSK-ee"—has about 500 full-time residents, most of whom ride around on golf carts or bikes (there's only one paved road, Haig Point Road). Once the home of rice and indigo plantations and rich oyster beds—the latter destroyed by pollution and overharvesting—the two upscale residential resort communities on the island, begun in the 1980s, give a clue as to where the future might lie, although the recent global economic downturn, perhaps thankfully, slowed development to a standstill.

The area of prime interest to visitors is the unincorporated western portion, or **Historic District,** the old stomping grounds of Pat Conroy during his stint as a teacher of resident African American children. His old

Who Are the Gullah?

A language, a culture, and a people with a shared history, Gullah is more than that—it's also a state of mind. Simply put, the Gullah are African Americans of the Sea Islands of South Carolina and Georgia. (In Georgia, the term *Geechee,* from the nearby Ogeechee River, is more or less interchangeable.) Protected from outside influence by the isolation of this coastal region after the Civil War, Gullah culture is the closest living cousin to the West African traditions of those brought to this country as slaves.

While you might hear that *Gullah* is a corruption of "Angola," some linguists think it simply means "people" in a West African language. In any case, the Gullah speak what is known as a creole language, meaning one derived from several sources. Gullah combines elements of Elizabethan English, Jamaican patois, and several West African dialects; for example, "goober" (peanut) comes from the Congo *n'guba.* Another creole element is a word with multiple uses; for example, Gullah's *shum* could mean "see them," "see him," "see her," or "see it" in either past or present tense, depending on context. Several white writers in the 1900s published collections of Gullah folk tales, but it wasn't until later linguistic research was done that the Gullah tongue was recognized as something more than just broken English. Lorenzo Dow Turner's groundbreaking *Africanisms in the Gullah Dialect,* published in 1949, traced elements of the language to Sierra Leone in West Africa and more than 300 Gullah words directly to Africa.

Gullah is typically spoken very rapidly, which of course only adds to its impenetrability to the outsider. Gullah also relies on colorful turns of phrase. *"E tru mout"* ("He true mouth") means the speaker is referring to someone who doesn't lie. *"Le een crack muh teet"* ("I didn't even crack my teeth") means "I kept quiet." A forgetful Gullah speaker might say, *"Mah head leab me"* ("My head left me").

Gullah music, as practiced by the world-famous Hallelujah Singers of St. Helena Island, also uses many distinctly African techniques, such as call-and-response (the folk hymn "Michael Row the Boat Ashore" is a good example). The most famous Americans with Gullah roots are late boxer Joe Frazier (Beaufort), hip-hop star Jazzy Jay (Beaufort), NFL great Jim Brown (St. Simons Island, Georgia), and Supreme Court justice Clarence Thomas (Pin Point, Georgia, near Savannah).

Upscale development continues to claim more and more traditional Gullah areas, generally by pricing the Gullah out through rapidly increasing property values. Today, the major pockets of living Gullah culture in South Carolina are in Beaufort, St. Helena Island, Daufuskie Island, Edisto Island, and a northern section of Hilton Head Island.

The old ways are not as prevalent as they were, but several key institutions are keeping alive the spirit of Gullah: the **Penn Center** (16 Martin Luther King Dr., St. Helena, 843/838-2474, www. penncenter.com, Mon.-Sat. 11am-4pm, $4 adults, $2 seniors and children) on St. Helena Island near Beaufort; the **Avery Research Center** (66 George St., Charleston, 843/953-7609, www. cofc.edu/avery, Mon.-Fri. 10am-5pm, Sat. noon-5pm) at the College of Charleston; and **Geechee Kunda** (622 Ways Temple Rd., Riceboro, Georgia, 912/884-4440, www.geecheekunda.com) near Midway off U.S. 17.

one-room schoolhouse of *The Water is Wide* fame, the **Mary Field School,** is still here, as is the adjacent 140-year-old **Union Baptist Church,** but Daufuskie students now have a surprisingly modern new facility (middle school students are still ferried to mainland schools every day). Farther north on Haig Point Road is the new **Billie Burn Museum,** housed in the old Mount Carmel Church and named after the island's resident historian.

On the southern end you'll find the **Bloody Point Lighthouse,** named for the vicious battle fought nearby during the Yamasee War of 1815 (the light was actually moved inland in the early 1900s). Other areas of interest throughout the island include Native American sites, tabby ruins, the old Baptist church, and a couple of cemeteries.

Download a very well-done, free self-guided tour of Daufuskie's historic sites at www.hiltonheadisland.org; look for the "Robert Kennedy Historic Trail Guide" (not a nod to the former attorney general and U.S. senator, but a longtime island resident and historian).

For overnight stays, you can rent a humble but cozy cabin at **Freeport Marina** (843/785-8242, $100-150, golf cart $60 extra per day), near the ferry dock and overlooking the water. There are vacation rental options island-wide as well; go to www.daufuskieislandrentals.com for info on a wide variety of offerings. Sorry, no camping available!

There are no grocery stores as commonly understood on Daufuskie, only a couple of general store-type places. So if you've booked a vacation rental, most grocery items will need to be brought in with you.

For the freshest island seafood, check out the **Old Daufuskie Crab Company** (Freeport Marina, 843/785-6652, daily 11:30am-9pm, $8-22). The deviled crab is the house specialty. The other place to dine out on the island is **Marshside Mama's** (15 Haig Point Rd., 843/785-4755, www.marshsidemamas.com, hours change frequently, $10-15), a laid-back spot to enjoy grouper, gumbo, and Lowcountry boil, and frequent live music. Reservations are strongly encouraged.

For hand-crafted island art, go to **Iron Fish Gallery** (168 Benjies Point Rd., 843/842-9448, call ahead for hours), featuring the work of Chase Allen. His "coastal sculptures" include fanciful depictions of fish, stingrays, and even mermaids.

Transportation and Services

The main public ferry between Daufuskie and Hilton Head is operated by **Calibogue Cruises** (18 Simmons Rd., 843/342-8687, www.daufuskiefreeport.com). Taking off from Broad Creek Marina on Hilton Head, the pleasant short ride—30 minutes each way—brings you in on the landward side of the island. Cost is $33 per person round-trip, or $64 per person round-trip including a meal at the Old Daufuskie Crab Company and a golf cart rental. Ferries run three times a day Monday, Wednesday, and Friday, and twice a day Tuesday, Thursday, Saturday, and Sunday. Ferry reservations are essential!

While the ferry trip and many vacation rentals include the rental of a golf cart, for *a la carte* service—get it?—rent one near Freeport Marina by calling 843/342-8687 (rates vary but hover around $30 per person per day). As the amount of golf carts is limited, I strongly recommend reserving yours in advance. All standard rules of the road apply, including needing a valid driver's license.

Points Inland

It's likely that at some point you'll find yourself traveling inland from Beaufort, given that region's proximity to I-95. While this area is generally more known for offering interstate drivers a bite to eat and a place to rest their heads, there are several spots worth checking out in their own right, especially Walterboro and the Savannah National Wildlife Refuge.

WALTERBORO

Walterboro is chiefly known to the world at large for being one of the best antiquing locales on the East Coast. Indeed, many of the high-dollar antiques shops on Charleston's King Street actually do their picking right here in the local stores, selling their finds at a significant markup in Charleston! (Another advantage Walterboro antiques shopping has over Charleston: plenty of free parking.)

Convenient and walkable, the two-block **Arts and Antiques District** on Washington Street centers on more than a dozen antiques and collectible stores, interspersed with a few gift shops and eateries. The best shop, though by no means the only one you should check out, is **Bachelor Hill Antiques** (255

E. Washington St., 843/549-1300, Mon.-Sat. 9am-6pm, Sun. 9am-4pm), which has several rooms packed with interesting and unique items, from collectibles to furniture to most everything in between.

Sights

★ SOUTH CAROLINA ARTISANS CENTER

Don't miss the **South Carolina Artisans Center** (334 Wichman St., 843/549-0011, www.scartisanscenter.com, Mon.-Sat. 9am-5pm, Sun. 1pm-5pm, free), an expansive and vibrant collection of the best work of local and regional painters, sculptors, jewelers, and other craftspeople, for sale and for enjoyment. The Artisans Center hosts numerous receptions, and every third Saturday of the month they hold live artist demonstrations 11am-3pm.

MUSEUMS

Walterboro boasts three small museums. The relocated and upgraded **Colleton Museum** (506 E. Washington St., 843/549-2303, www.colletonmuseum.org, Tues. noon-6pm, Wed.-Fri. 10am-5pm, Sat. 10am-2pm, free) is one of the best examples of a small-town museum you're likely to find. Adjacent is the farmers market, open Tuesday 2pm-6pm and Saturday 10am-2pm May-end of October.

The **Bedon-Lucas House Museum** (205 Church St., 843/549-9633, Thurs.-Sat. 1pm-4pm, $3 adults, free under age 8) was built by a local planter in 1820. An example of the local style of "high house," built off the ground to escape mosquitoes and catch the breeze, the house today is a nice mix of period furnishings and unadorned simplicity.

The **Slave Relic Museum** (208 Carn St., 843/549-9130, www.slaverelics.org, by appointment, $6 adults, $5 children) houses the Center for Research and Preservation of the African American Culture. It features artifacts, photos, and documents detailing the Atlantic passage, slave life, and the Underground Railroad.

TUSKEGEE AIRMEN MEMORIAL

Yes, the Tuskegee Airmen of World War II fame were from Alabama, not South Carolina. But a contingent trained in Walterboro, at the site of the present-day **Lowcountry Regional Airport** (537 Aviation Way, 843/549-2549), a little north of downtown on U.S. 17. A publicly accessible, low-security area of the airport hosts the **Tuskegee Airmen Memorial,** an outdoor monument

the South Carolina Artisans Center

Tuskegee Airmen in Walterboro

In a state where all too often African American history is studied in the context of slavery, a refreshing change is the tale of the Tuskegee Airmen, one of the most lauded American military units of World War II. Though named for their origins at Alabama's Tuskegee Institute, the pilots of the famed 332nd Fighter Group actually completed their final training in South Carolina at Walterboro Army Airfield, where the regional airport now sits.

The U.S. military was segregated during World War II, with African Americans mostly relegated to support roles. An interesting exception was the case of the 332nd, formed in 1941 as the 99th Pursuit Squadron by an act of Congress and the only all-black flying unit in the American military at the time. Mostly flying P-47 Thunderbolts and P-51 Mustangs, the pilots of the 332nd had one of the toughest missions of the war: escorting bombers over the skies of Germany and protecting them from Luftwaffe fighters. Though initially viewed with skepticism, the Tuskegee Airmen wasted no time in proving their mettle.

In fact, it wasn't long before U.S. bomber crews—who were, needless to say, all white—specifically requested that they be escorted by the airmen, who were given the nickname "Red-tail Angels" because of the distinctive markings of their aircraft. While legend has it that the 332nd never lost a bomber, this claim has been debunked. But as Tuskegee Airman Bill Holloman said, "The Tuskegee story is about pilots who rose above adversity and discrimination and opened a door once closed to black America, not about whether their record is perfect." The 332nd's reputation for aggressiveness in air combat was so widely known that the Germans also had a nickname for them—*Schwartze Vogelmenschen*, or "Black Birdmen."

Today Walterboro honors the airmen with a monument on the grounds of the Lowcountry Regional Airport, on U.S. 17 just northeast of town. In an easily accessible part of the airport grounds, the monument features a bronze statue and several interpretive exhibits. Another place to catch up on Tuskegee Airmen history is at the **Colleton Museum** (506 E. Washington St., 843/549-2303, www.colletonmuseum.org, Tues. noon-6pm, Wed.-Fri. 10am-5pm, Sat. 10am-2pm, free), which has a permanent exhibit on the pilots and their history in the Walterboro area.

Walterboro Army Airfield's contribution to the war effort was not limited to the Tuskegee Airmen. Seven of the famed Doolittle Raiders were trained here, there was a compound for holding German prisoners of war, and it was also the site of the U.S. military's largest camouflage school.

to these brave flyers. There's a bronze statue and several interpretive exhibits.

GREAT SWAMP SANCTUARY

Just south of town is the **Great Swamp Sanctuary** (www.thegreatswamp.org, daily dawn-dusk, free), a still-developing ecotourism project focusing on the Lowcountry environment. Located in one of the region's few braided-creek habitats accessible to the public, the 842-acre sanctuary has three miles of walking and biking trails, some along the path of the old Charleston-Savannah stagecoach route. Kayakers and canoeists can paddle more than two miles of winding creeks. There are three entry points to the Great Swamp Sanctuary, all off Jefferies Boulevard. In west-to-east order from I-95: north onto

Beach Road, north onto Detreville Street (this is considered the main entrance), and west onto Washington Street.

Festivals and Events

In keeping with South Carolina's tradition of towns hosting annual events to celebrate signature crops and products, Walterboro's **Colleton County Rice Festival** (http://thericefestival.org, free) happens every April. There's a parade, live music, a 5K run, and the crowning of the year's "Rice Queen."

Food

The story of food in Walterboro revolves around ★ **Duke's Barbecue** (949 Robertson Blvd., 843/549-1446, $7), one of the best-regarded barbecue spots in the Lowcountry and one of the top two joints named "Duke's" in the state (the other, by common consensus, is in Orangeburg). The pulled pork is delectable, cooked with the indigenous South Carolina mustard-based sauce.

Accommodations

If you're looking for big-box lodging, the section of Walterboro close to I-95 is chockablock with it. The quality is surprisingly good, perhaps because they tend to cater to Northerners on their way to and from Florida. A good choice is **Holiday Inn Express & Suites** (1834 Sniders Hwy., 843/538-2700, www.hiexpress.com, $85), or try the **Comfort Inn & Suites** (97 Downs Ln., 843/538-5911, www.choicehotels.com, $95).

If you'd like something with a bit more character, there are two B&Bs on Hampton Street downtown. **Old Academy Bed & Breakfast** (904 Hampton St., 843/549-3232, www.oldacademybandb.com, $80-115) has four guest rooms housed in Walterboro's first school building. They offer a full continental breakfast. Note that credit cards are not accepted. Although built recently (by local standards), the 1912 **Hampton House Bed and Breakfast** (500 Hampton St., 843/542-9498, www.hamptonhousebandb.com, $125-145) has three well-appointed

guest rooms and offers a full country breakfast. By appointment only, you can see its Forde Doll and Dollhouse Collection, with over 50 dollhouses and oodles of antique dolls.

SAVANNAH NATIONAL WILDLIFE REFUGE

Roughly equally divided between Georgia and South Carolina, the sprawling, 30,000-acre **Savannah National Wildlife Refuge** (912/652-4415, www.fws.gov/savannah, daily dawn-dusk, free) is one of the premier bird-watching and nature-observing locales in the Southeast. The system of dikes and paddy fields once used to grow rice now helps make this an attractive stopover for migrating birds. Bird-watching is best October-April. While you can kayak on your own on miles of creeks, you can also call **Swamp Girls Kayak Tours** (843/784-2249, www.swampgirls.com), who work out of nearby Hardeeville, for a guided tour. The wildlife refuge is about 20 minutes from Savannah, two hours from Charleston, and an hour from Beaufort. To get here, take exit 5 off I-95 onto U.S. 17. Go south to U.S. 170 and look for Laurel Hill Wildlife Drive. Be sure to stop by the **visitors center** (off U.S. 170 at Laurel Hill Wildlife Dr., Mon.-Sat. 9am-4:30pm).

Background

The Landscape

GEOGRAPHY

The story of the coastal Carolinas' geography begins, ironically enough, with the Appalachian Mountain chain. It's in Appalachia where so much of the coast's freshwater—in the form of rain—comes together and flows southeast—in the form of rivers—to the Atlantic Ocean.

Moving east, the next level down from the Appalachians is the **Piedmont** region. The Piedmont is a rolling, hilly area, the eroded remains of an ancient mountain chain now long gone.

At the Piedmont's eastern edge is the **fall line,** so named because it's there where rivers make a drop toward the sea, generally becoming navigable. This slight but noticeable change in elevation—which actually marked the shoreline about 60 million years ago—not only encouraged trade, but has provided water power for mills for hundreds of years. Many inland cities of the region trace their origin and commercial success to their strategic location on the fall line.

Around the fall line zone in the **Upper Coastal Plain** you can sometimes spot **sandhills,** usually only a few feet in elevation, generally thought to be the vestigial remains of primordial sand dunes and offshore sandbars. Well beyond the fall line and the sometimes nearly invisible sandhills lies the **Lower Coastal Plain,** gradually built up over a 150 million-year span by sedimentary runoff from the Appalachian Mountains, which were then as high or even higher than the modern-day Himalayas.

The Coastal Plain was sea bottom for much of the earth's history, and in some eroded areas you can see dramatic proof of this in prehistoric shells, sharks' teeth, and fossilized whale bones and oyster beds, often many miles inland. In some places, calcium from these ancient shells has provided a lush home for distinct groups of unique plants, called **dijuncts.**

At various times over the last 50 million years, the Coastal Plain has submerged, surfaced, and submerged again. At the height of the last major Ice Age, when global sea levels were very low, the east coast of North America extended out nearly 100 miles farther than the present shoreline. (We now call this former coastal region the **continental shelf.**) The Coastal Plain has been in roughly its current form for about the last 15,000 years.

In coastal North Carolina, above about Jacksonville, begins a sort of hybrid geography, mixing characteristics of the Coastal Plain with a series of massive river estuaries. Here the general salt marsh environment gives way to a more windswept, deeper-water topography that will find its ultimate expression in the remote feel and independent lifestyle of the Outer Banks themselves.

Rivers

Visitors from drier climates are sometimes shocked to see how huge the rivers can get in the South, how wide and voluminous as they saunter to the sea, their seemingly slow speed belying the massive power they contain. North and South Carolina's big **alluvial,** or sediment-bearing, rivers originate in the region of the Appalachian mountain chain.

The **blackwater river** is a particularly interesting Southern phenomenon, duplicated elsewhere only in South America and one example each in New York and Michigan. While alluvial rivers generally originate in highlands and carry with them a large amount of

---

sediment, blackwater rivers—the Edisto in South Carolina being a great example, along with North Carolina's Cape Fear River—tend to originate in low-lying areas and move slowly toward the sea, carrying with them very little sediment.

Rather, their dark tea color comes from the tannic acid of decaying vegetation all along their banks, washed out by the slow, inexorable movement of the river toward the sea. While I don't necessarily recommend drinking it, despite its dirty color blackwater is for the most part remarkably clean and hygienic.

Carolina Bays

An interesting regional feature of the Carolinas is the **Carolina Bay,** an elliptical depression rich with biodiversity, thousands of which are found all along the coast from Delaware to Florida. While at least 500,000 have been identified, new laser-based technology is enabling the discovery of thousands more, previously unnoticed.

Though not all Carolina Bays are in the Carolinas, many are and that's where they were first documented. They're called "bays" not for the water within them—indeed, many hold little or no water at all—but for the proliferation of bay trees often found inside. Carolina Bays can be substantially older than the surrounding terrain, with many well over 25,000 years old. Native Americans referred to the distinctive wetland habitat within a Carolina Bay as a *pocosin.*

Theories abound as to their origin. One has it that they're the result of wave action from when the entire area was underwater in primordial times. The most popular, if unproven theory, is that they are the result of a massive meteor shower in prehistoric times. Certainly their similar orientation, roughly northwest-southeast, makes this intuitively possible as an impact pattern. Further bolstering this theory is the fact that most Carolina Bays are surrounded by sand rims, which tend to be thicker on the southeast edge.

An old, once-discredited theory now gaining new credence is that Carolina Bays are the result of a disintegrating comet, which exploded upon entry into the earth's atmosphere somewhere over the Great Lakes. Apparently if you extend the axes of all the Carolina Bays, that's where they all converge. This theory takes on an ominous edge when one realizes that the same comet is also blamed for a mass extinction of prehistoric animals such as the mammoth.

The Intracoastal Waterway

You'll often see its acronym ICW on signs—and sadly you'll probably hear the locals mispronounce it "Intercoastal Waterway"—but the casual visitor might actually find the Intracoastal Waterway difficult to spot. Relying on a natural network of interconnected estuaries and channels, combined with manmade **cuts,** the ICW often blends in rather subtly with the already extensive network of creeks and rivers in the area.

Mandated by Congress in 1919 and maintained by the U.S. Army Corps of Engineers, the Atlantic portion of the ICW runs from Key West to Boston and carries recreational and barge traffic away from the perils of offshore currents and weather. Even if they don't use it specifically, kayakers and boaters often find themselves on it at some point during their nautical adventures.

Estuaries

Most biologists will tell you that the Coastal Plain is where things get interesting. The place where a river interfaces with the ocean is called an estuary, and it's perhaps the most interesting place of all. Estuaries are heavily tidal in nature (indeed, the word derives from *aestus,* Latin for tide), and feature brackish water and heavy silt content.

The Carolinas typically have about a six- to eight-foot tidal range, and the coastal ecosystem depends on this steady ebb and flow for life itself. At high tide, shellfish open and feed. At low tide, they literally clam up, keeping saltwater inside their shells until the next tide comes.

Waterbirds and small mammals feed on

shellfish and other animals at low tide, when their prey is exposed. High tide brings an influx of fish and nutrients from the sea, in turn drawing predators like dolphins, who often come into tidal creeks to feed.

It's the estuaries that form the most compelling and beautiful sanctuaries for the area's incredibly rich diversity of animal species. Many estuaries are contiguous with those of other rivers.

Salt Marsh

All this water action in both directions—freshwater coming from inland, saltwater encroaching from the Atlantic—results in the phenomenon of the salt marsh, the single most recognizable and iconic geographic feature of the Carolina coast, also known simply as "wetlands." (Freshwater marshes are more rare, Florida's Everglades being perhaps the premier example.)

Far more than just a transitional zone between land and water, marsh is also nature's nursery. Plant and animal life in marshes tends to be not only diverse, but encompasses multitudes. Though you may not see its denizens easily, on close inspection you'll find the marsh absolutely teeming with creatures. Visually, the main identifying feature of a salt marsh is its distinctive, reed-like marsh grasses, adapted to survive in brackish water. Like estuaries, marshes and all life in them are heavily influenced by the tides, which bring in nutrients.

The marsh has also played a key role in human history as well, for it was here where the massive rice and indigo plantations grew their signature crops, aided by the natural ebb and flow of the tides. While most marsh you see will look quite undisturbed, very little of it could be called pristine.

In the heyday of the rice plantations of the Carolinas, much of the entire coastal salt marsh was crisscrossed by the canal-and-dike system of the rice paddies. You can still see evidence almost everywhere in the area if you look hard enough (the best time to look is right after takeoff or before landing in an airplane, since many approaches to regional airports take you over wetlands). Anytime you see a low, straight ridge running through a marsh, that's likely the eroded, overgrown remnant of an old rice paddy dike. Kayakers occasionally find old wooden water gates, or "trunks," on their paddles.

In the Lowcountry of South Carolina, you'll often hear the term **pluff mud.** This refers to the area's distinctive variety of soft, dark mud in the salt marsh, which often has an equally distinctive odor that locals love, but some visitors have a hard time getting used to. Extraordinarily rich in nutrients, pluff mud helped make rice a successful crop in the marshes of the Lowcountry.

In addition to their huge role as wildlife incubators and sanctuaries, wetlands are also one of the most important natural protectors of the health of the coastal region. They serve as natural filters, cleansing runoff from the land of toxins and pollutants before it hits the ocean. They also help humans by serving as natural hurricane barriers, their porous nature helping to ease the brunt of the damaging storm surge.

Beaches and Barrier Islands

The beaches of the Carolinas are almost all situated on barrier islands, long islands parallel to the shoreline and separated from the mainland by a sheltered body of water. Because they're formed by the deposit of sediment by offshore currents, they change shape over the years, with the general pattern of deposit going from north to south (i.e., the northern end will begin eroding first).

Most of the barrier islands are geologically quite young, only being formed within the last 25,000 years or so. Natural erosion, by current and by storm, combined with the accelerating effects of dredging for local port activity has quickened the decline of many barrier islands. Many beaches in the area are subject to a mitigation of erosion called **beach renourishment,** which generally involves redistributing dredged material closely offshore so that it will wash up on and around the beach.

As the name indicates, barrier islands are another of nature's safeguards against hurricane damage. Historically, the barrier islands have borne the vast bulk of the damage done by hurricanes in the region. Like the marshes, barrier islands also help protect the mainland by absorbing the brunt of the storm's wind and surging water.

While the barrier islands of South Carolina are certainly much more heavily traveled, the most unique collection of them is off the North Carolina coast. Taking up the entire northern half of the Tarheel State's coast, the **Outer Banks** is a nearly 200-mile-long string of very narrow barrier islands, jutting much farther into the Atlantic Ocean than their southern counterparts.

As a result of this eastward positioning, not only do the Outer Banks have a much more lonely, windswept feel than more southerly barrier islands, they're also virtual hurricane magnets, with hundreds of the storms making contact with the Outer Banks since such records began.

This extreme vulnerability means that, even more than most barrier islands, the geography of the Outer Banks changes with each year's storm patterns. For example, Hatteras Island was literally cut in half by Hurricane Isabel in 2003. (The damage was later repaired by a U.S. Army Corps of Engineers' project).

The relative solitude of the Outer Banks has also contributed to its status as the "Graveyard of the Atlantic," a place where at least 2,000 shipwrecks have occurred in its nearly 500 years of recorded history.

Wiregrass and Longleaf Ecosystems

In prehistoric times, most of Carolina Upper Coastal Plain was covered by what's known as a wiregrass or longleaf pine ecosystem. Wiregrass (*Arista stricta*) is a foot-tall species of hardy grass which often coexists with forests of the longleaf pine (*Pinus palustrist*), a relative of the slash pine now used as a cash crop throughout the South. The longleaf pine is fire-dependent, meaning it only reproduces

after wildfire—usually started by lightning—releases its seed cones.

Wiregrass savanna and old-growth forests of longleaf pine once covered most of the Southeast to the tune of about 100 million acres. Within about 200 years, however, settlers had deforested the region to a shadow of its former self. Contrary to Hollywood portrayals, no one ever needed a machete to tear their way through an old-growth forest. Because the high, thick tree canopy allows little but wiregrass to grow on the forest floor, Native Americans and early settlers could simply walk through these primordial forests with ease.

CLIMATE

One word comes to mind when one thinks about Southern climate: hot. That's the first word that occurs to Southerners as well, but virtually every survey of why residents are attracted to the area puts the climate at the top of the list. Go figure.

How hot is hot? The average high for July, the region's hottest month, in Charleston is about 89°F. While that's nothing compared to Tucson or Death Valley, coupled with the region's notoriously high humidity it can have an altogether miserable effect.

Technically most of the Carolina coast has a **humid subtropical** climate. During summer the famous high-pressure system called the **Bermuda High** settles over the entire southeastern United States, its rotating winds pushing aside most weather coming from the west. This can bring drought, as well as a certain sameness that afflicts the area during summer. Heat aside, there's no doubt that one of the most difficult things for an outsider to adjust to in the South is the humidity. The average annual humidity in Charleston is about 55 percent in the afternoons and a whopping 85 percent in the mornings. The most humid months are August and September.

There is no real antidote to humidity—other than air conditioning, that is—though many film crews and other outside workers swear by the use of Sea Breeze astringent. If you and your traveling partner can deal with the strong minty odor, dampen a hand towel with the astringent, drape it across the back of your neck and go about your business. Don't assume that because it's humid you shouldn't drink fluids. Just as in any hot climate, you should drink lots of water if you're going to be out in the Southern heat.

If you're on the Carolina coast, you'll no doubt grow to love the steady ocean breeze during the day. But at night you may notice the wind changing direction and coming from inland. That's caused by the land cooling at night, and the wind rushing toward the warmer waters offshore. This shift in wind current is mostly responsible for that sometimes awe-inspiring, sometimes just plain scary phenomenon of a typical Southern **thunderstorm.** Seemingly within the space of a few minutes on a particularly hot and still summer day, the afternoon is taken over by a rapidly moving stacked storm cloud called a **thunderhead,** which soon bursts open and pours an unbelievable amount of rain on whatever is unlucky enough to be beneath it, along with frequent, huge lightning strikes. Then, almost as quickly as it came on, the storm subsides and the sun comes back out again as if nothing happened.

August and September are the rainiest months in terms of rainfall, with averages well over six inches for each of those months. July is also quite wet, coming in at over five inches on average. Winters here are pretty mild, but can seem much colder than they actually are because of the dampness in the air. The coldest month is January, with about a 58°F high for the month and a 42°F average low.

You're highly unlikely to encounter snow in the area, and if you do it will likely only be skimpy flurries that a resident of the Great Lakes region wouldn't even notice as snow. But don't let this lull you into a false sense of security. If such a tiny flurry were to hit, be aware that most people down here have no clue how to drive in rough weather and will not be prepared for even such a small amount of snowfall. Visitors from snow country are often surprised by how completely a Southern city will shut down when that rare few inches of snow finally hits.

Hurricanes

The major weather phenomenon for residents and visitors alike is the mighty hurricane. These massive storms, with counterclockwise-rotating bands of clouds and winds pushing 200 miles per hour, are an ever-present danger to the southeast coast June-November of each year (the real danger period is around Labor Day).

North Carolina's Outer Banks in particular have seen an incredible number of damaging storms. I remember seeing a map showing all the routes of all the hurricanes in recorded history known to make landfall in the United States. About a third of them crossed over the same point: Cape Hatteras, North Carolina.

As most everyone is aware now from the horrific, well-documented damage from such killer storms as Hugo, Andrew, and Katrina, hurricanes are not to be trifled with. Old-fashioned, drunken "hurricane parties" are a thing of the past for the most part, the images of cataclysmic destruction everyone has seen on TV having long since eliminated any lingering romanticism about riding out the storm.

Local TV, websites, and print media can be counted on to give more than ample warning in the event a hurricane is approaching the area during your visit. Whatever you do, do not discount the warnings. It's not worth it. If the locals are preparing to leave, you should too.

Typically when a storm is likely to hit the area, there will first be a suggested evacuation. But if authorities determine there's an overwhelming likelihood of imminent hurricane damage, they will issue a **mandatory evacuation order.** What this means in practice is that if you do choose to stay behind, you cannot count on any type of emergency services or help whatsoever.

Generally speaking, the most lethal

element of a hurricane is not the wind but the storm surge, the wall of ocean water that the winds drive before them onto the coast. During Hurricane Hugo, Charleston's Battery was inundated with a storm surge of over 12 feet, with an amazing 20 feet reported farther north at Cape Romain.

ENVIRONMENTAL ISSUES

The Carolina coast is currently experiencing a double whammy, environmentally speaking: Not only are its distinctive wetlands extraordinarily sensitive to human interference, this is one of the most rapidly developing parts of the country. New and often-poorly planned subdivisions and resort communities are popping up all over the place. Vastly increased port activity, too, is taking a devastating toll on the salt marsh and surrounding barrier islands. Combine all that with the South's often skeptical attitude towards environmental activism, and you have a recipe for potential ecological disaster.

Thankfully, there are some bright spots. More and more communities are seeing the value of responsible planning and not green-lighting every new development sight unseen. Land trusts and other conservation organizations are growing in size, number, funding, and influence. The large number of marine biologists in these areas at various research and educational institutions means there's a wealth of education and talent available in advising local governments and citizens on how best to conserve the area's natural beauty.

Marsh Dieback

The dominant species of marsh grass, *Spartina alterniflora* (pronounced Spar-TINE-uh) and *Juncus roemerianus* thrive in the typically brackish water of the coastal marsh estuaries, their structural presence helping to stem erosion of banks and dunes. While drought and blight have taken their toll on the grass, increased coastal development and continued channel deepening have also led to a steady creep of ocean saltwater farther and farther into remaining marsh stands.

The Paper Industry

Early in the 20th century, the Southeast's abundance of cheap, undeveloped land and plentiful, free water led to the establishment of massive pine tree farms to feed coastal pulp and paper mills. Chances are if you used a paper grocery bag recently, it was made in a paper mill in the South.

But in addition to making a whole lot of paper bags and providing lots of employment for residents through the decades, the paper industry also gave the area lots of air and water pollution, stressed local water supplies (it takes a lot of water to make paper from trees), and took away natural species diversity from the area by devoting so much acreage to a single crop, pine trees.

Currently the domestic paper industry is reeling from competition from cheaper Asian lumber stocks and paper mills. As a result, an interesting—and not altogether welcome—phenomenon has been the wholesale entering of Southeastern paper companies into the real estate business. Discovering they can make a whole lot more money selling or developing tree farms for residential lots than making paper bags, pulp and paper companies are helping to drive overdevelopment in the region by encouraging development on their land rather than infill development closer to urban areas. So in the long run, the demise of the paper industry in the South may not prove to be the net advantage to the environment that was anticipated.

Aquifers

Unlike parts of the western U.S., where individuals can enforce private property rights to water, the South has generally held that the region's water is a publicly held resource. The upside of this is that everybody has equal claim to drinking water without regard to status or income or how long they've lived there. The downside is that industry also has the same free claim to the water that citizens do—and they use a heck of a lot more of it.

Currently at least half of the population of North and South Carolina gets its water from aquifers, which are basically huge underground caverns made of limestone. Receiving **groundwater** drip by drip, century after century, from rainfall farther inland, the aquifers essentially act as massive, sterile warehouses for freshwater, accessible through wells.

The aquifers have human benefit only if their water remains fresh. Once saltwater from the ocean begins intruding into an aquifer, it doesn't take much to render all of it unfit for human consumption—forever. What keeps that freshwater fresh is natural water pressure, keeping the ocean at bay.

But nearly a century ago, paper mills began pumping millions and millions of gallons of water out of coastal aquifers. Combined with the dramatic rise in coastal residential development, that has decreased the natural water pressure of the aquifers, leading to measurable saltwater intrusion at several points under the coast.

Currently, local and state governments in both states are increasing their reliance on **surfacewater** (i.e., treated water from rivers and creeks) to relieve the strain on the underground aquifer system. But it's too soon to tell if that has contained the threat from saltwater intrusion.

Nuclear Energy

South Carolina has four nuclear power plants, though none on the coast, in the Greenville, Hartsville, and Jenkinsville areas, and in York County. The massive, Cold War-era nuclear bomb plant Savannah River Site is near Aiken, well inland.

North Carolina has three nuclear power plants: one in Brunswick County near the coast, one near Charlotte well inland, and one near Raleigh in the middle of the state.

Air Pollution

Despite growing awareness of the issue, air pollution is still a big problem in the coastal region. Paper mills still operate, putting out their distinctive rotten-eggs odor, and auto emissions standards are notoriously lax in South Carolina. The biggest culprit, though, are coal-powered electric plants, which are the norm throughout the region and which continue to pour large amounts of toxins into the atmosphere.

Plants and Animals

PLANTS

The most iconic plant life of the coastal region is the **Southern live oak** *(Quercus virginiana)*. Named because of its evergreen nature, a live oak is technically any one of a number of evergreens in the *Quercus* genus, many of which reside in the Carolinas, but in local practice almost always refers to the Southern live oak. Capable of living over 1,000 years and possessing wood of legendary resilience, the Southern live oak is one of nature's most magnificent creations. Though the timber value of live oaks has been well known since the earliest days of the American shipbuilding industry—when the oak dominated the entire coast inland of the marsh—their value as a canopy tree has finally been widely recognized by local and state governments as well.

Fittingly, the other iconic plant life of the coastal region grows on the branches of the live oak. Contrary to popular opinion, **Spanish moss** *(Tillandsia usnesides)* is neither Spanish nor moss. It's an air plant, a wholly indigenous cousin to the pineapple. Also contrary to folklore, Spanish moss is not a parasite nor does it harbor parasites while living on an oak tree—though it can after it has already fallen to the ground.

Also growing on the bark of a live oak, especially right after a rain shower, is the **resurrection fern** *(Polypodium polypodioides)*, which can stay dormant for amazingly long periods of time, only to spring back to life with the introduction of a little water. You can find live oak, Spanish moss, and resurrection fern anywhere in the **maritime forest** ecosystem of the coastal Carolinas, a zone generally behind the **interdune meadows,** which is itself right behind the beach zone.

Far and away the region's most important commercial tree is the pine, used for paper, lumber, and turpentine. Rarely seen in the wild today due to tree farming, the dominant species is now the **slash pine** *(Pinus elliottii),* often seen in long rows on either side of rural highways. Before the introduction of large-scale monoculture tree farming, however, a rich variety of native pines flourished in the **upland forest** inland from the maritime forest, chief among them the **longleaf** *(Pinus palustris)* and **loblolly** *(Pinus taeda)* pines. Longleaf forest covered nearly 100 million acres of the Southeast Coastal Plain upon the arrival of the Europeans; within 300 years most of it would be cut down and/ or harvested.

Right up there with live oaks and Spanish moss in terms of instant recognition would have to be the colorful, ubiquitous **azalea,** a flowering shrub of the *Rhododendron* genus. Over 10,000 varieties have been cultivated through the centuries, with quite a wide range of them on display during blooming season, March-April. The area's other great floral display comes from the **camellia** *(Camellia japonica),* a large, cold-hardy evergreen shrub with flowers that generally bloom in late winter (January-March). An import from Asia, the southeastern coast's camellias are close cousins to *Camellia sinensis,* from which tea is made (and also an import).

Other colorful ornamentals of the area include the ancient and beautiful **Southern magnolia** *(Magnolia grandiflora),* a native plant with distinctive large white flowers (evolved before the advent of bees); and the **flowering dogwood** *(Cornus florida),* which despite its very hard wood—great for daggers, hence its original name "dagwood"—is actually quite fragile. An ornamental imported

from Asia that has now become quite obnoxious in its aggressive invasiveness is the **mimosa** *(Albrizia julibrissin),* which blooms March-August.

Moving into watery areas, you'll find the remarkable **bald cypress** *(Taxodium distichum),* a flood-resistant conifer recognizable by its tufted top, its great height (up to 130 feet), and its distinctive "knees," parts of the root that project above the waterline and which are believed to help stabilize the tree in lowland areas. Much prized for its beautiful, pest-resistant wood, great stands of ancient cypress once dominated the marsh along the coast; sadly, overharvesting and destruction of wetlands has made the magnificent sight of this ancient, dignified species much less common.

Probably the most unique plant on the coast of the Carolinas—for a variety of reasons—is the **Venus flytrap** *(Dionaea muscipula).* This fascinating carnivorous species grows only in the bogs of the coastal Carolinas, generally within about a hundred-mile radius of Wilmington, North Carolina. Easily accessible areas where you can find Venus flytraps in the wild include Green Swamp Preserve in Brunswick County and Carolina Beach State Park south of Wilmington.

The acres of **smooth cordgrass** that comprise the coastal marsh are plants of the *Spartina alternaflora* species. (A cultivated cousin, *Spartina anglica,* is considered invasive.) Besides its simple natural beauty, *Spartina* is also a key food source for marsh denizens. Playing a key environmental role on the coast are **sea oats** *(Uniola paniculata).* This wispy, fast-growing perennial grass anchors sand dunes and hence is a protected species (it's a misdemeanor to pick them).

South Carolina isn't called the "Palmetto State" for nothing. Though palm varieties are not as common up here as in Florida, you'll definitely encounter several types along the coast. The **cabbage palm** *(Sabal palmetto),* for which South Carolina is named, is the largest variety, up to 50-60 feet tall. Its "heart of palm" is an edible delicacy, which coastal Native Americans boiled in bear fat as porridge. In dunes and sandhills you'll find clumps of the low-lying **saw palmetto** (*Serenoa repens*). The **bush palmetto** (*Sabal minor*) has distinctive fan-shaped branches. The common **Spanish bayonet** (*Yucca aloifolia*) looks like a palm, but it's actually a member of the agave family.

ANIMALS
On Land

Perhaps the most iconic land animal—or semi-land animal, anyway—of the Carolina coast is the legendary **American alligator** (*Alligator mississippiensis*), the only species of crocodile native to the area. Contrary to their fierce reputation, locals know these massive reptiles, 6-12 feet long as adults, to be quite shy.

If you come in the colder months you won't see one at all, since alligators require an outdoor temperature over 70°F to become active and feed. (Indeed, the appearance of alligators was once a well-known symbol of spring in the area.) Often all you'll see is a couple of eyebrow ridges sticking out of the water, and a gator lying still in a shallow creek can easily be mistaken for a floating log. But should you see one or more gators basking in the sun—a favorite activity on warm days for these cold-blooded creatures—it's best to admire them from afar. A mother alligator, in particular, will destroy anything that comes near her nest. Despite the alligator's short, stubby legs, they run amazingly fast on land—faster than you, in fact.

If you're driving on a country road at night, be on the lookout for **white-tailed deer** (*Odeocoileus virginianus*), which, besides being quite beautiful, also pose a serious road hazard. Because development has dramatically reduced the habitat—and therefore the numbers—of their natural predators, deer are plentiful throughout the area and, as you read this, are hard at work devouring vast tracts of valuable vegetation. No one wants to hurt poor little Bambi, but the truth is that area hunters perform a valuable service by culling the local deer population, which is in no danger of extinction anytime soon—far from it.

North and South Carolina host large populations of playful **river otter** (*Lutra Canadensis*). Not to be confused with the larger sea otters off the West Coast, these fast-swimming members of the weasel family inhabit inland waterways and marshy areas, with dominant males sometimes ranging as much as 50 miles within a single waterway. As strict carnivores, usually of fish, otters are a key indicator of the health of their ecosystem. If they're thriving, water and habitat quality is likely to be pretty high. If they're not, something's going badly wrong.

While you're unlikely to encounter an otter, if you're camping you might easily run into the **raccoon** (*Procyon lotor*), an exceedingly intelligent and crafty relative of the bear, sharing that larger animal's resourcefulness in stealing your food. Though nocturnal, raccoons will feed whenever food is available. Raccoons can grow so accustomed to the human presence as to almost consider themselves part of the family, but resist the temptation to get close to them. Rabies is prevalent in the raccoon population and you should always, always keep your distance.

Another common campsite nuisance, the **opossum** (*Didelphis virginiana*) is a shy, primitive creature that is much more easily discouraged. North America's only marsupial, a 'possum's usual "defense" against predators is to play dead. That said, however, they have an immunity to snake venom and often feed on the reptiles, even the most poisonous ones.

Opossums are native to the area, but another similarly slow-witted, slow-moving creature is not: the **nine-banded armadillo** (*Dasypus novemcinctus*). In centuries past, these armor-plated insect-eaters were mostly confined to Mexico, but they are gradually working their way northward. Obsessive diggers, armadillos cause quite a bit of damage to crops and gardens. Sometimes jokingly called "'possum on the half shell," armadillo, like opossum, are frequent roadkill on Carolina highways.

While you're highly unlikely to actually see a **red fox** *(Vulpes vulpes),* you might very well see their distinctive footprints in the mud of a marsh at low tide. These nocturnal hunters, a non-native species introduced by European settlers, range the coast seeking mice, squirrels, and rabbits.

Once fairly common in the Carolinas, the **black bear** *(Ursus americanus)* has suffered from hunting and habitat destruction and is extremely rare in the region.

In the Water

Humankind's aquatic cousin, the **Atlantic bottle-nosed dolphin** *(Ursiops truncates),* is a well-known and frequent visitor to the coast, coming far upstream into creeks and rivers to feed. Children, adults, and experienced seamen alike all delight in encounters with the mammals, sociable creatures who travel in family units. When not occupied with feeding or mating activities—both of which can get surprisingly rowdy—dolphins show great curiosity about human visitors to their habitat. They will gather near boats, surfacing often with the distinctive chuffing sound of air coming from their blowholes. Occasionally they'll even lift their heads out of the water to have a look at you; consider yourself lucky indeed to have such a close encounter. Don't be fooled by their cuteness, however. Dolphins live life with gusto and aren't scared of much. They're voracious eaters of fish, amorous and energetic lovers, and will take on an encroaching shark in a heartbeat.

Another beloved part-time marine creature of the barrier islands of the coast is the **loggerhead turtle** *(Caretta caretta),* which is South Carolina's state reptile. Though the species prefers to stay well offshore the rest of the year, females weighing up to 300 pounds come out of the sea each May-July to dig a shallow hole in the dunes and lay over 100 leathery eggs, returning to the ocean and leaving the eggs to hatch on their own after two months. Interestingly, the mothers prefer to nest at the same spot on the same island year after year. After hatching, the baby turtles then make a dramatic, extremely dangerous (and extremely *slow* trek) to the safety of the waves, at the mercy of various predators.

A series of dedicated research and conservation efforts are working hard to protect the loggerheads' traditional nursery grounds to ensure the survival of this fascinating, loveable, and threatened species. Cape Island within the Cape Romain National Wildlife Refuge accounts for about a quarter of all loggerhead nests in South Carolina, and is the leading nesting site north of Florida. Other key sites in South Carolina include Kiawah, Edisto, and Hilton Head Islands. Though their numbers are lower in the Tarheel State, the loggerheads do like to nest along the entire length of the coast, especially near Cape Hatteras.

Of course the coastal waters and rivers are chock-a-block with fish. The most abundant and sought-after recreational species in the area is the **spotted sea trout** *(Cynoscion nebulosus),* followed by the **red drum** *(Suaenops ocellatus).* Local anglers also pursue many varieties of **bass, bream, sheepshead,** and **crappie.** It may sound strange to some accustomed to considering it a "trash" fish, but many types of **catfish** are not only plentiful here but are a common and well-regarded food source. Many species of **flounder** inhabit the silty bottoms of estuaries all along the coast. Farther offshore are game and sportfish like **marlin, swordfish, shark, grouper,** and **tuna.**

Each March, anglers jockey for position on coastal rivers for the yearly running of the **American shad** *(Alosa sapidissima)* upstream to spawn. This large (up to eight pounds), catfish-like species is a regional delicacy as a seasonal entrée, as well as for its tasty roe. There's a limit of eight shad per person per season.

One of the more interesting fish species in the area is the endangered **shortnose sturgeon** *(Acipenser brevirostrum).* A fantastically ancient species that has evolved little in hundreds of millions of years, this small, freshwater fish is known to exist in the estuaries of the ACE Basin. Traveling up-river to spawn in the winter, the sturgeons remain around the mouths of waterways the rest of the year, venturing near the ocean only sparingly.

Crustaceans and shellfish have been a key food staple in the area for thousands of years, with the massive shell middens of the coast being testament to Native Americans' healthy appetite for them. The beds of the local variant, the **eastern oyster** *(Crassostrea virginica)*, aren't what they used to be due to overharvesting, water pollution, and disruption of habitat. In truth, most local restaurants import the little filter-feeders from the Gulf of Mexico these days. Oysters spawn May-August, hence the old folk wisdom about eating oysters only in months with the letter "r," so as not to disrupt the breeding cycle.

Each year April-January, shrimp boats up and down the southeastern coast trawl for **shrimp**, most commercially viable in two local species, the white shrimp *(Penaeus setiferus)*, and the brown shrimp *(Penaeus aztecus)*. Shrimp are the most popular seafood item in the United States and account for hundreds of millions of dollars in revenue in the coastal economy. While consumption won't slow down anytime soon, the Carolina shrimping industry is facing serious threats, both from species decline due to pollution and overfishing and from competition from shrimp farms and the Asian shrimp industry.

Another important commercial crop is the **blue crab** *(Callinected sapidus)*, the species used in such Lowcountry delicacies as crab cakes. You'll often see floating markers bobbing up and down in rivers throughout the region. These signal the presence directly below of a crab trap, often of an amateur crabber.

A true living link to primordial times, the alien-looking **horseshoe crab** *(Limulus polyphemus)*, is frequently found on beaches of the coast during the spring mating season (it lives in deeper water the rest of the year). More closely related to scorpions and spiders than crabs, the horseshoe has evolved hardly a lick in hundreds of millions of years.

Any trip to a local salt marsh at low tide will likely uncover hundreds of **fiddler crabs** *(Uca pugilator* and *Uca pugnax)*, so-named for the way the males wave their single enlarged claws in the air to attract mates. (Their other, smaller claw is the one they actually eat with.) The fiddlers make distinctive burrows in the pluff mud for sanctuary during high tide, recognizable by the little balls of sediment at the entrances (the crabs spit out the balls after sifting through the sand for food).

One charming beach inhabitant, the **sand dollar** *(Mellita quinquiesperforata)*, has seen its numbers decline drastically due to being entirely too charming for its own good. Beachcombers are now asked to enjoy these flat little cousins to the sea urchin in their natural habitat and to refrain from taking them home. Besides, they start to smell bad when they dry out.

The **sea nettle** *(Chrysaora quinquecirrha)*, a less-than-charming beach inhabitant, is a jellyfish that stings thousands of people on the coast a year (though only for those with severe allergies are the stings potentially life-threatening). Stinging their prey before transporting it into their waiting mouths, the jellyfish also sting when disturbed or frightened. Most often, people are stung by stepping on the bodies of jellyfish washed up on the sand. If you're stung by a jellyfish, don't panic. You'll probably experience a stinging rash for about half an hour. Locals say applying a little baking soda or vinegar helps cut the sting. (Some also swear fresh urine will do the trick, and I pass that tip along to you purely in the interest of thoroughness.)

In the Air

When enjoying the marshlands of the coast, consider yourself fortunate to see an endangered **wood stork** *(Mycteria americana)*, though their numbers are on the increase. The only storks to breed in North America, these graceful, long-lived birds (routinely living over 10 years) are usually seen on a low flight path across the marsh, though at some birding spots beginning in late summer you can find them at a **roost,** sometimes numbering over 100 birds. Resting at high tide, they fan out over the marsh to feed at low tide on foot. Old-timers sometimes call them "Spanish buzzards" or simply "the preacher."

Often confused with the wood stork is the gorgeous **white ibis** *(Eudocimus albus),* distinguishable by its orange bill and black wingtips. Like the wood stork, the ibis is a communal bird that roosts in colonies. Other similar-looking coastal denizens are the white-feathered **great egret** *(Ardea alba)* and **snowy egret** *(Egretta thula),* the former distinguishable by its yellow bill and the latter by its black bill and the tuft of plumes on the back of its head.

Egrets are in the same family as herons. The most magnificent is the **great blue heron** *(Ardea herodias).* Despite their imposing height—up to four feet tall—these waders are shy. Often you hear them rather than see them, a loud shriek of alarm that echoes over the marsh.

So how to tell the difference between all these wading birds at a glance? It's actually easiest when they're in flight. Egrets and herons fly with their necks tucked in, while storks and ibises fly with their necks extended.

Dozens of species of shorebirds comb the beaches, including **sandpipers, plovers,** and the wonderful and rare **American oystercatcher** *(Haematopus palliates),* instantly recognizable for its prancing walk, dark brown back, stark white underside, and long, bright-orange bill. **Gulls** and **terns** also hang out wherever there's water. They can frequently be seen swarming around incoming shrimp boats, attracted by the catch of little crustaceans.

The chief raptor of the salt marsh is the fish-eating **osprey** *(Pandion haliaetus).* These large grayish birds of prey are similar to eagles but are adapted to a maritime environment, with a reversible outer toe on each talon (the better for catching wriggly fish) and closable

nostrils so they can dive into the water after prey. Very common all along the coast, they like to build big nests on top of buoys and channel markers in addition to trees.

The **bald eagle** *(Haliaeetus leucocephalus),* is making a comeback thanks to increased federal regulation and better education of trigger-happy locals. Of course as we all should have learned in school, the bald eagle is not actually bald but has a head adorned with white feathers. Like the osprey, they prefer fish, but unlike the osprey they will settle for rodents and rabbits.

Inland among the pines you'll find the most common area woodpecker, the huge **pileated woodpecker** *(Dryocopus pileatus)* with its huge crest. Less common is the smaller, more subtly marked **red-cockaded woodpecker** *(Picoides borealis).* Once common in the vast primordial pine forests of the southeast, the species is now endangered, its last real refuge being the big tracts of relatively undisturbed land on military bases and on national wildlife refuges.

Insects

Down here they say that God invented bugs to keep the Yankees from completely taking over the South. And insects are probably the most unpleasant fact of life in the southeastern coastal region.

The list of annoying indigenous insects must begin with the infamous **sand gnat** *(Culicoides furens),* scourge of the lowlands. This tiny and persistent nuisance, a member of the midge family, lacks the precision of the mosquito with its long proboscis. No, the sand gnat is more torture-master than surgeon, brutally gouging and digging away at its victim's skin until it hits a source of blood. Most prevalent in the spring and fall, the sand gnat is drawn to its prey by the carbon dioxide trail of its breath.

While long sleeves and long pants are one way to keep gnats at bay, that causes its own discomfort because of the region's heat and humidity. The only real antidote to the sand gnat's assault—other than never breathing—is the Avon skin care product Skin So Soft, which has taken on a new and wholly unplanned life as the South's favorite anti-gnat lotion. Grow to like the scent, because the more of this stuff you lather on the better. And in calmer moments grow to appreciate the great contribution sand gnats make to the salt marsh ecosystem—as food for many species of birds and bats.

Running a close second to the sand gnat are the over three dozen species of highly aggressive **mosquito,** which breed anywhere a few drops of water lie stagnant. Not surprisingly, massive populations blossom in the rainiest months, in late spring and late summer. Like the gnat, the mosquito—the biters are always female—homes in on its victim by trailing the plume of carbon dioxide exhaled in the breath.

More than just a biting nuisance, mosquitoes are now vectoring West Nile disease, signaling a possibly dire threat to public health. Local governments in the region pour millions of dollars of taxpayer money into massive pesticide spraying programs from helicopters, planes, and trucks. While that certainly helps stem the tide, it by no means eliminates the mosquito population. (This is just as well, because like the sand gnat the mosquito is an important food source for many species, such as bats and dragonflies.) Alas, Skin So Soft has little effect on the mosquito. Try over-the-counter sprays, anything smelling of citronella, and wearing long sleeves and long pants when weather permits.

But undoubtedly the most viscerally loathed of all pests here, especially on the coast, is the so-called "palmetto bug," or **American cockroach** (Periplaneta

americana). These black, shiny, and sometimes grotesquely massive insects—up to two inches long—are living fossils, virtually unchanged over hundreds of millions of years. And perfectly adapted as they are to life in and among wet, decaying vegetation, they're unlikely to change a bit in 100 million more years.

While they spend most of their time crawling around, usually under rotting leaves and tree bark, the American cockroach can indeed fly—sort of. There are few more hilarious sights than a room full of people frantically trying to dodge a palmetto bug that has just clumsily launched itself off a high point on the wall. Because the cockroach doesn't know any better than you do where it's going, it can be a particularly bracing event—though the insect does not bite and poses few real health hazards.

Popular regional use of the term "palmetto bug" undoubtedly has its roots in a desire for polite Southern society to avoid using the ugly word "roach" and its connotations of filth and unclean environments. But the colloquialism actually has a basis in reality. Contrary to what anyone tells you, the natural habitat of the American cockroach—unlike its kitchen-dwelling, much-smaller cousin the German cockroach—is outdoors, often up in trees. They only come inside human dwellings when it's especially hot, especially cold, or especially dry outside. Like you, the palmetto bug is easily driven indoors by extreme temperatures and by thirst.

Other than visiting the Southeast during the winter, when the roaches go dormant, there's no convenient antidote for their presence. The best way to keep them out of your life is to stay away from decaying vegetation and keep doors and windows closed on especially hot nights.

History

BEFORE THE EUROPEANS

Based on studies of artifacts found throughout the area, anthropologists know the first humans arrived in the Carolinas at least 13,000 years ago, at the tail end of the Ice Age. However, a still-controversial archaeological dig in South Carolina, the Topper Site on the Savannah River inland near Allendale, has found artifacts that some scientists say are about 50,000 years old.

In any case, during this **Paleoindian Period,** sea levels were over 200 feet lower than present levels, and large mammals such as wooly mammoths, horses, and camels were hunted for food and skins. However, rapidly increasing temperatures, rising sea levels, and efficient hunting techniques combined to quickly kill off these large mammals, relics of the Pleistocene Era, ushering in the **Archaic Period** of history in what's now the southeastern United States. Still hunter-gatherers, Archaic Period Indians began turning to small game such as deer, bear, and turkey, supplemented with fruit and nuts.

The latter part of the Archaic era saw more habitation on the coasts, with an increasing reliance on fish and shellfish for sustenance. It's during this time that the great **shell middens** of the Carolina and Georgia coast trace their origins. Basically serving as trash heaps for discarded oyster shells, as the middens grew in size they also took on a ceremonial status, often being used as sites for important rituals and meetings. Such sites are often called **shell rings,** and the largest yet found was over nine feet high and 300 feet in diameter. Hilton Head Island, for example, has two remaining shell rings. Using ground-penetrating radar, archaeologists are finding more and more Archaic era shell middens and rings all the time.

The introduction of agriculture and improved pottery techniques about 3,000 years ago led to the **Woodland Period** of Native American settlement. Extended clan groups were much less migratory, establishing year-round communities of up to 50 people who began the practice of clearing land to grow crops. The ancient shell middens of their forefathers were not abandoned, however, and were continually added onto.

Native Americans had been cremating or burying their dead for years, a practice which eventually gave rise to the construction of the first **mounds** during the Woodland Period. Essentially built-up earthworks sometimes marked with spiritual symbols, often in the form of animal shapes, mounds not only contained the remains of the deceased, but items like pottery to accompany the deceased into the afterlife.

Increased agriculture led to increased population, and with that population growth came competition over resources and a more formal notion of warfare. This period, from about AD 800-1600, is termed the **Mississippian Period.** It was the Mississippians who would be the first Native Americans in what's now the continental United States to encounter European explorers and settlers after Columbus.

The Native Americans who would later be called **Creek Indians** were the direct descendants of the Mississippians in lineage, language, and lifestyle. Described by later European accounts as a tall, proud people, the Mississippians often wore elaborate body art and, like the indigenous inhabitants of Central and South America, used the practice of **head shaping,** whereby an infant's skull was deliberately deformed into an elongated shape by tying the baby's head to a board for about a year.

By about AD 1400, change came to the Mississippian culture for reasons that are still not completely understood. In some areas, large chiefdoms began splintering into smaller subgroups in an intriguing echo of the medieval feudal system going on concurrently in Europe. In other areas, however, the rise of a handful of more powerful chiefs subsumed smaller communities under their influence. In either case, the result was the same: The landscape of the Southeast became less peopled as many of the old villages, built around huge central mounds, were abandoned, some suddenly.

As tensions increased, the contested land became more and more dangerous for the poorly armed or poorly connected. Indeed, at the time of the Europeans' arrival much of the coastal area was more thinly inhabited than it had been for many decades.

THE EUROPEANS ARRIVE

The record of white European contact in the coastal Carolinas begins, suitably enough, with Amerigo Vespucci, the man for whom America was named. The Italian explorer came ashore somewhere in the Cape Hatteras area during his long-ranging first voyage to the new world in the 1490s.

Later, the Spanish arrived on the South Carolina coast in 1521, roughly concurrent with Cortez's conquest of Mexico. A party of Spanish slavers, led by Francisco Cordillo (sometimes spelled Gordillo), ventured to what's now Port Royal Sound from Santo Domingo in the Caribbean. Naming the area Santa Elena, he kidnapped a few dozen Indian slaves and left, ranging as far north as the Cape Fear River in present-day North Carolina, and by some accounts even further up the coast.

The first serious exploration of the coast came in 1526, when Lucas Vazquez de Ayllon and about 600 colonists made landfall at Winyah Bay near present-day Georgetown, South Carolina. They didn't stay long, however, immediately moving down the coast and trying to establish roots in the St. Catherine's Sound area of modern-day Georgia. That colony—called San Miguel de Gualdalpe—was the first European colony in America. (The continent's oldest continuously occupied settlement, St. Augustine, Florida, wasn't founded until 1565.) The colony also brought with it the seed of a future nation's dissolution: slaves from Africa. San Miguel lasted only six weeks due to political tension and a slave uprising.

Hernando de Soto's infamous expedition of 1539-1543 began in Florida and went through southwest Georgia before crossing the Savannah River somewhere near modern-day North Augusta, South Carolina. He immediately came in contact with emissaries from the Cofitachequi empire of Mississippian Indians. His subsequent route took him through the central Carolinas, westward over the Appalachians, and eventually to the Gulf of Mexico, where de Soto died of fever.

Long after his departure, de Soto's legacy was felt throughout the Southeast in the form of various diseases for which the Mississippian tribes had no immunity whatsoever: smallpox, typhus, influenza, measles, yellow fever, whooping cough, diphtheria, tuberculosis, and bubonic plague. While the barbaric cruelties of the Spanish certainly took their toll, far more damaging were these deadly diseases to a population totally unprepared for them. As the viruses they introduced ran rampant, the Europeans themselves stayed away for a couple of decades after the ignominious end of de Soto's quest. During that quarter-century, the once-proud Mississippian culture, ravaged by disease, disintegrated into a shadow of its former greatness.

The French Misadventure

The Spanish presence in the Carolinas was briefly threatened by the ill-fated establishment of Charlesfort in 1562 by French Huguenots under Jean Ribault. Part of a covert effort by the Protestant French Admiral Coligny to send Huguenot colonizing missions around the globe, Ribault's crew of 150 first explored the mouth of the St. Johns River near present-day Jacksonville, Florida before heading north to Port Royal Sound and present-day Parris Island, South Carolina.

After establishing Charlesfort, Ribault returned to France for supplies. During his absence, religious war had broken out in his home country. Ribault sought sanctuary in England but was clapped in irons anyway. Meanwhile, most of Charlesfort's colonists grew so demoralized they joined another French expedition led by Rene Laudonniere at Fort Caroline on the St. Johns River. The remaining 27 built a ship to sail from Charlesfort back to France. Only 20 of them survived the journey, which was cut short in the English Channel when they had to be rescued.

Ribault himself was dispatched to reinforce Fort Caroline, but was headed off by a contingent from the new Spanish fortified settlement at St. Augustine. The fate of the French presence on the southeast coast was sealed when not only did the Spanish take Fort Caroline, but a storm destroyed Ribault's reinforcing fleet. Ribault and all survivors were massacred as soon as they struggled ashore.

To keep the French away for good and cement Spain's hold on this northernmost part of their province of *La Florida,* the Spanish built the fort of Santa Elena directly on top of Charlesfort. Both layers are currently being excavated and studied today on Parris Island, near a golf course on the U.S. Marine camp.

The Mission Era

With Spanish dominance ensured for the near future, the lengthy mission era began. While it's rarely mentioned as a key part of U.S. history, the truth is that the Spanish missionary presence in Florida and on the Georgia coast was longer and more comprehensive than its much more widely known counterpart in California.

While the purpose of the missions was to convert as many Indians as possible to Christianity, they also served to further consolidate Spanish political control. It was a dicey proposition, as technically the mission friars served at the pleasure of the local chiefs. But the more savvy of the chiefs soon learned that cooperating with the militarily powerful Spanish led to more influence and more supplies. Frequently it was the chiefs themselves who urged for more expansion of the Franciscan missions.

The looming invasion threat to St. Augustine from the great English adventurer and privateer Sir Francis Drake was a harbinger of trouble to come. The Spanish consolidated their positions near St. Augustine and Santa Elena on Parris Island was abandoned. As Spanish power waned, in 1629 Charles I of England laid formal claim to what's now the Carolinas, Georgia, and much of Florida, but made no effort to colonize the area.

By 1706 the Spanish mission effort in the southeast had fully retreated to Florida. In an interesting postscript, 89 Native Americans—the sole surviving descendants of Spain's southeastern missions—evacuated to Cuba with the final Spanish exodus from Florida in 1763.

THE LOST COLONY

The first English settlement in the New World, the ill-fated "Lost Colony" of Roanoke Island, was in modern-day North Carolina. Somewhat confusingly, however, it was considered part of Virginia at the time. (The first permanent English settlement, Jamestown, happened two decades later in Virginia proper.)

Famed English maritime adventurer Sir Walter Raleigh received a charter from Queen Elizabeth I in the 1580s to establish a colony—to be called Virginia after the "Virgin Queen" herself—that would provide a base of operations from which to plunder Spanish treasure ships crossing the Atlantic.

The Outer Banks were considered the ideal place for such a naval base, and Raleigh sent an expedition to the modern-day Manteo area on Roanoke Island commanded by Phillip Amadas and Arthur Barlowe, followed a few months later in spring 1585 by Sir Richard Grenville's larger colonizing expedition.

While first contact between the English and the resident Native Americans went reasonably well, a bad omen came early, when a dispute over a silver cup stolen from the colonists led to the ransacking of an Indian village and the brutal execution by fire of the local chief.

Despite this, Grenville went ahead with his plan to leave about 75 colonists behind while he and his crew went back to England to re-provision. Though he promised to be back by April 1586, the only Englishman to visit during that time was the wide-ranging privateer Sir Francis Drake, who simply took the bulk of the colonists back to England with him.

That group, however, was not the Lost Colony. Raleigh—who eventually did return, albeit finding no one there—sent a second group of 117 settlers to the same spot, making landfall July 22, 1587. In a chilling harbinger of what was to come, this group found no trace of the 15 men left behind to maintain the Queen's claim to Virginia—save for the bones of a single man.

The group of 117 settlers—their ranks expanded by one with the birth of the first English baby in the Americas, Virginia Dare—immediately ran into trouble with some of the local tribes, whose memory of the violence of a year before was still vivid. Though relations were good with the Croatan tribe, others in the area were less friendly, and a dispute led to the killing of a colonist, George Howe.

In response, the colonists asked their leader, John White, to return to England to bring reinforcements. The timing couldn't have been worse.

The crisis induced by the attack of the Spanish Armada on England in 1588 meant White could find no decent ship in which to return to Roanoke. In desperation he contracted with the captains of two very small vessels. On the way back to America, the captains decided to indulge in a little piracy of their own, only to have the tables turned and have their own supplies taken from them. Thus humbled, White had to sail back to England.

Continuing war with the Spanish further delayed White's return to Roanoke by another three years. Finally hitching a ride with a privateer headed for the Caribbean, White made landfall in Roanoke on August 18, 1590.

The colony was totally deserted, with no sign of struggle and the fortifications carefully dismantled. The only clue he found was a cryptic word carved into a tree that would resonate through history: "Croatoan." On a nearby tree was apparently another attempt to write the same word: "Cro."

The tree-carvings weren't without context. Before he had left the colonists, White had told them to carve a Maltese cross into a tree as a sign that they'd left under duress.

Finding no such symbol, White could only assume that the colonists were trying to tell him they'd decamped for some reason to be near the Croatan tribe. He wanted to head north to find them, but a storm was brewing and White's men refused to go any further. Later fact-finding expeditions out of the Jamestown colony farther north were also fruitless.

Why did they leave? With no sign of struggle, it's hard to blame friction with local tribes for the move. However, scientists have proven through tree-ring study that the period of the colonists' departure coincided exactly with one of the worst droughts ever recorded.

Where did these possibly drought-stricken colonists go? To this day no one knows. The modern-day Lumbee Indians of southeastern North Carolina insist they are descended from Roanoke colonists who intermarried with their tribe, and indeed they still bear many of the historical surnames of the colonists.

Chief Powhatan of Virginia, however, told English settlers that the colonists had taken up with a tribe in his area, and that he had destroyed that tribe as well as the colonists wholesale.

Another theory has it that the colonists became assimilated into the Tuscarora tribe of the Carolinas, or maybe the Indians of Person County, long known for their European look and characteristics.

DNA testing is now ongoing, and so far the most promising explanation favors the longest-running claim of all—that of the Lumbees.

THE FOUNDING OF CAROLINA

With the settlement of Jamestown, Virginia, in 1607, the English focus moved farther north for awhile. Activity in what would later be called the Carolinas was further limited by continuing political unrest in England, which culminated in the savage English Civil War.

The colony of Carolina was a product of the **English Restoration,** when the monarchy returned to power after the grim 11-year tenure of Oliver Cromwell, who had defeated Royalist forces in the English Civil War. The attitude of the Restoration era was expansionist, confident, and mercantile.

Historians dispute exactly how close-minded Cromwell himself was, but there's no debating the puritanical tone of his reign as British head of state. Theater was banned, as was most music except for religious hymns. Hair was close-cropped and dress was extremely conservative. Most disturbing of all for the holiday-loving English, the observation of Christmas and Easter was strongly discouraged because of their supposedly pagan origins.

Enter Charles II, son of the beheaded Charles I. His ascent to the throne in 1660 signaled a release of all the pent-up creativity and energy of the British people, stagnant under Cromwell's repression. The arts returned to their previous importance. Foreign policy became aggressive and expansionist. Capitalists again sought profit. Fashion made a comeback, and dandy dress and long hair for both men and women were all the rage.

This then, is the backdrop for the first English settlement of the deep South. The first expedition was by a Barbadian colonist, William Hilton, in 1663. While he didn't establish a new colony, he did leave behind his name on the most notable geographic feature he saw—Hilton Head Island.

In 1665 King Charles II gave a charter to eight Lords Proprietors to establish a colony in the area, generously to be named Carolina after the monarch himself. (One of the Proprietors, Lord Ashley Cooper, would see not one but both rivers in the Charleston area named after him.) Remarkably, none of the Proprietors ever set foot in the colony they established for their own profit.

Before their colony was even established, the Proprietors themselves set the stage for the vast human disaster that would eventually befall it. They encouraged slavery by promising that each colonist would receive 20 acres of land for every black male slave and 10 acres for every black female slave brought to the colony within the first year.

In 1666 explorer Robert Sandford officially claimed Carolina for the king, in a ceremony on modern-day Seabrook or Wadmalaw Island. The Proprietors then sent out a fleet of three ships from England, only one of which, the *Carolina,* would make it the whole way. After stops in the thriving English colonies of Barbados and Bermuda, the ship landed in Port Royal. They were greeted without violence, but the fact that the local indigenous people spoke broken Spanish led the colonists to conclude that perhaps the site was too close to Spain's sphere of influence for comfort. A Kiawah chief, eager for allies against the fierce, slave-trading Westo tribe, invited the colonists north to settle instead.

So the colonists—148 of them, including three African slaves—moved 80 miles up the coast, and in 1670 pitched camp on the Ashley River at a place they dubbed Albemarle Point after one of their lost ships. Living within the wooden palisades of the camp, the colonists farmed 10-acre plots outside the walls for sustenance. The Native Americans of the area were of the large and influential Cusabo tribe of the Creeks, and are sometimes even today known as the Settlement Indians. Subtribes of the Cusabo whose names live on today in South Carolina geography were the Kiawah, Edisto, Wando, Stono, and Ashepoo.

A few years later some English colonists

from the Caribbean colony of Barbados, which was beginning to suffer overpopulation, joined the Carolinians. The Barbadian influence, with an emphasis on large-scale slave labor and a caste system, would have an indelible imprint on the colony in years to come. Indeed, within a generation a majority of settlers in the new colony would be African slaves.

By 1680, however, Albemarle Point was feeling growing pains as well, and the Proprietors ordered the site moved to Oyster Point at the confluence of the Ashley and Cooper Rivers (the present-day Battery). Within a year Albemarle Point was completely abandoned, and the walled fortifications of Charles Town were built a few hundred yards up from Oyster Point on the banks of the Cooper River.

The original Anglican settlers were quickly joined by various Dissenters, among them French Huguenots, Quakers, Congregationalists, and Jews. A group of Scottish Presbyterians established the short-lived Stuart Town near Port Royal in 1684. Recognizing this diversity, the colony in 1697 granted religious liberty to all "except Papists." The Anglicans attempted a crackdown on Dissenters in 1704, but two years later Queen Anne stepped in and ensured religious freedom for all Carolinians (again with the exception of Roman Catholics, who wouldn't be a factor in the colony until after the American Revolution).

The English settlements quickly gained root as the burgeoning deerskin trade increased exponentially. Traders upriver, using an ancient network of trails, worked with local Native Americans, mostly Cherokees, to exploit the massive numbers of deer in the American interior.

The Tuscarora War

The Tuscarora War was a remarkably bloody conflict in present-day North Carolina between settler and Indian that had the result of cementing the control of white settlers on the region.

In a similar story repeated throughout the region, the Tuscarora—demoralized by disease and tired of unscrupulous white traders—decided to take a stand and coordinate an attack. On Sept. 22, 1711, came the first attacks, near the town of Bath and the plantations on the Neuse and Trent rivers. Hundreds of settlers died.

The response was even more devastating. Gov. Edward Hyde called out the militia, and a combined force of settlers and Indian allies attacked the southern Tuscarora Indians at Fort Narhantes in Craven County in 1712. Over 300 Tuscarora were killed. Unrest continued, resulting in a clash at Fort Neoheroka in Greene County in which over a thousand Tuscarora were killed or captured.

By this time the tribe began emigrating to the New York area to escape further destruction. The remaining tribespeople signed a peace treaty in 1718, one of the terms of which was their removal to a tract of land in Bertie County.

The Yamasee War

South Carolina would have its own bloody conflict with Native Americans, also named after the tribe in opposition to the settlers.

Within 20 years the English presence expanded throughout the Lowcountry to include Port Royal and Beaufort. Charles Town became a thriving commercial center, dealing in deerskins with independent traders in the interior and with foreign concerns from England to South America. Its success was not without a backlash, as the local Yamasee tribe of the Creek Indians became increasingly disgruntled at the settlers and their allies' growing monopolies on deerskin and the slave trade.

Slavery was a sad and common fact of life from the earliest days of white settlement in the region. Indians were the most frequent early victims, with not only white settlers taking slaves from the tribes, but the tribes themselves conducting slaving raids on each other, often selling their hostages to eager colonists.

As rumors of war spread, on Good Friday, 1715, a delegation of six white Carolinians went to the Yamasee village of Pocataligo to address some of the tribe's grievances in the hopes of forestalling violence. Their effort was in vain, however, as Yamasee warriors murdered four in their sleep, the remaining two escaping to sound the alarm. The treacherous attack signaled the beginning of the two-year Yamasee War, which would claim the lives of nearly 10 percent of the colony's population and an unknown number of Native Americans—making it one of the bloodiest conflicts in American history.

Energized and ready for war, the Yamasee attacked Charles Town itself and killed about 90 of the 100 or so white traders in the interior, effectively ending all commerce in the area. As Charles Town began to swell with refugees from the hinterland, water and supplies ran low and the colony was in peril.

After an initially poor performance by the Carolina militia, a professional army—including armed African slaves—was raised. Well trained and well led, the new army more than held its own despite being outnumbered. A key alliance with local Cherokees was all the advantage the colonists needed to turn the tide for good. While the Cherokee never received the overt military backing from the settlers that they sought, they did garner enough supplies and influence to convince their Creek rivals, the Yamasee, to begin the peace process.

The war-weary settlers, eager to get back to life and to business, were eager to negotiate with them, offering goods as a sign of their earnest intent. By 1717 the Yamasee threat had subsided and trade in the region began flourishing anew.

No sooner had the Yamasee War ended, however, when a new threat emerged: the dread pirate Edward Teach, a.k.a. Blackbeard. Entering Charleston harbor in May 1718 with his flagship *Queen Anne's Revenge* and three other vessels, he promptly plundered five ships and began a full-scale blockade of the entire settlement. He took a number of prominent citizens hostage before finally departing northward along the coast, thinking he had a royal pardon. However, a Royal Navy flotilla tracked him down near Ocracoke Island in the Outer Banks and killed him.

Slavery Expands

While it was the Spanish who introduced slavery to America—of Indians as well as Africans—it was the English-speaking settlers who dramatically expanded the institution.

For the colonists of South Carolina, the Blackbeard episode was the final straw. Already disgusted by the lack of support from the Lords Proprietors during the Yamasee War, the humiliation of the pirate blockade was too much to take. So to almost universal agreement in the colony, the settlers threw off the rule of the Proprietors and strenuously lobbied in 1719 to become a crown colony, an effort that came to final fruition in 1729. While this outward-looking and energetic place—whose name would morph into Charlestown, and then simply Charleston—was originally built on the backs of merchants, with the introduction of the rice and indigo crops in the early 1700s it would increasingly be built on the backs of slaves.

For all the wealth gained through the planting of indigo, rice, and cotton seeds, another seed was sown by the Lowcountry plantation culture. The area's total dependence on slave labor would soon lead to a disastrous war, a conflict signaled for decades to those smart enough to read the signs.

By this time Charleston was firmly established as the key American port for the importation of African slaves, accounting for about 40 percent of the trade. As a result, the black population of the coast outnumbered the white population by more than three-to-one. The very real fear of violent slave uprisings had great influence over not only politics, but day-to-day affairs. These fears were eventually realized in the **Stono Rebellion.**

On September 9, 1739, 20 slaves, led by an Angolan known only as Jemmy, met near the Stono River 20 miles southwest of

Charleston. Marching with a banner that read "Liberty," they seized guns from a store, killing the proprietors, with the eventual plan of marching all the way to Spanish Florida and sanctuary in the wilderness. On the way they burned seven plantations and killed 20 more whites. A militia eventually caught up with them, killing 44 escaped slaves and losing 20 of their own. The prisoners were decapitated and had their heads spiked on every milepost between the spot of that final battle and Charleston.

The result was not only a 10-year moratorium on slave importation into Charleston, but a severe crackdown on the education of slaves—a move that would have damaging implications for generations to come.

Spain Vanquished

In 1729, Carolina was divided into north and south. In 1731, a colony to be known as Georgia, after the new English king, was carved out of the southern part of the Carolina land grant specifically to provide a military buffer to protect Carolina.

A young English general, aristocrat, and humanitarian named James Edward Oglethorpe gathered together a group of Trustees—similar to Carolina's Lords Proprietors—to take advantage of that grant. Like Carolina the Georgia colony also emphasized religious freedom. While to modern ears Charleston's antipathy towards "papists" and Oglethorpe's original ban of Roman Catholics from Georgia might seem incompatible with this goal, the reason was a coldly pragmatic one for the time: England's two main global rivals, France and Spain, were both staunchly Catholic countries.

In 1742 Oglethorpe defeated a Spanish force on St. Simons Island, Georgia in the **Battle of Bloody Marsh.** That clash marked the end of Spanish overtures on England's colonies in America. With first the French and then the Spanish effectively shut off from the American East Coast, the stage was set for an internal battle between England and its burgeoning colonies across the Atlantic.

REVOLUTION AND A NEW NATION

It's a persistent but inaccurate myth that the affluent elite on the southeastern coast were reluctant to break ties with England. While the coast's cultural and economic ties to England were certainly strong, the **Stamp Act** and the **Townshend Acts** combined to turn public sentiment against the mother country there as elsewhere in the colonies.

Militarily, the Carolinas were the key to the colonist's eventual victory. With George Washington in a stalemate with British troops in the northeast, the war hinged on the success or failure of the British **"Southern Strategy,"** an attempt to expand Redcoat ranks by enlisting support from loyalists in the area.

South Carolinian planters like Christopher Gadsden, Henry Laurens, John Rutledge, and Arthur Middleton were early leaders in the movement for independence. In 1773, North Carolina installed nonimportation agreements that forced local merchants to drop trade with Great Britain. The next year, North Carolina planters sent food and supplies to Massachusetts, then facing the brunt of the British crackdown.

At war's outbreak, North Carolina saw its first engagement at the Battle of Moore's Creek Bridge near Wilmington in early 1776. This clash of loyalist and patriot forces was a clear-cut patriot victory, and little fighting occurred on the North Carolina coast through the end of the conflict.

The poor showing of the loyalists prompted British General Sir Henry Clinton to head further south to attempt to take Charleston, South Carolina—fourth-largest city in the colonies—in June 1776. The episode gave South Carolina its "Palmetto State" moniker when Redcoat cannonballs bounced off the palm tree-lined walls of Fort Moultrie on Sullivan's Island. The British successfully took the city, however, in 1780, holding it until 1782.

Though the southeast coast's two major cities were captured—Savannah fell to the British in 1778—the war raged on throughout the surrounding area. With over 130 known military engagements occurring in South Carolina, that colony sacrificed more men during the war than any other—including Massachusetts itself.

The struggle became a guerrilla war of colonists vs. the British as well as a civil war between patriots and loyalists, or **Tories.** Committing what would today undoubtedly be called war crimes, the British routinely burned homes, churches, and fields, and killed recalcitrant civilians. In response, patriots of the Lowcountry bred a group of deadly guerrilla soldiers under legendary leaders such as Francis Marion, "the Swamp Fox," and Thomas Sumter, "the Gamecock." Using unorthodox tactics perfected in years of backcountry Indian fighting, the patriots of the Carolinas attacked the British in daring hit-and-run raids staged from the swamps and marshes, from the hills and forests.

The Cotton Boom

True to form, the new nation wasted no time in asserting its economic strength. Rice planters from Wilmington, North Carolina, on down to the St. Johns River in Florida built on their already-impressive wealth, becoming America's richest men by far—with fortunes built, of course, on the backs of the slaves working in the fields and paddies.

Charleston was still by far the largest, most powerful, and most influential city in the southeast. While most Lowcountry planters spent the warmer months away from the mosquito-and-malaria-infested coast, Charleston's elite grew so fond of their little peninsula that they took to living in their "summer homes" year-round, becoming absentee landlords of their various plantations. As a result of this affluent, somewhat hedonistic atmosphere, Charleston became an early arts and cultural center for the United States.

In 1786, a new crop was introduced that would only enhance the financial clout of the coastal region: cotton. A former loyalist colonel, Roger Kelsal, sent some seed from Anguilla in the West Indies to his friend

James Spaulding, owner of a plantation on St. Simons Island, Georgia. This crop, soon to be known as **Sea Island cotton** and considered the best in the world, would eventually supplant rice as the crop of choice for coastal plantations. Plantations on Hilton Head, Edisto, Daufuskie, and Kiawah islands would make the shift to this more profitable product and amass even greater fortunes for their owners.

With the boom in cotton there needed to be a better way to get that cash crop to market quickly. In 1827, the South Carolina Canal and Rail Road Company was chartered to build a line that would expedite cotton trade from the Upcountry down to the port of Charleston. The resulting 137-mile Charleston-Hamburg line, begun in 1833, was at the time the longest railroad in the world.

Up in North Carolina, New Bern was at this time the state's most populous city, though it had lost its capital status to Raleigh in 1794.

Secession

Though much of the lead-in to the Civil War focused on whether or not slavery would be allowed in America's newest territories in the West, all figurative roads eventually led to South Carolina.

During Andrew Jackson's presidency in the 1820s, his vice president, South Carolina's John C. Calhoun, became a thorn in Jackson's side with his aggressive advocacy for the concept of **nullification,** which Jackson strenuously rejected. In a nutshell, Calhoun said that if a state decided that the federal government wasn't treating it fairly—in this case with regards to tariffs that were hurting the cotton trade in the Palmetto State—it could simply nullify the federal law, superseding it with law of its own.

As the abolition movement gained steam and tension over slavery rose, South Carolina Congressman Preston Brooks took things to the next level. On May 22, 1856, he beat fellow Senator Charles Sumner of Massachusetts nearly to death with his walking cane on the Senate floor. Sumner had just given a speech criticizing pro-slavery forces—including a relative of Brooks—and called slavery "a harlot." (In a show of support, South Carolinians sent Brooks dozens of new canes to replace the one he broke over Sumner's head.)

In 1860, the national convention of the Democratic Party, then the dominant force in U.S. politics, was held in—where else?—Charleston. Rancor over slavery and state's rights was so high that they couldn't agree on a single candidate to run to replace President James Buchanan. Reconvening in Maryland, the party split along sectional lines, with the northern wing backing Stephen A. Douglas. The southern wing, fervently desiring secession above all else, deliberately chose its own candidate, John Breckenridge, in order to split the Democratic vote and throw the election to Republican Abraham Lincoln, an outspoken opponent of slavery.

During that so-called **Secession Winter** before Lincoln took office, seven states seceded from the union, first among them the Palmetto State, followed by Mississippi, Florida, Alabama, Georgia, Louisiana, and Texas.

Ironically, South Carolina's neighbor to the north was the last Southern state to secede, leaving the union after the war had already begun. Known as being quite reluctant to the cause, the Tarheel State may have even gotten its nickname for having metaphorical feet that were too sticky to take a step.

Not nearly as dependent on slave labor as South Carolina, North Carolinians for the most part saw no reason to be hasty about dissolving a union that for the most part had been quite good to it. Once committed, however, they were fully devoted to the Confederacy, and indeed lost more troops in the conflict than any other Southern state.

A UNION DISSOLVED

Five days after South Carolina's secession on December 21, 1860, U.S. Army Major Robert Anderson moved his garrison from Fort Moultrie in Charleston harbor to nearby Fort Sumter. Over the next few months and into the spring, Anderson would ignore many calls to surrender the fort and Confederate forces would prevent any Union resupply or reinforcement. Shortly before dawn on April 12, 1861, Confederate batteries around Charleston—ironically none of which were at the Battery itself—opened fire on Fort Sumter for 34 straight hours, until Anderson surrendered on April 13.

In a classic example of why you should always be careful what you wish for, the secessionists had been too clever by half in pushing for the election of Lincoln. Far from prodding the North to sue for peace, the fall of Fort Sumter instead caused the remaining states in the Union to rally around the previously unpopular tall man from Illinois. Lincoln's skillful—some would say cunning—management of the Fort Sumter standoff meant that from then on out, the South would bear history's blame for initiating the conflict that would claim over half a million American lives.

After Fort Sumter, the remaining four states of the Confederacy—Arkansas, Tennessee, North Carolina, and Virginia—seceded. The Old Dominion was the real prize for the secessionists, as Virginia had the South's only ironworks and by far its largest manufacturing base.

War on the Coast

In November 1861, a massive Union invasion armada landed in Port Royal Sound in South Carolina, effectively taking the entire Lowcountry and Sea Islands out of the war. Charleston, however, did host two battles in the conflict. The **Battle of Secessionville** came in June 1862, when a Union force attempting to take Charleston was repulsed on James Island with heavy casualties. The next battle, an unsuccessful Union landing on Morris Island in July 1863, was immortalized by the movie *Glory*.

The 54th Massachusetts Regiment, an African American unit with white commanders, performed so gallantly in its failed assault on the Confederate Battery Wagner that it inspired the North and was cited by abolitionists as further proof that African Americans should be given freedom and full citizenship rights. Another invasion attempt on Charleston would not come, but it was besieged and bombarded for nearly two years (devastation made even worse by a massive fire, unrelated to the shelling, which destroyed much of the city in 1861).

In other towns, white Southerners evacuated the coastal cities and plantations for the hinterland, leaving behind only slaves to fend for themselves. In many coastal areas, African Americans and Union garrison troops settled into an awkward but peaceful coexistence.

While the ironclad *USS Monitor* gained fame for its sea battle with the Confederate ironclad *CSS Virginia* (formerly the *Merrimac*) farther north in Virginia waters, it was actually lost at sea off Cape Hatteras in December 1862. The underwater site is now a National Historic Landmark.

In Savannah to the south, General William Sherman concluded his **March to the Sea** in 1864, famously giving the city to Lincoln as a Christmas present. While staunch Confederates, city fathers were wise enough to know what would happen to their accumulated wealth and fine homes should they be foolhardy enough to resist Sherman's army of war-hardened veterans, most of them farm boys from the Midwest with a pronounced distaste for the "peculiar institution" of slavery.

In North Carolina, Wilmington remained in Confederate hands until very late in the war, February 1865, acting as the South's de facto main base for blockade runners due to the quick fall of New Orleans and the effective blockading of Charleston, Beaufort, and Savannah.

Aftermath

The only military uncertainty left was in how badly Charleston, the "cradle of secession," would suffer for its sins. Historians and local wags have long debated why Sherman spared Charleston, the hated epicenter of the Civil War. Did Sherman fall in love with the city during his brief posting there as a young lieutenant? Did he *literally* fall in love there, with one of its legendarily beautiful and delicate local belles?

We may never know for sure, but it's likely that the Lowcountry's marshy, mucky terrain simply made it too difficult to move large numbers of men and supplies from Savannah to Charleston proper. So Sherman turned his terrifying, battle-hardened army inland toward the state capitol of Columbia, which would not be so lucky. Most of Charleston's outlying plantation homes, too, would be put to the torch.

For the African American population of South Carolina, however, it was not a time of sadness but the great Day of Jubilee. Soon after the Confederate surrender, black Charlestonians held one of the largest parades the city has ever seen, with one of the floats being a coffin bearing the sign, "Slavery is dead."

As for the place where it all began, a plucky Confederate garrison remained underground at Fort Sumter throughout the war, as the walls above them were literally pounded into dust by the long Union siege. The garrison quietly left the fort under cover of night on February 17, 1865. Major Robert Anderson, who surrendered the fort at war's beginning, returned to Sumter in April 1865 to raise the same flag he'd lowered exactly four years earlier. Three thousand African Americans attended the ceremonies, including the son of Denmark Vesey himself.

Later that same night, Abraham Lincoln was assassinated in Washington, D.C.

Reconstruction

A case could be made that slavery need not have led America into Civil War. The U.S. had banned the importation of slaves long before, in 1808. The great powers of Europe would soon ban slavery altogether (Spain in 1811, France in 1826, and Britain in 1833). Visiting foreign dignitaries in the mid-1800s were often shocked to find the practice in full swing in the American South. Even Brazil, the world center of slavery, where four out of every 10 African slaves were brought (less than 5 percent came to the U.S.), would ban slavery in 1888.

Still, the die was cast, the war was fought, and everyone had to deal with the aftermath. For a brief time, Sherman's benevolent dictatorship on the coast held promise for an orderly post-war future. In 1865, he issued his sweeping "40 Acres and a Mule" order seeking dramatic economic restitution for free blacks of the Sea Islands of South Carolina and Georgia. However, politics reared its ugly head in the wake of Lincoln's assassination and the order was rescinded, ushering in the chaotic Reconstruction era, echoes of which linger to this day.

Nonetheless, that period of time in the South Carolina and Georgia Sea Islands served as an important incubator of sorts for the indigenous African American culture of the coast—called Gullah in South Carolina and Geechee in Georgia. Largely left to their own devices, these insulated farming and oystering communities held to their old folkways, many of which exist today.

Even as the trade in cotton and naval stores hit even greater heights than before, urban life and racial tension became more and more problematic. Urban population swelled as freed blacks from all over the depressed countryside rushed into the cities. As one, his name lost to history, famously said: "Freedom was free-er in Charleston."

It was during this time that some gains were made by African Americans, albeit with little support from the indigenous white population. Largely under duress, the University of South Carolina became the first Southern university to grant degrees to black students. The historically black, Methodist-affiliated Claflin College in Orangeburg was founded in 1869.

While the coast and urban areas saw more opportunity for African Americans, tension remained high in the countryside.

Largely with the support of white militia groups, in 1876 the old guard of the Democratic Party returned to power in South Carolina with the election of former Confederate General Wade Hampton III to the governor's office. Supported by a violent paramilitary group called the "Red Shirts," Hampton used his charisma and considerable personal reputation to attempt to restore South Carolina to its antebellum glory—and undo Reconstruction in the process.

The Wilmington Insurrection

Despite its laidback, friendly reputation, Wilmington was the site of one of the bloodiest racial incidents in American history, and by some accounts the only time a U.S. municipal government has ever been removed by force.

In the late 19th century, Wilmington was North Carolina's largest city and had a reasonably well-functioning Republican-led government that featured the input of many free African American citizens. One was Alexander Manly, editor of the *Wilmington Daily Record*, at the time the only black-owned newspaper in the United States.

On the morning of November 10, 1898, a mob largely comprising former Confederate soldiers attacked the newspaper office, motivated by Manly's recent rebuttals against accusations that local African American men were guilty of raping white women. Manly left town in fear of his life as the mob burned the newspaper building down.

Led by Alfred Moore Waddell, the mob then gave the elected city government, which included both white and black officials, an ultimatum: Resign or face a similar fate. Literally at gunpoint, the municipal government was dissolved and a new city council "appointed." By four o'clock in the afternoon of the same day, Waddell was declared mayor.

RENAISSANCE

While the aftermath of the Civil War was painful, it was by no means bereft of activity or profit. The reunion of the states marked the coming of the Industrial Revolution to America, and in many quarters of the South the cotton, lumber, and naval stores industries not only recovered, but exceeded antebellum levels.

A classic South Carolina example was in Horry County, where the town of Conway exploded as a commercial center for the area logging industry. By 1901 the first, modest resort had been built on nearby Myrtle Beach, and the area rapidly became an important vacation area—a role it serves to this day.

The **Spanish-American War of 1898** was a major turning point for the South. For most Southerners, it was the first time since the Civil War that they were enthusiastically patriotic about being Americans. The southeastern coast felt this in particular, as it was a staging area for the invasion of Cuba. Charlestonians cheered the exploits of their namesake heavy cruiser the USS *Charleston,* which played a key role in forcing the Spanish surrender of Guam.

A South Carolinian himself, Wall Street financial wizard and presidential advisor Bernard Baruch would make many Americans more familiar with the state's natural beauty. After his acquisition of the old Hobcaw Barony near Georgetown in 1905, he hosted many a world leader there, including President Franklin D. Roosevelt and British Prime Minister Winston Churchill.

Charleston would elect its first Irish-American mayor, John Grace, in 1911. Though it wouldn't open until 1929, the first Cooper River Bridge joining Charleston with Mount Pleasant was the child of the Grace administration, which is credited today for modernizing the Holy City's infrastructure (as well as tolerating high levels of vice during Prohibition) and making possible much of the civic gains to follow.

A major change that came during this time is rarely remarked upon in the history books: This was when South Carolina became a majority white state. With thousands of African Americans leaving for more tolerant pastures and more economic opportunity in the North and the West—a move known as the **Great Migration**—the demographics of the state changed accordingly.

The arrival of the tiny but devastating boll weevil all but wiped out the cotton trade on the coast after the turn of the century, forcing the economy to diversify. Naval stores and lumbering were the order of the day at the advent of **World War I,** the combined patriotic effort for which did wonders in repairing the wounds of the Civil War, still vivid in many local memories.

A major legacy of World War I that still greatly influences life in the Lowcountry is the Marine Corps Recruiting Depot Parris Island, which began life as a small Marine camp in 1919.

First in Flight
The lonely Outer Banks of North Carolina hosted one of the seminal events in human history, with the **Wright Brothers'** first powered flight.

Born in Indiana and raised in Dayton, Ohio, neither Orville and Wilbur Wright graduated from college. They opened a bicycle shop in Dayton and used the profits to fund their growing interest in aviation.

Wilbur, the more aggressive of the two, was inspired by the flight of birds to make groundbreaking research into wing design. Another key difference between the Wrights' work and other concurrent aviation minds was that the brothers insisted on the pilot having total control over the aircraft, as opposed to being totally dependent on prevailing winds.

To bring their ideas to fruition, in 1900 the Wrights traveled to remote and then barely-inhabited Kitty Hawk, North Carolina, which they picked for two reasons: First, the sea breeze and soft sand were conducive to flight experiments; and just as importantly, no reporters were likely to follow them there and prematurely reveal their designs and methods.

For two full years, they worked on nothing but gliders, launching them off of Kill Devil Hill, the highest point on this part of the Outer Banks. In late 1903, however, the "Wright Flyer One" was ready for takeoff. Wilbur won a coin toss to see who would pilot the first flight, an ill-fated three-second trip that damaged the craft.

When the Flyer was repaired, it was quiet Orville who would pilot the historic "real" first flight, a 12-second, 120-foot trip across the sandy scrub at the base of Kill Devil Hill on December 17, 1903. It is this flight which is recorded in the famous photograph instantly recognizable the world over.

Fame was long in coming, however. Despite the presence of a handful of witnesses—not to mention the photo—no one quite believed the Wright Brothers had actually managed controlled, powered flight.

For a time, this suited the Wrights just fine, since they had not yet received a patent for their revolutionary wing design and were still fearful their work would be pirated by others. They continued working in relative anonymity back in Dayton, until finally receiving a patent in 1906, after which a whirlwind of transatlantic business negotiations followed.

The skeptical French were wowed by a display in August 1908, which stunned a crowd at Le Mans with a nearly two-minute powered flight that included several graceful banked turns.

The famously protective Wrights continued to defend their patents, with mixed results, against other businesspeople. While they never profited as much as they wanted from their invention, history still reveres the brilliant, oddball brothers as the fathers of aviation.

In the kind of win-win situation that was unfortunately lacking in the Wright Brothers' business activities, the states of Ohio and North Carolina have worked out a compromise of sorts to share the Wright legacy. Ohio calls itself "The Birthplace of Aviation Pioneers" (a nod to the fact that astronauts John Glenn and Neil Armstrong are also Ohioans), whereas the Tarheel State claims as its motto "First in Flight."

The Roaring Twenties

In the boom period following World War I, North Carolina was the most industrialized state in the South, chiefly due to its healthy textile trade. The tobacco crop as well was particularly profitable.

During this time, Charleston, South Carolina, entered the world stage and made some of its most significant cultural contributions to American life. The "Charleston" dance, originated on the streets of the Holy City and popularized in New York, would sweep the world. The Jenkins Orphanage Band, often credited with the dance, traveled the world, even playing at President Taft's inauguration.

In the visual arts, the "Charleston Renaissance" took off, specifically intended to introduce the Holy City to a wider audience. Key work included the Asian-influenced work of self-taught painter Alice Ravenel Huger Smith and the etchings of Elizabeth O'Neill Verner. Edward Hopper was a visitor to Charleston during that time and produced several noted watercolors. The Gibbes Art Gallery, now the Gibbes Museum of Art, opened in 1905.

Recognizing the cultural importance of the city and its history, in 1920 socialite Susan Pringle Frost and other concerned Charlestonians formed the Preservation Society of Charleston, the oldest community-based historic preservation organization in America.

In 1924, lauded Charleston author DuBose Heyward wrote the locally set novel *Porgy*. With Heyward's cooperation, the book would soon be turned into the first American opera, *Porgy and Bess*, by George Gershwin, who labored over the composition in a cottage on Folly Beach, South Carolina. Ironically, *Porgy and Bess*, which premiered with an African American cast in New York in 1935, wouldn't be performed in its actual setting until 1970 because of segregation laws.

And in a foreshadowing of a future tourist boom to come, the Pine Lakes golf course opened in Myrtle Beach, South Carolina, in 1927, the first on the Grand Strand.

A NEW DEAL

Alas, the good times didn't last. The Great Depression hit the South hard, but since wages and industry were already behind the national average, the economic damage wasn't as bad as elsewhere in the country. As elsewhere in the South and indeed across the country, public works programs in President Franklin D. Roosevelt's New Deal helped not only to keep locals employed, but contributed greatly to the cultural and archaeological record of the area.

The Public Works of Art Project stimulated the visual arts. The Works Progress Administration renovated the old Dock Street Theatre in Charleston, and theatrical productions once again graced that historic stage. You can still enjoy the network of state parks built in South Carolina by the Civilian Conservation Corps.

As important and broadly supported as the New Deal was in the Carolinas, the primarily rural nature of both states meant a less vigorous and concentrated lobbying effort in Washington DC, to free up funding. Hence, the per capita benefit of the New Deal in the Carolinas was actually significantly less than for other states.

WORLD WAR II AND THE MODERN ERA

With the attack on Pearl Harbor and the coming of World War II, life in America and the Carolinas would never be the same. Military funding and facilities swarmed into the area, and populations and long-depressed living standards rose as a result. Here are some key wartime developments on the coast:

- In 1941 construction began in Onslow County on what would become Marine Corps Base Camp Lejeune near Jacksonville, North Carolina. A satellite facility of Camp Lejeune, Montford Point (now called Camp Gilbert H. Johnston), trained 20,000 African American Marines 1942-1947, when the U.S. military was still segregated.

- Also in 1941, construction began on what would become Marine Corps Air Station Cherry Point, which trained Marine aviators for service in the Pacific theater of operations.

- Though Fort Bragg in Fayetteville, North Carolina, was begun in 1918, it really got on the map during World War II as a major training facility. Immediately following World War II, Fort Bragg became the operations and training center for the U.S. Army Special Forces, and it remains so to this day.

- The Charleston Navy Yard became that city's largest employer, and the population soared as workers crowded in.

- Down in Walterboro, South Carolina, the Tuskegee Airmen, a highly-decorated group of African American fighter pilots, trained for their missions escorting bombing raids over Germany. Walterboro also hosted a large German POW camp.

- The Marine Corp Recruiting Depot Parris Island in South Carolina expanded massively, training nearly a quarter-million recruits 1941-1945.

- The entire 1944 graduating class of The Citadel in Charleston was inducted into the armed forces—possibly the only time an entire class was drafted at once.

The war particularly hit home in North Carolina, which trained more soldiers than any other state in its 24 bases. The hottest spot for German U-boat attacks on the U.S. eastern seaboard was off the Outer Banks. Residents—living in blackout conditions at night—would often see explosions just offshore as American merchant ships were sunk by the submarines. To this day the sea bottom on the coast is littered with over 60 sunken vessels from this dark time—including at least three destroyed U-boats.

Then of course there's the famous battleship *USS North Carolina,* which participated in every major naval campaign of the war's Pacific theater of operations. When commissioned in April 1941, it was considered the most advanced, if not the largest, battleship in the world. Decommissioned after the war, the ship spent 14 years anchored in New Jersey. Scheduled to be scrapped, it was saved by a conservation and fundraising effort in the late 1950s, which brought the great warship back to its namesake state in 1961. Today berthed in Wilmington, the *North Carolina* is a major tourist attraction and a stirring tribute to a key chapter in U.S. naval history.

The Postwar Boom

Myrtle Beach and the Grand Strand were already the breeding ground of that unique South Carolina dance called the shag. The postwar era marked the shag's heyday, as carefree young South Carolinians flocked to beachfront pavilions to enjoy this indigenous form of music, sort of a white variation on the regional black rhythm 'n' blues of the time.

America's post-war infatuation with the automobile—and its troublesome child, the suburb—brought exponential growth to the great cities of the coast. The first bridge to Hilton Head Island was built in 1956, leading to the first of many resort developments on the island, Sea Pines, in 1961. In many outlying Sea Islands, electricity came for the first time.

With rising coastal populations came pressure to demolish more and more fine old buildings to put parking lots and highrises in their place; a backlash grew among the cities' elites, aghast at the destruction of so much history. The immediate postwar era brought about the formation of the Historic Charleston Foundation, which began the financially and politically difficult work of protecting the historic districts from the wrecking ball of "progress."

They weren't always successful, but the work of these organizations—mostly comprising older women from the upper crust—laid the foundation for the successful coastal tourist industry to come, as well as preserved important American history for the ages.

Civil Rights

Contrary to popular opinion, the civil rights era wasn't just a blip in the 1960s. The gains of that decade were the fruits of efforts begun decades prior.

Many of the efforts involved expanding black suffrage. Though African Americans secured the nominal right to vote years before, primary contests were not under the jurisdiction of federal law. As a result, Democratic Party primary elections—the *de facto* general elections because of that party's total dominance in the South at the time—were effectively closed to African American voters.

In Charleston, the Democratic primary was opened to African Americans for the first time in 1947. In 1960, the Charleston Municipal Golf Course voluntarily integrated to avoid a court battle. Lunch counter sit-ins happened all over South Carolina, including the episode of the "Friendship Nine" in Rock Hill. Martin Luther King Jr. visited South Carolina in the late 1960s, speaking in Charleston in 1967 and helping reestablish the Penn Center on St. Helena Island as not only a cultural center, but a center of political activism as well.

The hundred-day strike of hospital workers at the Medical University of South Carolina in 1969—right after King's assassination—got national attention and was the culmination of Charleston's struggle for civil rights. By the end of the 1960s, the city council of Charleston had elected its first black alderman, and the next phase in local history began.

A Coast Reborn

While the story of the South Carolina coastal boom actually begins in the 1950s with Charles Fraser's development of Sea Pines Plantation on Hilton Head—forever changing that barrier island—the decade of the 1970s was pivotal to the future success of the South Carolina coast.

In Charleston, the historic tenure of Mayor Joe Riley began in 1975, continuing to this day as of this writing. The Irish American would break precedents and forge key alliances, reviving not only the local economies but tamping down age-old racial tensions. Beginning with downtown's Charleston Place, Riley embarked on a series of high-profile public works projects to reinvigorate the then-moribund Charleston historic area. King Street would soon follow. In the years 1970-1976, tourism in the Holy City would increase 60 percent.

The coast's combination of beautiful scenery and cheap labor proved irresistible to the movie and TV industry, which began filming many shows and films in the area in the 1970s, and continue to do so to this day.

Wilmington, North Carolina, remains a key movie location, often calling itself "Hollywood East." Some of the 300 feature films made there include *Blue Velvet, I Know What You Did Last Summer, Enchanted, Weekend at Bernies,* and *Divine Secrets of the Ya-Ya Sisterhood.* Beaufort, South Carolina, would also emerge from its stately slumber as the star of several popular films, such as *The Great Santini* and *The Big Chill.*

Of course, Myrtle Beach had been a leisure getaway for generations. But with the 1980s and the building of the Barefoot Landing retail/lodging development—followed by many others like it—the Grand Strand entered the first tier of American tourist destinations, where it remains.

Charleston received its first major challenge since the Civil War in 1989 when Hurricane Hugo slammed into the South Carolina coast just above Charleston. The Holy City, including many of its most historic locations, was massively damaged, with hardly a tree left standing. However, in a testament to the toughness beneath Charleston's genteel veneer, the city not only rebounded but came back stronger. In perhaps typically mercantile fashion, Charlestonians used the devastation of Hugo as a reason to introduce a new round of residential construction to the entire area, particularly the surrounding islands.

Government and Economy

GOVERNMENT

For many decades, the South was completely dominated by the Democratic Party. Originally the party of slavery and segregation, the Democratic Party began attracting Southern African American voters in the 1930s with the election of Franklin D. Roosevelt. The allegiance of black voters was further cemented in the Truman, Kennedy, and Johnson administrations.

The region would remain solidly Democratic until a backlash against the civil rights movement of the 1960s drove many white Southerners, ironically enough, into the party of Lincoln, the Republicans. This added racial element, so confounding to Americans from other parts of the country, remains just as potent today.

The default mode in the South is that white voters are massively Republican, and

black voters massively Democratic. Because both states are predominantly white, the GOP currently controls the governor's mansion and both houses of the state legislature.

But don't make the mistake of assuming that local African Americans are particularly liberal because of their voting habits. Deeply religious and traditional in background and upbringing, African Americans in the Carolinas are among the most socially conservative people in the region, even if their choice of political party does not always reflect that.

ECONOMY

The coastal Carolinas have experienced a century's worth of profound changes in economy and business. The rice crop moved offshore in the late 1800s and the center of the cotton trade moved to the Gulf states in the early 1900s. That left timber as the main cash crop all up and down the coast, specifically huge pine tree farms to feed the pulp and paper business.

For most of the 20th century, the largest employers along the coast were massive, sulfur-smelling paper mills, which had as big an effect on the local environment as on its economy. But even that's changing, as Asian competition is driving paper companies to sell off their tracts for real estate development—not necessarily a more welcome scenario from an environmental perspective.

Since World War II, the U.S. Department of Defense has been a major employer and economic driver in the entire South. Of course, tourism is also an important factor in the local economies of the area, particularly in seasonal, resort-oriented areas like Hilton Head, Myrtle Beach, Kiawah, and Seabrook Islands.

Charleston also has a well-honed tourist infrastructure, bringing at least $5 billion a year into the local economy, and is routinely voted as one of the top three American cities to visit.

Almost all parts of the Carolina coast have become havens for transplants and retirees looking for better weather and/or cheaper housing, as well as generally high quality of life (except for the hurricanes!). The so-called Inner Banks of North Carolina is particularly bullish on attracting retirees from other areas of the country, as is the Beaufort-Bluffton-Hilton Head area of South Carolina.

Another huge economic development on the coast has been the exponential growth of the Charleston seaport. From the 1990s on, the quickened pace of globalization has brought enormous investment, volume, and expansion to area port facilities.

People and Culture

Contrary to how they are often portrayed in the media, the Carolinas are hardly exclusive to natives with thick, flowery accents who still obsess over the Civil War and eat grits three meals a day. As you will quickly discover, the entire coastal area is becoming heavily populated with transplants from other parts of the country. In some of these places you can actually go quite a long time without hearing even one of those Scarlett O'Hara accents.

Some of this is due to the region's increasing attractiveness to professionals and artists, drawn by the temperate climate, natural beauty, and business-friendly environment. Part of it is due to its increasing attractiveness to retirees, most of them from the frigid Northeast. Indeed, in some places, chief among them Hilton Head, the most common accent is a New York or New Jersey one, and a Southern accent is rare.

In any case, don't make the common mistake of assuming you're coming to a place where footwear is optional and electricity is a recent development (though it's true that

many of the islands didn't get electricity until the 1950s and '60s). Because so much new construction has gone on in the South in the last quarter-century or so, you might find some aspects of the infrastructure—specifically the roads and the electrical utilities—actually superior to where you came from.

POPULATION

The 2010 U.S. Census put South Carolina's population at 4,679,230. Population statistics for individual cities in the state can be misleading because of South Carolina's notoriously strict annexation laws, which make it nearly impossible for a city to annex growing suburbs.

In rough order of rank, the largest official metropolitan areas in South Carolina are Columbia (767,000), Charleston/North Charleston/Summerville (664,000), Greenville/Mauldin/Easley (636,000), Myrtle Beach/North Myrtle Beach/Conway (329,000), Florence (200,000), and Hilton Head/Beaufort (170,000).

Although its coast often seems less populated than the Palmetto State's, North Carolina is actually a much more populous state, coming in at number 10 in the nation with a total population of 9,222,000. Its largest metro areas tend to be clusters of several cities, for example Charlotte-Gastonia-Salisbury (population 2.3 million), Raleigh-Durham-Chapel Hill (1.6 million), and Greensboro-Winston-Salem-High Point (1.5 million).

The Fayetteville metropolitan area (population just over 350,000) and the Wilmington metro area (just under 350,000) are the two most populous North Carolina cities covered in this book. Otherwise coastal North Carolina is quite sparsely populated compared to the middle of the state. New Bern, a large town for the area, has only about 120,000 people. The entire Outer Banks has a year-round population of less than 60,000.

Racial Makeup

Its history as the center of the U.S. slave trade and plantation culture means that South Carolina continues to have a large African-American population, nearly 30 percent of the total. The coastal percentage is generally higher, with Charleston being about 31 percent African American and Georgetown about 40 percent.

North Carolina's African American population comes in around 21 percent, but again, the number is higher along the coast.

One unfortunate remnant of the Carolinas' history is the residual existence, even to this day, of a certain amount of de facto segregation. Visitors are often shocked to see how some residential areas even today still break sharply on racial lines—as do schools, with most public schools in the area being majority black and most private schools overwhelmingly white.

The Hispanic population, as elsewhere in the U.S., is growing rapidly in the coastal Carolinas. But statistics can be misleading. Though Hispanics are growing at a triple-digit clip throughout the region, they still remain under 3 percent of South Carolina's total population and about 7 percent of North Carolina's, with most of the latter population not along the coast at all. Bilingual signage is becoming more common but is still quite rare.

RELIGION

The South Carolina Lowcountry, and Charleston in particular, is unusual in the Deep South for its wide variety of religious faiths. While South Carolina remains overwhelmingly Protestant—over 80 percent of all Christians in the state are members of some Protestant denomination, chief among them Southern Baptist and Methodist—the coast's cosmopolitan, polyglot history has made it a real melting pot of faith.

Though the Lowcountry was originally dominated by the Episcopal Church (known as the Anglican Church in England), from early on they were also havens for those of other faiths. Various types of Protestant offshoots soon arrived, such as French Huguenots and Congregationalists. Owing to vestigial prejudice from the European *realpolitik* of the founding era, the Roman Catholic presence in South Carolina was late in arriving, but once it came it was there to stay, especially on the coast.

Most unusually of all for the deep South, Charleston had not only a large Jewish population, but one that was a key participant in the city from the very first days of settlement. Sephardic Jews of primarily Portuguese descent were among the first settlers. One of them, Judah Benjamin, spent a lot of time in the Carolinas and became the Confederacy's secretary of state. Indeed, up to about 1830 South Carolina had the largest Jewish population of any state in the union.

The North Carolina coast also has an interesting religious history. While the Southern Baptist and Methodist churches are the top two Christian denominations in the state, the coast—as is the case in South Carolina—has quite a large Episcopal representation, a legacy of the original English colonization.

In and around the New Bern area there is a large concentration of Calvinist-affiliated churches, a legacy of the original Swiss and German settlers of this second-oldest city in North Carolina.

More recently, Roman Catholicism has been on the increase along the North Carolina coast, due to the influx of northeastern transplants as well as a growing Latino population. An exception exists in certain counties on the sparsely populated extreme northeast coast, where there are no reported Catholic congregations at all.

MANNERS

The prevalence and importance of good manners is the main thing to keep in mind about the South. While it's tempting for folks from more outwardly and assertive parts of the world to take this as a sign of weakness, that would be a major mistake. Bottom line: Good manners will take you a long way here.

Southerners use manners, courtesy, and chivalry as a system of social interaction with one goal above all: to maintain the established order during times of stress. A relic from a time of extreme class stratification, etiquette and chivalry are ways to make sure that the elites are never threatened—and on the other hand, that even those on the lowest rungs of society are afforded at least a basic amount of dignity.

But as a practical matter, it's also true that Southerners of all classes, races, and backgrounds rely on the observation of manners as a way to sum up people quickly. To any Southerner, regardless of class or race, your use or neglect of basic manners and proper respect indicates how seriously they should take you—not in a socio-economic sense, but in the big picture overall.

The typical Southern sense of humor—equal parts irony, self-deprecation, and good-natured teasing—is part of the code. Southerners are loathe to criticize another individual directly, so often they'll instead take the opportunity to make an ironic joke. Self-deprecating humor is also much more common in the South than in other areas of the country. Because of this, you're also expected to be able to take a joke yourself without being too sensitive.

Etiquette

The most basic rules are that it's rude here to inquire about personal finances, along with the usual no-go areas of religion and politics. Here are some other specific etiquette tips.

Basics: Be liberal with "please" and "thank you," or conversely, "no, thank you" if you want to decline a request or offering.

Eye contact: With the exception of elderly African Americans, eye contact is not only accepted in the South, it's encouraged. In fact, to avoid eye contact in the South means you're likely a shady character with something to hide.

Handshake: Men should always shake hands with a *very* firm, confident grip and appropriate eye contact. It's okay for women to offer a handshake in professional circles, but otherwise not required.

Chivalry: When men open doors for women here—and they will—it is not thought of as a patronizing gesture, but as a sign of respect.

The elderly: Senior citizens—or really anyone obviously older than you—should be called "sir" or "ma'am." Again, this is not a patronizing gesture in the South, but is considered a sign of respect. Also, in any situation where you're dealing with someone in the service industry, addressing them as "sir" or "ma'am" regardless of their age will get you far.

Bodily contact: Interestingly, though public displays of affection by romantic couples are generally frowned upon here, Southerners are otherwise pretty touchy-feely once they get to know you. Full-on body hugs are rare, but Southerners who are well acquainted often say hello or goodbye with a small hug.

Driving: With the exception of the interstate perimeter highways around the larger cities, drivers in the South are generally less aggressive than in other regions. Cutting sharply in front of someone in traffic is taken as a personal offense. If you need to cut in front of someone, poke the nose of your car a little bit in that direction and wait for a car to slow down and wave you in front. Don't forget to wave back as a thank-you! Similarly, using a car horn can also be taken as a personal affront, so use your horn sparingly, if at all. In rural areas, don't be surprised to see the driver of an oncoming car offer a little wave. This is an old custom, sadly dying out. Just give a little wave back; they're trying to be friendly.

THE GUN CULTURE

One of the most misunderstood aspects of the South is the value the region places on the personal possession of firearms. No doubt, the Second Amendment to the U.S. Constitution ("A well regulated Militia, being necessary to the security of a free State, the right of the people to keep and bear Arms, shall not be infringed") is well known here and fiercely protected, at the governmental and at the grassroots level.

But while guns are indeed more casually accepted in everyday life in the South, the reason for this has less to do with personal safety than with the rural background of the region and its long history of hunting. If you're traveling a back road and you see a pickup truck with a gun rack in the back containing one or more rifles or shotguns, this is not intended to be menacing or intimidating. Chances are the driver is a hunter, nothing more.

State laws do tend to be significantly more accommodating of gun owners here than in much of the rest of the country. It is legal to carry a concealed handgun in North and South Carolina with the proper permit, and you need no permit at all to possess a weapon for self-defense. However, there are regulations regarding how a handgun must be conveyed in automobiles.

Both North Carolina and South Carolina feature versions of the so-called "stand your ground" law, whereby if you're in imminent lethal danger you do not have to first try to run away before resorting to deadly force to defend yourself. South Carolina's goes one step further, however, in that their stand-your-ground law extends to lethal danger in public places as well as in the home or car.

Essentials

Transportation

AIR

There are five international airports serving the coastal Carolinas:

- **Norfolk International Airport** (NIA, 2200 Norview Ave., Norfolk, Virginia, 757/857-3351, www.norfolkairport.com): Though in Virginia, this airport is close enough to the northern portion of North Carolina to make it a good choice for those wanting to concentrate on that area.

- **Wilmington International Airport** (ILM, 1740 Airport Blvd., Wilmington, 910/341-4125, www.flyilm.com): This is a good choice for those needing a central embarkation point on the Carolina coast.

- **Charleston International Airport** (CHS, 5500 International Blvd., 843/767-1100, www.iflychs.com): This is a primary gateway to the entire coast.

- **Myrtle Beach International Airport** (MYR, 1100 Jetport Rd., 843/448-1589, www.flymyrtlebeach.com): Because of the lack of interstate highway coverage in this area, the Myrtle Beach airport is best used only if Myrtle Beach is your primary destination.

- **Savannah/Hilton Head International Airport** (SAV, 400 Airways Ave., 912/964-0514, www.savannahairport.com): Although it is located in Georgia, because of its location near the extreme southern tip of South Carolina, this airport is perhaps the best access point to enjoy the lower portion of the South Carolina coast, and definitely Hilton Head.

CAR

The distance between the Great Dismal Swamp in North Carolina to Hilton Head Island, South Carolina, is about 500 miles, roughly 10-12 hours of drive time. Due to the spread-out nature of the coastal Carolinas and the general lack of public transportation, auto travel is integral to enjoying the region.

While the road infrastructure in the Outer and Inner Banks regions of North Carolina is in pretty good shape, driving from one place to another always takes longer than it looks on a map because there are so many waterways to cross and so few direct routes anywhere. Always budget more time than you think you'll need for auto travel in this area.

The main interstate arteries into and through the region are the north-south I-95 and the east-west I-26 and I-40. The bulk of your travel, however, will not be on interstate highways, but rather various state highways, most of which are quite well maintained and which I do recommend using, for the most part.

Keep in mind that despite being very heavily traveled, the Myrtle Beach area is not served by any interstate. A common landmark road throughout the coastal region is U.S. 17, which used to be known as the Coastal Highway and currently goes by a number of local incarnations as it winds its way along the coast.

Unfortunately, the stories you've heard about speed traps in small towns in the South are often correct. Always strictly obey the speed limit, and if you're pulled over always deal with the police respectfully and truthfully, whether or not you agree with their judgment.

Car Rentals

Unless you're going to hunker down in one city, you will need auto transportation to enjoy the coastal Carolinas. Renting a car is

---

Previous: aerial view of Charleston; Venus flytraps in the South Carolina wetlands.

easy and fairly inexpensive as long as you play by the rules, which are simple. You need either a valid U.S. driver's license from any state or a valid International Driving License from your home country, and you must be at least 25 years old.

If you do not either purchase insurance coverage from the rental company or already have insurance coverage through the credit card you rent the car with, you will be 100 percent responsible for any damage caused to the car during your rental period. While purchasing insurance at the time of rental is by no means mandatory, it might be worth the extra expense just to have that peace of mind.

Key rental car companies include **Hertz** (www.hertz.com), **Avis** (www.avis.com), **Thrifty** (www.thrifty.com), **Enterprise** (www.enterprise.com), and **Budget** (www.budget.com). Some rental car locations are in cities proper, but the vast majority of outlets are in airports, so plan accordingly. The airport locations have the bonus of generally holding longer hours than their in-town counterparts.

TRAIN

Passenger rail service in the car-dominated United States is far behind other developed nations, both in quantity and quality. For the most part, the national rail system, **Amtrak** (www.amtrak.com), runs well inland from the areas covered by this book. Exceptions include Amtrak stations in Charleston and Yemassee in South Carolina and Fayetteville, Wilson, and Rocky Mount in North Carolina. You could use this quasi-coastal route to access points of entry for the coast, but you would need other transportation to make it the rest of the way.

BUS

With the exception of the Outer Banks, the large bus service, **Greyhound** (www.greyhound.com), has decent coverage in coastal North Carolina, including stations in Elizabeth City, Fayetteville, Jacksonville, New Bern, and Wilmington. In coastal South Carolina, the bus company has stations in Beaufort, Charleston, Georgetown, Myrtle Beach, and Walterboro. Due to the frequent stops and relatively leisurely pace, this is by far the slowest form of travel in the region—as well as somewhat rustic—and should only be considered as an extreme budget option.

BOAT

One of the coolest things about the coastal Carolinas is the prevalence of the Intracoastal Waterway, a combined man-made/natural sheltered seaway going from Miami to Maine. Many boaters enjoy touring the coast by simply meandering up or down the Intracoastal, putting in at marinas along the way.

Key cities and towns along the ICW in North Carolina are Wilmington, Swansboro, Southport, Morehead City, Hatteras, Elizabeth City, Calabash, Belhaven, and Beaufort.

Key cities and towns along the ICW in South Carolina are Beaufort, Charleston, Georgetown, Hilton Head, Murrells Inlet, Myrtle Beach, and Port Royal.

If you've got a boat, you might want to traverse the entire coast for yourself. An excellent online resource is www.cruisingtheicw.com, which includes comprehensive marina and docking information. You can sleep onboard the whole time or occasionally tie up for the night and go into town for a stay at a nearby B&B.

For a hilarious and informative account of an oddball journey down the ICW in a restored English canal boat (or "narrow dog"), read Terry Darlington's 2009 account, *Narrow Dog to Indian River*.

Recreation

STATE PARKS AND NATURAL AREAS

The Carolinas have two of the best state park systems in the United States, many built by the Civilian Conservation Corps during FDR's New Deal and boasting distinctive, rustic, and well-made architecture.

While primitive camping is available, the general preference here is for more plush surroundings more conducive to a family vacation. Many state parks offer fully-equipped rental cabins with modern amenities that rival a hotel's. Generally speaking, such facilities tend to sell out early in the calendar, so make reservations as soon as you can. Keep in mind that during the high season, March-November, there are minimum rental requirements.

Dogs are allowed in state parks, but they must be leashed at all times.

NATIONAL WILDLIFE REFUGES

Coastal North Carolina has the following U.S. Fish and Wildlife Service National Wildlife Refuges (NWR), from north to south:

- **Mackay Island NWR**(www.fws.gov/mackayisland)
- **Currituck NWR**(www.fws.gov/currituck)
- **Pocosin Lakes NWR**(www.fws.gov/pocosinlakes)
- **Roanoke River NWR**(www.fws.gov/roanokeriver)
- **Alligator River NWR**(www.fws.gov/alligatorriver)
- **Pea Island NWR**(www.fws.gov/peaisland)
- **Mattamuskeet NWR**(www.fws.gov/mattamuskeet)
- **Swanquarter NWR**(www.fws.gov/swanquarter)
- **Cedar Island NWR**(www.fws.gov/cedarisland)

Coastal South Carolina has the following National Wildlife Refuges, from north to south:

- **Waccamaw NWR**(www.fws.gov/waccamaw)
- **Cape Romain NWR**(www.fws.gov/caperomain)
- **ACE Basin NWR**(www.fws.gov/acebasin)
- **Pinckney NWR** (www.fws.gov/pinckneyisland)
- **Savannah NWR**(www.fws.gov/savannah)

Admission is generally free. Access is limited to daytime hours, from sunrise to sunset. Keep in mind that some hunting is allowed on some refuges.

BEACHES

Some of the best beaches in America are in the region covered in this book. While the upscale amenities aren't always there and they aren't very surfer-friendly, the area's beaches are outstanding for anyone looking for a relaxing, scenic getaway.

By law, beaches in the United States are fully accessible to the public up to the high-tide mark during daylight hours, even if the beach fronts are private property and even if the only means of public access is by boat.

It is a misdemeanor to disturb the sea oats, those wispy, waving, wheat-like plants among the dunes. Their root system is vital to keeping the beach intact. Also never disturb a turtle nesting area, whether it is marked or not.

The **North Carolina Outer Banks** feature many miles of long, comparatively uncrowded beaches. For a more commercial experience, there's **Nags Head,** but for something more wild, check out the National Seashores of **Cape Hatteras** and **Cape Lookout.**

The **Wilmington** area features several fun, beautiful, and high-trafficked beach areas, especially **Wrightsville Beach, Kure Beach,** and **Carolina Beach.**

The busy **Grand Strand,** of course, has many miles of beach, from North Myrtle Beach on down to Huntington Beach State Park. Charleston-area beaches, generally less crowded, include **Folly Beach, Sullivan's Island,** and **Isle of Palms.** Moving down the coast, some delightful beaches are at **Edisto Island** and **Hunting Island,** which both feature state parks with lodging.

Hilton Head Island has about 12 miles of beautiful, family-friendly beaches, and while most of the island is devoted to private golf resorts, the beaches remain accessible to the general public at four points with parking: **Driessen Beach Park, Coligny Beach Park, Alder Lane Beach Access,** and **Burkes Beach Road.**

KAYAKING AND CANOEING

In North Carolina, sea kayakers enjoy many areas in the Outer Banks, including Bald Head Island, Cape Hatteras, and Ocracoke Island. Just to the north is the Great Dismal Swamp, a haven for kayaking and canoeing.

Down the coast, hot spots include Albemarle Sound, Alligator River NWR, and the Cape Fear and Cashie Rivers.

In the Grand Strand of South Carolina, you can enjoy kayaking on the Waccamaw River and Winyah Bay. Some key kayaking and canoeing areas in the Charleston area are Cape Romain National Wildlife Refuge, Shem Creek, Isle of Palms, Charleston Harbor, and the Stono River.

Farther south in the Lowcountry are the Ashepoo, Combahee, and Edisto blackwater rivers, which combine to form the ACE Basin. Next is Port Royal Sound near Beaufort.

The Hilton Head/Bluffton area have good kayaking opportunities at Hilton Head's Calibogue Creek and Bluffton's May River.

FISHING AND BOATING

In the coastal Carolinas, because of the large number of islands and wide area of salt marsh, life on the water is largely inseparable from life on the land. Fishing and boating are very common pursuits, with species of fish including spotted sea trout, channel bass, flounder, grouper, mackerel, sailfish, whiting, shark, amberjack, and tarpon.

Freshwater anglers will find largemouth bass, bream, catfish, and crappie, among many more.

To fish legally in North Carolina, if you're over 16 years old you'll need to get a Coastal Recreational Fishing License. A 10-day nonresident license is $15. Go to www.ncwildlife.org for more information or to purchase a license online.

In South Carolina, if you're over 16 years old, you'll need to get a nonresident fishing license. A seven-day license is $11. Go to www.dnr.sc.gov for more information or to purchase a license online.

Fishing charters and marinas are ample throughout the region, for both inshore and offshore trips. Details for each destination are in their dedicated chapters.

GOLF

The first golf club in America was formed in Charleston, and South Carolina as a whole is one of the world's golf meccas. There is a great variety of courses to choose from here, from tony courses like the Pete Dye-designed Ocean Course at the **Kiawah Island Golf Resort** or **Harbour Town** on Sea Pines Plantation in Hilton Head, to the more **budget-conscious courses** in the Santee Cooper region, Myrtle Beach, and North Myrtle Beach.

Don't be shy about pursuing golf packages which combine lodging with links. South Carolina, especially the coastal area, is currently suffering from something of a glut in courses, and you can find some great deals online.

Travel Tips

TRAVELING WITH CHILDREN

The coastal Carolinas are extremely kid-friendly, with the possible exception of some B&Bs that are clearly not designed for younger children. If you have any doubts about this, feel free to inquire. Otherwise, there are no special precautions unique to this area.

WOMEN TRAVELING ALONE

Women should take the same precautions they would take anywhere else. Many women traveling to this region have to adjust to the prevalence of traditional chivalry. In the South, if a man opens a door for you, it's considered a sign of respect, not condescension.

Another adjustment is the possible assumption that two or three women who go to a bar or tavern together might be there to invite male companionship. This misunderstanding can happen anywhere, but in some parts of the South it might be slightly more prevalent.

While small towns in the Carolinas are generally very friendly and law-abiding, some are more economically depressed than others and hence prone to higher crime. Always take common-sense precautions, no matter how bucolic the setting may be.

TRAVELERS WITH DISABILITIES

While the vast majority of attractions and accommodations make every effort to comply with federal law regarding those with disabilities, as they're obliged to do, the very historic nature of this region means that some structures simply cannot be retrofitted for maximum accessibility. This is something you'll need to find out on a case-by-case basis, so call ahead. The sites administered by the National Park Service in this book are as wheelchair-accessible as possible.

GAY AND LESBIAN TRAVELERS

North Carolina is one of the more progressive Southern states, and gay and lesbian travelers will generally feel quite comfortable there. Because of its large college-age population and heavy arts component, Wilmington is particularly gay-friendly.

While South Carolina is typically more conservative in outlook, Charleston, in particular, is quite accepting, and generally speaking, gay and lesbian travelers shouldn't expect anything untoward to happen.

In small towns all over the Carolinas, the best approach is to simply observe dominant Southern mores for anyone here, gay or straight. In a nutshell, that means keep public displays of affection and politics to a minimum. Southerners in general have a low opinion of anyone who flagrantly espouses a viewpoint too obviously or loudly.

SENIOR TRAVELERS

Both because of the large proportion of retirees in the region and because of the South's traditional respect for the elderly, the area is quite friendly to senior citizens. Many accommodations and attractions offer a senior discount, which can add up over the course of a trip. Always inquire *before* making a reservation, however, as check-in time is sometimes too late.

TRAVELING WITH PETS

While the United States is very pet-friendly, that friendliness rarely extends to restaurants and other indoor locations. More and more accommodations are allowing pet owners to bring pets, often for an added fee, but please inquire *before* you arrive. In any case, keep your dog on a leash at all times. Some beaches in the area permit dog-walking at certain times of the year, but as a general rule keep dogs off beaches unless you see signage saying otherwise.

Health and Safety

CRIME

While crime rates are indeed above national averages in much of the Carolinas, especially in inner city areas, incidents of crime in the more heavily trafficked tourist areas are no more common than anywhere else. In fact, these areas might be safer because of the amount of foot traffic and police attention.

By far the most common crime against visitors here is simple theft, primarily from cars. (Pickpocketing, thankfully, is quite rare in the United States). Always lock your car doors. Conversely, only leave them unlocked if you're absolutely comfortable living without whatever's inside at the time. As a general rule, I try to lock valuables—such as CDs, a recent purchase, or my wife's purse—in the trunk. (Just make sure the "valet" button, allowing the trunk to be opened from the driver's area, is disabled.)

Should someone corner you and demand your wallet or purse, just give it to them. Unfortunately, the old advice to scream as loud as you can is no longer the deterrent it once was, and in fact may hasten aggressive action by the robber.

If you are the victim of a crime, *always call the police.* Law enforcement wants more information, not less, and the worst thing that can happen is you'll have an incident report in case you need to make an insurance claim for lost or stolen property.

Remember that in the United States as elsewhere, no good can come from a heated argument with a police officer. The place to prove a police officer wrong is in a court of law, perhaps with an attorney by your side, not at the scene.

For emergencies, always call 911.

AUTO ACCIDENTS

If you're in an auto accident, you're bound by law to wait for police to respond. Failure to do so can result in a "leaving the scene of an accident" charge, or worse. In the old days, cars in accidents had to be left exactly where they came to rest until police gave permission to move or tow them. However, many U.S. states have recently loosened regulations so that if a car is blocking traffic as a result of an accident, the driver is allowed to move it enough to allow traffic to flow again. That is, if the car can be moved safely. If not, you're not required to move it out of the way.

Since it's illegal to drive without auto insurance, I'll assume you have some. And because you're insured, the best course of action in a minor accident, where injuries are unlikely, is to patiently wait for the police and give them your side of the story. In my experience, police react negatively to people who are too quick to start making accusations against other people. After that, let the insurance companies deal with it. That's what they're there for.

If you suspect any injuries, call 911 immediately.

ILLEGAL DRUGS

Marijuana, heroin, methamphetamine, and cocaine and all its derivatives are illegal in the United States with only a very few, select exceptions, none of which apply to the areas covered by this book. The use of ecstasy and similar mood-elevators is also illegal. The penalties for illegal drug possession and use in the Carolinas are *extremely severe.* Just stay away from them entirely.

ALCOHOL

The drinking age in the United States is 21. Most restaurants that serve alcoholic beverages allow those under 21 inside. Generally speaking, if only those over 21 are allowed inside, you will be greeted at the door by someone asking to see identification. These people are often poorly trained and anything other than a state driver's license may confuse them, so be forewarned.

Drunk driving is a problem on the highways of America, and the Carolinas are no exception. Always drive defensively, especially late at night, and obey all posted speed limits and road signs—and never assume the other driver will do the same. You may *never* drive with an opened alcoholic beverage in the car, even if it belongs to a passenger.

Generally speaking, both Carolinas have so-called **blue laws** allowing Sunday retail purchase of beer and wine after noon, but no hard liquor the entire day. Closing times at bars generally vary by municipality.

Both Carolinas feature ABC, or **Alcohol Beverage Control,** stores, which are the only places to buy liquor outside a restaurant or bar setting.

ILLNESS

Unlike most developed nations, the United States has no comprehensive national health care system (there are programs for the elderly and the poor). Visitors from other countries who need non-emergency medical attention are best served by going to free-standing medical clinics. The level of care is typically very good, but you'll be paying out of pocket for the service, unfortunately.

For emergencies, however, do not hesitate to go to the closest hospital emergency room, where generally the level of care is also quite good, especially for trauma. Worry about payment later. Emergency rooms in the United States are required to take true emergency cases whether or not the patient can pay for services.

Pharmaceuticals

Unlike many European nations, antibiotics are available in the United States only on a prescription basis and are not available over the counter. Most cold, flu, and allergy remedies are available over the counter. While homeopathic remedies are gaining popularity in the United States, they are nowhere near as prevalent as in Europe.

Drugs with the active ingredient ephedrine are available in the United States without a prescription, but their purchase is often tightly regulated to cut down on the use of these products to make the illegal drug methamphetamine.

Vaccinations

As of this writing, there are no vaccination requirements to enter the United States. Contact your embassy before coming to confirm this before arrival, however.

In the autumn, at the beginning of flu season, preventive influenza vaccinations, simply called "flu shots," often become available at easily accessible locations like clinics, health departments, and even supermarkets.

Humidity, Heat, and Sun

There is only one way to fight the South's high heat and humidity, and that's to drink lots of fluids. A surprising number of people each year refuse to take this advice and find themselves in various states of dehydration, some of which can land you in a hospital. Remember: If you're thirsty, you're already suffering from dehydration. The thing to do is keep drinking fluids *before* you're thirsty, as a preventative action rather than a reaction.

Always use sunscreen, even on a cloudy day. If you do get a sunburn, get a pain relief product with aloe vera as an active ingredient. On extraordinarily sunny and hot summer days, don't even go outside between the hours of 10am and 2pm

HAZARDS

Insects

Because of the recent increase in the mosquito-borne and often deadly West Nile virus, the most important step to take in staying healthy in the coastal Carolinas is to keep **mosquito bites** to a minimum. Do this with a combination of mosquito repellent and long sleeves and long pants, if possible. Not every mosquito bite will give you the virus; in fact, chances are quite slim that one will. But don't take the chance if you don't have to.

The second major step in avoiding insect nastiness is to steer clear of **fire ants,** whose large, gray or brown-dirt nests are quite common in this area. They attack instantly and in great numbers, with little or no provocation. They don't just bite, they inject you with poison from their stingers. In short, fire ants are not to be trifled with.

While the only real remedy is the preventative one of never coming in contact with them, should you find yourself being bitten by fire ants, the first thing is to stay calm. Take off your shoes and socks and get as many of the ants off you as you can. Unless you've had a truly large amount of bites—in which case you should seek medical help immediately—the best thing to do next is wash the area to get any venom off, and then disinfect with alcohol if you have any handy. Then a topical treatment such as calamine lotion or hydrocortisone is advised. A fire ant bite will leave a red pustule that lasts about a week. Try your best not to scratch it so that it won't get infected.

Outdoor activity, especially in woodsy, undeveloped areas, may bring you in contact with another unpleasant indigenous creature, the tiny but obnoxious **chigger,** sometimes called the redbug. The bite of a chigger can't be felt, but the enzymes it leaves behind can lead to a very itchy little red spot. Contrary to folklore, putting fingernail polish on the itchy bite will not "suffocate" the chigger, because by this point the chigger itself is long gone. All you can do is get some topical itch or pain relief and go on with your life. The itching will eventually subside.

For **bee stings,** the best approach for those non-allergic to them is to immediately pull the stinger out, perhaps by scraping a credit card over the bite, and apply ice if possible. A topical treatment such as hydrocortisone or calamine lotion is advised. In my experience the old folk remedy of tearing apart a cigarette and putting the tobacco leaves directly on the sting does indeed cut the pain. But that's not a medical opinion, so do with it what you will. A minor allergic reaction can be quelled by using an over-the-counter antihistamine. If the sting victim is severely allergic to bee stings, go to a hospital or call 911 for an ambulance.

Threats in the Water

While enjoying area beaches, a lot of visitors become inordinately worried about **shark attacks.** Every couple of summers there's a lot of hysteria about this, but the truth is that you're much more likely to slip and fall in a bathroom than you are to even come close to being bitten by a shark in these shallow Atlantic waters.

A far more common fate for area swimmers is to get stung by a **jellyfish,** or sea nettle. They can sting you in the water, but most often beachcombers are stung by stepping on beached jellyfish stranded on the sand by the tide. If you get stung, don't panic; wash the area with saltwater, not freshwater, and apply vinegar or baking soda.

Lightning

The southeastern United States is home to some vicious, fast-moving thunderstorms, often with an amazing amount of electrical activity. Death by lightning strike occurs often in this region and is something that should be taken quite seriously. The general rule of thumb is if you're in the water, whether at the beach or in a swimming pool, and hear thunder, get out of the water immediately until the storm passes. If you're on dry land and see lightning flash a distance away, that's your cue to seek safety indoors. Whatever you do, do not play sports outside when lightning threatens.

Information and Services

MONEY

Automated Teller Machines (ATMs) are available in all urban areas covered in this guide. Be aware that if the ATM is not owned by your bank, not only will that ATM likely charge you a service fee, but your bank may charge you one as well. While ATMs have made traveler's checks less essential, traveler's checks do have the important advantage of accessibility, as some rural and less-developed areas covered in this guide have few or no ATMs. You can purchase traveler's checks at just about any bank.

Establishments in the United States only accept the national currency, the U.S. dollar. To exchange foreign money, go to any bank.

Generally, establishments that accept credit cards will feature stickers on the front entrance with the logo of the particular cards they accept, although this is not a legal requirement. The use of debit cards has dramatically increased in the United States. Most retail establishments and many fast-food chains are now accepting them. Make sure you get a receipt whenever you use a credit card or a debit card.

Tipping

Unlike many other countries, service workers in the United States depend on tips for the bulk of their income. In restaurants and bars, the usual tip is 15 percent of the pretax portion of the bill for acceptable service, 20 percent (or more) for excellent service. For large parties, usually six or more, a 15-18 percent gratuity is automatically added to the bill.

It's also customary to tip bellboys about $2 per bag when they assist you at check-in and checkout of your hotel; some sources recommend a minimum of $5.

For taxi drivers, 15 percent is customary as long as the cab is clean, smoke-free, and you were treated with respect and taken to your destination with a minimum of fuss.

INTERNET ACCESS

Visitors from Europe and Asia are likely to be disappointed at the quality of Internet access in the United States, particularly the area covered in this book. Fiber-optic lines are still a rarity, and while many hotels and B&Bs now offer in-room Internet access—some charge, some don't, so make sure to ask ahead—the quality and speed of the connection might prove poor.

Wireless (Wi-Fi) networks also are less than impressive, although that situation continues to improve on a daily basis in coffeehouses, hotels, and airports. Unfortunately, many hot spots in private establishments are for rental only.

PHONES

Generally speaking, the United States is behind Europe and much of Asia in terms of cell phone technology. Unlike Europe, where "pay-as-you-go" refills are easy to find, most American cell phone users pay for monthly plans through a handful of providers. Still, you should have no problem with cell phone coverage in urban areas. Where it gets much less dependable is in rural areas and on beaches. Bottom line: Don't depend on having cell service everywhere you go. As with a regular landline, any time you face an emergency, call 911 on your cell phone.

All phone numbers in the United States are seven digits preceded by a three-digit area code. You may have to dial a 1 before a phone number if it's a long-distance call, even within the same area code.

Resources

Suggested Reading

NONFICTION

Carlson, Tom. *Hatteras Blues: A Story from the Edge of America.* Chapel Hill, NC: University of North Carolina Press, 2005. A poignant chronicle of the ups and downs of one family's sportfishing business on the Outer Banks.

Click, Patricia. *Time Full of Trial: The Roanoke Island Freedmen's Colony, 1862-1867.* Chapel Hill, NC: University of North Carolina Press, 2001. An insightful exploration, based on primary sources, of this underreported, major chapter of African-American history in coastal North Carolina.

Darlington, Terry. *Narrow Dog to Indian River.* New York, NY: Delta, 2009. A British couple and their whippet dog Jim navigate an English canal boat down the Intracoastal Waterway from Virginia to Florida, with long, hilarious sections about their travels in North and South Carolina.

Ferling, John E. *Almost a Miracle: The American Victory in the War of Independence.* New York, NY: Oxford University Press, 2007. Not only perhaps the best single volume detailing the military aspects of the Revolutionary War, but absolutely indispensable for learning about the Carolinas' key role in it. In a dramatic departure from most New England-focused books of this genre, fully half of *Almost a Miracle* is devoted to an in-depth look at the Southern theater of the conflict.

Hudson, Charles M. *The Southeastern Indians.* Knoxville, TN: University of Tennessee Press, 1976. Though written decades ago, this seminal work by the noted University of Georgia anthropologist remains the definitive work on the life, culture, art, and religion of the Native Americans of the Southeast region.

Klein, Maury. *Days of Defiance: Sumter, Secession, and the Coming of the Civil War.* New York, NY: Vintage, 1999. A gripping and vivid account of the lead-up to war, with Charleston as the focal point.

Pilkey, Orrin H. *How to Read a North Carolina Beach: Bubble Holes, Barking Sands, and Rippled Runnels.* Chapel Hill, NC: University of North Carolina Press, 2006. Fascinating and user-friendly guide to taking an up-close look at the ebb and flow of the typical North Carolina maritime ecosystem.

Reed, John Shelton. *Holy Smoke: The Big Book of North Carolina Barbecue.* Chapel Hill, NC: University of North Carolina Press, 2009. The title says it all: everything you ever needed or wanted to know about North Carolina 'cue.

Robinson, Sally Ann. *Gullah Home Cooking the Daufuskie Island Way.* Chapel Hill, NC: University of North Carolina Press, 2007. Subtitled "Smokin' Joe Butter Beans, Ol' 'Fuskie Fried Crab Rice, Sticky-Bush Blackberry Dumpling, and Other Sea

Island Favorites," this cookbook by a native Daufuskie Islander features a foreword by Pat Conroy.

Rogers Jr., George C. *Charleston in the Age of the Pinckneys,* Columbia, SC: University of South Carolina Press, 1980. This 1969 history is a classic of the genre.

Rosen, Robert. *A Short History of Charleston.* Columbia, SC: University of South Carolina Press, 1997. Quite simply the most concise, readable, and entertaining history of the Holy City I've found.

Whedbee, Charles Harry. *Blackbeard's Cup and Stories of the Outer Banks.* Winston-Salem, NC: John F. Blair, 1989. Funny and engaging collection of folklore in and around the Outer Banks.

Woodward, C. Vann (ed.). *Mary Chesnut's Civil War.* New Haven, CT: Yale University Press, 1981. The Pulitzer Prize-winning classic compilation of the sardonically funny and quietly heartbreaking letters of Charleston's Mary Chesnut during the Civil War.

FICTION

Conroy, Pat. *The Lords of Discipline.* New York, NY: Bantam, 1985. For all practical purposes set at the Citadel, this novel takes you behind the scenes of the notoriously insular Charleston military college.

Conroy, Pat. *The Water is Wide.* New York, NY: Bantam, 1987. Immortal account of Conroy's time teaching African-American children in a two-room schoolhouse on "Yamacraw" (actually Daufuskie) Island.

Frank, Dorothea Benton. *Sullivan's Island.* New York, NY: Berkley, 2004. This South Carolina native's debut novel, and still probably her best, chronicles the journey of a Charleston woman through the breakup of her marriage to eventual redemption.

Kidd, Sue Monk. *The Secret Life of Bees.* New York, NY: Penguin, 2003. Set in South Carolina in the 1960s, this best-seller delves into the role of race in the regional psyche. It gained critical acclaim due to the unusual fact that the author, a white woman, features many African-American female characters.

Poe, Edgar Allan. *The Gold Bug.* London: Hesperus Press, 2007. Inspired by his stint there with the U.S. Army, the great American author set this classic short story on Sullivan's Island, South Carolina, near Charleston.

Siddons, Anne Rivers. *Outer Banks.* New York, NY: HarperTorch, 1992. The Outer Banks are the backdrop for this gripping, character-driven novel by this best-selling author.

Index

QR

S

List of Maps

Photo Credits

Also Available

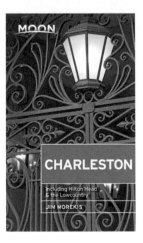

MAP SYMBOLS

▦ Expressway	○	City/Town	✈	Airport	♟	Golf Course
▦ Primary Road	◉	State Capital	✗	Airfield	Ⓟ	Parking Area
▦ Secondary Road	⊛	National Capital	▲	Mountain	⚑	Archaeological Site
▦ Unpaved Road	★	Point of Interest	✚	Unique Natural Feature	▮	Church
— Feature Trail	●	Accommodation				Gas Station
-- Other Trail	▼	Restaurant/Bar	⟲	Waterfall		Glacier
⋯ Ferry	■	Other Location	▲	Park		Mangrove
▦ Pedestrian Walkway			▣	Trailhead		Reef
▦ Stairs	▲	Campground	⛷	Skiing Area		Swamp

CONVERSION TABLES

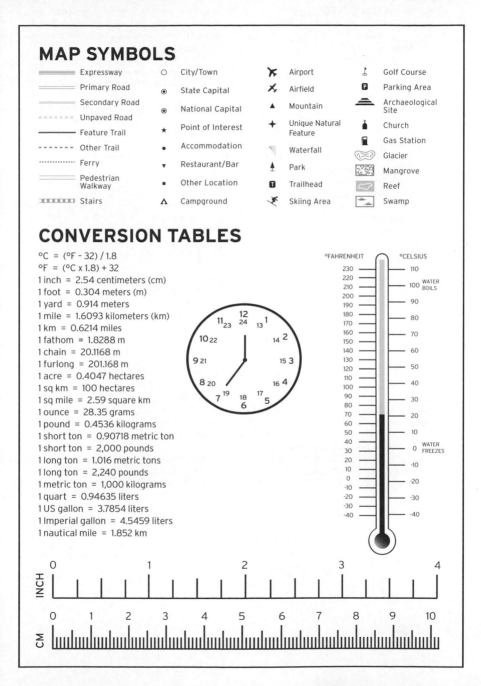

$°C = (°F - 32) / 1.8$

$°F = (°C × 1.8) + 32$

1 inch = 2.54 centimeters (cm)
1 foot = 0.304 meters (m)
1 yard = 0.914 meters
1 mile = 1.6093 kilometers (km)
1 km = 0.6214 miles
1 fathom = 1.8288 m
1 chain = 20.1168 m
1 furlong = 201.168 m
1 acre = 0.4047 hectares
1 sq km = 100 hectares
1 sq mile = 2.59 square km
1 ounce = 28.35 grams
1 pound = 0.4536 kilograms
1 short ton = 0.90718 metric ton
1 short ton = 2,000 pounds
1 long ton = 1.016 metric tons
1 long ton = 2,240 pounds
1 metric ton = 1,000 kilograms
1 quart = 0.94635 liters
1 US gallon = 3.7854 liters
1 Imperial gallon = 4.5459 liters
1 nautical mile = 1.852 km

MOON COASTAL CAROLINAS
Avalon Travel
Hachette Book Group
1700 Fourth Street
Berkeley, CA 94710, USA
www.moon.com

Editor: Rachel Feldman
Series Manager: Kathryn Ettinger
Copy Editor: Brett Keener
Graphics and Production Coordinator:
 Elizabeth Jang
Cover Design: Faceout Studios, Charles Brock
Interior Design: Domini Dragoone
Moon Logo: Tim McGrath
Map Editor: Kat Bennett
Cartographers: Stephanie Poulain, Karin Dahl
Proofreader: Ann Seifert
Indexer: Greg Jewett

ISBN-13: 978-1-64049-245-5

Printing History
1st Edition — 2001
4th Edition — February 2018
5 4 3 2 1

Front cover photo: sea oats on North Carolina's Outer Banks © Will & Deni McIntyre/Getty

Back cover photo: a wood stork at Pinckney Island National Wildlife Refuge, South Carolina © Zachary Dalzell | Dreamstime

Printed in China by RR Donnelley